Beginning SQL Server 2012 Administration

Rob Walters
Grant Fritchey

Apress®

Beginning SQL Server Administration

ISBN-13 (pbk): 978-1-4302-3981-9

ISBN-13 (electronic): 978-1-4302-3982-6

President and Publisher: Paul Manning
Lead Editor: Jonathan Gennick
Developmental Editor: Jonathan Gennick, Douglas Pundick
Technical Reviewer: Matt Eddinger
Editorial Board: Steve Anglin, Ewan Buckingham, Gary Cornell, Louise Corrigan, Morgan Ertel, Jonathan Gennick, Jonathan Hassell, Robert Hutchinson, Michelle Lowman, James Markham, Matthew Moodie, Jeff Olson, Jeffrey Pepper, Douglas Pundick, Ben Renow-Clarke, Dominic Shakeshaft, Gwenan Spearing, Matt Wade, Tom Welsh
Coordinating Editor: Brent Dubi
Copy Editor: Heather Lang
Production Support: Patrick Cunningham
Indexer: SPi Global
Artist: SPi Global
Cover Designer: Anna Ishchenko

Distributed to the book trade worldwide by Springer Science+Business Media New York, 233 Spring Street, 6th Floor, New York, NY 10013. Phone 1-800-SPRINGER, fax (201) 348-4505, e-mail orders-ny@springer-sbm.com, or visit www.springeronline.com.

For information on translations, please e-mail rights@apress.com, or visit www.apress.com.

Apress and friends of ED books may be purchased in bulk for academic, corporate, or promotional use. eBook versions and licenses are also available for most titles. For more information, reference our Special Bulk Sales–eBook Licensing web page at www.apress.com/bulk-sales.

Any source code or other supplementary materials referenced by the author in this text is available to readers at www.apress.com. For detailed information about how to locate your book's source code, go to www.apress.com/source-code/.

Contents at a Glance

Contents

About the Authors

Rob Walters is a data platform technology specialist with Microsoft. In this role, he helps customers see the value of Microsoft SQL Server by leading proof-of-concept and architectural design sessions. Mr. Walters's extensive experience with Microsoft SQL Server started more than 12 years ago when he worked as a consultant for Microsoft Consulting Services in Denver, CO. Shortly after the dot-com bubble burst, Mr. Walters returned to Microsoft's headquarters and worked as a program manager in the SQL Server product unit. There, he owned various features within SQL Server including SQL Server Agent, several management features, and the security for the database engine. Mr. Walters has coauthored three patents on technologies that are used within Microsoft SQL Server.

Mr. Walters has coauthored *Programming Microsoft SQL Server 2005* (Microsoft Press, 2006) and *Pro SQL Server 2005* (Apress, 2007). He is also the lead author of *Accelerated SQL Server 2008* (Apress, 2008) and *Beginning SQL Server 2008 Administration* (Apress 2009).

Mr. Walters holds a bachelors of science degree in electrical engineering from Michigan State University and a master's degree in business administration from Seattle University.

Outside of work, he enjoys spending time with his wife, Julie, and children. Mr. Walters is also a certified firefighter and emergency medical technician and volunteers his time when needed.

Grant Fritchey works for Red Gate Software, a market-leading software tools vendor, as a product evangelist. Grant has been awarded as a Microsoft SQL Server MVP since 2009. He's developed large-scale applications in languages such as VB, C#, and Java and has worked in SQL Server since version 6.0. In addition, he has worked in the insurance, finance, and consulting industries and for three failed dot-coms. He is the author of *SQL Server Execution Plans* (Simple Talk Publishing, 2008), *SQL Server 2008 Query Performance Tuning Distilled* (Apress, 2008), and *SQL Server 2012 Query Performance Tuning* (Apress, 2012). Grant is a coauthor of *Beginning SQL Server Administration* (Apress, 2009) and wrote one chapter in *SQL Server MVP Deep Dives Volume 2* (Manning, 2011).

About the Technical Reviewer

Matt Eddinger has over 15 years of experience from several facets of the information technology field. He currently works for Microsoft Consulting Services, where he specializes in SQL Server and SharePoint engagements. He holds a bachelor's degree from Shepherd University, a master's degree from Mountain State University, and dozens of technical certifications, which include CISSP, MCTS, MCITP, and MCT. He resides in Rocky Hill, CT, when he is not on the road (which is a lot).

Acknowledgments

Thank you to Jonathan Gennick for giving me the many opportunities to write for Apress. I would also like to say thank you to my wife, Julie, for supporting me throughout this effort.

Rob Walters

I just want to thank Rob and the folks at Apress for allowing me the opportunity to take part in this project. But since I'm here, I'll also take the time to thank my lovely wife and my kids for putting up with me while I work on these books.

Grant Fritchey

Introduction

The SQL Server product has been around since the late 1980s. Back then, Microsoft worked together with Sybase to create a database on the OS/2 platform. Shortly after this effort was completed, Microsoft realized it wanted to tightly couple SQL Server with Windows. By 1993, Microsoft had released Windows NT 3.1, and with it came the option of using a well-integrated version of SQL Server called SQL Server 4.2. This was to be the last version of SQL Server made jointly between the two companies. By 1995, Microsoft left the partnership with Sybase and released SQL Server version 6.0, followed a year later by version 6.5. These two versions were still on the original Sybase platform.

As a DBA today, you will rarely see a production server running any of these three versions of SQL Server. If you do, chances are the servers are probably running a database application from a company that no longer exists. Either way, if you encounter these systems in production, it may be worthwhile to do a few web searches and learn a bit more about how to administer these kinds of SQL Server instances.

By 1997, Microsoft decided to rewrite the database engine and effectively move away from the old Sybase design. This rewrite effort led to the release of SQL Server's next version, 7.0. To some, this version marked the first generation of SQL Server. By rewriting the database engine, Microsoft was able to provide key features to customers, including the ability for offline users to update data and merge it back to live data when they reconnected to the server (merge replication). DBAs could also grow and shrink databases as needed, as well as use new wizards such as the Copy Database wizard to easily perform administrative tasks. SQL Server 7.0 also made online analytical processing (OLAP) capabilities affordable to the market by including OLAP services as part of the SQL Server 7.0 license. This was SQL Server's initial entry into the data warehousing market. With SQL Server 7.0, users could easily design, build, and manage data marts and data warehouses.

Seeing SQL Server 7.0 in production isn't as uncommon as seeing a Sybase-style version, but is still rare since that version is no longer being serviced or supported by Microsoft.

SQL Server 2000, released in 1999, built on the success and lower total cost of ownership value that SQL Server 7.0 introduced to the market. Major parts of the database engine were rewritten again to accommodate features such as multi-instances, where DBAs could run more than one instance of SQL Server per server. Microsoft made continued investments in scalability and availability with features such as log shipping. Log shipping allowed DBAs to automatically copy and load transaction log backups from one database to one or more databases, enabling a highly available environment. Investments were also made for developers, including XML support and the ability to create user-defined functions. In the business intelligence (BI) space, a more mature version of Data Transformation Services was shipped as well as Reporting Services for SQL Server 2000. There was a large effort around the integration of Microsoft Office applications and Analysis Services. For example, it was possible to use Excel pivot tables loaded with data from cubes created with Analysis Services.

Although SQL Server 2000 is no longer supported, many organizations still use it in production today. There is a good chance you, as a DBA, will be involved with managing and eventually upgrading these servers to SQL Server 2012.

Between the release of SQL Server 2000 and SQL Server 2005, there was about a five-year gap. The result of this long wait was a product that contained many new enterprise capabilities, such as database mirroring, online indexing, online restore, and table partitioning.

If your company has been using SQL Server for a while, it is highly likely to have some installations of various versions of SQL Server including SQL Server 2005 and SQL Server 2008 in production.

SQL Server 2012 is the latest and most significant release of SQL Server to date. This version is all about mission-critical confidence, breakthrough business intelligence insight, and leveraging the cloud on your terms. In this book, you will be exposed to a lot of the key features of SQL Server 2012 from a database administration perspective.

Who This Book Is For

Are you considering a career as a database administrator? Are you an IT professional who is curious about what SQL Server is and how to manage it? Are you a database administrator for a non–SQL Server platform like Oracle, Sybase, or DB2 who has an interest in SQL Server? Do you want to learn about SQL Server? If you answered "yes" to any of these questions, you will have invested your money wisely in this book. This book provides you with a solid foundation of the fundamental skills and concepts of managing a SQL Server instance.

How This Book Is Structured

If you are not familiar with databases, it is probably best to work through each chapter sequentially, because topics in later chapters build on ones described in earlier chapters. This is what each chapter covers:

Chapter 1: This chapter explores the database administration profession. Topics include typical tasks of DBAs as well as input from experienced real-life DBAs.

Chapter 2: SQL Server is an enterprise-ready database platform. Simply installing it onto a production server without much planning is a surefire way of getting shown the door by your current employer. This chapter explores some of the key issues to consider when installing SQL Server. Microsoft provides multiple editions of SQL Server, so this chapter also reviews these editions as well as walks you through an installation of the evaluation edition of SQL Server.

Chapter 3: Getting familiar with a new server application like SQL Server can be a daunting task for most. Many different applications are installed such as management and development tools, Performance Monitor counters, and numerous other new things to learn about. This chapter will explore these bits that SQL Server installs.

Chapter 4: There are a few tools that you, as a DBA developer, can use in your quest to code against SQL Server. In this chapter, you will explore the development capabilities of SQL Server Management Studio and SQL Server Data Tools.

Chapter 5: In this chapter, you get your hands dirty by using the database for its most fundamental purpose: creating tables and storing some data. You'll also learn to create indexes to help ensure efficient access to that data when you later want to retrieve it.

Chapter 6: This chapter covers Transact SQL (T-SQL) syntax. You'll learn to write and use stored procedures, functions, and triggers, as well as to perform many other common functions within SQL Server.

Chapter 7: This chapter gives you a heads up on how a SQL Server installation is organized. You'll learn that a SQL Server install includes several databases used by the system in support of those databases that you create for your own use. These databases include the master database containing user logins and the tempdb database used for temporary storage. You'll also learn about the Windows services that run in the background that make up a running SQL Server installation.

Chapter 8: If you know nothing else as a DBA, you better know how to perform a database backup. This is a core task that almost all DBAs are involved with. This chapter covers the different types of backups and when to use each. Additional topics include special backups, such as compressed and encrypted.

Chapter 9: Backing up a database is only half the battle. If a disaster occurs, DBAs need to know how to restore the database and get the server back online or restored to a specific point in time. The overall plan for recovering from a disaster is the disaster recovery plan, and this chapter will cover what kind of information this plan should contain as well as how to perform database restores.

Chapter 10: Effectively backing up and restoring databases are critical skills for DBAs to possess. However, a DBA performs many other functions, including tuning indexes, creating maintenance scripts, and scheduling jobs. This chapter covers the key tools within SQL Server that help DBAs perform these kinds of tasks.

Chapter 11: This chapter covers the SQL Server security model. You'll learn how users authenticate to SQL Server and are granted access to objects within the server.

Chapter 12: DBAs who work for publicly traded companies, health-care companies, or companies that stored and use credit card information will undoubtedly be asked into a few meetings with some auditors. These folks, if they are external to your company, are hired specifically to make sure your company complies with the applicable regulations such as Sarbanes-Oxley, Payment Card Industry (PCI), and others. This chapter describes how SQL Server enables features that help DBAs configure their servers to be compliant.

Chapter 13: This chapter covers the basic tools used for performance measurement as well as the tools used to tune databases. These key improvements in SQL Server 2012 will be covered in this chapter.

Chapter 14: Fault tolerance is an important concept for the DBA to understand. This chapter will cover service level agreements (SLA) and how to leverage the various high-availability features within SQL Server 2012 to accommodate your own SLA.

Chapter 15: Companies around the world are continuing to embrace cloud computing for specific workloads. This chapter will introduce SQL Azure, Microsoft's database as a service offering.

Chapter 16: With the advent of high-core-count processors came a large push for database consolidation and virtualization. Today, SQL Server DBAs are being tasked with building or contributing to the design of private cloud SQL Server clusters. This chapter will cover the concepts of what makes up a SQL Server private cloud environment.

Chapter 17: This chapter provides valuable references that will help you as a new DBA continue to build your foundation of knowledge about SQL Server conventions.

Contacting the Authors

You can contact the book's lead author, Rob Walters, via his e-mail address at `Robert.Walters@Microsoft.com`.

CHAPTER 1

The Database Administration Profession

Why is this damn application so slow?
I accidentally deleted my customer's order a few days ago. Can you retrieve it?
The auditor is coming in tomorrow to review our security access list. Please have something ready.
Here is your pager; enjoy the weekend!

The life of a database administrator (DBA) can be quite interesting. To some nontechnical folks within a company, a DBA is a necessary evil. They can look at a developer and say, "Oh, this is what you created." When they look at a DBA, what can they see? Usually, they don't think much about the DBA until they have a problem. When this occurs, you are more important than anyone else, including most executives. In these situations, you, as a DBA, can make or break your career.

Why Do We Need a DBA? Access Runs Great!

We are in the heart of the Information Age. The global economy has shifted from the manufacturing of physical goods to the storing, managing, and mining of information. It is amazing to think about how much information is being recorded every second.

Some grocery store chains in the United States offer "savings cards," which, when presented to the cashier upon checkout, may give buyers some additional savings on the various products they purchased. To the customer, this simple chore of carrying around a little plastic card and remembering to give it to the cashier is worth the potential dollars in savings. To the store, this savings card program is worth far more than the few dollars it will cost the store per transaction. First, it encourages customer loyalty, since customers want to get the discount and so shop at that store. The second, and arguably the most important, benefit to the store is it allows the store to perform data mining.

Take a look at the kind of data that can easily be obtained. For every customer checkout (transaction), the store gets the list of items purchased as well as who bought them. With some analysis and mining through products such as SQL Server Analysis Services, the grocery store can answer questions like "what is the most popular product sold each day?" and "how often are hot dogs and hot dog buns sold together?" If you, as the customer, provided some more information on your savings card application, the store could also answer questions like "what is the most popular product sold to a married person with children?" and "how much do single females spend per visit compared to single males?" Having the answers to these questions allows the store to target advertising campaigns to various demographics as well as give customers occasional coupons that align with their buying behavior.

All of this data gathered from transactions is stored in a database. You can imagine the potentially large amount of information that could be obtained over time in this example. Had the grocery store owners simply asked their business analysts to put the data into a database in something like Microsoft Access or, more commonly, Microsoft Excel, they wouldn't be able to easily derive the important answers they need for the business. Without a centrally managed relational database, there would be no single version of the truth. The company would have data scattered throughout the organization, and that data would be difficult to secure. Competitors and high-tech criminals would love to get hold of a customer list or a store's sales data. For these reasons and many others, companies hire smart DBAs like you to help store, manage, and protect their data.

What Exactly Does a DBA Do Anyway?

Much like other technical jobs, defining exactly what DBAs do is difficult because each company may use them in different ways. In the previous example, information from the grocery store's cash register could be fed into a database. A business intelligence tool like SQL Server Analysis Services could be used to create multidimensional models of shopping data. Other tools such as SQL Server Reporting Services could be used to create reports that business analysts would use to make business decisions from. As a DBA, you might be responsible for backing up, restoring, and securing the data within the data warehouse, or you might even be responsible for maintaining the reporting server. Your exact role really depends on the organization you work for. Some DBAs spend more time on production servers and others on development servers. In an effort to make a generalization about the role, the following sections describe some of things people working in the database administration field might expect to be responsible for.

Database Maintenance

Maintenance of the database encompasses a variety of different tasks. It is perhaps one of the most important skills to develop as a DBA. Proper database maintenance starts with doing regular database backups to ensure that valuable company data can be easily retrieved should something happen to the production database or server. There is nothing like the feeling when a server goes down and you realize that you don't have a current backup handy. If this ever happens to you, there are some great web sites that can help you get a new job.

Periodically, the database itself will need some tuning and optimization. Indexes are a vital part of the database, and you may occasionally need to evaluate them for their effectiveness. New ones may need to be added, and others may be irrelevant. Microsoft SQL Server provides some tools to make index maintenance and management easier for the database administrator. Indexes will be discussed more in Chapter 3.

It is impossible to make a claim that software is 100 percent bug free. For this reason, we have service packs. Service packs contain cumulative updates of a product since the original version was released. Most organizations have a process for deploying service packs because, although they are not supposed to change the behavior of SQL Server, in some rare cases, they have been known to do so. Even something as innocent as a performance enhancement to an application may cause problems. As a DBA, you may be asked to set up a test environment to test a new service pack with your organization's existing applications. If your organization does not have a test environment, you should lead an effort to make one. Also, as soon as you find an issue in your test environment that ultimately saves downtime in production, you may get an instant promotion.

Security and Regulatory Compliance

To some, working on security is about as glamorous and fun as cleaning up after a party when you are hung over. However, to a company, security is as important as the alcohol is to the party itself. Without these beverages, no one will come, and without security, no customers will feel safe giving their information to you.

So, what does security mean to a database administrator? Security means managing the user access to SQL Server and the corresponding databases it contains. This user management may be as specific as configuring permissions on objects within the database, or it can be as general as specifying surface area settings such as disabling the use of `xp_cmdshell` within SQL Server.

With the advent of the corporate scandals in the early part of this century came an increased awareness and requirement for companies to be in compliance with various government and industry regulatory standards. Some of these regulatory standards may be familiar and include Sarbanes-Oxley (SOX), the Health Insurance Portability and Accountability Act (HIPAA), and Payment Card Industry Data Security Standards (PCI DSS). SQL Server contains a lot of features to help mitigate the requirements imposed by these regulations. Some companies need to comply, and some do not. Auditing your company's compliance with relevant regulation is one area where you, as a DBA, may need to help out.

If you study security, you will realize that there are many kinds of attacks against SQL that intruders can perform. These include SQL injection, repudiation, and even janitor attacks. These attacks can come not only from the outside world but from internal employees and contractors as well. A complete discussion on security and auditing is available in Chapter 11.

Disaster Recovery

Disasters can happen at any time and can take the form of many different types of events. In the case of a natural disaster or terrorist attack, more things may be damaged or destroyed than your database server. Thankfully, the more common scenario is a catastrophic hardware failure. As a DBA, you will either create or be responsible for reading and understanding the disaster recovery plan. To help mitigate a disaster, companies usually back up their databases and copy or transport these backups to a different physical site. In addition, companies depending more on real-time data may configure database replication between two physically separate locations. Other technologies within SQL Server that help in disaster recover include AlwaysOn Availability Groups, which is the ability to have a live or near-live copy of the database ready in case of a problem on the primary server. This copy can be used for active read-only connections.

Design and Performance Improvement

As you gain more experience as a DBA, you may be asked to help architects and developers design schemas. A proper schema design is critical to the efficiency of the applications that will utilize the database, and a lot of tools and techniques are available to help model data.

Outside of designing the schema for the database, more often, a DBA will be asked to troubleshoot poorly performing queries. SQL Server 2012 comes with tools to help find and troubleshoot these problem queries. First, the Database Tuning Advisor will take a look at a workload and suggest improvements that can be made such as creating indexes on certain columns used by a query. The data collector can collect historical performance information, which can be used to easily discover trend information. Trends can show you, the DBA, when a particular query started to slow down and at what rate the degradation occurred. You'll find a thorough discussion on the Database Tuning Advisor, data collector, and many more performance-tuning and optimization tools in Chapter 13.

Documentation

As a DBA, you may have to document the configuration of your database servers, disaster recovery plans, schemas, and best practices. You also may be asked to establish a standard configuration for SQL Server. This configuration and instructions on how to use it are usually written by—guess who?—you. If you are not familiar with the idea or need for a standard SQL Server configuration, consider the case where you, as the DBA, own and are responsible for the database server. An outside group wants to use SQL Server, and if you didn't require them to use your "standard SQL Server configuration," you could potentially end up with custom maintenance and security scripts. Not defining and using standard SQL Server configurations may increase your workloads by a larger amount than you expect, so do not be afraid to start defining standards and documenting them.

■ **Note** As a technical person, it took a long time for me to realize the importance of documentation. As a software test engineer back in the mid-1990s, my philosophy was something to the effect of "Can't you just look at my test cases? Why do I have to spend the time writing a Word document?" It wasn't until I started working as a program manager on the SQL Server Management Tools team that I realized the importance of writing down information. The specifications I wrote would be read by many other folks. By having a well-written specification, I found it was easier to answer people's questions with, "It's in the spec! Read it!"

—Robert Walters

Salary Information

The U.S. Department of Labor and Statistics has an occupational handbook that describes different professions and their perspective job growth, average earnings, and other interesting bits of information. You can find the DBA profession at `www.bls.gov/oco/ocos042.htm`. The annual earnings for a DBA, according to the handbook, range between $50,000 and $85,000. Still dislike writing documentation? This salary, though, is subject to the local cost of living, to supply and demand, and to other factors. With that aside, DBAs make a nice income.

Words from Real-World DBAs

Rather than give you only our opinions about DBAs and what they do, we'll share with you different perspectives of this profession from other people who are performing this role today. The following sections contain interviews with practicing and successful database administrators.

Grant Fritchey, Principal DBA

Grant Fritchey has been a DBA for 10 years and has been working in the IT field for about 20 years. Grant works for Red Gate Software as their product evangelist.

Robert Walters: How did you end up as a DBA? Were you always interested in this career?

Grant Fritchey: My first job as a DBA came about by accident. I had been working for years as a developer. During that time, I had worked quite a lot with databases in smaller shops that sometimes didn't have a DBA. I picked up a lot of the basics. I was working a startup that was undergoing a lot of turmoil. Our DBA had a quit a couple of months earlier. Because he quit, we had started running into all kinds of problems with our databases. One day, I got really upset and went into my boss, Vipul Minocha, great guy, and started hollering about all the issues. Vipul wrote them all down and talked to me a minute about the priorities, which ones were more important, and so on. After a bit he said, "OK, so now you've got your priorities; let me know if you run into any issues working them out." After I picked my jaw up off the floor, I was a DBA.

Robert Walters: What do you like about the job?

Grant Fritchey: My principal job now is to help other DBAs to do their jobs better. That's great fun. I get to find out what kinds of problems that DBAs and data professionals run into during the day and come up with methods to help them do their jobs better. I spend a hefty chunk of every day documenting best practices and approaches for all sorts of things—backups, deployments, disaster recovery, all that. It's constantly challenging and extremely hard work and I absolutely love it.

The thing I like the most about being a database professional is that things constantly change. We can't sit back on our previous accomplishments and declare ourselves finished. There are always new challenges and new problems to solve. Best of all, the technology is constantly changing so that we have new solutions to both the new and old problems. There's no sitting still or even slowing down. You have to constantly learn. That makes this a thrilling position to be in.

Robert Walters: What is the most challenging part of the job?

Grant Fritchey: There are two really big challenges to this job, and they can be summed up in two different words: "technology" and "people." You have to keep your technology running. This means learning everything you can about it and creating appropriate monitors and checks and best practices—all to help keep it running. Further, you have to know what to do when the technology fails. All that taken together can be very hard. Add on to that, you have to work with people. This job straddles the normal IT hierarchy. You have to work closely with development teams and the infrastructure teams. That means talking to people. People can be very hard to work with. You may have to tell developers that the query they spent two weeks writing just won't scale and has to be completely rewritten. That's like calling their baby ugly. You may have to request disk space from SAN managers who just don't understand why you need more space when they gave you space last week. All these negotiations require soft skills that aren't taught in college or at the local IT school. You have to develop them through other means. That's hard too.

Robert Walters: How many server/databases or organizations do you support?

Grant Fritchey: None. Or, you could say, thousands. I don't have to support any databases for the company, but I'm involved with tuning queries on our products that go out to thousands of databases all over the world, so you could say I support all of those. I do have a couple of servers running locally that I break and rebuild on a regular basis so that I know how to do disaster recovery and database restores and backups better than I ever did before.

Robert Walters: What is a typical day for you at your company like?

Grant Fritchey: Fortunately, there is no typical day. I may be performance tuning a database compression algorithm in the morning and then documenting a better way to do object-level recovery in the afternoon. I do spend a certain amount of time most days answering questions on forums like Ask SQL Server Central, SQL Server Central, and the Red Gate forums. I also travel quite a bit and present at user groups, SQL Saturdays, and various conferences. The presentations are mostly on exactly the types of things we talk about in this book, setting up servers, performance tuning, backups and restores, consistency checking, and all the rest.

But my focus remains on standard DBA and data professionals' issues. I want to come up with solutions to common problems. I want to identify common problems. So I spend my time interacting with other DBAs and doing research and testing.

Robert Walters: Do you have any advice for new DBAs?

Grant Fritchey: First, and most important, make sure you know how to do a backup, a log backup, a differential backup, and any other kind of backup that's available. Once that's done, learn how to do a restore, a log restore, a restore to a point in time, system database restores . . . you get the picture. Don't just learn this stuff; practice this stuff. If you learn nothing else as a DBA, know how to back up and restore your systems.

After that, keep learning. Pick up books on the various topics of T-SQL, SQL Server, data warehousing, whatever, and learn them. Take part in your local user group. You can learn stuff there. Take part in online communities like SQL Server Central. Keep learning all the time. There's a lot to learn for any given version of SQL Server, and just about when you've got it reasonably well in hand, an upgrade will come along, and you'll have to start all over again. But that's the fun part.

Roman Rehak, Principal Database Architect

Roman Rehak has been working with databases for the past ten years. He currently works for MyWebGrocer, a provider of online grocery services.

Robert Walters: How did you end up as a DBA? Were you always interested in this career?

Roman Rehak: For some reason, I always liked databases. I remember when, as a student at the University of Vermont, I was working at the school lab and launched Microsoft Access just to see what it did. I started as a C++ developer. My company developed a product similar to Visual Basic, and once the product was done, aside from selling it, we started doing custom development for companies using that same RAD environment. I was not happy about being downgraded from a C++ guy to a RAD type of guy, but luckily, our applications were using SQL Server as the back end, and I quickly fell in love with it.

At my next job, I was offered a position of a development DBA, where the work was split between SQL Server and coding in Visual Basic 6, ASP, and later .NET. As a developer, I prefer coding the background stuff—things like components, middle layer, web services, and of course, T-SQL. My current position is the first DBA-only type of job, but I still sneak in some C# coding to develop my own tools and utilities or to code complex XML imports. Right now, aside from supporting our development team, I am responsible for several 24/7 production servers, the development and QA environments, and everything else that goes along with that.

Robert Walters: What do you like about the job?

Roman Rehak: There is never a dull moment in the database world. I like the feeling I get when I resolve a production problem or avert a potentially dangerous situation. I love query tuning more than anything else, especially if I can make a huge difference in execution time and resource usage. Being a good DBA involves a lot of different skills, so you need a solid background in coding, relational theory, networking, and hardware; plus, you need solid people and communication skills. On top of that, you need to develop pretty good detective skills to resolve what I call "evasively obvious issues" like "This code behaves differently when I run it on its own and when I execute it in a stored procedure." (Answer: You have different ANSI null settings.) I love the variety I get as a DBA. Every day is different from another. I also enjoy the mentoring part of the job—helping developers with their database tasks and teaching them best practices. I got bored doing just regular web development from a spec, and this is much different.

Robert Walters: What is the most challenging part of the job?

Roman Rehak: Balancing and prioritizing what needs to be done. I usually have a long list of items I need to work on, both my own stuff and requests from developers or operations. I use a whiteboard and constantly modify my daily, weekly, and long-term to-do lists. But when there is a problem in production, it takes precedence over anything else, so these interruptions add to the challenge.

Robert Walters: How many server/databases or organizations do you support?

Roman Rehak: We have about 60 employees. We have ten production database servers, six standby servers, and six development/QA servers.

Robert Walters: What is a typical day for you at your company like?

Roman Rehak: I check my e-mail about 20 times a day, including in the evening. We have pretty extensive monitoring in place, so we get notifications about free disk space, long-running transactions, job failures, replication problems, application timeouts, and many other things. I often have to respond to those issues right away or the same day, and that takes precedence over anything else. I attend a few meetings a week with the development or operations teams. When things are quiet, I can work on regular stuff, like coding stored procedures, creating new tables, creating SSIS packages, or putting together deployment scripts. Once in a while, I work from home half a day so that nobody bugs me, and I can think about the big-picture stuff, like architecture. Things are slower on Fridays, so I often work on some proof-of-concept stuff or spend an hour reading SQL Server blogs.

Robert Walters: Do you have any advice for new DBAs?

Roman Rehak: This is a good field to be in, if you are cut out for the job. I survived a total of six layoffs at my three previous jobs mainly because of my database skills, since those are harder to replace, so I can say that my choice to make SQL Server my main skill has served me well. My most important advice would be to have a good disaster recovery plan in place. Make sure backups are done and stored in multiple places. If you are shipping to a standby server, remember that a database is not enough to get your application running again. Make sure all SQL Agent jobs and all dependent objects in system databases are there and ready to go if needed. The other advice I have is to stay current. The technology changes quickly, and SQL Server is becoming more and more complex, so you need to read magazines, blogs, and books and attend conferences and local user group meetings.

Charlie Pyne, Senior DBA

Charlie has been a DBA for the past ten years at Partners Healthcare in Boston. His team supports the database servers for many Boston hospitals.

Robert Walters: How did you end up as a DBA? Were you always interested in this career?

Charlie Pyne: After working in the construction management field for a few years, I went to Worcester Poly Tech for a certificate program in client server application development. My first SQL related job was in 1999 for Partners Healthcare supporting a terrible MS Access–based work order system that happened to have a SQL back end. In the process of working with this system, I was exposed to T-SQL programming and eventually transferred to the DBA team at Partners. I've worked here ever since.

Robert Walters: What do you like about the job?

Charlie Pyne: I like how DBA work is a mix of programming, hardware, and systems administration. All three are areas I have always been interested in. DBA work is the perfect mix for someone who can't pick one computer field.

Robert Walters: What is the most challenging part of the job?

Charlie Pyne: The most challenging part is finding the right balance between the perfect system and "good enough." Customers, server owners, and vendors often want to do things "their way," which almost never fits nicely into a DBA's plan for how a server should be configured. We spend a lot of time coming up with configurations that are solid and secure but are also as flexible enough to accommodate everyone.

Robert Walters: How many server/databases or organizations do you support?

Charlie Pyne: Approximately 500 servers and 5,000 databases in 15 hospitals.

Robert Walters: What is a typical day for you at your company like?

Charlie Pyne: Every day is different, but here's a typical day.

- *Morning:* Check backups and fix any issues that may have appeared in our monitoring system

- *Afternoon:* Meetings with programmers, vendors, and business owners to plan upgrades and new systems.

- *Night (from home):* Upgrades and work that can't be done during business hours.

Robert Walters: Do you have any advice for new DBAs?

Charlie Pyne: Be sure you learn to write SQL and write it well. This will not only help you be a better SQL Server DBA but also directly relates to programming and use of other database systems. I'm always amazed by how many DBAs can barely write a basic SQL statement. You'll be at a distinct disadvantage if you can't write SQL well.

Ed Clapper, Database Product Architect Manager

Ed has been in the IT field for 35 years, with 31 years at CIGNA Corporation. He spent the first seven years of his career with mainframe–based application programming. Following this, he moved into IMS

DB\DC support then DB2. For the past 20 years, he has worked with SQL Server as a DBA and in product support within CIGNA.

Robert Walters: How did you end up as a DBA? Were you always interested in this career?

Ed Clapper: Starting out as an application programmer, I learned early that I was much more interested in the technical aspects of IT than the business components. This led me to system design and consulting for applications utilizing relational database systems. Early on, I transitioned to providing SQL Server DBA support, as there was a sizable push to move off the mainframe platform, as there was a perception that Wintel deployment was less expensive then mainframe. Providing DBA consulting for a variety of internal businesses and then subsequent DBMS product support positioned me to stay in the forefront of the technology directions.

Robert Walters: What do you like about the job?

Ed Clapper: I am constantly confronted with new and changing situations requiring a continued passion for learning new and challenging technologies. It provides opportunities to provide major impacts to my customers' bottom lines.

Robert Walters: What is the most challenging part of the job?

Ed Clapper: Enforcing standards across the distributed enterprise including security and object management.

Robert Walters: How many server/databases or organizations do you support?

Ed Clapper: My team supports approximately 1,100 production databases and 3,500 additional databases for various levels of testing and certification. We provide DBMS product support for an additional 1,500 databases.

Robert Walters: What is a typical day for you at your company like?

Ed Clapper: A typical day involves mix of activities:

- Responding to application DBMS–related issues that arise on a daily basis
- Designing architecture for new applications and cost effective solutions
- Providing knowledge transfer to DBAs and developers
- Managing the flow of product enhancements and fixes for both the DBMS and all supporting products
- Designing new solutions to improve availability for critical business applications
- Researching technology trends and their viability for my corporation

Robert Walters: Do you have any advice for new DBAs?

Ed Clapper:

- Automate, automate, automate.

- Stay clear of dependence on GUI tools.

- Develop solid relationships with your partner software and hardware support teams.

- Expect the problem to be perceived to always be the database until it is proven otherwise.

- Enforce standards above all else.

Michael Esposito, Senior Technical Consultant and DBA

Michael has been in IT for about 30 years. He has been a DBA off and on for about 25 years.

Robert Walters: How did you end up as a DBA? Were you always interested in this career?

Michael Esposito: I was not always interested in being a DBA. In college, I do not think they even mentioned the position. When I got out into the professional world, I was an application developer working with a DBMS system called Integrated Database Management System (IDMS). One of my applications was having locking issues, so I started working closely with our DBA team. I had done a lot of research about the issue, and I was telling the DBAs how the locking system in the DBMS worked. My relationship with DBA team developed to the point where, when a job posting came up for a DBA, they asked me to post. One of the big reasons they wanted me was that most of them had come from OS system support, so having someone on the team who could talk to application developers easily was a big plus.

Robert Walters: What do you like about the job?

Michael Esposito: I like being able to a have a foot in the OS/systems world and in the application world. One day, I might be tuning a query, and the next, I am designing the layout of instances and databases for a new release of the DBMS. The variety of tasks keeps things interesting.

Robert Walters: What is the most challenging part of the job?

Michael Esposito: The most challenging task for me is dealing with costs. Cost issues have become very tough because consumers of IT resources want everything for free or at least for less, but IT management wants to charge back the consumer directly for everything possible. It is challenging to come up with fair chargeback schemes that do not cost the company more as a whole. Also, as certain technologies decline, the consumers who still use those technologies can see charges go up for the same service. It is difficult to have that conversation with a customer and still keep them satisfied.

Robert Walters: How many server/databases or organizations do you support?

Michael Esposito: We about 100 servers and 2,000 databases. We have databases from 10MBs to 300GBs.

Robert Walters: What is a typical day for you at your company like?

Michael Esposito: There really is no typical day, which is good because I like the variety, but there are tasks that must be done like checking your backups, checking filesystem space, being sure there are no production problems, etc. It is like doing your homework before you can go out and play.

Robert Walters: Do you have any advice for new DBAs?

Michael Esposito: If you can, do some code development along the way. It always helps to walk a mile in another person's shoes. Also, be flexible and open to opportunities. At one point in my career, databases on the Unix environment were rare, but my company wanted to be ready for them so they were looking for "volunteers" to join the Unix admin group. A few people refused, but I said OK. I did not do anything database-related for a few years, but I learned so much about Unix that when the Unix database environment started to take off, I was an instant expert.

Summary

Throughout the years, we have found the best thing to do to learn about a new job is to do an informational interview with someone who is currently in that role, like the ones in the final section of this chapter. Make sure you ask them the tough questions about the job. Depending on where you currently live, another great resource is the local SQL Server users group. These groups usually meet once a month to cover a topic. They are great for meeting other IT professionals as well as getting job leads! Although there is no official Microsoft web site that lists all of the SQL Server users groups, there is one that lists quite a few worldwide: `www.mssqltips.com/tip.asp?tip=949`. SQL Saturdays are also a great way to meet people and learn about SQL Server. More information can be found at `www.sqlsaturday.com`.

CHAPTER 2

Planning and Installing SQL Server 2012

For some reason, during my time as an application development consultant, I (Rob Walters) ended up working on a few projects where I was writing an InstallShield or Windows Installer package for a client. As a former developer working in various environments, I have made my own hypothesis that, in general, whoever gets stuck writing install scripts must feel like the little kid who got picked last for a kickball team in fifth grade. There is nothing glamorous about setup. Your code is run only when the application is installed, updated, or removed. If my hypothesis is correct and writing setup scripts is not the most exciting task for developers, one can assume that, in general, the overall experience to the end user might not be optimal. After all, as a developer, why should you put much effort in something that is going to run only a few times in the life of the product?

The reason you, as a developer, should put a lot of effort into setup is that it's the first impression of your product to the customer! A flimsy install might leave the impression that the rest of the product is shoddy, which may or may not be true. Setup is also incredibly complex with multiple requirements, including providing support for multiple operating systems and editions of SQL Server and for upgrading, repairing, and uninstalling. Getting all these right is a tough task.

Until SQL Server 2008, setting up and installing the product was an average experience at best. In general, the product would install most of the time, but there was massive room for improvement. SQL Server 2008 was part of the third generation of SQL Server products, and SQL Server 2012 builds on this great setup experience. This version contains the absolute best installation and configuration experience of any previous version of the product. The user interface is informative and intuitive, and on top of all that, there are wizards to help you perform advanced tasks such as setting up and removing cluster nodes.

In this chapter, we will discuss several aspects of planning and installing SQL Server:

- SQL Server editions and resource requirements
- Installation planning for SQL Server
- Step-by-step install of the evaluation edition of SQL Server 2012

To get the most out of this chapter, it is best to walk through an installation of the evaluation edition yourself. This edition is a free download and functions for 180 days. You can find it at the following URL: www.microsoft.com/sqlserver/en/us/get-sql-server/try-it.aspx.

Understanding the Editions

There are three main editions of SQL Server: Enterprise, Business Intelligence, and Standard. Beyond these, there are a variety of specialized editions: Developer, Express, and Evaluation edition. Before diving into the differences between each of these, it is important to first discuss 32- and 64-bit architectures, because each edition may or may not support your preferred hardware configuration.

Demystifying 32-Bit and 64-Bit Architectures

If you are relatively new to working with technology, you may have seen servers on the x86 or x64 or IA64 processor platform. If not, you will see that nomenclature once you read which platforms each SQL Server edition supports. Historically, x86 comes from the 86 part of the Intel 8086 chip. This chip design dates back the late 1970s and has been dramatically transformed over the years, increasing in performance and capabilities. Lately, the x86 in servers has been on 32-bit architecture. With 32-bit servers, one of the more significant limitations is the relatively small amount of addressable memory. Having large amounts of memory is good because it allows you to have more active connections and increases performance in memory-hungry applications like Analysis Services, SQL Server Integration Services, and the SQL Server database engine.

So, in a perfect world, manufacturers would give you a 64-bit chip to allow you to address greater amounts of memory. And they have provided 64 bits, just with some bumps in the road. Up until 64-bit chips, two main chip manufacturers supported the Windows operating system: AMD and Intel. In terms of market share, hardware vendors appeared to prefer Intel's implementation of x86. When it was time for 64-bit, Intel veered off into a totally new direction, away from its popular x86 architecture. This new chipset was called Itanium, or IA64. AMD also wanted to produce a 64-bit chip, but it produced a chip that was just like the x86 except the instruction sets were 64-bit. In effect, AMD made a true 64-bit version of the popular x86 chip; it's referred to as x86-64. In the end, hardware vendors and users of these chips found it much easier and quicker to leverage AMD's implementation than Intel's Itanium. This was because, with AMD, the vendors did not have to rewrite major parts of their implementations to run on a 64-bit platform. With the minimal success of its Itanium brand of processors, Intel was forced to make an x86-64 chip as well. Together, both AMD and Intel's version of x86-64 are known to Microsoft as x64. Various editions of SQL Server support specific architectures, and chances are, if your company is buying new hardware, it's probably 64-bit. SQL Server 2012 supports the x86 and x64 platforms. At the time of this writing, there is no planned support for the Itanium IA64 platform. Also note that if you are planning on installing SQL Server 2012 on 32-bit hardware, you will not be able to use addressable windowing extensions (AWE). This feature was introduced to allow SQL Server to use more than the 2GB memory normally capped by 32-bit operating systems.

Server Editions

Before SQL Server 2008, there was not much difference between the features in Standard edition and the ones in Enterprise edition. Enterprise edition traditionally has had features that focus on solving the needs of very large and highly available database systems. Features such as table partitioning, unlimited CPU usage, online indexing, and online restore are examples of enterprise features. If companies had unconstrained budgets, chances are they would probably just buy Enterprise edition and go on with life. In reality, most organizations are always under tight budget constraints, so companies were more likely to purchase Standard edition, which costs about one-fourth as much as Enterprise edition. Starting with SQL Server 2008, the differences between Standard and Enterprise editions are quite substantial. In fact, the changes added to the Standard edition of SQL Server 2012 are minimal. Most of the work has been placed in Enterprise edition and in a new edition called Business Intelligence edition. The feature sets work a lot like a Russian doll, where Standard edition is a subset of Business Intelligence edition, which is a subset of the Enterprise edition features.

Most of the key features, such as AlwaysOn Availability Groups and columnar indexing, are in Enterprise edition only. SQL Server Books Online has a great article called "Features Supported by the Editions of SQL Server 2012" at http://msdn.microsoft.com/en-us/library/cc645993(v=SQL.110).aspx. If you are asked to evaluate which edition to use, consider the capabilities that Enterprise edition offers, because it may be more economical to consolidate servers and applications and simply purchase a single Enterprise license.

Let's take a look at these editions in detail.

Standard Edition

Standard edition is designed for departmental applications. This edition contains some basic business intelligence capabilities as well as the fundamental relational database features. Most of the enhancements to SQL Server are found in the other two editions; however, you will notice some minor improvements, such as native auditing support at the server instance level.

Business Intelligence Edition

Business Intelligence Edition contains all the functionality of Standard edition and includes a full suite of business intelligence capabilities including the new Power View feature. This edition contains functionality to integrate well with your SharePoint environment.

Enterprise Edition

Enterprise Edition is the most comprehensive offering. It includes all the mission-critical OLTP capabilities as well as end-to-end business intelligence capabilities. Unlike other database platform vendors, there are not any add-ons to SQL Server. When you choose Enterprise edition, you have everything that SQL Server has to offer.

Specialized Editions

Enterprise edition, Business Intelligence edition, and Standard edition are the core offerings for SQL Server. If those editions were all you could buy, you probably wouldn't be too happy. There are situations where you need to have access to all the functionality of Enterprise edition but you can't afford it. A development environment is a perfect example of when you might need all the features available. For this reason and others, several specialized editions are available. Each of these editions has some restrictions that are mentioned in the following subsections.

Developer Edition

Developer edition is really Enterprise edition with some extra development-oriented content and licensing restrictions on how it can be used. This edition is intended for users to build and test applications and is not allowed to be run as a production server. In the event you want to upgrade your Developer edition to Enterprise edition, this is also possible.

Express Edition

Express edition is Microsoft's free version of SQL Server. A long time ago, Microsoft had a free version of a database called Microsoft Desktop Engine (MSDE). A major issue with MSDE was that there was no user interface, so it was very difficult to manage. Microsoft did away with MSDE and introduced the Express edition starting with SQL Server 2005. Functionally, Express edition is almost the same as Standard edition except that is limited on CPU and memory use. There are other differences, such as the absence of the SQL Server Agent job scheduler and a reduced replication story. After all, what do you expect for free?

There are a few more versions of Express. One is called Express with Advanced Services. The name is not really catchy, but it includes everything in Express plus a version of Reporting Services. The other is Express with Tools, which is the SQL Server database engine and SQL Server Management Studio Express version. You can also download just the SQL Server Management Studio Express version as a stand-alone install.

SQL Server Express LocalDB

SQL Server Express edition is a free version of SQL Server that is basically a throttled-down version of the full SQL Server engine. For SQL Server development, the idea was to include this free version for developers to use and learn with. One of the problems with SQL Server Express is it's a heavyweight in a fight requiring a featherweight. SQL Server Express is a Windows Service and requires network configuration and attention.

For developers, there is something better in SQL Server 2012 called SQL Server Express LocalDB (LocalDB). LocalDB is a version of SQL Server that installs faster, has fewer prerequisites and doesn't require management of a database instance. LocalDB is not an in-proc DLL that you bind to, rather it's an application that runs in the user mode as a separate process. LocalDB is not appropriate for server-based or multiuser environments, because its opens the database files for exclusive use. It is, however, ideal for development environments since it's fully supports T-SQL.

Evaluation Edition

The evaluation edition is a 180-day free version of Enterprise edition. You can download it for free from `www.microsoft.com/sqlserver/en/us/get-sql-server/try-it.aspx`. Note that at the end of the 180-day period, you will either have to upgrade to a paid edition or uninstall SQL Server.

SQL Server Terminology

Before we get too much in depth on describing how to install and use SQL Server, it is good to introduce some key concepts about this relational database at this point. In particular, you should understand the term *instance* as it is used with respect to SQL Server.

Prior to SQL Server 2000, you could have only one installation or instance of SQL Server installed on the server. You can think of an instance of SQL Server as a complete SQL Server installation including objects like system and user databases, logins, and SQL Server Agent jobs. Starting with SQL Server 2000, you can install multiple instances of SQL Server on the same server. These additional instances will simply listen for user connections on different ports. Since each instance is effectively a completely isolated database server, using multiple instances allows for easy application consolidation.

Planning Your Installation

If you are planning on installing SQL Server on your desktop to just play with it, you probably don't create a plan, review it with other folks in your organization, and schedule a time to implement the plan. Chances are you load `setup.exe` and click the Next button a bunch of times until the wizard starts installing SQL Server.

Although installing SQL Server 2012 can be as simple as clicking a few buttons, it is a good idea to step back first and create an installation plan. This plan will help you answer questions that are critical to the success of the installation. Some of these questions are as follows: Do we meet the hardware requirements of SQL Server 2012? Are the systems engineering folks aware of our new installation of SQL Server? The last question is very important. In some organizations, measures are in place to automatically block network ports if new applications appear to be running on them. This is an effort to reduce the risk and damages of viruses. Always get the necessary people involved when planning an installation of SQL Server. These people include not only your database administrators but other folks from IT, such as the people who are responsible for the network and for the operating systems. The specific list depends on how your organization is structured.

Assessing the Environment

Most organizations have a good idea of all the servers that they currently have. However, the larger the organization, the more likely that there are instances of SQL Server that exist that may or may not be accounted for or managed by the DBA staff. That situation may come about for a variety of reasons, even some legitimate ones. In the end, as a DBA, it is a good idea to keep an active inventory of which servers and SQL instances you manage. Not only is this a best practice but it's a good way to prevent you and your company from getting into legal trouble. There are a variety of tools that can help you with SQL Server instance discovery. Microsoft ships a tool called the Microsoft Assessment and Planning (MAP) Toolkit. This toolkit is not designed for just SQL Server; rather, it helps users simplify the planning process for migrating to Windows 8, Microsoft Office 2010, Windows Server 2008 R2, and other Microsoft products. You can find more information about this tool at `www.microsoft.com/MAP`.

With respect to SQL Server, the MAP tool will discover and inventory all the SQL Server instances in your organization. Data collected about each instance includes the version, edition, and current service pack applied. This tool also captures the hardware and platform details for computers that are running SQL Server instances, including determining whether the machines are virtual or physical. Figure 2-1 shows a screen shot of the MAP tool.

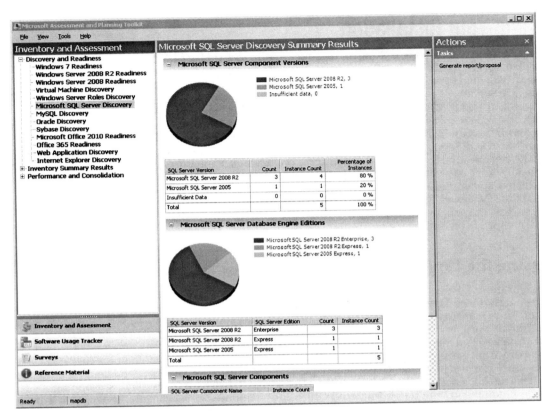

Figure 2-1. Microsoft SQL Server discovery summary

The MAP tool creates both a Word document and Excel workbook that are much more detailed than the report shown in Figure 2-1. Information gathered from this tool includes SQL Server service packs installed, editions, disk free space, database names, database sizes, users and much more. This tool is covered in greater depth in Chapter 16.

Choosing the Right Edition

Earlier, you read about the various editions available with SQL Server. Unless you know your organization is purchasing Enterprise edition, you need to determine whether the features and functionality you need are in any of the other versions. After all, there's no need to spend money unnecessarily.

SQL Server Books Online offers a plethora of great information on SQL Server, including a nice table that lists which edition contains which of the key features within the product. You can find this "Features Supported by the Editions of SQL Server 2012" article at `http://msdn.microsoft.com/en-us/library/cc645993(v=SQL.110).aspx`.

Once your organization or team has decided which edition to use, you need to verify the hardware and software requirements for SQL Server.

Validating Hardware and Software Requirements

Going to college in the great state of Michigan, I had the opportunity to do an internship with an independent software vendor that was working on a project for one of the big three automobile manufacturers. I learned a lot from that experience, and it wasn't just Visual Basic and COM development. Rather, it was what was learned from the water cooler discussions. One time, I overheard a few folks talking about an investigation into why brakes were wearing out much faster than they did when tested in their lab. Apparently, the vehicles running those brakes that had this problem all had aftermarket rims, and these rims couldn't dissipate the heat that the brakes generated. The heat buildup caused the brakes to wear more quickly than with the stock rims. The moral of this story in relation to SQL Server is to check that the hardware you plan to install SQL Server on can support the requirements and thus provide a great end-user experience.

SQL Server Books Online does another great job going into detail on each of the editions in the article "Hardware and Software Requirements for Installing SQL Server 2012" at `http://msdn.microsoft.com/en-us/library/ms143506(v=SQL.110).aspx`. You can see from the article that the requirements vary between editions. Thus, it is important to consider the edition you plan to use.

In an enterprise environment, change happens. You'll frequently be faced with new requirements and user demand. In the Enterprise edition of SQL Server, it is possible to hot-add memo
ry and CPUs, provided both the hardware and the operating system support this capability. By being able to add memory and CPU without restarting the server or the SQL Server service, you can maintain high levels of availability for your database.

Installing SQL Server Evaluation Edition

In this section, we will perform the initial install of SQL Server, which simply installs the support files, including the .NET Framework and SQL Server Installation Center. If you already have SQL Server installed or choose not to install SQL Server at this time, you can skip this section. Throughout this book, the examples will use the evaluation edition of SQL Server.

■ **Note** Developer and Enterprise editions provide the same capabilities as the evaluation edition. If you have either Developer or Enterprise edition available to you already, you can go ahead and use it rather than installing the evaluation edition.

Step 1: Downloading SQL Server Evaluation Edition

You can download the evaluation edition from `www.microsoft.com/sqlserver/en/us/get-sql-server/try-it.aspx`. When you navigate to this link, you will have the option to download a 32-bit or 64-bit version.

You can download either a DVD image of the product or a single executable. Either one will work, and for the sake of simplicity, I'll assume you chose the x64 executable. Once a selection is made, the download begins, and depending on your Internet connection speed, you may want to consider grabbing a drink. The download is more than 1GB.

Once you have your own copy of the 1GB executable, you are ready to run it. Upon execution, you are asked for a folder name. Once you provide this folder path, the installation application will take about five minutes to extract all the files within the single file archive and re-create the entire SQL Server installation directory structure. When this process is complete, you will be greeted with a simple Extraction Complete dialog box.

It is at this point where you are ready to actually run the installation of Setup.

Step 2: Understanding the SQL Server Installation Center

If you look at the files that are contained on the SQL Server setup media, you can see a `readme.htm` file. Readme files are provided with every release of the product and contain a lot of valuable information. In the SQL Server 2012 readme file, there are links to the Upgrade Advisor tool and to various SQL Server Books Online topics regarding installing SQL Server.

At this point, you are ready to begin installing SQL Server. As with most Microsoft products, a `setup.exe` executable is located in the root folder of the SQL Server media. This program will first verify that you have the correct .NET Framework version installed as well as other prerequisites. If it is determined that you are missing any of these prerequisites, `setup.exe` will install them for you at this time. You may be required to reboot the machine depending on which operating system and which prerequisites you have already installed.

Once the prerequisites are installed, running the `setup.exe` program will simply launch the SQL Server Installation Center dialog box. This small application is the graphical launch point for all kinds of setup tasks. Here, you can install a stand-alone instance of SQL Server or even add a node to an existing SQL Server cluster. The installation center consists of seven tabs, each providing values to an aspect of installing SQL Server. Let's take a look at each of these tabs in more detail.

Planning Tab

The Planning tab (see Figure 2-2) is the first tab that is displayed when the SQL Server Installation Center is started.

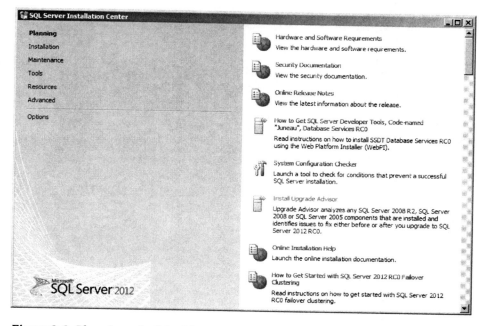

Figure 2-2. Planning tab of the SQL Server Installation Center

Previously in this chapter, we discussed issues to think about when you install SQL Server, such as figuring out whether your current hardware and software are compatible with SQL Server 2012. The Planning tab helps you plan your installation of SQL Server by making it easy to quickly access this kind of information. This tab also provides links to other important information, such as online release notes and online installation help. In addition to hyperlinks, there are two tools within this tab, the System Configuration Checker and the Upgrade Advisor. The System Configuration Checker (see Figure 2-3) will check the state of your server and determine whether Setup can proceed. Examples of these tests include determining whether your server needs to be restarted or whether you meet the minimum operation system version to install SQL Server.

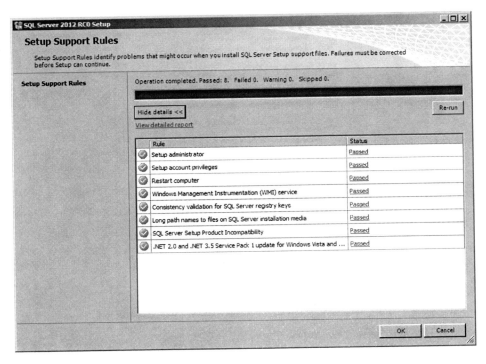

Figure 2-3. System Configuration Checker

There are other times within Setup where this System Configuration Checker will run for you. For example, when you are installing a stand-alone instance of SQL Server, this utility will be run at the beginning of that task.

The other tool on the Planning tab is the Upgrade Advisor. Use the Upgrade Advisor when you have an existing SQL Server installation and want to upgrade it to SQL Server 2012. The tool will check, from a syntactical standpoint, the integrity of your SQL Server installation. For example, if your application has referenced a deprecated stored procedure or function, this tool will tell you. Knowing and acting on this information before actually upgrading the server can save a lot of time and pain. This tool is discussed in more detail in the "Upgrading SQL Server" section of this chapter.

One of the last links on the Planning tab is the "How to get started with SQL Server 2012 Failover Clustering" link. Clustering is a big deal in most enterprise environments, and this link is an effort to help users with installing SQL Server on clustered servers.

Installation Tab

The Installation tab (see Figure 2-4) provides a series of wizards to help users install or upgrade SQL Server.

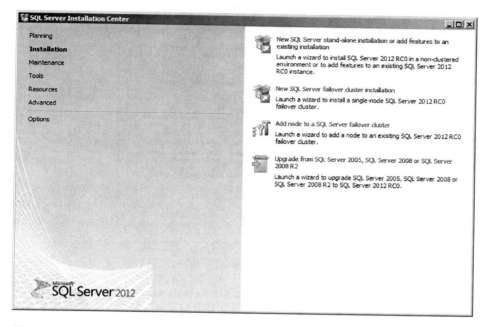

Figure 2-4. *Installation tab of the SQL Server Installation Center*

The Setup experience with SQL Server contains a lot of wizards in key areas. On the Installation tab, you can see links to launch wizards that help users. The first option, "New SQL Server stand-alone installation or add features to an existing installation," is self-explanatory; it launches the wizard you will use later in this chapter to install your instance of SQL Server. The next option is "New SQL Server failover cluster installation." The act of setting up and configuring a clustered SQL Server has traditionally been a tedious process. This version of SQL Server relieves some of the frustration by providing easy-to-use wizards to help the process along. Even common tasks, such as adding a node to a cluster, can be done using the "Add node to a SQL Server failover cluster" link, which also launches a wizard. There is even a wizard that will walk you through an upgrade of SQL Server 2005, SQL Server 2008, or SQL Server 2008 R2. This would be, you probably guessed it, the "Upgrade from SQL Server 2005, SQL Server 2008 or SQL Server 2008 R2" link.

Maintenance Tab

The Maintenance tab (see Figure 2-5) has four more features for you to enjoy.

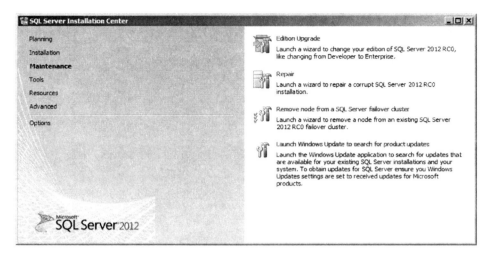

Figure 2-5. *Maintenance tab in the SQL Server Installation Center*

The Edition Upgrade Wizard allows you to upgrade an installation from a lower edition to a higher one. If you don't know what is meant by "lower edition," just think of how much each edition costs. For example, you can upgrade from Standard to Enterprise, but you cannot upgrade from Enterprise to Standard edition. This feature isn't here just to up-sell you on the bigger and faster vehicle; it does have some use in the upgrade scenario. Although it is possible to upgrade directly from SQL Server 2005 Standard to SQL Server 2012 Enterprise, the best practice would be to upgrade to SQL Server 2012 Standard first and then perform this edition upgrade once your existing applications are verified.

The Repair Wizard is the second of the three wizards available on the Maintenance tab. It runs through and checks the integrity of the installation, making any necessary changes to get you back to the original installation. Use this wizard if you had a previously failed installation of SQL Server.

The "Remove node from a SQL Server failover cluster" wizard guides you in removing a node from a SQL Server cluster. This task was once a pain to perform, but this wizard makes node removal much easier in SQL Server 2012.

Searching for product updates within setup makes it easy to install the latest bits the first time. Although this check is performed when you install an instance of SQL, you can check for updates whenever you want using the, "Launch Windows Update to search for product updates" link.

Tools Tab

The Tools tab (see Figure 2-6) contains four tools that will help users in their installations of SQL Server.

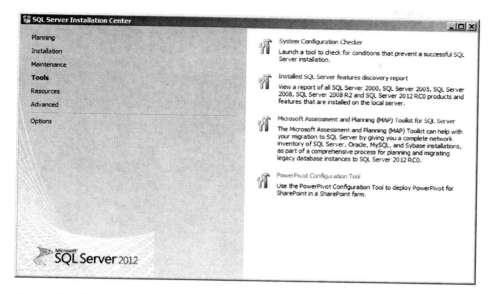

Figure 2-6. Tools tab in SQL Server Installation Center

The System Configuration Checker tool is the same one as was described on the Planning tab. The link to the tool is included on this tab also, just for convenience's sake.

On some occasions, you may be installing SQL Server 20012 on a server that may already have components of SQL Server or other instances of SQL Server installed. The "Installed SQL Server features discovery report" option does a quick inventory of the SQL Server instances and components that are installed on the local server. The tool presents these findings in an HTML document format for easy reading.

The discovery report obtains this information only for the local server. However, it is possible to run a different utility—the MAP toolkit—to obtain this kind of inventory information across your enterprise. You'll find an example of using the MAP toolkit in Chapter 16.

Finally, the PowerPivot Configuration Tool allows you to deploy PowerPivot into an existing SharePoint 2010 farm. PowerPivot for SharePoint enables the sharing of PowerPivot workbooks (created in Excel) via the SharePoint platform.

Resources Tab

The Resources tab (see Figure 2-7) contains a plethora of links to online resources related to SQL Server 2008.

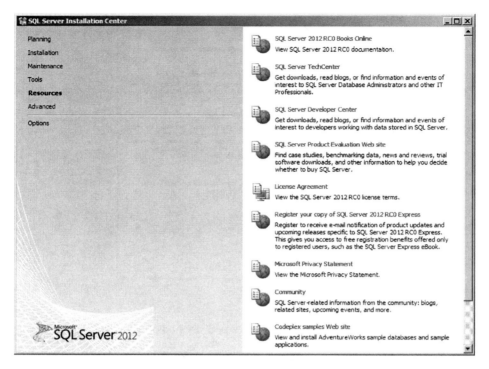

Figure 2-7. Resources tab in SQL Server Installation Center

SQL Server Books Online will be your best friend. Books Online contains an immense amount of SQL Server information. From T-SQL statement definitions to how-to articles, you will find yourself frequently referring to it. SQL Server Books online can always be accessed for free from the Web at `http://msdn.microsoft.com/en-us/library/ms130214(v=SQL.110).aspx`.

The other link on the Resources tab that is worth mentioning is the link to the CodePlex samples web site. In previous versions of SQL Server, samples were included on the install media. SQL Server 2012 does not include any samples; rather, all samples and example databases like AdventureWorks are available from CodePlex. The CodePlex web site isn't just for SQL Server; it is actually a multiproduct open source project workspace (`www.codeplex.com`).

Advanced Tab

The Advanced tab (see Figure 2-8) contains links to wizards that will assist the user in special-case installations.

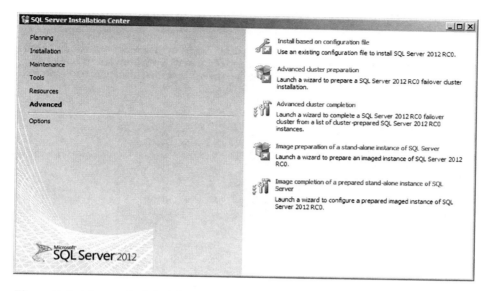

Figure 2-8. Advanced tab in SQL Server Installation Center

One of the more common techniques for installing SQL Server is to do it without a user interface (UI). This technique is called a *scripted install* and is very useful when you have to install multiple SQL Server instances. Imagine trying to run through the setup wizard on each one of your 20 SQL Server instances. Not only would that process take a long time but you would be spending a lot of time sitting at the server waiting for the installation to finish. Scripted installs leverage a configuration file that specifies all the properties you would have set while walking through the wizard. The end result is you don't have to sit there and wait to click the Next button.

Creating the configuration file by hand is a bit tedious. A SQL Server Books Online how-to article called "How to: Install SQL Server 2012 Using a Configuration File" at `http://msdn.microsoft.com/en-us/library/dd239405(v=SQL.110).aspx` makes a few key points about using configuration files. The most important one is that you don't have to sit and launch Notepad and write one of these configuration files from scratch. You can simply run through the setup wizard once and, instead of proceeding past the Ready to Install page, just copy the file path provided on this page and click Cancel. The file path is the location of a configuration file based on the options you selected in the wizard.

The "Image preparation of a stand-alone instance of SQL Server" option invokes a wizard that helps you create a Sysprep image of SQL Server. Sysprep is a tool that is used to help deploy images of system across multiple servers. Imagine if you had 30 brand new servers and you wanted to install Windows Server and SQL Server on all of them. This would take a lot of time. However, if we install one and then use Sysprep on that server, we could take that the resulting image and deploy it across the 29 other servers. The "Image completion of a prepared stand-alone instance of SQL Server" option invokes the wizard you run to finalize this Sysprep image. By "finalize," we mean setting the specific computer name for that server and other instance specific information.

Once you have a configuration file, you can simply pass this file to Setup on the command line (`setup.exe/ConfigurationFile=myCustomSQLInstall.ini`) and come back when it's finished.

Options Tab

The Options tab (see Figure 2-9) allows the user to select a processor architecture as well as the location of the installation media. This option is useful in a consolidation scenario where you want to install an x86 32-bit install on an x64 system. The x64 option is disabled because this screen shot was taken on a 32-bit virtual machine.

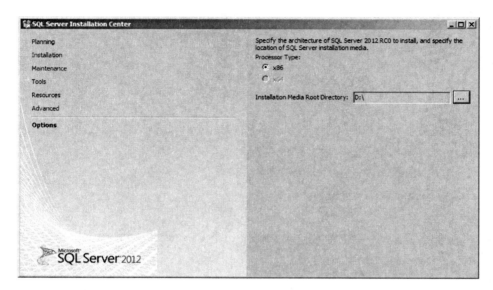

Figure 2-9. *Options tab in SQL Server Installation Center*

Step 3: Installing an Instance of SQL Server

Begin your installation of SQL Server by clicking the "New SQL Server stand-alone instance" link on the Installation tab of the SQL Server Installation Center. This link will launch a wizard that you can use to install a single instance of the SQL Server database engine. When you launch the wizard, Setup will run the System Configuration Checker tool, the same one that can be launched from the Tools tab. This checker will make sure that the server is in a state that can handle the installation of SQL Server. Some of the issues that could prevent an install include situations where the server is pending a reboot or the user is trying to install SQL Server on an unsupported operating system. Next, SQL Server will check for Product Updates and install SQL Server setup files.

After the check is performed, you will be asked for the product key. In the case of the evaluation edition, you will be asked either to enter the product key or to simply choose which free edition you want to install. To enable all the features in the product, make sure Enterprise Evaluation is selected in the "Specify a free edition" drop-down list.

Upon continuing the wizard, some additional SQL Server installation files will be installed; after that, you will be presented with the actual installation wizard. The first page of this wizard will be another system configuration check, which will check some different properties than the first configuration check. Once this completes, you are now ready to start telling the wizard exactly what you want.

Setup Role Page

SQL Server and its components like Analysis Services are not just their own products. They are sometimes integrated within other products like SharePoint 2010. It is the Setup Role Page shown in Figure 2-10, from which setup is asking you if you want to install all the SQL Server components, install the analysis services components within a SharePoint farm, or install everything with default options. For purposes of this chapter, we will keep the default radio button, SQL Server Feature Installation, selected.

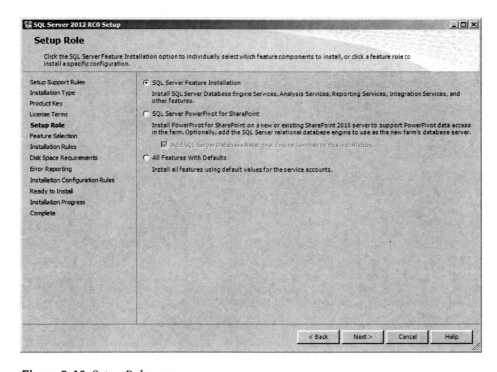

Figure 2-10. Setup Role page

Feature Selection Page

The Features Selection page (see Figure 2-11) allows you to specify which components of the product you want to install.

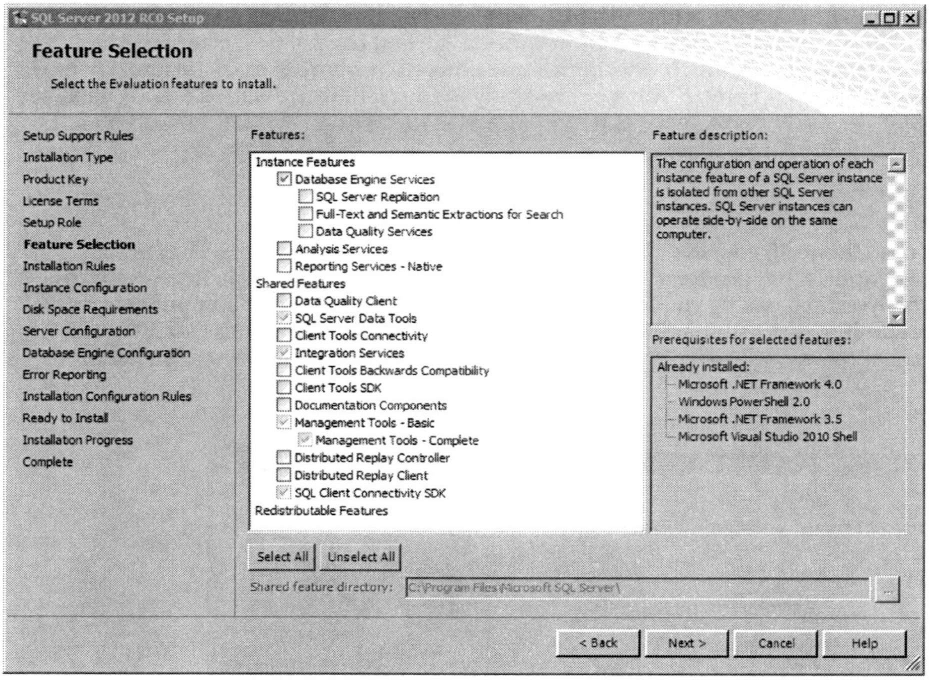

Figure 2-11. *Feature Selection page*

By selecting an instance feature, you are asking Setup to install a new instance of the database engine, Analysis Services engine, or Reporting Services. These options will install a new instance regardless of whether there is already one on the server. There are some components, though, that don't require more than one instance on the server. These components are called *shared components* and include things like SQL Server Management Studio (would you really want two different copies of SQL Server Management Studio on the same server or client machine?). If you took a good look at Figure 2-11, you may have noticed that one of the items, Redistributable Features, does not have any items under it. This is by design, and it includes features like MSXML version 6.0 and Error and Usage Reporting.

For the purposes of our walkthrough, select Database Engine Services from the Instance Features node as well as the default selected shared features shown in the above figure.

Instance Configuration Page

The Instance Configuration page (see Figure 2-12) allows users to select which type of instance to install—either a default instance or a named one. Per server, there can be just one default instance. However, you can install multiple named instances. In fact, you can have up to 50 instances installed on a server. These instances could all be SQL Server 2012 or a mix of SQL Server 2005 and SQL Server 2008.

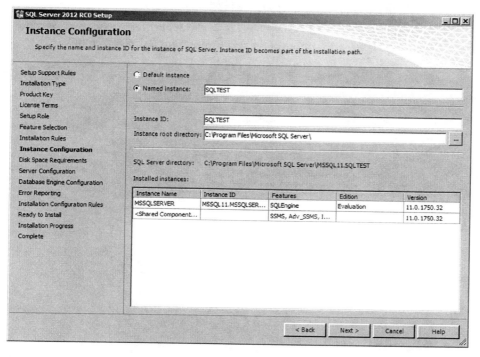

Figure 2-12. *Instance Configuration page*

There are some restrictions on the name of a named instance, including a 16-character limit and the inability to use SQL Server reserved words, such as *default*. These are all documented in the "Instance Configuration" article in SQL Server Books Online.

When SQL Server creates a new instance, it creates various registry key entries and folders within the file system. Since you can install more than one instance of the SQL Server database engine on a server, SQL Server needs to uniquely name these registry keys and directories. The instance ID is the text that will be used to help create the unique name for these objects. By default, the instance ID is the same as the instance name. The instance root directory is the folder that will contain the binaries for the SQL Server database engine.

If there were existing instances of SQL Server installed on this server, the Installed Instances grid would be populated with these. This grid is useful when it's midnight and you can't remember whether or not you installed the new instance on your server.

Disk Space Requirements Page

The Disk Space Requirements page simply summarizes how much disk space will be required to install the selected features. The space usage is broken up into space required on the system drive, space required in the shared feature folder, and space required by the instance directory itself. There are no options to select on this page; it is informative only.

Server Configuration Page

The Server Configuration page (see Figure 2-13) is one of the more important pages within this installation wizard.

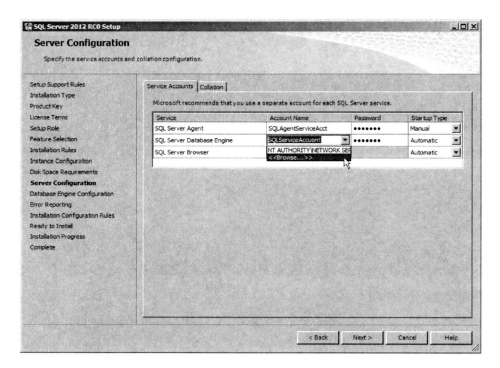

Figure 2-13. *Server Configuration page*

A service account can be built-in, like the Network Service account, or it can be a Windows User account. One thing to keep in mind is that whatever account is used for these services, that account has a high privilege. If you are not using Windows 7 or Windows Server 2008, you should refrain from using the built-in system accounts and instead use a regular domain user account.

The reason is that if your SQL Server instance is compromised and the attackers gain access to the sysadmin account, they are effectively running as whatever user is listed as the SQL Server service account. If you have only a single domain user account for SQL Server and a different one for other services, it would be much more difficult for attackers to obtain information from the other services. Similarly, if SQL Server is running under the Local System built-in account, that account has access to everything on the server. Thus, if your server is compromised and you are running under Local System, your whole server could be exposed to the attacker. If you are using Windows 7 or Windows Server 2008, you can use the Network Service account because it is more secure and easier to administrate than a domain account. The Service Accounts grid allows the user to specify a built-in account or a user account to use for each of the services that will be installed.

The Startup Type drop-down options are Automatic, Manual, or Disabled. This setting determines the state of the service upon a server reboot. Automatic means this service will be automatically started when the operating system starts. Manual means that an administrator will have to explicitly start the service. Disabled means that the service will not be available. A best practice is to set services that you know you will not use to either Manual or Disabled. By stopping or disabling a service, you are reducing the surface area for attack.

Next to the Service Accounts tab is the Collation tab. Collation is all about language support for SQL Server. A collation setting defines how SQL Server sorts and compares characters that are stored in non-Unicode data types. Image what should happen if you issued the statement SELECT * FROM Customers where State='MA' and your state column data within the table was stored in lowercase, as in ma. Depending on which collation you were using, this query should either return all the rows as expected or return nothing. The result depends on if the collation was case insensitive or case sensitive. For more information on using collations, check out the SQL Server Books Online topic "Working with Collations."

Database Engine Configuration Page

The Database Engine Configuration page (see Figure 2-14) contains important security-related parameters that need to be addressed.

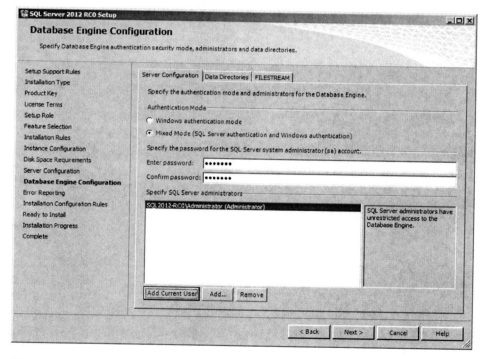

Figure 2-14. Database Engine Configuration page

This page in the wizard has three tabs: Account Provisioning, Data Directories, and FILESTREAM. The Account Provisioning tab allows you to define the kind of authentication mode SQL Server will support. If you select just Windows Authentication mode, only Windows users can connect to SQL Server. This situation is problematic if you can't use Active Directory or the local user store in Windows. The other option in this case is Mixed Mode. In mixed mode, you can still have Windows-authenticated users connect, but you could also have a user credential that exists only within SQL Server. These kinds of principals are called *SQL logins.*

SQL logins are very helpful in heterogeneous environments when you have non-Microsoft clients connecting to SQL Server. SQL Server authenticated accounts are easier to set up and use, and for that reason, they are used within the examples throughout this book. Thus, you need to select the Mixed Mode radio button.

When SQL Server is installed, a few accounts are created before anyone connects to SQL Server. The SA account is the system administrator account and has access to everything within SQL Server. This is the highest privileged account, and its credentials should be protected. This tab allows you to enter a password for the SA account; be sure to provide a complex one.

The "Specify SQL Server administrators" list box contains all the users that you want to give system administrator access. For some customers, Windows administrator users who install SQL Server are not necessarily those who will manage it. In this case, the Windows administrators would simply add whomever the DBA will be in the "Specify SQL Server accounts" list box. For the purposes of our evaluation of SQL Server, just click the Add Current User button, and your Windows User account will be added as an administrator.

The Data Directories page (see Figure 2-15) within this wizard page is where you can specify the default folder paths of various databases within SQL Server.

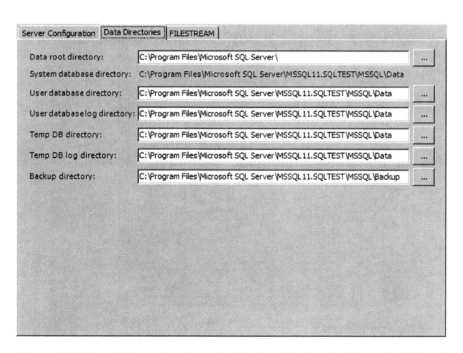

Figure 2-15. Data Directories tab on the Database Engine Configuration Wizard page

In this example, all of the directories are on the local C drive. For demonstration purposes, this is fine, but on a production system, it's best to spread different database files on different physical hard drives. This is important for user databases but is equally important for a system database called tempdb, which is SQL Server's scratch pad and is used by the server to sort data in queries and perform many other data-intensive operations. Thus, it is good to put tempdb on its own physical disk if possible.

The FILESTREAM tab is used to enable the Filestream feature, which allows users to exceed the 2-GB storage limit by placing the data on the file system. The Filestream feature manages the integrity of the file and ensures that no one can directly affect the data on the file system. As an added bonus, if you back up the database, the files stored and managed by the Filestream feature will also be included in the backup. You do not need to enable the Filestream feature at this time. If you want to enable it after you install SQL Server, you can do so using the SQL Server Configuration Manager. You can find details in the SQL Server Books Online article "How to: Enable FILESTREAM."

Error and Usage Reporting Page

This page displays two options. The first option is to opt in to send error information to Microsoft. The other option is to send feature usage information anonymously to Microsoft. Although some may be hesitant to do this because they fear sending sensitive information over the Internet, this issue isn't a concern, because these options do not send raw data. Rather, these options will send error codes and feature usage to Microsoft anonymously. This data is extremely valuable to the SQL Server product team because it can answer questions like "how often is this feature used?" In the end, by enabling these options, you will indirectly improve the user experience of the product.

Installation Rules Page

The Installation Rules page will perform another system configuration check, but this time, using yet a different set of rules. You specify parameters such as whether the WMI service is on and whether the file system is NTFS. There are no user-customizable actions on this page.

Ready to Install Page

The Ready to Install page (see Figure 2-16) is the page you have probably been waiting for. It gives a detailed summary of what Setup plans to do.

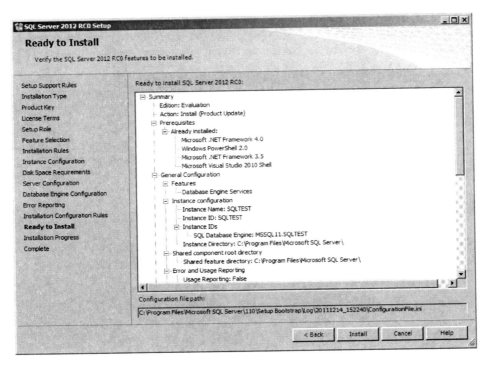

Figure 2-16. *Ready to Install page*

At this point, you could click the Install button and have the Setup application start performing the install, or you could obtain the installation script by locating the file at the bottom of the page. The "Configuration file path" setting points to a configuration file that is automatically created based on your selections on the previous wizard pages. If you wanted to perform a silent or remote install, you could now use this configuration file.

If you are following along with this installation, you can click the Install button now. This action will start the install process. The duration of installation depends on how many options you selected to be installed and what kind of platform you are installing onto. When Setup is complete, you will be presented with the Complete page. Here, you will find a link to the setup log file. If bad things happened in the setup and it failed, the setup summary log file is the first place to go to look into what might be wrong. If you ever call Microsoft product support for any installation issues, finding and sending this log will be one of the first tasks you will be asked to do. The Complete page (see Figure 2-17) shows the location of the setup log files.

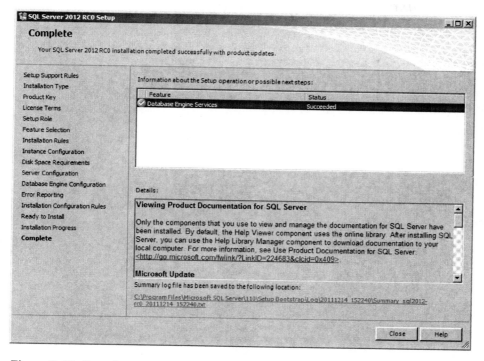

Figure 2-17. Complete page

Upgrading SQL Server

Chances are that if your organization has existing SQL Server implementations, you may eventually need to upgrade them. Each version of SQL Server (and almost any other software product) is officially supported for a limited number of years. Once this time is up (as it was in April 2008 for SQL Server 2000), customers can purchase extended support agreements. You can find detailed information on the life cycles of Microsoft products at www.microsoft.com/lifecycle.

Upgrading servers in your organization is probably not a spur-of-the-moment decision. A lot of planning should be done beforehand to make sure the upgrade goes smoothly. When thinking about upgrading a SQL Server database, it is important to first consider the following questions:

- *Is the server hardware capable of running this new version of SQL Server?* If you are planning on using the same hardware you were using to run SQL Server 2005, this may not be suitable for SQL Server 20012. Complete requirements can be found in the "Hardware and Software Installation Requirements for SQL Server 2012" article in SQL Server Books Online at http://msdn.microsoft.com/en-us/library/ms143506(v=SQL.110).aspx.

- *Are you planning on using the right edition of SQL Server?* A lot of the bright and shiny features of SQL Server 2012 are in the Enterprise edition. If you are currently running the Standard edition and want to upgrade because you want to leverage the new AlwaysOn Availability Groups feature, simply upgrading to SQL Server 2012 Standard edition will be disappointing. On the bright side, it's very easy to upgrade editions within SQL Server's Setup application. If this is your scenario and you wanted to go from SQL Server 2005 or SQL Server 2008 Standard edition to SQL Server 2012 Enterprise, the best practice is to go through the setup process and upgrade the server to SQL Server 2012 Standard first. Once SQL Server is upgraded, test your applications against it. When you're satisfied, rerun Setup, and run the Edition Upgrade Wizard on the Maintenance tab of the SQL Server Installation Center. SQL Server Books online includes an article called "Features Supported by the Editions of SQL Server 2012" located at `http://msdn.microsoft.com/en-us/library/cc645993(v=SQL.110).aspx` This article has a table that lists the high-level features and which editions they're available in.

■ **Note** Other than feature availability between editions, the development interfaces are the same for all editions of SQL Server.

- *Which upgrade strategy should you implement?* When it comes time to actually perform the upgrade, you have two options to actually upgrade the bits on the server to SQL Server 2012. You can implement an in-place upgrade that's basically running Setup and replacing the old SQL Server bits on the disk with the new SQL Server 2012 ones. Alternatively, you could do a side-by-side upgrade where you do not touch the old installation at all and instead install a new instance of SQL Server 2012. With this new instance, you will copy databases and objects from the old database into the new one. There are pros and cons to either one of these kinds of upgrades. An in-place upgrade is the fastest and least resource intensive, but it incurs more downtime of the server, and if something bad happens, it will take a long time to reinstall the old server version again. The side-by-side upgrade is resource intensive and more of a manual operation, but the benefit is you don't have to move clients over until the new server is ready. If something bad happens on upgrade, there is no downtime.

- *Are you using deprecated features?* As new versions of SQL Server are released, sometimes an existing feature or functionality is no longer needed. Since users and third-party software developers may have extensively used the feature, Microsoft cannot simply remove the feature from the product upon upgrade to the newer version. This action would break the user's applications and make the incentive of upgrading much less desirable. For this reason, Microsoft has a three-release deprecation policy.

Consider the `sp_renamedb` stored procedure. This stored procedure's functionality was replaced by the introduction of a `MODIFY NAME` parameter in the `ALTER DATABASE` statement. Since having two ways of renaming a database is not desirable, Microsoft officially deprecated the `sp_renamedb` stored procedure starting in SQL Server 2005. This means that SQL Server 2012 will be the last version that this stored procedure exists in the product. So, if you don't upgrade your scripts by this future version, they will not work anymore.

Microsoft does a good job at warning users of these deprecated features; a SQL Server Books Online article lists all the deprecated features for the release. This article is called "Deprecated Database Engine Features in SQL Server 2012" and is located at `http://msdn.microsoft.com/en-us/library/ms143729(v=SQL.110).aspx`.

Before you perform an upgrade, you can launch the free Upgrade Advisor from the Planning tab of the SQL Server Installation Center. This tool runs through your existing databases, SQL Server trace files, and T-SQL scripts and produces a report of issues that should be addressed before you upgrade. One of the issues the tool reports on is the use of deprecated features.

If, after you upgrade, you are still concerned that you may have some deprecated features being used, you can use the Windows Performance Monitor tool and monitor the SQL Server: Deprecated Features performance object counter. Figure 2-18 shows the Add Counters dialog box of the Windows Performance Monitor tool.

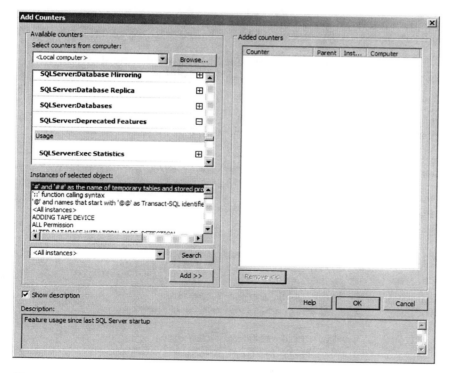

Figure 2-18. Windows Performance Monitor: Add Counters dialog box

In the Add Counters dialog box, you can collect specific deprecated features, or you can select "All instances" and collect any occurrence of a deprecated feature.

As you can see, there are a number of questions to ask and issues to deal with when upgrading. Your organization may also have additional standard operating procedures for upgrading servers that may involve the use of test servers and other processes.

Summary

64-bit installations of SQL Server are more often becoming the standard for SQL Server databases. Their large address space makes memory-intensive applications like SQL Server Analysis Services and SQL Server Integration Services work extremely well. Although using 64-bit hardware may be an acceptable standard for your organization, choosing which edition of SQL Server to use may be a political issue to solve. The key issue in this decision from a nontechnical standpoint is the cost differential between the Standard and Enterprise editions. This extra cost is negligible compared to the performance and productivity gains you get from Enterprise features such as Resource Governor and data compression.

When installing SQL Server, it's best to have a plan. Without a plan, you may be ill prepared if bad things happen. Having a plan is even more critical when you are upgrading an existing SQL Server database with active user databases.

If you did not install SQL Server because of lack of time or hardware resources and want to quickly test it out, you can easily launch a Microsoft virtual lab on SQL Server 20012. These virtual labs teach many aspects of SQL Server including tasks relating to both DBAs and developers. The virtual labs are run through the web browser in a virtual server environment, so you are free to do whatever you choose to do. You can find the virtual labs at `www.microsoft.com/sqlserver/en/us/learning-center/virtual-labs.aspx`.

Finally, I've mentioned a number of URLs in this chapter that take you to various online resources such as Books Online, samples, and more. Table 2-1 lists these URLs and online resources in one place for convenient reference.

Table 2-1. *SQL Server Resources*

Resource	Description
SQL Server Evaluation edition	`www.microsoft.com/sqlserver/en/us/get-sql-server/try-it.aspx`
Microsoft Assessment and Planning Toolkit	`www.microsoft.com/MAP`
"Features Supported by the Editions of SQL Server 2012"	`http://msdn.microsoft.com/en-us/library/cc645993(v=SQL.110).aspx`
"Hardware and Software Requirements for Installing SQL Server 2012"	`http://msdn.microsoft.com/en-us/library/ms143506(v=SQL.110).aspx`
SQL Server Books Online	`http://msdn.microsoft.com/en-us/library/ms130214(v=SQL.110).aspx`
CodePlex samples	`www.codeplex.com`

Resource	Description
"How to Install SQL Server 2012 Using a Configuration File"	http://msdn.microsoft.com/en-us/library/dd239405(v=SQL.110).aspx
Life cycle of Microsoft products	www.microsoft.com/lifecycle
Microsoft virtual labs	www.microsoft.com/sqlserver/2008/en/us/virtual-labs.aspx
"Deprecated Database Engine Features in SQL Server 2012"	http://msdn.microsoft.com/en-us/library/ms143729(v=SQL.110).aspx

CHAPTER 3

What's in the Toolbox?

If installing Microsoft SQL Server gave you only a database engine and nothing else, the management experience would be dismal at best. Luckily, Microsoft has shipped some relatively useful tools in conjunction with the database engine. In this chapter, you will explore most of the tools that are installed in a full installation of SQL Server.SQL Server Management Studio

For a DBA, SQL Server Management Studio (SSMS) is arguably the most frequently used tool of any provided by Microsoft for use with SQL Server. SSMS is the main tool for querying and managing all the products in SQL Server, including the SQL Server database engine, SQL Server Compact, SQL Server Reporting Services, SQL Server Integration Services, and SQL Server Analysis Services. Some of these products, such as Analysis Services, Integration Services, and Reporting Services, require the use of another tool called SQL Server Data Tools to maximize their value.

To a developer or someone familiar with the Microsoft Visual Studio line of products, SSMS may look a lot like Visual Studio. This is because SSMS is leveraging the shell of Visual Studio for hosting its dialog boxes and controls. By using the Visual Studio shell, SSMS is able to provide some advanced capabilities, such as the ability to debug stored procedures and script check-in and check-out capabilities via a source control product like Visual Studio Team Foundation Server.

Connecting to SQL Server

When you launch SSMS, the connection dialog box shown in Figure 3-1 will pop up and ask you which server you want to connect to.

Figure 3-1. Connection dialog box

The default server type is Database Engine, but if you click the "Server type" drop-down, you can connect to other server types, such as Analysis Services and Integration Services. The Authentication drop-down allows you to specify the authentication type you will use to connect to SQL Server. Your options for connecting to SQL Server are Windows authentication and SQL Server authentication. With Windows authentication, you do not have to specify your password when connecting to SQL Server. Since you are already logged into the client machine as a Windows user, SSMS relies on Windows to pass your security token to SQL Server. If you select SQL Server authentication, you need to provide a username and password combination, which would be sent to SQL Server for authentication. This username and password combination is unique to SQL Server.

The Options button enables two additional tabs, Connection Properties and Additional Connection Parameters. Figure 3-2 shows the Connection Properties tab. On this tab, you can force the connection to use a specific network protocol. You can also force the connection to be encrypted by selecting the "Encrypt connection" check box. You will learn more about encryption and certificate use in Chapter 12.

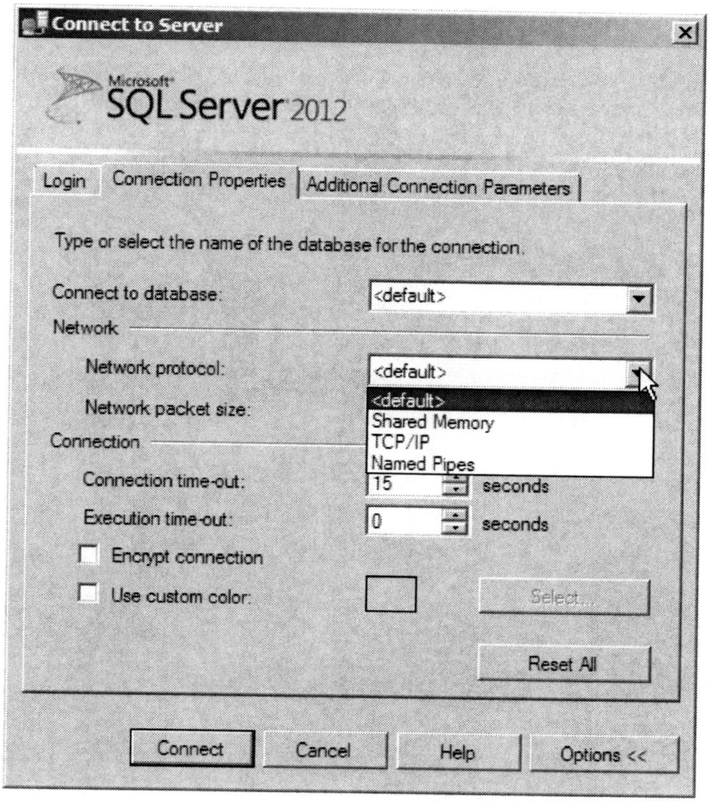

Figure 3-2. Connection Properties tab of the connection dialog box

In some cases, you may need to add parameters to the connection string. The Additional Connection Parameters tab allows you to specify these parameters. Once the server name and authentication information are entered, simply click the Connect button to make a connection to SQL Server.

■ **Note** One of the historical security issues with using SQL Server authentication was the fact that username and passwords were always sent in clear text over the network. Starting with SQL Server 2005, this behavior has been addressed. The initial credential passing for connections that use SQL Server authentication will always be encrypted regardless of whether the "Encrypt connection" check box is selected. This is true as long as you are using the Microsoft SQL Server Native Client (SNAC) libraries. SSMS uses SNAC, but other application vendors may still use Microsoft Data Access Components (MDAC), which will not automatically encrypt credential passing when using SQL Server authentication.

Issuing Queries Using SSMS

After establishing a connection to a server, SSMS will populate the Object Explorer tree. Object Explorer is just one of a few key components of SSMS. Figure 3-3 shows an SSMS window annotated with three of the main components: Object Explorer, document windows, and the Results pane. Note that the Results pane is showing a results grid; this area can also return results as text or as XML. Also note that Robert Walters has indeed made it in life; he is officially an AdventureWorks employee.

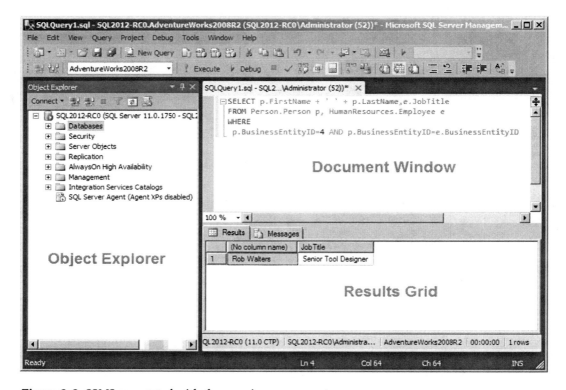

Figure 3-3. *SSMS annotated with three major components*

Object Explorer

Object Explorer is a tree view populated with information from the connected server and the corresponding objects contained within it. This tree view will show different nodes based on the server type to which you are connected. For example, when you connect to Analysis Services, you will see a Cubes node within a specific database node.

You can have multiple connections open to either the same or different server types. Figure 3-4 shows a connection to a SQL Server instance, to an integration server, and to Analysis Services.

■ **Note**   To see the Integration Services and Analysis Services nodes, you would need to have these products installed. The installation detailed in Chapter 2 did not cover installing these products.

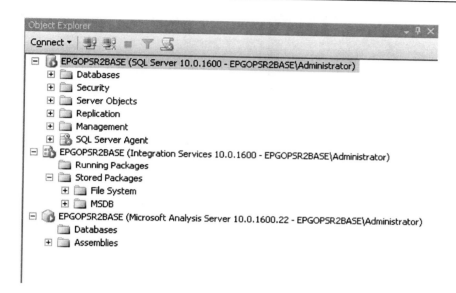

Figure 3-4. Object Explorer showing multiple connections to different server types

Not only is Object Explorer meant to display objects, but it is also a launch point for various tasks. These tasks change depending on the object that is selected and can be accessed by the context menu of the object selected. Figure 3-5 shows the context menu of the Databases node within a SQL Server instance connection.

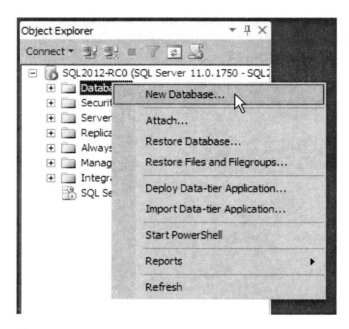

Figure 3-5. *Databases node context menu*

From the Databases node, you can create a new database, attach or restore a database, and perform other useful tasks. To demonstrate some of the other capabilities of Object Explorer and SSMS, let's create a new database. This database will be used throughout the remainder of this book. To create a new database using SSMS, select the New Database context menu item from the Databases node. This will launch the New Database dialog box, as shown in Figure 3-6.

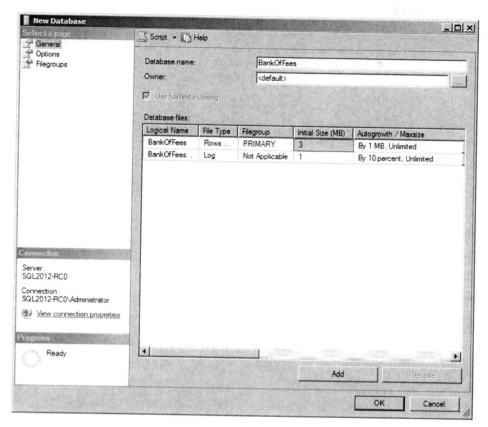

Figure 3-6. *New Database dialog box*

Almost all SSMS dialog boxes share some capabilities that are worth mentioning. The left side of a dialog box shows one or more pages. Usually, the most common or required information is displayed on the first page. In the case of the New Database dialog box, this first page is the General page. In this dialog box, once you fill in the database name, you could just click OK and run with all the preset defaults. For the purposes of demonstrating this dialog box, type **BankOfFees** in the "Database name" text box, and use the horizontal scrollbar to explore the additional columns of options. One of the options is Path. For simplicity in finding the database files that you'll use within this book, change that path to C:\Data for both the data and log files.

▓ **Note** If you are following along with this example, you will need to create the C:\Data folder if it does not already exists.

Clicking the Options page will show you a number of options available for creating a database. Here, you can specify the recovery mode, compatibility mode, and many other options. Once you have reviewed these settings and are ready to create the database, you can click OK. However, if you did not want to actually create the database at this time, you have a number of options. Most of the dialog boxes in SSMS support the Script button located at the top of the dialog box. Clicking the down arrow, you will be presented with four options: Script Action to New Query Editor Window, Script Action to File, Script Action to Clipboard, and Script Action to Job. By selecting Script Action to Job, you will create a SQL Server Agent job, which will schedule the execution of the actions within this dialog box. If you just want to see what T-SQL is generated by the dialog box, you could use any of the other options.

Once you create the database, it will show up as a child node to the Databases node. Object Explorer and all previous versions of SQL Server have a tough time automatically refreshing on changes to objects. If you do not immediately see the new database, you can select Refresh from the context menu of the Databases node. Also notice that if you selected the newly created database, the context menu list would be expanded as compared to the Databases container node. Some of these new menu options include tasks such as the following:

- Back up a database

- Shrink a database

- Import data

- Export data

■ **Note** Selecting multiple objects is not supported within Object Explorer. To select multiple items of the same type, you need to use Object Explorer's Details document window. To show Object Explorer's Details window, select it from the View menu, or simply press the F7 key.

Writing the Query

Now that you have created the BankOfFees database, you are ready to start issuing queries. To create a new query, you can click the New Query button above the Object Explorer window. This will create a new document window, which is formally called the Query Editor. You could also select New Query as a context menu item of the BankOfFees database node. If you select the command from within a specific database node, that database will be the active database for the query. If you launch the query from somewhere else, you may have another database, such as the master database, as the active database. You can see what your active database is by looking at the available databases drop-down box, as shown in Figure 3-7.

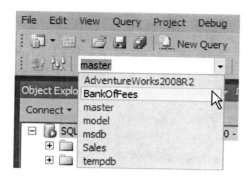

Figure 3-7. *Available database drop-down showing master as the current database*

If we had a dollar for every time someone executed a query and accidentally executed a script against an unintended database, we would not have any personal debt! It is very important that you double-check what the active database is before executing your query. The way most folks make sure they are executing T-SQL statements against the correct database is to place the USE command within their script. The following is an example:

```
USE BankOfFees
GO
--Rest of script goes here
```

To execute a script like this, you can click the "! Execute" button, or press the F5 key. You can also highlight just a portion of your script using the mouse or keyboard, and this same button will execute only what is highlighted. If you don't want to run the query but just want to know whether it's syntactically correct, you can click the Parse button (the blue check box near the Execute button) or press Ctrl+F5.

Some users new to SSMS have mistakenly thought the green right-facing arrow button would execute a query. Although clicking that button will execute a query, it will do so in debug mode, allowing you to step through each T-SQL statement.

■ **Note** SSMS provides the ability to debug or step through the execution of T-SQL statements. This feature is very useful when trying to troubleshoot stored procedures or user-defined functions.

Let's add some useful content to your new database using the Query Editor document window. To create a new table and fill the table with useful data, type the following script:

```
USE BankOfFees
GO
CREATE TABLE Customers
(customer_id INT NOT NULL,
first_name VARCHAR(50) NOT NULL,
last_name VARCHAR(50) NOT NULL)
GO
```

```
INSERT INTO Customers
VALUES (1,'Barack','Obama'),
VALUES (2,'George','Bush'),
VALUES (3,'Bill','Clinton')
GO
```

Next, click the "! Execute" button, or press the F5 key to run this script. If everything was typed correctly, you should see a successful message in the Results pane.

To view the data you just inserted into the table, you can use the SELECT statement as follows:

```
SELECT * FROM Customers
```

Executing this statement will yield the following result in the Results pane:

customer_id	first_name	last_name
1	Barack	Obama
2	George	Bush
3	Bill	Clinton

Document Windows

Document window is the technical term used within SSMS to describe the multiple-tab capabilities that exist. SSMS creates a document window for various features and spawns a dialog box at other times. Some of the different kinds of uses of document windows include the Query Editor, Object Explorer's Details window, and the Activity Monitor tool.

Clicking the New Query button will create a new document window that hosts a Query Editor. However, if you select Properties from the context menu of a database, you will get a dialog box. There is some reasoning behind the two different approaches. When you want to create or edit a query, you probably want a rich development experience, and because of technical reasons, these features can be leveraged only while inside a document window. If you are simply looking at database properties, though, you don't need any rich-experience capabilities, so you will just have a dialog box. One of the other reasons for using dialog boxes is the usability issue with having multiple document windows. Every time you create a new query, SSMS will create another document window. If SSMS created a document window for every other action, such as looking at database properties, that could result in a lot of windows. Depending on your screen resolution, SSMS will show only two or three document windows at a time; the rest will be located under a small drop-down, as shown in Figure 3-8.

Figure 3-8. Document window drop-down showing additional queries

Results Pane

When you issue queries against a SQL Server instance, the results are returned in the Results pane. The results can be in either text or grid form. This option can be toggled using the "Results to" context menu item of the Query menu option in SSMS.

Usually, more than one tab is available in the Results pane after you issue a query. The Results tab shows you the results of the query. The Messages tab shows you information that SQL Server returned about the query such as how many rows were returned and whether there were any errors. When you start digging into query execution plans, there will be a third tab, Execution Plan, to show you how SQL Server will go about executing your query. Execution plans tell you which indexes, if any, will be used and how much I/O will occur as a result of your query.

▦ **Tip**   For an in-depth look at execution plans and how to read them, pick up a copy of Grant Fritchey's book, *Dissecting SQL Server Execution Plans* (Simple Talk Publishing, 2008), which is about reading the plans. Another helpful book is *SQL Server 2008 Query Performance Tuning Distilled* (Apress, 2009), coauthored by Grant Fritchey and Sajal Dam, which helps you make changes to improve those plans.

Obtaining information from the results grid is easy. With a mouse, you can right-click and copy data to the clipboard. One of the nice new features within SQL Server is the ability to "copy with headers." This context menu item will copy the column headers in addition to the data you selected.

Managing Multiple Servers

SQL Server has been designed to handle enterprise workloads. Chances are these types of enterprises have more than one instance of SQL Server that needs to be managed. In the following sections, you will learn about three of the many features within SSMS that enhance the multiserver management experience.

Registered Servers

Being able to keep a list of all the servers that you need to manage is important. The Registered Servers window enables you to keep and maintain that list all in one place. You can open the Registered Servers window by selecting View   Registered Servers.

When you open the Registered Servers window for the first time, you may see only two folders under the Database Engine node. The Local Server Groups child node will contain local definitions of servers that are local to the client machine from which you are running SSMS. If you used another SSMS on someone else's client machine, your Local Server Groups node would not show up. If you want to create a shared list of SQL Server instances, you want to consider creating these in the Central Management Servers node.

A central management server is not another type of server that requires its own licensing; rather, it's simply a SQL Server instance that you designate as a central management server (CMS). The CMS serves two main purposes. The first purpose is to simply retain a list of registered servers. Having a central place that contains registered servers allows you to tell other DBAs where to connect for the latest list of servers. It eliminates the need for exporting the list, e-mailing it around to all the DBAs, and then running the risk of someone having an outdated list. The next purpose of the CMS has to do with easily evaluating policies against multiple servers. Policy-based management is discussed in more detail in the upcoming section "Policy-Based Management."

The Registered Servers window also applies to other server types. Take a look at the buttons right below the title bar in Figure 3-9. Each of these icons represents a different server connection type. These different types include SQL Server Analysis Services, SQL Server Reporting Services, SQL Server Compact Edition, and SQL Server Integration Services. For example, you can now create a list of all your reporting servers.

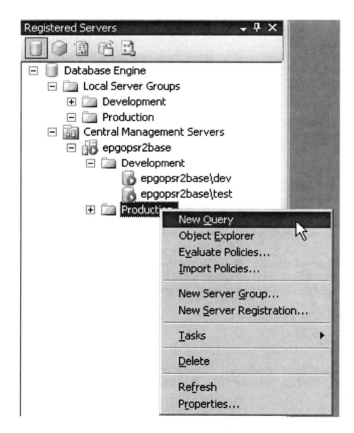

Figure 3-9. *Registered Servers window*

To add a server to the list of registered servers, right-click the Local Server Groups node, and select New Server Registration. This will launch the New Server Registration dialog box. Simply type in a server name, or use localhost if your server is on the same machine as SSMS. When you click OK, your server will show up under the Local Server Groups node. If you want to be neat about things, you could create folders or server groups under the Local Server Groups node.

Queries Against Multiple Servers

In Figure 3-9, the Production folder is selected, and you have the option of issuing a new query. Being able to issue queries against multiple instances without any additional setup and configuration work is extremely valuable.

■ **Note** When you launch a new query for more than one SQL Server instance, the yellow banner located on the bottom of the Query Editor document window will turn pink. This is just a visual cue that whatever you plan to do within that Query Editor window will affect multiple server instances.

Policy-Based Management

Group policies within the Windows operating system allow administrators to define policies governing password expiration, desktop backgrounds, available printers to use, and a bunch of other items. Policy-based management (PBM) is SQL Server's version of Windows group policies. Although there is no integration between the two policy engines, DBAs will no doubt be pleased at the flexibility and power of PBM.

With PBM, a DBA can define a policy and either periodically evaluate that policy or schedule the evaluation. If the policy is based on a Data Definition Language (DDL) operation such as creating a table, the policy can either log a violation of the policy to the error log at the time of statement execution or roll back the transaction, preventing execution of the change.

There are many scenarios for using PBM. For security compliance, you could create a policy that ensures encryption is enabled on the database. You could also check that certain tables are audited and perform other security-related checks.

In a multiserver scenario, SSMS makes it easy to evaluate policies across all servers either by leveraging the Registered Servers window through SSMS or by using PowerShell from the command line. PowerShell is a scripting framework for Windows. SQL Server includes a PowerShell provider that enables you to do actions such as evaluate policies from PowerShell scripts. PowerShell will be discussed in more detail later in this chapter.

PBM supports down-level servers: it is possible to create a policy and evaluate it against older version SQL Servers like SQL Server 2005 and SQL Server 2008. The exception to the experience is that you cannot proactively prevent actions that cause policy violations. For example, in SQL Server 2008, you could roll back the transaction if a user tried to create a table that didn't start with the letters *TBL*. Since SQL Server 2005 does not know about PBM, you can evaluate your policies only against this server version.

Monitoring Server Activity

Many software development companies make money selling server monitoring software. Microsoft has its own enterprise-wide monitoring solution called Microsoft System Center Operations Manager (SCOM). SCOM does provide capabilities to bubble up information about all your SQL Server instances. However, if you don't have the budget for these enterprise-wide solutions, you can still leverage some of the great features within SQL Server to answer some of the same questions.

Activity Monitor

Activity Monitor (AM) allows you to monitor the state of SQL Server including active connections, active processes, resource contention including any locks, and many more valuable bits of information. AM can be launched from the toolbar by clicking the Activity Monitor icon. This icon is located to the right of the Print icon; Figure 3-10 shows the Recent Expensive Queries collection expanded.

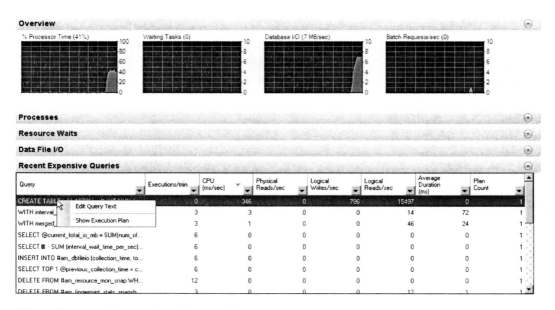

Figure 3-10. Activity Monitor showing the Recent Expensive Queries collection

In Figure 3-10, a **CREATE TABLE** statement has been issued, and it is causing a lot of logical reads and writes. If you wanted to investigate this further, you would simply right-click the statement and edit the query text or view the execution plan. Having the ability to easily see the most expensive queries without having to set up a special trace is incredibly valuable. If a user comes to your desk and tells you that an application is running slowly, this is one of the first things you can do to see whether a query is having problems.

AM has a few more expand and collapse regions that add a lot of value for the DBA. The Overview region shows CPU time as well as database I/O. The Process region shows all the active SQL Server processes, along with their corresponding Security Identifiers (SIDs). From here, you can kill a process or set up a SQL trace to trace the process using the SQL Server Profiler tool. The Resource Waits collection shows the number of active wait states such as locking or buffer I/Os. The Data File I/O region provides performance information on a per-database basis. You can tell how many megabytes per second are being read from and written to your database.

Performance Data Collector

Activity Monitor is great at giving you an accurate representation of what is happening currently with your SQL Server. However, trend information, such as how fast your log file is growing or what the most expensive query is over the past week, is difficult to obtain from Activity Monitor. Performance Data Collector (PDC) is the solution to gathering and analyzing performance information for your SQL Server enterprise. PDC collects performance information gathered from various T-SQL statements, Windows System Monitor counters, and Windows Management Instrumentation (WMI) classes. It stores this information on the local server, and periodically, it will upload this information to a management data warehouse. A *management data warehouse* is simply a database on a server you designate. Performance information is gathered from all the servers in your organization and stored in the warehouse. Since you have a single place with all this valuable information, you can run really useful reports.

To start collecting performance data, you need to first define the management database. You can do this by selecting the Configure Management Data Warehouse menu item from the Data Collection node of the Management node in Object Explorer. This action launches a wizard that will simply create the database used to store the performance results. Once this database is created, you need to rerun this wizard on each instance for which you want to collect data. When the wizard is run again, be sure to select the "Set up data collection" option. The wizard will ask where the management data warehouse is, and then it will create the four system collection sets: Disk Usage, Query Statistics, Server Activity, and Utility Information. Although adding your own collection sets is possible, SQL Server provides these four out of the box. The word from the product team is that much thought went into exactly what counters and queries each collection set makes. The product team asked Microsoft Product Support which queries and counters were used when customers called in with SQL Server questions. The team also asked a number of their partners and customers. Together, this information was rolled up into these three counters.

You will find value in simply enabling all three counters with the default settings. Doing so uses only about 300MB to 500MB on your local server. The default setting for data retention is 14 days. If you want to keep the historical data around longer than that, you can easily modify this property in the Properties dialog box of each collection set.

After you enable the collector and run it for enough time to gather some useful data, you can view some useful reports out of the box. You can find these reports in the Reports context menu of the database that is the management data warehouse. Figure 3-11 shows a subset of the Server Activity report.

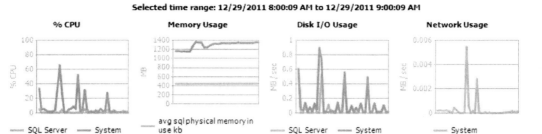

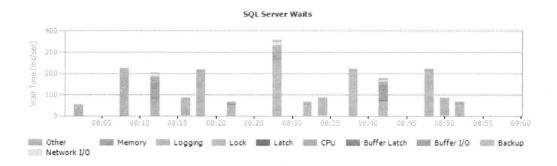

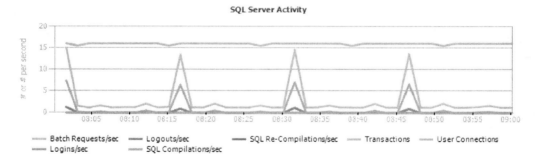

Data for this report has been collected by the Server Activity collection set.
Collection set state: Running.

Figure 3-11. *Subset of the Server Activity report*

From the report in Figure 3-11, you can easily obtain critical information such as the occurrence of some locking around 16:30. Since these activity reports are interactive, you can click any of the blue locking bars to obtain another report detailing the SQL Server waits. Figure 3-12 shows parts of this subreport.

Navigate through the historical snapshots of data using the time line below.

Selected time range: 12/29/2011 8:00:09 AM to 12/29/2011 9:00:09 AM

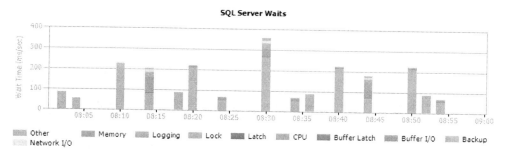

Wait Category	Completed Waits	Wait Time (ms/sec)	% of Total Wait Time
⊞ Backup	15,454	52.099	65.62%
⊞ Other	415	12.535	15.79%
⊞ CPU	4,176	10.464	13.18%
⊞ Logging	1,846	2.592	3.26%
⊞ Network I/O	6,871	1.237	1.56%
⊞ Buffer I/O	89	0.464	0.58%
⊞ Lock	3	0.006	0.01%
⊞ Buffer Latch	332	0.001	0.00%
⊞ Latch	0	0.000	0.00%
⊞ Memory	0	0.000	0.00%

Data for this report has been collected by the Server Activity collection set.

Collection set state: Running.
Last upload time: 12/29/2011 9:15:17 AM

Figure 3-12. *A portion of the SQL Server Waits subreport*

As you click through, you obtain more detail about the selected objects. In this case, you can see details on the various wait states that occurred for this time series. Clicking the Lock hyperlink will link to another report detailing the connections that were causing the locking behavior.

Query Statistics is another report provided out of the box. With Query Statistics, you get a graphical report showing query information across the time series you specified. Figure 3-13 shows a portion of the Query Statistics report.

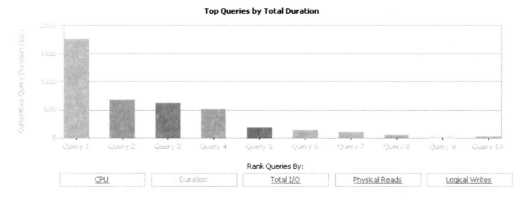

Figure 3-13. *A portion of Query Statistics report*

Figure 3-13 shows that query 1 took more than 1,700 seconds. Clicking that query will produce yet another report detailing information on the query, including physical reads and writes and a link to the execution plan.

The Disk Summary report is the third report provided out of the box. This report shows trend information for data and log files of all databases within the server. It is a useful report to run to see how fast or slow your files are growing.

Reports

SQL Server comes with a lot of reports for the DBA to run. These reports provide additional insight into your database. For example, clicking the Reports context menu within a specific database will yield a number of useful reports. Some of these reports include Disk Usage by Table, Top Transactions by Age, and Backup and Restore Events.

Figure 3-14 shows the Server Dashboard report for my new installation of SQL Server.

Server Dashboard

on SQL2012-RC0 at 12/28/2011 10:38:24 AM

This report provides overview data about the SQL Server instance, its configuration, and activity on it.

⊟ **Configuration Details:**

Server Startup Time	Dec 25 2011 6:30AM		Server Collation	SQL_Latin1_General_CP1_C I_AS
Server Instance Name	SQL2012-RC0		Is Clustered	No
Product Version	11.0.1750.32		Is Full Text Installed	No
Edition	Enterprise Evaluation Edition		Is Integrated Security Only	No
Scheduled Agent Jobs	13		# Processors (used by instance)	1

⊞ **Non Default Configuration Options:**

⊟ **Activity Details:**

Active Sessions	1		Idle Sessions	23
Active Transactions	7		Blocked Transactions	0
Active Databases	8		Distinct Connected Logins on Sessions	2
Total Server Memory (KB)	264664		Traces Running	1

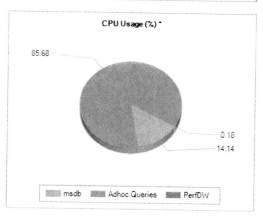

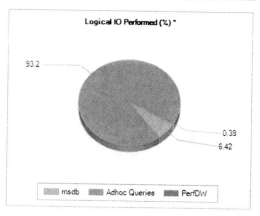

* : "CPU Usage" and "IO Performed" charts show the cumulative share of all objects by databases.

***Figure 3-14.** Disk usage for the master database*

The report in Figure 3-14 shows the disk usage of the master database in the newly created SQL Server instance. At this point, since we just created this instance, there is not much activity, and the master is really small. However, you can still see the usefulness of the information provided on the report.

Other Tools from the Start Menu

Although SSMS is the most frequently used of the tools supplied in a standard install, there are other tools that you should be aware of. In this section, we'll talk about other tools available from the Start menu. These are largely GUI-based tools. Then, in the next major section, we'll talk about command-line tools that you access via the Windows command prompt.

In Chapter 2, you performed a minimal installation of SQL Server. That installation is enough to go through the relational database engine examples in this book. However, in this section, you will learn about some of the additional tools that are available when you install other components like Analysis Services and Reporting Services. If you want to experiment with these features, simply run the SQL Server Installation Center application under the Configuration Tools Start menu. This will launch the Installation Center, and from there, you can click the Installation panel and click the "add features to an existing installation" link. This will launch a wizard that allows you to add the rest of the tools to your recent SQL Server installation.

The Microsoft SQL Server 2010 folder is where the bulk of the tools available to SQL Server users reside. Figure 3-15 shows the SQL Server 2012 folder within the Start menu.

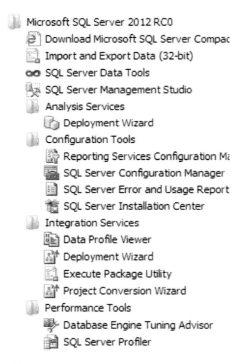

Figure 3-15. SQL Server 2012 Start menu

It may be a surprise to some folks to see Visual Studio 2010 installed when you install SQL Server 2012. This is because some of the business intelligence tools such as Analysis Services, Integration Services, and Reporting Services leverage the Visual Studio shell, and thus, you also have Visual Studio 2010 installed. Don't get too excited, though; it's just the shell and doesn't contain any programming languages like Visual C#.

Analysis Services Folder

SQL Server Analysis Services (SSAS) is Microsoft's business intelligence workhorse. It enables users to easily perform online analytical processing (OLAP) analysis, develop key performance indicator (KPI) scorecards, and perform data mining on existing data. OLAP has traditionally been a specialty skill among DBAs. However, with SQL Server providing rich out-of-the-box analytical functionality, companies are taking advantage and requiring their otherwise relational DBA to be more involved in OLAP and data warehousing.

In the Analysis Services folder, you find a single application called Deployment Wizard. This tool takes projects made with the SQL Server Data Tools and deploys them to the specified server.

Configuration Tools Folder

The Configuration Tools folder contains the following four applications: SQL Server Installation Center, SQL Server Error and Usage Reporting, Reporting Services Configuration Manager, and SQL Server Configuration Manager.

SQL Server Installation Center

The SQL Server Installation Center is the same application you saw when you initially launched `setup.exe` in Chapter 2. This link just makes finding this application more convenient, so you're not spending time digging around the file system.

SQL Server Error and Usage Reporting

Have you ever wondered why Microsoft is so persistent at asking its customers whether error reports and usage information can be sent to Microsoft for analysis? Some may think it's an attempt to obtain information with an eye toward spying on customers, but in reality, this is far from the truth. The dumps that are sent out do not contain user data and are used essentially to fix bugs within the product. You can probably guess that if Microsoft sees thousands of the same kind of error dumps, it might realize that it has an issue with something. The usage reporting piece of this also does not send any customer-sensitive data; rather, it simply provides answers to questions such as, "How many times did you access a certain dialog box?" or "How many tables do you have in each database?" This usage information helps SQL Server product development in a number of ways. For example, if the trend for customers is to have a really large number of tables, SQL Server Management Tools should provide features that make managing numerous tables within a database easier. The SQL Error and Usage Reporting application within the Configuration Tools folder allows you to specify whether you want to store and send error and usage information to Microsoft. Figure 3-16 shows this application.

▨ **Note**   Figure 3-16 is shown with the options expanded.

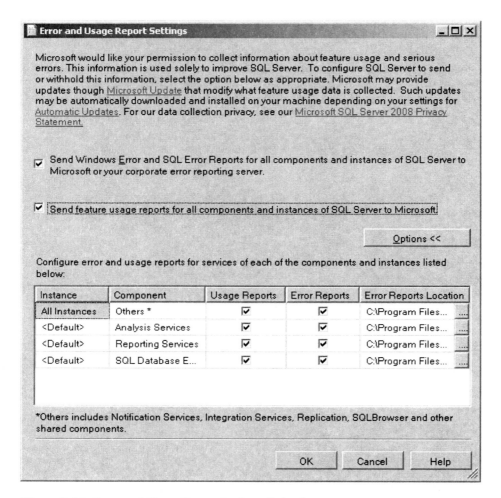

Figure 3-16. *Error and Usage Report Settings dialog box*

The Error and Usage Report Settings dialog box also allows for the selection of specific components within SQL Server. If you were curious about what data is collected, you can read these reports right from the file path specified in the Error Reports Location column. This valuable information is available once you click the Options button.

Reporting Services Configuration Manager

The Reporting Services Configuration Manager is also available from the Configuration Tools folder. This tool is used to manage the configuration of Reporting Services and is shown in Figure 3-17.

Note When you launch the Reporting Services Configuration Manager application, you will be asked to connect to a server instance.

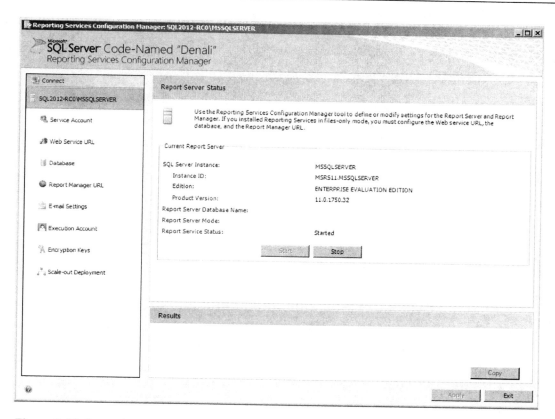

Figure 3-17. Reporting Services Configuration Manager

Reporting Services originally shipped as an add-on to SQL Server 2000. Since then, it has undergone a plethora of changes and improvements and has now become an enterprise reporting platform. The Reporting Services Configuration Manager shown in Figure 3-17 allows administrators to define or change the setting of Reporting Services components. This tool is not responsible for managing specific reports; rather, it's focused on the general configuration of Reporting Services.

SQL Server Configuration Manager

The SQL Server Configuration Manager is an important tool to become familiar with if you are a DBA. This tool is a Microsoft management console (MMC) snap-in and allows you to manage three important aspects of SQL Server. First, it allows you to manage all the services that are related to SQL Server. Figure 3-18 shows the SQL Server Services node of SQL Server Configuration Manager.

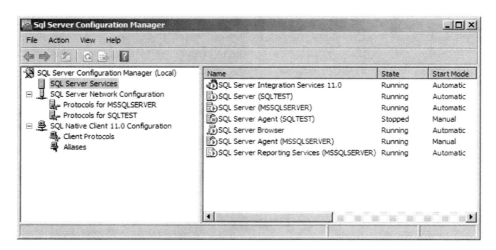

Figure 3-18. *SQL Server Services node in SQL Server Configuration Manager*

Managing the services from this snap-in instead of the Services control applet in Windows is a very important habit to start. The main reason for this has to do with the actions required to change the service account. Simply changing the username for the service, which is what the Windows Services applet in Control Panel does, is not enough. SQL Server has various folders and registry keys that need to have their access control lists (ACLs) updated upon this new change. If you decide not to listen to us and insist on changing the service account using the Windows Services applet, depending on the rights of the new account used, your service may simply fail to start because of a lack of permissions on either the file system or the registry. Thus, make your life simple, and use the SQL Server Configuration Manager only to manage services related to SQL Server.

The Services node does provide a lot more features other than simple service account management. If you wanted to enable the Filestream feature, you could do so through the Properties dialog box of the SQL Server service. Another important feature within the Properties dialog box of the SQL Server service itself is that of startup parameters. To view or modify these for the SQL Server service, click the Startup Parameters tab. In some rare occasions, if you had to start SQL Server in single-user mode or start SQL Server with a special trace flag, you would do this by passing a startup parameter.

The next significant behavior of SQL Server you can manage from this tool is network configuration. The question this node is going to answer is, "Which protocols will you allow SQL Server to allow connections from?" Figure 3-19 shows the Protocols node.

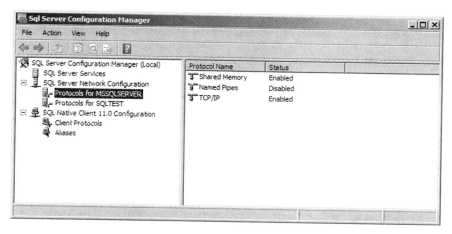

Figure 3-19. *Protocols node in SQL Server Configuration Manager*

Since you installed the evaluation edition, the only protocol that is enabled is Shared Memory. This is also the default behavior for new installations of Developer and Express editions of SQL Server. Shared Memory can make connections only when the client is physically on the same machine as the user. Thus, if you had tried and failed to remotely connect to this server (perhaps through another client machine), having only Shared Memory enabled is probably the reason. If you want to connect from a remote machine, you should use any of the other protocols. The most common one used to communicate with SQL Server is TCP/IP.

If you want to encrypt the flow of traffic to and from SQL Server, the Properties dialog box of the Protocols node allows you to force all traffic coming to and from SQL Server to be encrypted.

The discussion up until now involves the scenario where clients make connections to SQL Server. SQL Server can also be a client. Figure 3-20 shows the Client Protocols node.

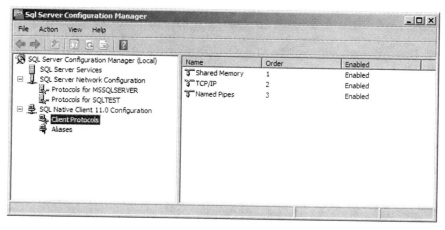

Figure 3-20. *The Client Protocols node within SQL Server Configuration Manager*

In this default behavior, all three protocols are enabled. In addition, a column called Order describes the order of priority of protocols. An order of 1 means that the protocol should be used first to establish a connection.

Each one of these protocols has a different purpose. For example, to communicate on the Internet, you use TCP/IP. TCP/IP is the most frequently used protocol, because most LANs are set up to use it. Shared Memory is special, because it works only within the same server. Thus, you cannot make a remote machine connection using Shared Memory. For more information on SQL Server protocols, check out the SQL Server Books Online article called "Choosing a Network Protocol" at `http://msdn.microsoft.com/en-us/library/ms187892.aspx`. If you want to get deep into protocols, there are some good articles on the SQL Protocols blog site at `http://blogs.msdn.com/sql_protocols`.

Documentation and Community Folder

The Documentation and Community folder contains useful resources for learning more about SQL Server. This folder contains a hyperlink to the SQL Server 2012 resource center, which is a web site containing a variety of information on SQL Server such as forums and other discussion groups. The folder also contains Community Project and Samples and SQL Server Documentation. Note that this folder and its components are installed when you select the Documentation Components feature option in setup. If you did not do this when installing SQL Server, you can simply rerun the setup and install just the documentation components.

Community Projects and Samples

The CodePlex web page contains SQL Server code samples and sample databases. All samples are available as downloads through the CodePlex web site at `www.codeplex.com`. CodePlex is Microsoft's effort at an open source developer community. You can download not only SQL code but also code from a variety of other products and projects uploaded by users just like yourself.

SQL Server Documentation

Books Online is by far the most useful resource readily available to you. This set of documentation covers a plethora of topics such as how to implement a database mirror and the T-SQL syntax for the `CREATE DATABASE` statement. This documentation will be your best friend, so it's best to spend some time getting familiar with this resource.

SQL Server Books Online can be installed locally on your server or client machine. You can also access this content through Microsoft's web site (`http://msdn.microsoft.com/en-us/library/ms130214(v=SQL.110).aspx`). Note that Books Online content changes more frequently than the product does; it appears to be refreshed once every few months. The latest version can always be downloaded from Microsoft via `www.microsoft.com/downloads`. Simply type **sql server books online 2012** in the search box, and find the most recent date.

Integration Services Folder

SQL Server's Integration Services is Microsoft's extract, transform, and load (ETL) platform for SQL Server. A data warehouse consists of data that comes from multiple sources and multiple formats. An ETL tool is used to extract this information from all these different sources, transform it into a common format (if necessary), and load it into the data warehouse. As we mentioned, SQL Server's version of an

ETL tool is called SQL Server Integration Services. The capabilities that this tool exposes yield use cases that are far beyond the simple ETL operation of a data warehouse. SSIS is so extensible that features like maintenance plans within SQL Server Management Studio leverage the powerful workflow designer. Most of the functionality, including the ability to create SSIS packages, is contained within the SQL Server Data Tool.

Data Profiler Viewer

The Data Profiler task in SSIS allows you to quickly assess key statistics about data in a database table. Statistics include data points such as column value and length distribution, column null ratio, column patterns, and functional dependencies. Since SSIS has no native way to view the output of the Data Profiler task, the Data Profiler Viewer tool can be used in this scenario.

Execute Package Utility

This utility provides you with a graphical way to execute a package. When you run an SSIS package, a lot of options are available such as where to load the package from, where to write log files to, and so on. All of these options can be specified on the command line as well, but this tool makes doing so easier.

Project Conversion Wizard

A lot of improvements and changes were made to how SSIS packages can be deployed in SQL Server 2012. This wizard generates a project development file, which is a compiled project consisting of packages and parameters. This project development file can then easily be used to deploy your SSIS project to an Integration Services catalog. For more information on the changes to SSIS with respect to deployment, check out the SQLServerPedia article, "SSIS 2012: Deploying Projects" located at `http://sqlserverpedia.com/blog/sql-server-bloggers/sql-university%e2%80%93-ssis-2012-deploying-projects-%e2%80%93lesson-one`.

Performance Tools Folder

Performance is one of the most common questions and investigations fielded by database administrators. SQL Server 2008 comes with two GUI-based tools out of the box: Database Engine Tuning Advisor and SQL Server Profiler.

Database Engine Tuning Advisor

Database performance is affected by a variety of factors. One of the initial investigations when troubleshooting performance is to analyze the execution plan of the query. The execution plan tells you things such as which indexes were used, if any were used at all. The Database Engine Tuning Advisor will analyze a workload against a given database and suggest ways to improve the performance. More commonly, it will suggest indexes where they do not currently exist. It will even provide the script to use, so all you have to do is click the button to use the new index.

SQL Server Profiler

One of the event engines within SQL Server Profiler is called SQL Trace. SQL Trace is primarily used for performance tuning and optimization efforts. With SQL Trace, you could set up the trace to collect every T-SQL statement executed. With these data collected, you could analyze and view the results to see things such as how long the query took and under what security context it was running. You can find a more in-depth discussion of SQL Server Profiler in Chapter 11. Note that SQL Trace is now deprecated in SQL Server 2012. Its replacement is a feature called Extended Events. Although SQL Profiler is still in the product, you should invest the time learning the new eventing model.

Import and Export Data Wizard

The Import and Export Data Wizard makes moving data from a source to a destination easy. The wizard will not move any objects over as part of the deployment. To move objects, you need to use another tool like the Copy Database Wizard. The end product of this wizard is a functional SSIS package that will import or export data. This package can be used as a great starting point for you to modify and work it into your own requirements.

SQL Server Data Tools

SQL Server Data Tools (SSDT) is the main development environment used by SQL Server Analysis Services, SQL Server Integration Services, and SQL Server Reporting Services. In earlier versions, this tool was called the Business Intelligence Development Studio (BIDS). Microsoft changed the name most likely due to the inclusion of additional relational database development capabilities. With SSDT, you can also create database projects that can be deployed on-premise against a SQL Server relational database engine or in the cloud via SQL Azure.

The look and feel of SSDT is similar to SQL Server Management Studio. These products all leverage the Visual Studio shell, so if you already have Visual Studio 2010 installed, these products just show up. If you do not have Visual Studio 2010, a lightweight version of Visual Studio is installed for you when you install SSDT. That is why you see a Visual Studio 2010 menu item when you install the SQL Server Data Tools. Although a discussion on each of these products may require a book itself, it's helpful if you spend the time to learn these technologies.

Command-Line Tools

There are two kinds of people in this world: those who do everything using a command-line interface and those who love using a graphical user interface (GUI) (some of you may fall somewhere in between, and thus violate our hypothesis). SQL Server has traditionally shipped with a few command-line tools. Perhaps the most popular scripting application is `SQLCMD`, a replacement to the aging `osql.exe` command-line tool. Another scripting tool that is more application agnostic is PowerShell. PowerShell is an extensible scripting engine that is part of the Windows operating system. Some of the other products in the box, like SQL Server Integration Services, have command-line interfaces as well. `DTEXEC.exe` is an example of an SSIS package execution utility.

SQLCMD

SQLCMD, pronounced "SQL command," is a command-line tool used to connect to SQL Server and submit T-SQL queries and commands. With SQLCMD, you can do the following:

- Execute SQL scripts against any SQL Server instance.
- Define and pass variables from the command line as well as within scripts.
- Use predefined system variables.
- Include multiple SQL scripts inline.
- Dynamically change connections within the same script.
- Connect to SQL Server via the dedicated administrator connection (DAC).

Connecting to SQL Server

SQLCMD allows users to make multiple connections to different servers within the same script. For example, suppose you had a few simple backup database scripts that each backed up a database on a specific server. On SERVERONE, the administrator could run the following backup script to back up the ReportServer database:

```
File: backup_ReportServer.sql
BACKUP DATABASE [ReportServer] TO DISK='C:\backups\ReportServer.bak'
```

On SERVERTWO, the administrator could run the following script to back up the Products database:

```
File: backup_Products.sql
BACKUP DATABASE [Products] TO DISK='D:\SQLServer\Backups\Products.bak'
```

In the real world, you know that administrators tend to have lots of scripts, and each perform its own functions on a specific server. With SQLCMD, you can now consolidate these into a single script using the :CONNECT command. Let's see this same scenario of backing up multiple databases using a single script:

```
File: backup_databases.sql
--Make a connection to SERVERONE using Windows Authentication
:CONNECT SERVERONE -E
--Issue a backup database command for ReportServer
BACKUP DATABASE [ReportServer] TO DISK='C:\backups\ReportServer.bak'
GO

--Make a connection to SERVERTWO using Windows Authentication
:CONNECT SERVERTWO -E
--Issue a backup database command for Products database
BACKUP DATABASE [Products] TO DISK='D:\SQLServer\Backups\Products.bak'
GO
```

Issuing the SQLCMD command `sqlcmd -E -i backup_databases.sql` yields the following result:

```
Sqlcmd: Successfully connected to server 'SERVERONE'.

Processed 280 pages for database 'ReportServer', file 'ReportServer' on file 4.

Processed 1 pages for database 'ReportServer', file 'ReportServer_log' on file 4.

BACKUP DATABASE successfully processed 281 pages in 0.369 seconds (6.238 MB/sec).

Sqlcmd: Successfully connected to server 'SERVERTWO'.

Processed 144 pages for database 'Products', file 'Products' on file 6.

Processed 1 pages for database 'Products', file 'Products_log' on file 6.

BACKUP DATABASE successfully processed 145 pages in 0.237 seconds (5.011 MB/sec)
```

Passing Variables

SQLCMD also provides the ability to pass variables from the command line and within the script itself. For example, assume you have a generic "backup database" script called `backup_database_generic.sql` that can be reused:

```
File: backup_database_generic.sql
:CONNECT $(myConnection)
BACKUP DATABASE $(myDatabase) TO DISK='C:\backups\$(myDatabase).bak'
```

At this point, you could call this script from the command line using the new **-v** parameter. This parameter tells SQLCMD that the following text is a variable, an example of which is shown here:

```
C:\>SQLCMD -E -i backup_database_generic.sql
 -v myConnection="." myDatabase="ReportServer"
```

When the `backup_database_generic.sql` script is run, it will have two variables defined: myConnection, which is equal to ".", and myDatabase, which is equal to "ReportServer". Alternatively, if you wanted to use variables, you also could have set the parameters within another script, as shown here:

```
File: backup_database_main.sql
:SETVAR myConnection .
:SETVAR myDatabase ReportServer

:R "backup_database_generic.sql"

GO
```

When this script is executed, SQLCMD will set the myConnection variable to "." (the period is an alias for the local server—you could have used "localhost" or the actual name of the server as well) and the myDatabase variable to "ReportServer"; then, it will insert the contents of the backup_database_generic.sql script inline.

PowerShell Provider for SQL Server

PowerShell is a command-line shell and scripting language designed with significant improvements in power and functionality when compared with VBScript and the Windows command prompt. PowerShell is available in Windows Server 2008 and is also available as a download (www.microsoft.com/powershell) for other versions of Windows. SQL Server 2012 provides a PowerShell provider that enables you to easily access SQL Server instances, SMO objects, and evaluate policies within the PowerShell environment.

> ■ **Note** You can launch PowerShell with the SQL Server provider using sqlps.exe.

Not only can you easily write a script that interacts with a SQL Server instance, but in that same script, you can easily access other PowerShell providers like the one for Exchange Server. You now have a consistent, seamless experience for scripting across Microsoft products.

Consider the following example:

```
#Use WMI to obtain the AT Scheduler job list
$colItems = get-wmiobject -class "Win32_ScheduledJob"
-namespace "root\CIMV2" -computername "."

foreach ($objItem in $colItems)
{
$JobId = $objItem.JobID
$JobStatus = $objItem.JobStatus
$JobName = $objItem.Command

#Use the SQL Provider Invoke-SqlCmd cmdlet to insert our
## result into the JobReports table
Invoke-SqlCmd -Query "INSERT INTO master..JobReports
(job_engine, job_engine_id, job_name, job_last_outcome)
 VALUES('NT','$JobId','$JobName','$JobStatus')"
}

#Now let's obtain the job listing from the JobServer object
#REPLACE the <SERVERNAME> with your own server name!
Set-Location "SQL:\<SERVERNAME>\default\JobServer"

$jobItems = get-childitem "Jobs"

foreach ($objItem in $jobItems)
{
$JobId =  $objItem.JobID
$JobStatus = $objItem.LastRunOutcome
$JobName = $objItem.Name
```

```
Invoke-SqlCmd -Query "INSERT INTO master..JobReports
(job_engine, job_engine_id, job_name, job_last_outcome)
 VALUES('AGENT','$JobId','$JobName','$JobStatus')"
}
```

■ **Note**   You will have to have the SQL Server Agent service running in order for this script to work. You can start the SQL Server Agent by selecting Start from the SQL Server Agent context menu in SSMS.

This example assumes you have a table in the master database that is defined as follows:

```
CREATE TABLE JobReports
(job_engine CHAR(6),
job_engine_id VARCHAR(50),
job_name VARCHAR(255),
job_last_outcome VARCHAR(50),
report_time datetime DEFAULT GETDATE())
```

After running your code, the JobReports table would be filled with entries of both the Windows Task scheduled jobs and SQL Agent jobs. An example result set follows:

job_engine	job_engine_id	job_name	last_outcome	report_time
NT	1	ntbackup.exe	Success	2008-01-22 15:32:29.270
NT	4	CustomApp.exe	Success	2008-01-22 15:32:29.280
AGENT	3226bb84-4e…	BackupTestDB	Succeeded	2008-01-22 15:32:29.290
AGENT	642f4e27-66…	BackupDevDB	Unknown	2008-01-22 15:32:29.300
AGENT	ddc03a7b-45…	ReIndxTestDB	Unknown	2008-01-22 15:32:29.300

This script enumerates the jobs defined within the Windows Task Scheduler as well as the SQL Server Agent jobs and inserts these lists in a table. This is just one example of the seamless scripting experience that can be obtained by using PowerShell.

Summary

As a new user to SQL Server, you will probably spend most of your time using SQL Server Management Studio. This chapter covered SSMS in depth and touched on some of the features that support SSMS, including policy-based management, the Performance Data Collector, and reporting.

Microsoft also has a number of virtual labs available online. Each of these SQL Server 2012 labs drops you into a Remote Desktop connection session with a server that has SQL Server installed. In addition to the lab, you are free to explore other features within the product. You are not bound to doing only what is in the lab, although launching a lab can be a quick way to kick the tires of the product without going through the time and resource of installation.

Finally, Table 3-1 lists some resources supporting the content discussed in this chapter. It's good to do some outside reading, and you'll find these resources helpful as you progress with SQL Server.

Table 3-1. *Helpful Resources*

Resource	Description
SQL Server Books Online	http://msdn.microsoft.com/en-us/library/ms130214(v=SQL.110).aspx
SQL Server 2012 Query Performance Tuning Distilled	www.apress.com/9781430242031
"Choosing a Network Protocol"	http://msdn.microsoft.com/en-us/library/ms187892.aspx
PowerShell	www.microsoft.com/powershell
SQL Server 2012 virtual labss	www.microsoft.com/sqlserver/en/us/learning-center/virtual-labs.aspx

CHAPTER 4

SQL Server Development

There is no standard job description for the DBA; it varies depending on their employer. Some DBAs tend to monitor their environments and maintain the maintenance jobs. In other companies, DBAs may perform more developer-oriented tasks, such as creating stored procedures and metadata within databases. While the focus of this book is on database administration, understanding the tools available for developers (and yourself) to use with SQL Server is also important. After reading through this chapter, you may find yourself secretly writing some code once you've seen what great tools Microsoft has provided for the development community.

Touring SSMS Through the Eyes of a Developer

SQL Server Management Studio (SSMS) is the main GUI tool used by most DBAs to administer their database environments. Throughout the releases of SQL Server, this tool (known as Enterprise Manager previous to SQL Server 2005) has provided increasing amounts of functionality around database development. Although SSMS is not a database development tool, it's important to know what kind of development-related tasks it can handle.

IntelliSense

One of the first features you notice when using the Query Editor in SSMS is IntelliSense. IntelliSense makes it very easy for the user to know what objects or statements are valid and allows for easy auto-completion of statements. For example, we have a copy of the AdventureWorks database installed on SQL Server, and IntelliSense lets us navigate and explore that database, as we'll show next.

■ **Note** AdventureWorks database can be downloaded from the CodePlex web site at http://msftdbprodsamples.codeplex.com.

To use IntelliSense, simply navigate to a database—in our example, AdventureWorks—right click the node, and select, New Query. Begin typing the query shown in Figure 4-1. After you type the period in the statement "SELECT * FROM Sales." a context menu will appear, as shown in Figure 4-1.

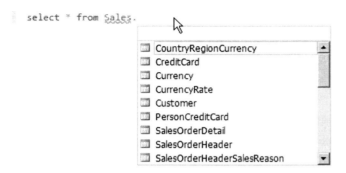

Figure 4-1. *IntelliSense content menu in the SSMS Query Editor*

Notice that the context menu lists the applicable objects that you can use to finish this part of the query. If you scroll down to CreditCard and press the Tab key, SSMS will auto-complete the input of that object name in the Query Editor window. IntelliSense is useful in many situations—when you can't remember the object name you are looking for or the acceptable parameters of a stored procedure, to name a few.

Query Designer

In addition to IntelliSense, another richer feature can help users write queries—the Query Designer. If you have used Microsoft Access, you may recognize some similarities with the Query Designer tool that is available in both SSMS and Visual Studio. The Query Designer helps users build queries by allowing them to graphically adding tables and views together and simply click the desired columns. To launch the Query Designer, click the New Query button to get a clean Query Editor window, and select Design Query in Editor from the Query menu on the SSMS toolbar. This will launch the Query Designer, as shown in Figure 4-2.

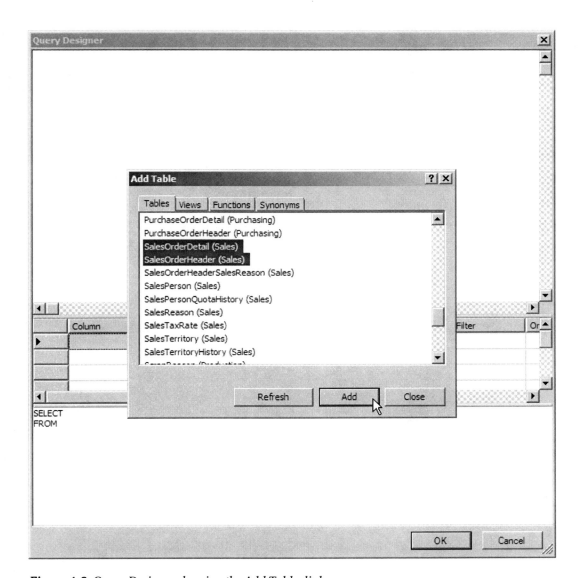

Figure 4-2. *Query Designer showing the Add Table dialog*

Let's add both the `SalesOrderDetail` and `SalesOrderHeader` tables to the Query Designer. Click each table's name, and click the Add button. When you have finished adding the tables or views, click the Close button. The Query Designer knows that these two tables share a relationship and has visually marked this in the UI. From here, you can go ahead and add the search criteria information to the query by checking the desired columns and typing any "group by" or "sort" information related to the desired query. For this example, we are interested in the sum of orders for each day, so we have configured the Query Designer as shown in Figure 4-3.

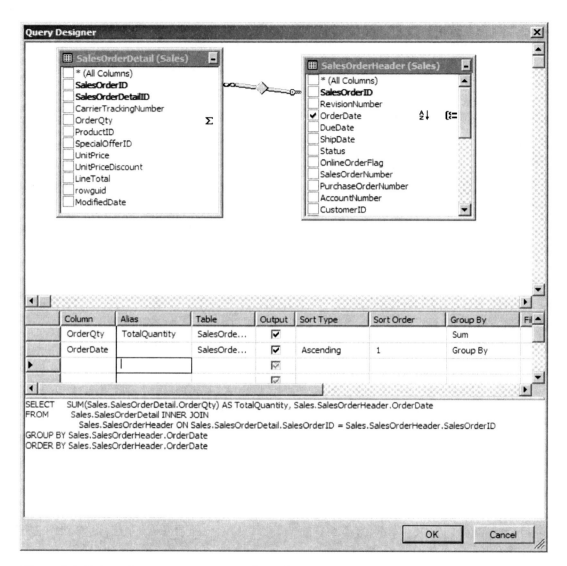

Figure 4-3. Sales order summary query configured in Query Designer

When you click the OK button, the Query Designer yields the following T-SQL text based on the settings in Figure 4-3:

```
SELECT       SUM(Sales.SalesOrderDetail.OrderQty) AS TotalQuantity,
Sales.SalesOrderHeader.OrderDate

FROM         Sales.SalesOrderDetail INNER JOIN

                 Sales.SalesOrderHeader ON Sales.SalesOrderDetail.SalesOrderID =
Sales.SalesOrderHeader.SalesOrderID

GROUP BY Sales.SalesOrderHeader.OrderDate

ORDER BY Sales.SalesOrderHeader.OrderDate
```

Even through the Query Designer brought us to back to the Query Editor window, you can always go back to the designer for help with the query by highlighting the query and selecting Design Query in Editor from the context menu of the highlighted query.

Templates

SSMS comes with a plethora of templates to use to create database objects. These are especially handy when you want to create a stored procedure and cannot remember the exact syntax. To see a complete list of templates, select Template Explorer from the View menu in the SSMS toolbar. This will launch the Template Explorer shown in Figure 4-4.

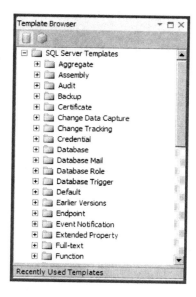

Figure 4-4. Template Explorer

To create a new stored procedure using a template expand the Stored Procedures node, and double-click Create Stored Procedure (New Menu). This will populate a new query editor window with the following template script:

```
-- ==================================================
-- Template generated from Template Explorer using:
-- Create Procedure (New Menu).SQL
--
-- Use the Specify Values for Template Parameters
-- command (Ctrl-Shift-M) to fill in the parameter
-- values below.
--
-- This block of comments will not be included in
-- the definition of the procedure.
-- ==================================================
SET ANSI_NULLS ON
GO
SET QUOTED_IDENTIFIER ON
GO
-- =============================================
-- Author:      <Author,,Name>
-- Create date: <Create Date,,>
-- Description: <Description,,>
-- =============================================
CREATE PROCEDURE <Procedure_Name, sysname, ProcedureName>
        -- Add the parameters for the stored procedure here
        <@Param1, sysname, @p1> <Datatype_For_Param1, , int> = <Default_Value_For_Param1, ,↵
  0>,
        <@Param2, sysname, @p2> <Datatype_For_Param2, , int> = <Default_Value_For_Param2, , 0>
AS
BEGIN
        -- SET NOCOUNT ON added to prevent extra result sets from
        -- interfering with SELECT statements.
        SET NOCOUNT ON;

    -- Insert statements for procedure here
        SELECT <@Param1, sysname, @p1>, <@Param2, sysname, @p2>
END
GO
```

In this script, you replace all the stub values like @Param1 and Datatype_For_Param1 individually, or you can use the Specify Values for Template Parameters dialog box, shown in Figure 4-5. To launch this dialog box, press Control, Shift, and the letter "M" together, or select Specify Values for Template Parameters from the Query menu in the SSMS toolbar.

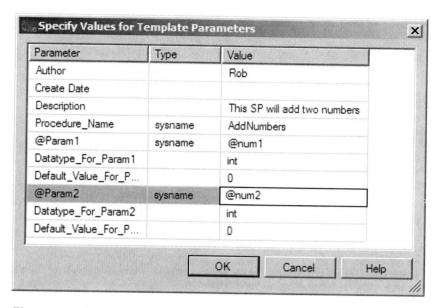

Figure 4-5. The Specify Values for Template Parameters dialog box

Let's begin with the preceding template and create a simple stored procedure that adds two numbers. In the template parameters dialog, type **AddNumbers** for the Procedure Name; type **@num1** for the @Param1 value and **@num2** for @Param2. Click the OK button, and the Query Editor window will be updated with a script that contains the values that you entered in the dialog box. From here, you can further modify this script as needed. To make our `AddNumbers` procedure meaningful, we will have to add an output parameter `@result` and perform the addition by appending SELECT `@result=@num1 +@num2` to the body of the stored procedure. The updated stored procedure follows, with changes in bold:

```
CREATE PROCEDURE AddNumbers
        -- Add the parameters for the stored procedure here
        @num1 int = 0,
        @num2 int = 0,
        @result int OUTPUT
AS
BEGIN
        -- SET NOCOUNT ON added to prevent extra result sets from
        -- interfering with SELECT statements.
        SET NOCOUNT ON;

    -- Insert statements for procedure here
        SELECT @result=@num1 +@num2
END
GO
```

To test this procedure, you can run the following code:

```
DECLARE @i INT
EXECUTE AddNumbers 1,4,@i OUTPUT
SELECT @i
```

The result will be 5. This stored procedure is very simple, but stored procedures used in regular applications can be very complex. Troubleshooting stored procedures has, until recently, been very difficult, so developers had many tactics to debug one that misbehaved—injecting code within the stored procedure to track values and adding code to force the values to name a few. If a problematic procedure was written in C# or VB.NET, developers could easily set up break points in the code, so that when the program hit that break point, the execution would stop and control would be given to the develop to step through the code line by line. It's this advanced debugging capability that is also part of SSMS for both T-SQL code and CLR code within T-SQL stored procedures and user-defined functions.

Debugging in T-SQL

In the previous section, we created a stored procedure called **AddNumbers**. Suppose we want to troubleshoot this procedure within SSMS. To do so, we can add a breakpoint by clicking to the left of the statement where we want SQL Server to pause or moving the cursor to the statement and pressing the F9 key. The red circle added to the line indicate a breakpoint; see Figure 4-6.

Figure 4-6. *Breakpoint set on a T-SQL statement*

To start debugging, click the debug button on the toolbar or press Alt+F5. The first statement will execute, and then the application will pause. A yellow arrow will show you the next statement to be executed, which, in our example, is the **EXECUTE** stored procedure statement. If you wanted SQL Server to execute the stored procedure in its entirety without stepping into the procedure and through each and every statement in it, you would click the Step Over button or press F10.

Since we want to peek inside the stored procedure and evaluate every line, click Step Into, or hit F11. Once you click Step Into, you can see the source of the stored procedure and the yellow arrow indicating the line to be executed next. Notice the Locals pane on the bottom of the screen. The Locals window shows variables and values in the given context. If you want to test a certain code path, you can simply overwrite the value here and see how the stored procedure behaves. Let's change the value of **@num2** to 5 instead of 4. Make sure that the "5" is colored red in the Locals window by pressing the Enter key after you change the value. Press F11 repeatedly to step through the code, and you will see the result come back as 6 (so one plus four really equals six). Being able to set breakpoints and step through code is just one small example of the power of debugging within SSMS. If you don't want a breakpoint at every iteration of the stored procedure, you can specify one of many breakpoint conditions. For example, you can choose to only break only when the value of a number is greater than 10. Then too, you could set a breakpoint filter to break only on specific computers, processes, or threads. Breakpoints can also be exported via an XML file so that you can share them with others.

Note In this chapter, we only touch on the debugging capabilities within SSMS. Visual Studio and the new SQL Server Developer Tools also perform debugging of code. Servers running SQL Server 2005 Service Pack 2 and above can be debugged using Visual Studio.

Data-Tier Applications

Politics, project plans, and budgets—these are some of the major tension areas within many IT departments. DBAs and developers, in particular, seem to clash often, because they generally have different priorities. Consider the DBA who is concerned with maintaining a specific service level agreement (SLA) and the developer who needs to update an application to support integration of a new widget. A DBA hears not the need for the update but that the developer wants to take the application off line, which would violate the SLA.

Software can't solve the politics of IT, but it can mitigate some of the conflicts by providing features and functionality that help developers focus on developing code and DBAs focus on maintaining databases and ensuring compliance with the SLAs they are given. This scenario applies often to data-tier applications.

Defining a Data-Tier Application

A *data-tier application* contains all of the database and instance objects used by an application. This entity is in reality is a ZIP file known as a `dacpac` file because of its `.dacpac` file extension. Theoretically, the developer creates this `dacpac` file and gives it to the DBA. The DBA then deploys this application to one or more instances of SQL Server, on premise or in the cloud via SQL Azure. The DBA's job is not so much about micromanaging that specific application but rather managing all the applications as they relate to core performance factors like CPU, memory, and disk utilization. This division of labor is similar to what has happened with system administrators and the operating system. Given the recent industry push for virtualization of operating systems, system administrators do not spend their time managing a specific instance of an operating system; rather, they look more at the big picture (in their case, at the virtual host machine) and ensure its health and performance.

You can create a `dacpac` file out of an existing database via SSMS. To illustrate the data-tier application, let's create a new database for a used car company. To start, open SSMS, and connect to your test database server. Next, open a New Query window, and type the following code:

```
USE MASTER
GO
CREATE LOGIN BobLogin WITH PASSWORD='pass@word1'
GO
CREATE DATABASE UsedCars
GO
```

```
USE UsedCars
GO
CREATE USER Bob FOR LOGIN BobLogin
GO
CREATE SCHEMA Sales
AUTHORIZATION Bob
GO
CREATE SCHEMA Product
AUTHORIZATION Bob
GO
CREATE TABLE Product.Inventory
(car_id INT NOT NULL PRIMARY KEY,
car_make VARCHAR(50) NOT NULL,
car_model VARCHAR(50) NOT NULL,
car_year SMALLINT NOT NULL)
GO
CREATE TABLE Sales.Orders
(order_id INT NOT NULL PRIMARY KEY,
order_date DATETIME NOT NULL,
order_carsold INT REFERENCES Product.Inventory(car_id),
order_saleprice SMALLMONEY NOT NULL)
GO
INSERT INTO Product.Inventory VALUES (1,'Saab',
'9-3',1999),(2,'Ford','Mustang',2003),(3,'Nissan','Pathfinder',2005)
GO
```

At this point, we have a very crude design with two simple tables. The `Product.Inventory` table contains a list of all cars available for sale. The `Sales.Orders` table lists when the car was sold. (This schema has some inherent problems that we will address later in this chapter. For now, assume this is the backend to our used car application.)

We can create a data-tier application out of an existing database by simply right-clicking the UsedCars database in SSMS object explorer and selecting Tasks and then "Extract Data-tier application". This will launch a wizard that will help us create the `dacpac` file. The first page where we can enter input is the Set Properties page shown in Figure 4-7.

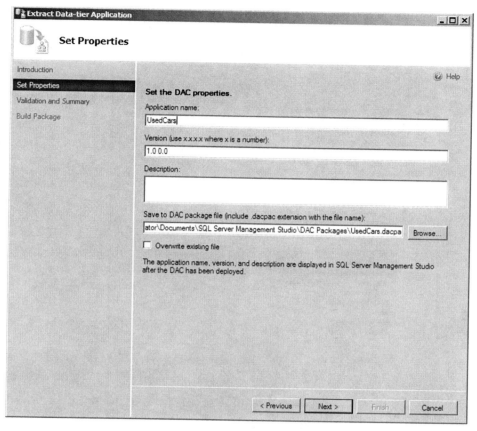

Figure 4-7. *The Set Properties page in Extract Data-tier Application wizard*

On this page, we can give the application a formal name and provide a description and a version number. The default location of our `dacpac` file will be in a subdirectory within the Documents path. In this example the default path is `C:\Users\Administrator\Documents\SQL Server Management Studio\DAC Packages`.

The next page in the wizard performs a check to see if the objects within the database can be exported into a data-tier application. After these checks are performed, the wizard gives you a summary of the findings, as shown in Figure 4-8.

Not all objects within a database can be used in a data-tier application; this is one of the limitations of using data-tier applications. SQL Server Books Online contains a list of the objects that are supported at `http://msdn.microsoft.com/en-us/library/ee210549(v=SQL.110).aspx`. On this web page, flip between the SQL Server 2008 R2 and SQL Server 2012 documentation, and you will see that in SQL Server 2012, more objects are supported. It's a good bet that as future editions of SQL Server come out that this list gets even longer.

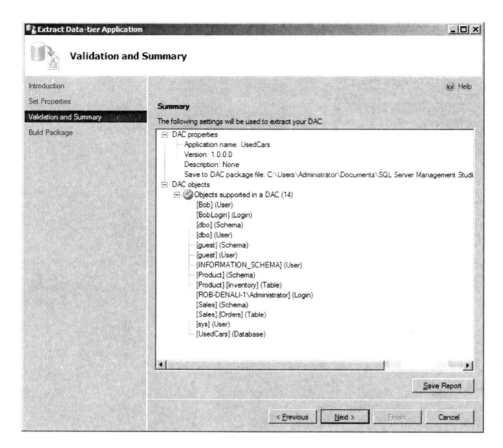

Figure 4-8. The Validation and Summary page of the Extract Data-tier Application wizard

After you've completed the wizard's steps, the `dacpac` file will be created. If you navigate to the folder where the `dacpac` file was created, you can see a single file called `UsedCars.dacpac`.

■ **Note** If you are curious about the contents of the dacpac file, simply rename it to have a `.zip` extension and unzip its contents. In our UsedCar application example, the dacpac contained four XML files: `[Content_Types]`, `DacMetadata`, `LogicalObjectStream`, and `PhysicalObjectStream`. If you load one of these XML files, you'll see that its contents do not include the actual data of the database, just the database shell. If you are interested in learning more about the schema of the files, go to `http://go.microsoft.com/fwlink/?LinkId=158286` to view the Data-Tier Application Schema File Format Structure Specification.

This data-tier application packages now contains all the objects needed for the UsedCars application. If you wanted to deploy the UsedCar application, simply connect to another SQL Server instance and deploy it.

Deploying a Data-Tier Application

Now that we have created the dacpac file for our UsedCars application, let's connect to another instance of SQL Server and deploy it. To start, connect to another SQL Server instance using SSMS. Navigate to the Management and then Data-Tier Applications nodes in Object Explorer. Right-click the Data-Tier Applications node, and select "Deploy Data-tier application" to launch a wizard that asks you which dacpac file to deploy. This wizard is shown in Figure 4-9.

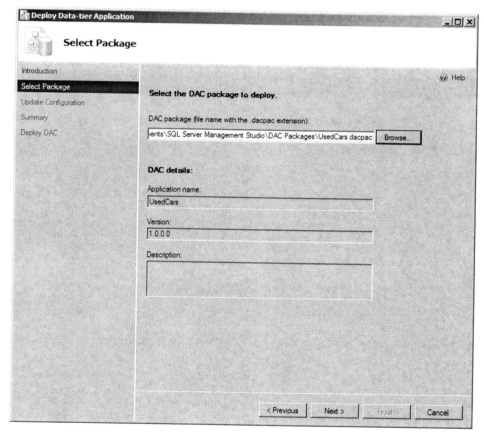

Figure 4-9. The Select Package page of the Deploy Data-tier Application wizard

After the wizard inspects the package, it asks you for the name of the new database and location to store the database files (see Figure 4-10).

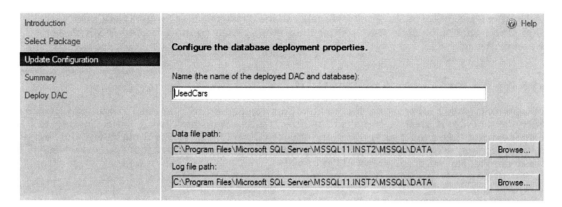

Figure 4-10. *The Update Configuration page of the Deploy Data-tier Application wizard*

Next, the wizard will provide you with a summary page and deploy your application. When the wizard completes, you will have a new node under "Data-tier applications" called UsedCars. Notice that you also have the UsedCars database created in this instance. At this point, our UsedCar application is deployed to the new server.

Registering an Existing Database as a Data-Tier Application

In the original SQL Server instance, we ran the Extract Data-tier Application wizard to create the dacpac file. If all you want to do is take an existing database and make a data-tier application on the same server, you can run the Register as Data-tier Application wizard. To help showcase the monitoring piece of data-tier applications, let's register the UsedCar database on the original SQL Server instance we used to create the dacpac file. To do this, connect to the original instance of SQL Server, and navigate to the UsedCar database in Object Explorer. Next, right-click the database, and select Tasks and then "Register as Data-tier Application". This will launch a wizard. The first page of this wizard will ask you to set the properties of the application. Much like we did in the wizard shown in Figure 4-7, we can enter a name, version number, and description. Once this wizard completes, our UsedCar application will appear in the Data-tier Application node of the Management node in Object Explorer for this instance of SQL Server as well.

Monitoring a Data-Tier Application Using the SQL Server Utility

Today, more applications in our datacenters need to be managed than in previous years. Not all of these are Tier 1, mission-critical applications. On the contrary, many are departmental Tier 2 and Tier 3 applications that support a subset of an organization. Data-tier applications allow the database administrator to focus on management at scale as opposed to micromanaging each individual application. In the example in this section, we have two instances of SQL Server: the default instance and an instance with a name of INST2. Since these applications are deployed, we can easily manage them through the SQL Server Utility.

In SQL Server 2008, the Performance Data Collector feature was introduced. This feature allowed DBAs to periodically poll a SQL instance for disk usage, query statistics, and server health information. Data from these queries would automatically be pushed into a database called the management data warehouse. This powerful tool gave DBAs a quick view of the health of a particular SQL Server instance. In SQL Server 2008 R2, this feature was expanded to include a concept called the utility control point (UCP). The UCP is a SQL Server instance designated as the central place to store and report on performance information. To create a UCP in SSMS, select the Utility Explorer menu item from the View menu in the SSMS toolbar. This will display a Getting Started document window containing a hyperlink to Create a Utility Control Point. Clicking this link will launch the Create Utility Control Point wizard. The first input screen is shown in Figure 4-11; it asks for a SQL Server instance to be used to create the UCP.

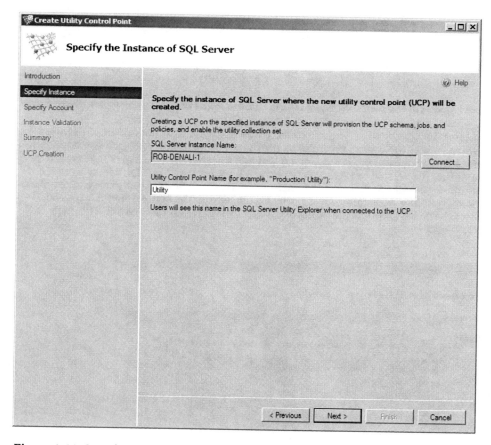

Figure 4-11. *Specifying the SQL Server instance for the Create Utility Control Point wizard*

The next page, shown in Figure 4-12, asks you for the Windows account that will be used to run the utility collect sets. Note that SQL Server Agent needs to be started on the instance you select to be the UCP. If you forget to start SQL Agent, the validation page will tell you and won't allow you to proceed until you start the service. Once the wizard has passed the validation checks, the next page will create the UCP, as shown in Figure 4-12.

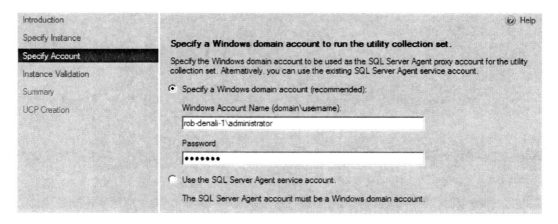

Figure 4-12. The Specify Account page of the Create Utility Control Point wizard

When the wizard has finished, it will bring you to the Utility Explorer Content document window. This window gives you a view of the overall health of all the managed instances and data-tier application components that the UCP is monitoring. Let's go ahead and add a second instance of SQL Server to be monitored. Remember that the SQL Server Agent service must be started on any SQL Server instance that we want to monitor. To enroll a SQL Server instance, in the Utility Explorer Utility node, right-click the Managed Instances container node, and select Enroll Instance from the context menu. This will launch a wizard for which the first input is the name of the SQL Server instance to enroll. This page is shown in Figure 4-13.

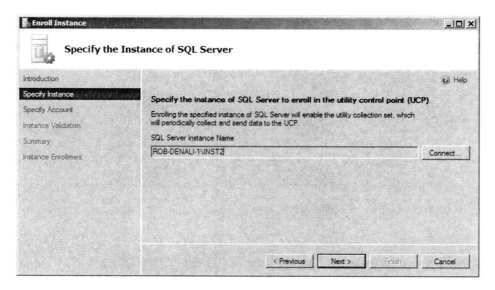

Figure 4-13. Specifying the instance of SQL Server in the Enroll Instance wizard

Next, we specify the Windows credentials for the account that will be obtaining the data on that instance of SQL Server; this page is similar to Figure 4-12. The wizard will then perform checks, and if these are passed, it will enroll the instance.

The UCP will be updated periodically from all the managed instances. At first, the new managed instance will be shown, but since no data has been collected, the display will show a gray circle as opposed to a green or red circle. This initial state for the second instance, `ROB-DENALI-1\INST2`, is shown in Figure 4-14.

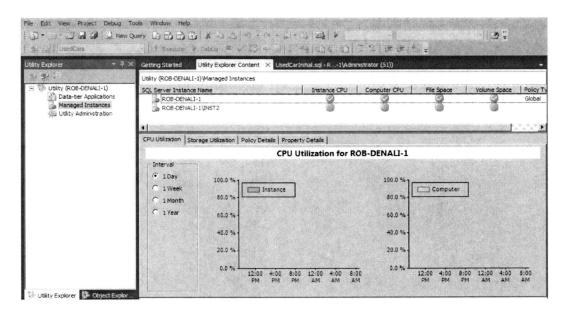

Figure 4-14. *Managed instances*

After a few minutes, both managed instances will report data to populate the Utility Explorer Content page. The real power of the UCP comes not only in its ability to get a snapshot of a server instance with respect to disk volume size and CPU trends over the past few days but in its ability to define a policy based on these statistics. For example, we can create a policy that says to mark a SQL Server instance as being overutilized if it's CPU usage is over 70 percent when sampled four times an hour. These policies are flexible and can be managed by clicking the Utility Administration node in the Utility Explorer. If a policy has been violated, the green circle shown in Figure 4-14 would be red.

Up until now, we have been discussing using UCPs to manage instances of SQL Server. UCPs can also manage data-tier applications. Once you've enrolled a SQL Server instance into a UCP, any data-tier applications that were defined within that instance will show up in the Data-Tier Applications node in the Utility Explorer. Since we have registered the UsedCars application on both of our SQL Server instances, we can see the performance of this application by clicking the Data-Tier Application node. This node is shown in 4-15.

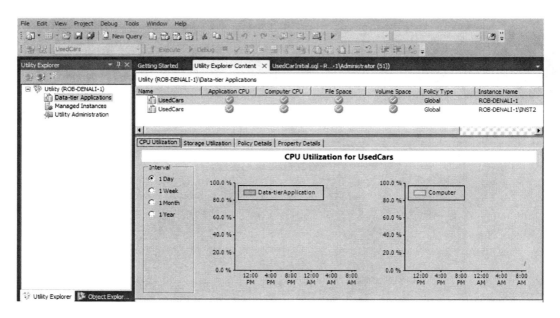

Figure 4-15. *Data-tier Applications*

We can now define policies like CPU and disk space limits to the application, just as we could for the instance.

Once we have all our managed instances enrolled, we can get a good, quick view of the health of our environment by clicking the Utility root node in the Utility Explorer. The resulting report is shown in Figure 4-16.

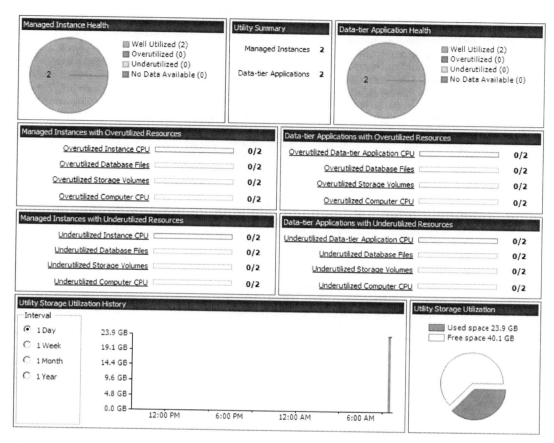

Figure 4-16. *A utility node report*

Since we only have two instances and not a lot of time has elapsed for data to be collected, this report looks fairly blank, but you can see the kind of content that you will be able to obtain from a real production environment.

SQL Server Utility is a great feature that allows DBAs to easily monitor their ever-expanding environments. For more information on SQL Server Utility, check out the "SQL Server Utility Features and Tasks" article located at `http://msdn.microsoft.com/en-us/library/ee210548(v=SQL.110).aspx`.

SQL Server Developer Tools

SQL Server is not just a relational database; it contains many other components including SQL Server Reporting Services, SQL Server Analysis Services, and SQL Server Integration Services. Each one of these components solves completely different problems, and for the most part, each is managed and developed differently than SQL Server itself. In earlier versions of SQL Server, developers who wish to develop reports for Report Server, cubes for Analysis Services, or packages for Integration Services used a tool called the Business Intelligence Development Studio. This tool was essentially a Visual Studio shell with snap-ins to provide the development experience. The experience is the same as having Visual C# or Visual Basic.NET within a Visual Studio shell. SQL Server developers could use Visual Studio itself, and depending on the version Visual Studio, would have advanced database tools to perform tasks like comparing schemas and data. Starting in SQL Server 2012, a new feature called SQL Server Development Tools (SSDT) attempts to bind Business Intelligence Studio and the database development capabilities within a traditional Visual Studio environment. At the time of this writing, the tool is in the Community Technology Preview 3 (CTP3) stage of development and can be downloaded from `http://msdn.microsoft.com/en-us/data/gg427686`.

The focus of SSDT is to accelerate the development of data-based applications against SQL Server and SQL Azure. SSDT supports development in the following platforms: SQL Server 2005, SQL Server 2008, SQL Server 2008 R2, SQL Server 2012, and SQL Azure.

Until now, we have been discussing development of SQL Server via SSMS. SSMS makes an active connection to SQL Server to obtain the necessary information to populate the IntelliSense context menus and to function usefully in general. If you're wearing your development hat, you want a source-code–driven development model as opposed to a database-driven model. With SSDT, this is possible, since SSDT supports a robust, offline set of development features. Before we get into the offline experience, let's look at SSDT in connected mode.

Working with SSDT in Connected Mode

Once you install SSDT, launch it from the Start Menu. To create a new project, click File, followed by New, and then Project from the main menu bar. Select SQL Server Database Project, and name it UsedCar Application. To connect to a SQL Server instance, click the View menu in the toolbar, and select Server Explorer. This will launch the Server Explorer (note that you may see a connection to a database called LocalDB; we will explain this later in this chapter). For now, click the Add Server button in the Server Explorer toolbar, and connect to the local SQL Server instance. The Server Explorer window will populate just like Object Explorer, as shown in Figure 4-17.

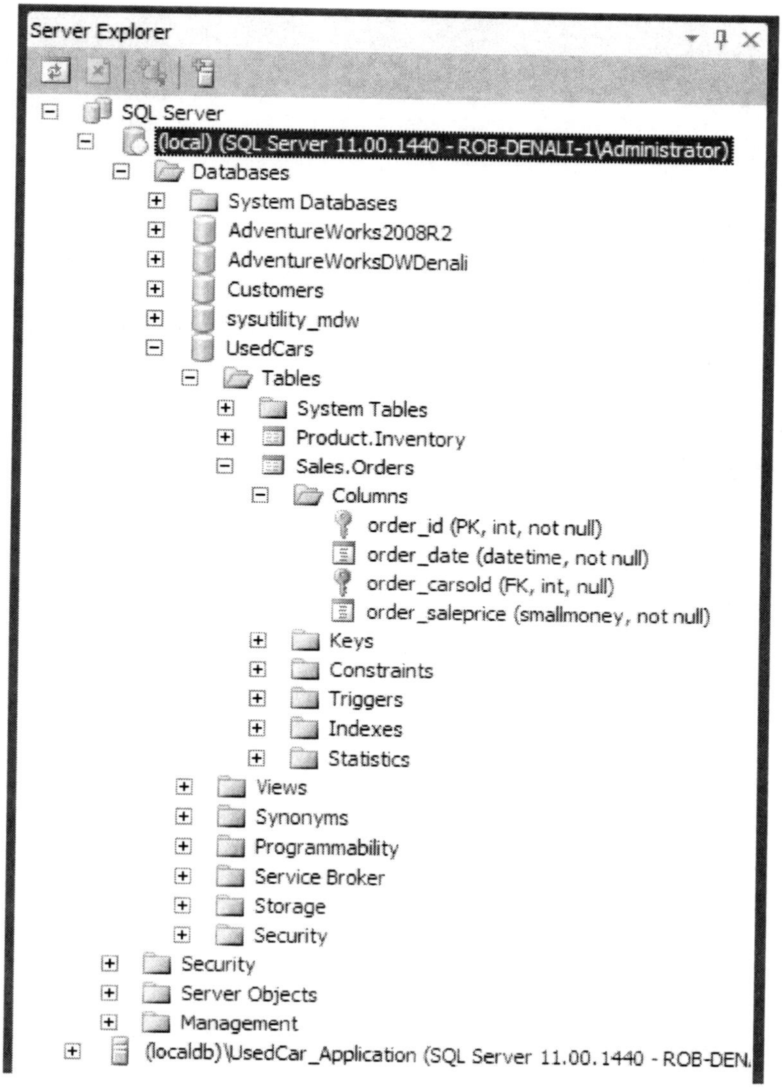

Figure 4-17. Server Explorer

Right-click the server node, and select New Query. On this sample server, we have the UsedCar database and data-tier application installed. In connected mode, we have IntelliSense, just as we had with SSMS. For example, if you type **SELECT * FROM SALES.**, you will get a drop-down list of available objects. If you select the `Orders` table and use your mouse to hover over the asterisk, you see additional information, such as all the columns that would be returned and their respective data types, as shown in Figure 4-18.

```
select * from Sales.Orders
         order_id(PK, int, not null),
         order_date(datetime, not null),
         order_carsold(int, null),
         order_saleprice(smallmoney, not null)
```

Figure 4-18. *Table definition within the query*

What if you wanted to delete or change an object but were not clear of its impact? One very useful feature of the tool is that it will tell you exactly what must happen to delete that object. Since our UsedCar schema is relatively small, to help illustrate this, we went to the AdventureWorks database and tried to delete the `Product.Products` table. Figure 4-19 shows the dialog that popped up when we tried to delete this object.

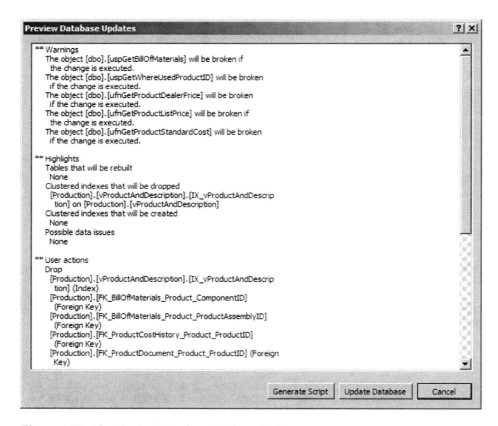

Figure 4-19. *The Preview Database Updates dialog*

In the dialog shown in Figure 4-19, you can see which functions would be broken, which indexes would be dropped and lots of other helpful information.

Working with SSDT in Offline Mode

A lot of power from SSDT comes in the offline mode. This is where developers can create projects that are source-code driven as opposed to database driven. To start, let's create a project based on our UsedCar database. Right-click the UsedCar database node in the Server Explorer, and select, New Project to launch the Import Database dialog shown in Figure 4-20.

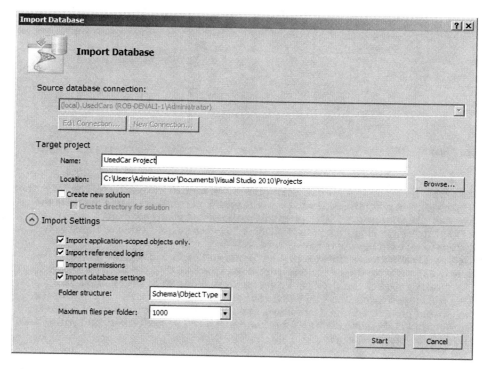

Figure 4-20. Import Database dialog

Type **UsedCar Project** for the name, and click the Start button. The dialog will go away for a minute and come back with a summary pane of the objects it created. When you click Finish, you can see that the Solution Explorer on the right-hand side of the screen has the schema that defines our database. In fact, it has .sql script files for all the objects including Bob and Bob User, our SQL login and database users, respectively.

Suppose we now want to add a column to the Inventory table to identify the asking price for the vehicle. To launch the table designer shown in Figure 4-21, you can double-click Inventory.sql in the Solution Explorer.

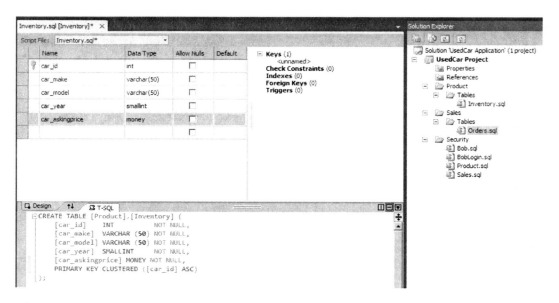

Figure 4-21. *Table designer*

The designer is interactive: to add a new column, click an empty cell below car_year, and define the column name and data type, for example, type **car_askingprice** and **money**, respectively. The TSQL that makes up the object is updated in real time with what is in the grid. You can also update the table the other way around: for example, change the TSQL statement in the bottom window from "car_askingprice MONEY" to "car_askingprice SMALLMONEY". Notice the grid value changed as well.

Click the Save button to save changes to the `Inventory.sql` file.

Suppose the developers made a lot of changes to the schema and had no idea if the tables on production server were the same as on their development server. One way they could check is to compare schemas. To do so, right-click the UsedCar Project node in Solution Explorer, and select Schema Compare. This will launch a dialog asking you for the source and destination. For the source, leave it pointed to the current project. For the destination, make a connection to the local SQL Server instance and UsedCar database. When you click OK, the comparison will be performed, and you will see our change in the UI shown in Figure 4-22.

Figure 4-22. Schema Compare document window

From this UI, we can generate the T-SQL Script to make an update or issue the update immediately to sync both servers.

SSDT also supports refactoring. For example, if you want to change the name of a column of a table from CustomerID to Customer_ID, it will look through every object in the application and tell you what will be affected. It will then provide the update script needed to make those corrections.

Application Versioning

If we dive a bit deeper into the pain points of developing a database application, we can see that a database is challenging to code and master. Developers have to maintain script libraries for the application. These scripts do things like initialize database objects, update schemas, and other things to mitigate the fact that a database is stateful. Think of the scenario where a developer updates an application. The database targeted by the application is still the same database that existed before the update, so it now needs to be updated to accommodate the changes to the application. Since there is no versioning within SQL Server, it's hard to tell for which version of the application the database is configured. The update scripts the developer writes are complex and critical to the success of the application, so once the new application is deployed, the DBA has to inspect these scripts to ensure they conform to the server instance that the application is deployed to. As you can see from this example, there are a lot of moving parts and issues to consider when developing a database application.

With SSDT, you can build a **dacpac** file out of the project to help with versioning. For our example, let's build a **dacpac** file of the UsedCar project and deploy to our server. To start, right-click the UsedCar Project, and select Properties. In the "Output types" group box, check the "Data-tier application" check box, and click Build. This will create the **dacpac** file in the output directory of your solution. At this point, you could go to SSMS and import the data-tier application.

Assume that we did connect to a SQL Server instance and deploy this **dacpac** package. If we made any updates to the solution, we can set a new version of the **dacpac** and deploy it again on the same instance of SQL Server. The existing database that is a part of the **dacpac** on the SQL Server would be upgraded to the new version.

SQL Server LocalDB

SQL Server Express edition is a free version of SQL Server that is basically a throttled-down version of the full SQL Server engine. Despite hard limits on CPU and memory consumption, it is almost the same as Standard edition from a relational engine perspective. For SQL Server development, the idea was to include this free version for developers to use and learn with. In fact, Visual Studio includes SQL Server Express as an option to install. One of the problems SQL Server Express is that it is a heavyweight in a fight requiring a featherweight. SQL Server Express is a Windows service, which requires network configuration and attention. For developers, there is something better in SQL Server 2012 called LocalDB. LocalDB is a version of SQL Server that installs faster, has fewer prerequisites, and doesn't require management of a database instance. Unlike SQL Server Compact edition, LocalDB is not an in process DLL that you bind to; rather, it's an application that runs in the user mode as a separate process. LocalDB is not appropriate for server-based or multiuser environments because its opens the database files for exclusive use. It is, however, ideal for development environments because it fully supports T-SQL.

When we created a project in SSDT and navigated to the Server Explorer, you may have noticed that LocalDB was attached. This is the default deployment database for SSDT solutions.

■ **Note** If you want to read more about LocalDB, check out the following blog:

http://blogs.msdn.com/b/sqlexpress/archive/2011/07/12/introducing-localdb-a-better-sql-express.aspx.

Summary

SQL Server Management Studio is a tool that has been used historically by just the DBA community. Throughout the iterations of SSMS, additional functionality has been placed in the application that makes development easier. Although not classified as a development tool, SSMS gives you the ability to perform development-related tasks like debugging Common Language Runtime (CLR) and T-SQL stored procedures. A fairly new deployment paradigm called data-tier applications are used to package database application code and objects for easy deployment, management, and updates. For developers, a new tool called the SQL Server Developer Tools was introduced in SQL Server 2012 as a Visual Studio experience that makes it easy to develop data applications and deploy them to SQL Server or to SQL Azure.

CHAPTER 5

Creating Tables and Other Objects

In this chapter, you will learn how to create various objects within the SQL Server database. Primarily, we'll focus on creating tables and objects, such as indexes and constraints, that are closely related to tables. To get the most out of this chapter, you should follow along using SQL Server Management Studio and the instance of SQL Server you installed in Chapter 2. It is important to note that there are multiple ways to create object in SQL Server. Two of the most common ways are by issuing Transact SQL (T-SQL) statements directly to SQL Server using a tool such as SSMS or SQLCMD and by using the management dialogs in a management tool like SSMS.

Navigating the Object Explorer Tree

You can find SQL Server Management Studio in the Microsoft SQL Server 2012 folder in the Start menu. When this application launches, it will ask you for the server you want to connect to. If you need help, please read the "Connecting to SQL Server" section in Chapter 3.

Once you are connected to the SQL Server instance, the Object Explorer tree within SQL Server Management Studio will populate with a root node, which will be the server instance you just connected to. This node will have a series of child nodes all exposing specific objects and features related to the specific SQL Server instance. Figure 5-1 shows the Object Explorer tree just after a connection was made to a local server instance.

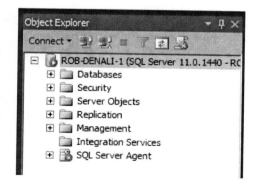

Figure 5-1. Object Explorer showing active connection to the local server instance

As you learned in Chapter 3, expanding any one of these child nodes brings up the specific objects related to the content of that particular child node. Right-clicking the container node or an actual object brings up dynamic context menus that allow you to perform actions on the objects. These context menus change depending on what you select. For example, the context menu for the Databases node gives the ability to launch the Create Database dialog box, while the context menu for the Security node allows you to create a new login to SQL Server. In this chapter, you will learn how to create various objects using both the user interface in SQL Server Management Studio and T-SQL statements.

Scripting the Actions of an SSMS Dialog Box

One of the most useful features within a typical SSMS dialog box is the ability to script the actions of a dialog box instead of actually executing the action against the server. For example, launch the New Database dialog box from the Databases node in Object Explorer. This will launch the dialog box shown in Figure 5-2. As an example, enter **SmartCommunityBank** in the "Database name" text box.

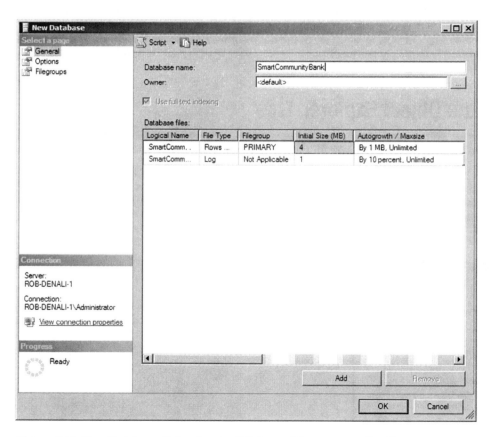

Figure 5-2. New Database dialog box in SQL Server Management Studio

If you click the OK button, the database will be created, and the dialog box will close. However, if you want to know exactly what T-SQL statements will be executed as a result of what you input in this dialog box, click the downward-facing arrow on the Script button at the top of the dialog box. This will pop up a list of destinations for the script, as shown in Figure 5-3.

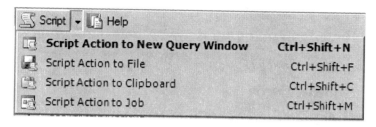

Figure 5-3. *Script options*

If you select Script Action to New Query Window, this will open a new Query Editor window and populate it with the CREATE DATABASE script shown here:

```
CREATE DATABASE [SmartCommunityBank]
 CONTAINMENT = NONE
 ON  PRIMARY
( NAME = N'SmartCommunityBank', FILENAME = N'C:\Program Files\Microsoft SQL Server\
MSSQL11.MSSQLSERVER\MSSQL\DATA\SmartCommunityBank.mdf' , SIZE = 4096KB , FILEGROWTH
= 1024KB )
 LOG ON
( NAME = N'SmartCommunityBank_log', FILENAME = N'C:\Program Files\Microsoft SQL Server\
MSSQL11.MSSQLSERVER\MSSQL\DATA\SmartCommunityBank_log.ldf' , SIZE = 1024KB , FILEGROWTH
= 10%)
GO
ALTER DATABASE [SmartCommunityBank] SET COMPATIBILITY_LEVEL = 110
GO
ALTER DATABASE [SmartCommunityBank] SET ANSI_NULL_DEFAULT OFF
GO
ALTER DATABASE [SmartCommunityBank] SET ANSI_NULLS OFF
GO
ALTER DATABASE [SmartCommunityBank] SET ANSI_PADDING OFF
GO
ALTER DATABASE [SmartCommunityBank] SET ANSI_WARNINGS OFF
GO
ALTER DATABASE [SmartCommunityBank] SET ARITHABORT OFF
GO
ALTER DATABASE [SmartCommunityBank] SET AUTO_CLOSE OFF
GO
ALTER DATABASE [SmartCommunityBank] SET AUTO_CREATE_STATISTICS ON
GO
ALTER DATABASE [SmartCommunityBank] SET AUTO_SHRINK OFF
GO
ALTER DATABASE [SmartCommunityBank] SET AUTO_UPDATE_STATISTICS ON
GO
```

```
ALTER DATABASE [SmartCommunityBank] SET CURSOR_CLOSE_ON_COMMIT OFF
GO
ALTER DATABASE [SmartCommunityBank] SET CURSOR_DEFAULT  GLOBAL
GO
ALTER DATABASE [SmartCommunityBank] SET CONCAT_NULL_YIELDS_NULL OFF
GO
ALTER DATABASE [SmartCommunityBank] SET NUMERIC_ROUNDABORT OFF
GO
ALTER DATABASE [SmartCommunityBank] SET QUOTED_IDENTIFIER OFF
GO
ALTER DATABASE [SmartCommunityBank] SET RECURSIVE_TRIGGERS OFF
GO
ALTER DATABASE [SmartCommunityBank] SET  DISABLE_BROKER
GO
ALTER DATABASE [SmartCommunityBank] SET AUTO_UPDATE_STATISTICS_ASYNC OFF
GO
ALTER DATABASE [SmartCommunityBank] SET DATE_CORRELATION_OPTIMIZATION OFF
GO
ALTER DATABASE [SmartCommunityBank] SET PARAMETERIZATION SIMPLE
GO
ALTER DATABASE [SmartCommunityBank] SET READ_COMMITTED_SNAPSHOT OFF
GO
ALTER DATABASE [SmartCommunityBank] SET  READ_WRITE
GO
ALTER DATABASE [SmartCommunityBank] SET RECOVERY FULL
GO
ALTER DATABASE [SmartCommunityBank] SET  MULTI_USER
GO
ALTER DATABASE [SmartCommunityBank] SET PAGE_VERIFY CHECKSUM
GO
ALTER DATABASE [SmartCommunityBank] SET TARGET_RECOVERY_TIME = 0 SECONDS
GO
USE [SmartCommunityBank]
GO
IF NOT EXISTS (SELECT name FROM sys.filegroups WHERE is_default=1 AND name = N'PRIMARY')↵
 ALTER DATABASE [SmartCommunityBank] MODIFY FILEGROUP [PRIMARY] DEFAULT
GO
```

Note Choosing to script the action of a dialog box is a great way to learn which T-SQL statements perform which actions.

In this case, you can see that the CREATE DATABASE statement is used to create a database. To create the database, click the Execute button the toolbar.

Transact-SQL (T-SQL) Primer

Before you learn how to create various objects within the database, it is important to review the general constructs of the T-SQL language. T-SQL is Microsoft's version of the Structured Query Language (SQL) programming language. SQL is a declarative programming language, which means that the SQL code describes what information should be returned, or what the end goal is, as opposed to how to go about retrieving information or doing some work. The SQL language contains categories of statements. These categories are Data Definition Language (DDL), Data Manipulation Language (DML), and Data Control Language (DCL).

Data Definition Language (DDL)

DDL statements describe the creation or modification of objects within the database server. In our previous example using SSMS, you noticed that when you created the SmartCommunityBank database, SSMS really executed a T-SQL script using the CREATE DATABASE DDL statement. The script that SSMS generates is sometimes more verbose than what is required at a minimum. For example, the minimum code that is needed to create a database is as follows:

```
USE [master]
GO
CREATE DATABASE [VetClinic]
GO
```

This will create a database named VetClinic using default values (you can find the default values for any of the T-SQL statements in SQL Server Books Online).

DDL statements also deal with the modification of objects. An example of modifying an existing object using the ALTER DDL statement is as follows:

```
USE [master]
GO
ALTER DATABASE VetClinic
SET RECOVERY FULL
GO
```

The previous example changes the database recovery mode to FULL for an existing database.

DDL statements also apply to the creation of security principals and objects. For example, if you wanted to create a new SQL Server login named ReceptionistUser, you would execute the following script:

```
USE [master]
GO
CREATE LOGIN ReceptionistUser WITH PASSWORD='hj2(*h2hBM!@jsx'
GO
```

Data Manipulation Language (DML)

DML statements read and modify the actual data within the database. For example, assume you created the following table using DDL statements within the VetClinic database:

```
USE [VetClinic]
GO
CREATE TABLE [Pets]
(pet_id       INT   PRIMARY KEY,
pet_name      VARCHAR(50)  NOT NULL,
pet_weight    INT           NOT NULL)
GO
```

Now, let's add some data to the Pets table using the INSERT DML statement. The code follows:

```
USE [VetClinic]
GO
INSERT INTO Pets VALUES
 (1,'Zeus',185),
(2,'Lady',155),
(3,'Deno',50)
GO
```

If you want to query the data, you can use the SELECT DML statement as follows:

```
SELECT * FROM Pets
```

If you execute this statement within SSMS, it will return the three pets defined previously in the results grid. Other DML statements include UPDATE and DELETE, which are two important actions to perform against data.

You can find a more in-depth discussion of these DML statements in Chapter 5.

Data Control Language (DCL)

DCL statements control access to data. For example, if you wanted to give SELECT access to ReceptionistUser, you could use the GRANT DCL statement as follows:

```
USE [VetClinic]
GO
GRANT SELECT ON Pets TO ReceptionistUser
GO
```

Other DCL statements include REVOKE and DENY. These are used to either remove a previously granted permission or deny someone access to a particular object. Note that DENY takes precedence over GRANT at a higher scope. For example, ReceptionistUser is granted SELECT on the Pets table. This enables ReceptionistUser to read all the columns within the table. The administration could DENY that user specific access to a column, and even though ReceptionistUser has SELECT access for the entire table, the specific column would not be available.

Creating Tables

You can create tables by using DDL or by using the table designer within SSMS. No matter which approach you choose to use, it all comes down to T-SQL. If you create tables from the table designer, the designer generates and executes T-SQL on your behalf. That's convenient, because it saves you a lot of tedium in writing the T-SQL yourself. But sometimes writing your own T-SQL has advantages.

Creating Tables from the Table Designer

To launch the table designer, simply navigate to the Tables node of the VetClinic database, right-click the node, and select New Table from the context menu. This will launch the table designer, shown in Figure 5-4.

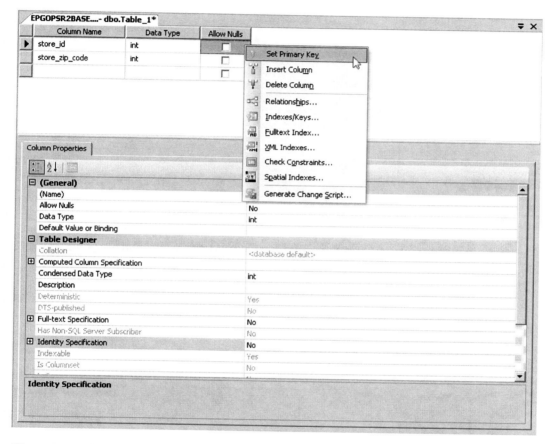

Figure 5-4. *Table designer in SSMS*

From the options visible in Figure 5-4, you can see that the majority of the common configuration options are available, such as the data type of the column and whether nulls are allowed. Both of these particular concepts will be discussed in detail in Chapter 5. The table designer provides you with the ability to easily configure a new table by exposing the most common options used for table creation.

To start adding columns, click the first empty row. Type **store_id** in the Column Name column, and select int for the data type. Deselect the Allows Nulls check box. Right-click the row, and select Set Primary Key. You will learn more about primary keys later in this chapter.

In the second row, type **store_zip_code** in the Column Name column, and select int for the data type.

To create the table, click the disk icon, and press Ctrl+S or select Save Table_1 from the File menu in SSMS. The table designer launches, giving the new table a name of Table_1. When you save the table, SSMS will ask you for a different name. It is in this save dialog box that you can specify Store Location for the table name.

When the table is saved, it is actually now created within the database.

Issuing the CREATE TABLE Statement

To create the Store Location table, you also could have used the CREATE TABLE statement. SSMS allows you to generate scripts based on existing objects. Thus, you can generate a CREATE TABLE script for the table you created with the table designer. To generate the CREATE script, right-click the Store Location table, and go to Script Table as CREATE To New Query Editor Window, as shown in Figure 5-5.

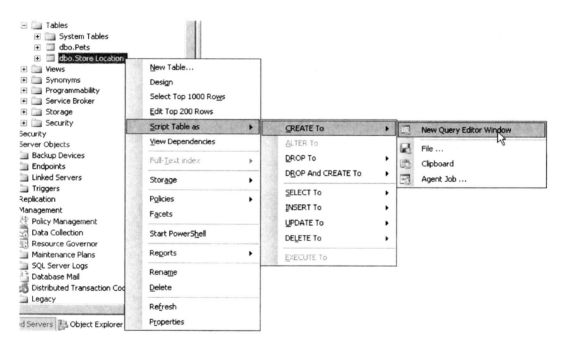

Figure 5-5. *Ad hoc scripting options available in SSMS*

The action New Query Editor Window will produce the following T-SQL script in a new Query Editor window:

```
USE [VetClinic]
GO
```

```
/****** Object:  Table [dbo].[Store Location]    ******/
SET ANSI_NULLS ON
GO

SET QUOTED_IDENTIFIER ON
GO

CREATE TABLE [dbo].[Store Location](
    [store_id] [int] NOT NULL,
    [store_zip_code] [int] NULL,
 CONSTRAINT [PK_Store Location] PRIMARY KEY CLUSTERED
(
    [store_id] ASC
)WITH (PAD_INDEX  = OFF, STATISTICS_NORECOMPUTE  = OFF,
IGNORE_DUP_KEY = OFF, ALLOW_ROW_LOCKS  = ON,
ALLOW_PAGE_LOCKS  = ON) ON [PRIMARY]
) ON [PRIMARY]

GO
```

Normally, when you create a table, you do not need to keep specifying the ANSI_NULLS or QUOTED_IDENTIFIER setting. These are in this script only because it was generated by SQL Server. For reference, the SET ANSI_NULL statement tells SQL how to deal with null values when used in equality or comparison operators. In a future version of SQL Server, you will not be able to set this value to OFF, so plan on keeping it set to ON, which is the default value. The QUOTED_IDENTIFER setting tells SQL Server how to handle quotation marks within query strings. You can find more information about this setting in the SQL Server Books Online article "SET QUOTED_IDENTIFIER (Transact-SQL)" located at http://msdn.microsoft.com/en-us/library/ms174393.aspx.

Let's examine the CREATE TABLE statement generated in the script. As with most DDL statements, the first value you need to specify is the name. In the example, the table name is Store Location, and it is created in the dbo schema.

```
CREATE TABLE [dbo].[Store Location]
```

The next two lines in the script supply the column definitions. In this table, we have two integer columns: store_id and store_zip_code. In T-SQL, these are defined within the CREATE TABLE statement as follows:

```
[store_id]              [int]  NOT NULL,
[store_zip_code]        [int]  NULL,
```

The keyword int specifies the integer data type. There are many different types of data types available to use. Data types will be discussed in more detail in Chapter 5. An integer allows the user to specify a number between –2,147,483,648 and 2,147,483,647. Different data types require different amounts of storage space. For example, storing the value of an integer takes 4 bytes. Unless you anticipate there being more than 32,768 stores, you could save 2 bytes of storage by using a smallint instead of an int to define the store_id column. SQL Server Books Online describes data types in the article "Data Types (Transact-SQL)" located at the following URL: http://msdn.microsoft.com/en-us/library/ms187752.aspx.

Altering Tables

Tables can be altered using SSMS or through DDL statements. To alter an existing table using SSMS, simply select Design from the context menu of the desired table. This will launch the table designer shown in Figure 5-4 populated with details from the table definition. You can freely modify the table using the UI, or you can modify a table using a DDL statement.

ALTER TABLE is the DDL statement used to change tables using T-SQL. A plethora of options are available for ALTER TABLE. For a complete list, see the SQL Server Books Online article "ALTER TABLE (Transact-SQL)" located at http://msdn.microsoft.com/en-us/library/ms190273.aspx.

To see ALTER TABLE in action, add a column called Store Manager to the Store Location table you just created:

```
ALTER TABLE [Store Location]
    ADD [Store Manager] VARCHAR(50)
```

In the following sections, you will also see other examples of altering a column including adding a constraint to an existing column.

Adding Constraints

With data types, you can limit the kind of data that can be stored within the column. For example, once you defined the store_id column as an integer, you could not insert the word boston for the store_id since a word is a sequence of characters and not an integer value. However, what if you had a column such as the weight of a pet that was an integer, and you knew your application would provide integers, but you wanted to make sure that only realistic or valid values were entered? This is where constraints come into play.

NULL Constraints

The keywords NOT NULL and NULL tell SQL Server whether a null value is allowed to be entered as a valid value for the column.

■ **Note** A null value is unknown and not meant to be confused with a zero value or empty value.

In some cases, you might have required value, such as a store ID, where a null value might not make any sense, because, for example, a store must have one specific ID to be a store. In this case, the column store_id must not allow null values; thus, you give NOT NULL as a parameter to the column definition. In other cases, you might be storing answers to a survey. Perhaps this survey accepts answers of yes or no, but the respondent didn't answer a particular question. The absence of an answer is a null value, and you should allow the answer column to have NULLs.

CHECK Constraints

Previously, we defined the Pets table as follows:

```
CREATE TABLE [Pets]
(pet_id        INT      PRIMARY KEY,
pet_name       VARCHAR(50)  NOT NULL,
pet_weight     INT          NOT NULL)
```

To make sure that the user cannot enter an unrealistic weight for a pet, such as a negative weight or a weight greater than 1,000 pounds, you can define a CHECK constraint. A CHECK constraint requires that the value entered passes an arbitrary expression. To restrict the list of valid values for the pet_weight column, you can apply the CHECK constraint as follows:

```
ALTER TABLE Pets  WITH CHECK
    ADD  CONSTRAINT [CK_Pets]
        CHECK  (([pet_weight]>0 AND [pet_weight]<1000))
GO
```

The keyword WITH CHECK means that existing data in the table will be checked against the constraint. If any values violate the constraint, the ALTER TABLE statement will fail. If you wanted to apply this constraint only for new data added to the table, you would specify WITH NOCHECK.

Primary Keys and Unique Constraints

In the Pets table defined earlier, notice pet_id is an integer data type, and it has a PRIMARY KEY constraint defined on it. The purpose of a primary key is to ensure that each row of data is unique for the given column or columns where the primary key is defined. In our example, we want a pet to appear only once in this table, so defining a primary key is one way to ensure this behavior.

Without a primary key, the data in Table 5-1 would be valid.

Table 5-1. *Defining Data Without a Primary Key*

Pet_id	pet_name	pet_weight
10	Sasha	30
10	Jake	23

If pet_id is used as a reference throughout the database application, how would you know if you were referring to Sasha or Jake, given a pet_id of 10? To mitigate this problem, you would define a primary key or unique constraint.

There can be only one primary key defined on a table, and the row value for a primary key column can never be null. The reason for this is that, when you define a primary key, SQL Server will create an index on the column or columns that you specify. Depending on whether an existing index is already defined, SQL Server may create a clustered index that physically sorts the data within the database files with respect to the key value. If there is already a clustered index defined on the table and you add a primary key, SQL Server will create a UNQIUE constraint to ensure that the values for the primary key column are unique. You will learn more about indexing later in this chapter.

A UNIQUE constraint is similar to a PRIMARY KEY constraint in that it enforces uniqueness of the data. However, the UNIQUE constraint creates a nonclustered index and does not physically change the structure of the data within the data files. You can have multiple unique constraints per table.

To illustrate the UNIQUE constraint, let's create a table called Medication. Since the veterinary practice can stock drugs from only one manufacturer, you need to define a unique constraint on the med_name column. The code for the table creation is as follows:

```
CREATE TABLE Medication
(med_id INT PRIMARY KEY,
med_name VARCHAR(50) CONSTRAINT u_med_name UNIQUE,
med_supplier VARCHAR(50) NOT NULL)
GO
```

From the previous code, you can define constraints at the time of creation and after the fact using the ALTER TABLE statement. Now that the Medication table is created, try to insert a medication that has the same name but from a different manufacturer, as follows:

```
INSERT INTO Medication VALUES (1, 'Cyclosporine 5mg', 'Generic Drugs Inc')
INSERT INTO Medication VALUES (2, 'Cyclosporine 5mg', 'ACME Vet Drugs')
```

When this code is executed, the first medication from Generic Drugs Inc will be successfully inserted, but the second will fail because of the violation of the constraint. The actual error message is as follows:

```
(1 row(s) affected)

Msg 2627, Level 14, State 1, Line 2

Violation of UNIQUE KEY constraint 'u_med_name'.

Cannot insert duplicate key in object 'dbo.Medication'.

The statement has been terminated.
```

Foreign Key Constraints

Notice that the Pets table you created previously in this chapter contains both primary and unique constraints. Now, you can create an Owners table that will reference the Pets table. The table creation code follows:

```
CREATE TABLE [Owners]
(owner_id   INT    PRIMARY KEY,
pet_id      INT    REFERENCES Pets(pet_id),
owner_name  VARCHAR(50) NOT NULL)
GO
```

There can be only one owner for each pet, so you create a primary key on the owner_id column. You create a foreign key on the pet_id column to enforce a link between the Owners table's pet_id column and the Pets table's pet_id column. This link is important in this scenario because you always want to ensure that pets belong to owners. There is a logical connection between these two entities. You cannot arbitrarily add a value to the pet_id column in the Owners table; the value must match an existing value in the pet_id column in the Pets table. This behavior is known as *referential integrity*.

To observe this behavior, add an owner associated with a pet that doesn't exist yet in the Pets database, as follows:

```
INSERT INTO Owners VALUES (1,20,'Julie')
```

Upon execution of the statement, you will get the following error:

```
Msg 547, Level 16, State 0, Line 1

The INSERT statement conflicted with the FOREIGN KEY constraint

 "FK__Owners__pet_id__1FCDBCEB". The conflict occurred in database

 "VetClinic", table "dbo.Pets", column 'pet_id'.

The statement has been terminated.
```

Dropping Tables

When you drop a table, you are deleting it from the database. When you perform this action, you are also deleting the table data, indexes, triggers, constraints, and permissions that were defined on the table. In certain circumstances, you are not allowed to drop a table. For example, if your table is referenced by another table via a foreign key constraint, the foreign key constraint must be removed from the referring table first before the table in question can be deleted. Also, any stored procedures or views that reference the table will need to be dropped or changed before the table in question can be dropped.

To help illustrate deleting a table, let's create two tables: Customers and Accounts. The Accounts table will contain a column customer_id that references the customer_id column in the Customers table. The script to create these tables is as follows:

```
CREATE TABLE Customers
(customer_id INT PRIMARY KEY,
customer_name NVARCHAR(50) NOT NULL)
GO

CREATE TABLE Accounts
(customer_id INT REFERENCES Customers(customer_id),
account_balance MONEY)
GO
```

To drop the Customers table using SSMS, simply right-click Customers in Object Explorer and select Delete. This will launch the Delete Object dialog box shown in Figure 5-6.

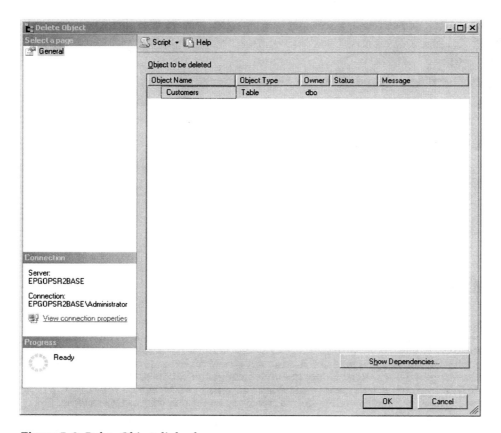

Figure 5-6. *Delete Object dialog box*

If you click OK to delete, you will get an error stating "Drop failed for Table 'dbo.Customers'. (Microsoft.SqlServer.Smo)." If you click the error link, you will find more details, including the following text: "Could not drop object 'dbo.Customers' because it is referenced by a FOREIGN KEY constraint. (Microsoft SQL Server, Error: 3726)." Since the Customers table is referenced by the Accounts table, you can't drop it until you address the foreign key reference. To determine these issues before you actually issue the drop command, you can click the Show Dependencies button. This will launch the Customers Dependencies dialog box shown in Figure 5-7.

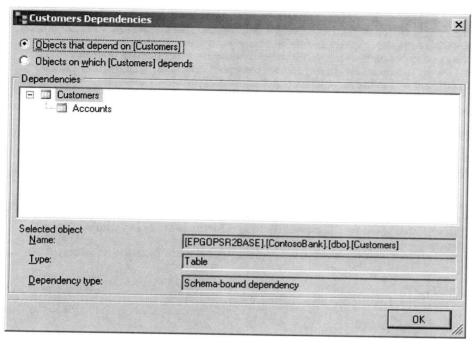

Figure 5-7. *Customers Dependencies dialog box*

Figure 5-7 clearly shows that the Accounts table references the Customers table.

The DDL statement for dropping a table is the DROP TABLE statement. To drop both tables, use the following script:

```
DROP TABLE Accounts
GO
DROP TABLE Customers
GO
```

Creating Indexes

Creating indexes on tables or views provides fast access to data by allowing the data to be organized in a way that allows for optimum query performance. You can think of an index within SQL Server just like the index of a book. If you were looking for the discussion of indexes, you could scan each page in this book, or you could go to the index and look up all the pages where indexes are mentioned. Obviously, looking through every page is tedious and takes the longest time of the two options mentioned. Without an index defined, SQL Server takes longer to do these scans for data as well.

The two most popular types of indexes are clustered and nonclustered. A *clustered index* physically changes the actual data pages stored in the database files themselves. This allows SQL Server to quickly go directly to the page where the requested data resides. Since we are physically ordering the data, you can have only one clustered index per table. If you wanted to optimize other queries that might not leverage the clustered index, you could create a nonclustered index. A *nonclustered index* is a separate data structure that keeps pointers to the actual data pages instead of physically changing the data page itself.

To help illustrate the value of the index, let's use the following script to create a Products table. This table will have an id column and a column for the price of the product. The setup script is as follows:

```
CREATE TABLE Products
(product_id INT IDENTITY(1,1) NOT NULL,
product_price DECIMAL(9,2) NOT NULL)
```

Note that you are not going to create a primary key on the product_id column. Instead, the IDENTITY property will be used to ensure every insert into the Products table has a unique value. You are not creating a primary key on the product_id column, because when you create a primary key, SQL Server creates a clustered index for that given key. This clustered index for the primary key would adversely affect your index versus nonindex performance results.

Now that the table is created, you can use the following script to create 100,000 test values:

```
DECLARE @i INT;
DECLARE @price DECIMAL(9,2);

SET @i=0;
WHILE (@i<100000)
BEGIN
SET @price= ROUND((RAND()*1000),2)

INSERT INTO Products(product_price) VALUES (@price)

SET @i=@i+1

END
```

The previous script will create 100,000 different prices ranging from 0 to less than 1,000.

■ **Note** This query may take a few minutes to run.

At this point, you have not created any indexes on the Products table. To easily determine whether SQL Server is performing a table scan or using an index, you can click the Include Actual Execution Plan button shown in Figure 5-8. Alternatively, you can include the actual execution plan by hitting Ctrl+M or selecting Include Actual Execution Plan from the Query menu in SSMS.

Figure 5-8. *Include Actual Execution Plan button*

When you include the actual execution plan, SSMS will add an extra tab called Execution Plan to the Results pane. The query results will still be displayed on the Results tab, but you can view the execution plan that SQL Server's query optimizer generated using the Execution Plan tab.

■ **Note** Execution plans are covered in more detail in Chapter 13.

Now, let's find all the products that cost between 400 and 700 using the following query:

```
SELECT COUNT(product_id) FROM Products WHERE
product_price BETWEEN 400 AND 700
```

When you click the Execution Plan tab in the Results pane, you will see something similar to Figure 5-9.

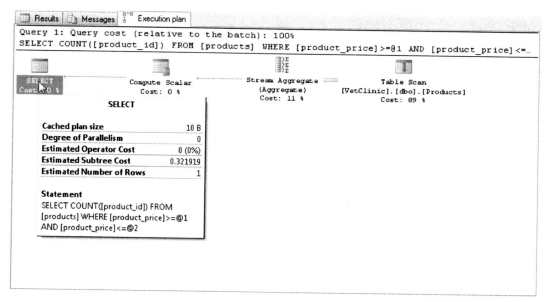

Figure 5-9. *Execution plan showing a table scan*

You can derive two important pieces of information from Figure 5-4. First, SQL Server performed a table scan. This means that it scanned a large portion of the 100,000 rows to satisfy this query. The second important information is the cost of the query. The estimated subtree cost was .321919 for this query.

Since you are querying based on the product_price column, create a clustered index on the column by issuing the following T-SQL script:

```
CREATE CLUSTERED INDEX CI_Price ON Products(product_price)
```

Now, when you reissue the same query:

```
SELECT COUNT(product_id) FROM Products WHERE
product_price BETWEEN 400 AND 700
```

the execution plan will show something similar to Figure 5-10.

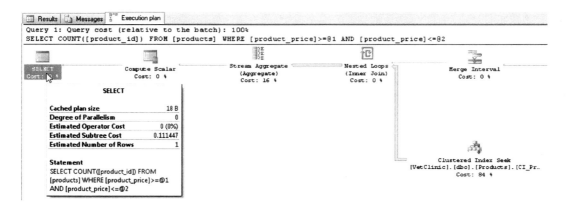

Figure 5-10. *Execution plan showing clustered index seek*

In this figure, you can see that a clustered index seek was performed instead of a table scan. Second, the estimated cost of the subtree was only .11147. This query executed more than twice as fast as the query without the index.

■ **Note** Even though an index may be defined for a given table or view, the SQL Server query optimizer may find it more efficient to just do a table scan for smaller row sizes instead of leveraging the index.

In our example, you created a clustered index. This type of index changes the actual data pages stored in the database. Thus, you can have only one clustered index per table. If you wanted to optimize other queries that might not leverage the clustered index, you could create a nonclustered index. Recall that a nonclustered index is a separate data structure that keeps pointers to the actual data pages instead of physically changing the data page itself. You will learn more about index fragmentation and rebuilding indexes in Chapter 10.

Summary

SQL Server Management Studio can be a very helpful tool to use when learning SQL Server. The dialog boxes allow you to script almost all of the actions you're performing. From these scripts, you can learn how your changes to the dialog box via SSMS affect the actual T-SQL statements. The Object Explorer tree exposes a context menu with a script option that allows you to script the creation, modification, or deletion of the selected objects; it's another great tool to help you learn T-SQL syntax.

One of the most important concepts to learn as a DBA is proper indexing. It's a topic that performance tuning and optimization books cover in great depth. Without indexing, SQL Server may have to issue table scans, which are quite costly from a disk I/O standpoint.

A solid understanding of the core relational database principals will help you tremendously in your DBA career. Now that you are finished with this chapter, practice using SSMS to create your own tables and try to integrate them within the Pets database. Practice creating and using indexes. The time you spend on these core concepts will be valuable.

CHAPTER 6

Transact-SQL

Transact-SQL (T-SQL) is the dialect of the Structured Query Language (SQL) adopted by Microsoft's SQL Server database engine. T-SQL has been around since the early days of the Sybase code in the early 1990s. It has evolved throughout the years and today is a robust programming language based on the ANSI SQL: 2008 standard. In this chapter, you will learn how to access data using T-SQL statements as well as how to use many of the programming capabilities within the database engine, including stored procedures and functions.

The VetClinic Sample Database Revisited

Before diving in, let's revisit the VetClinic database that you created in the previous chapter. You'll use that database for all of the examples in this chapter. If you haven't already created that database, you can create it now by executing the following code:

```
USE [master]
GO

CREATE DATABASE [VetClinic]
GO

USE [master]
GO

ALTER DATABASE VetClinic
SET RECOVERY FULL
GO

USE [VetClinic]
GO

CREATE TABLE [Pets]
(pet_id        INT                          PRIMARY KEY,
pet_name      VARCHAR(50)     NOT NULL,
pet_weight    INT                      NULL)
GO
```

```
ALTER TABLE [Pets]
ADD [MicroChipID] VARCHAR(100) NOT NULL
CONSTRAINT [MicroChip_Unique] UNIQUE
GO

USE [VetClinic]
GO

INSERT INTO Pets
VALUES(1,'Zeus',185,'398BF49'),
(2,'Lady',155,'191ABBC'),
(3,'Deno',50,'790AG441'),
(4,'Rex',44,'CDD81322'),
(5,'Rover',15,'A8719841')
GO

CREATE TABLE [Owners]
(owner_id        INT                     PRIMARY KEY,
pet_id           INT                         REFERENCES Pets(pet_id),
owner_name       VARCHAR(50)    NOT NULL)
GO

INSERT INTO Owners VALUES(1,2,'Bryan'),
(2,3,'Rob'),
(3,1,'Rob')

CREATE TABLE MicroChips
(MicroChipID VARCHAR(100) UNIQUE)
GO

INSERT INTO MicroChips VALUES('34BA123')
GO
```

Data Types

By now, you should be familiar with some of the data types available. The common ones that are used throughout this book are INT and VARCHAR. SQL Server Books Online has a complete list of all the data types that are supported within SQL Server. You can find the "Data Types (Transact-SQL)" article at http://msdn.microsoft.com/en-us/library/ms187752(v=SQL.110).aspx. Data types are used in many places within SQL Server, including as column definitions, as parameters to functions and stored procedures, and as variables. Table 6-1 describes a few of the common data types you may use in everyday tasks.

Table 6-1. *Common Data Types*

Data Type	Description
INT	Ranges from –2,147,483,648 to 2,147,483,647.
DECIMAL(p,s)	Stores decimal numbers; p is for precision (the maximum number that can be stored), and s is for scale (the maximum number that can be stored to the right of the decimal point).
DATETIME	Stores date and time, similar to the DATE and TIME data types, which store only the date or time, respectively.
CHAR, NCHAR	Stores fixed-length non-Unicode (CHAR) or Unicode (NCHAR) character data.
VARCHAR, NVARCHAR	Stores variable-length non-Unicode (VARCHAR) or Unicode (NVARCHAR) character data.
BINARY, VARBINARY	Stores fixed-length (BINARY) or variable-length (VARBINARY) binary data.

Each data type has different characteristics, including how much space on disk each value takes up. A VARCHAR data type can be defined for 20 characters but takes up only a few bytes on disk. A quick way to determine how many bytes are used is to use the DATALENGTH function. In the following example, the @name variable has the text Rob:

```
DECLARE @name VARCHAR(20)
SET @name='Rob'
SELECT DATALENGTH(@name)
```

When this script is run, the size of @name is 3 bytes. If you were to change it to SET @name='Robert' and rerun the query, the size would be 6 bytes.

Fixed data types, such as integers and money, always take the same storage space regardless of the value. Taking up more storage space than is needed not only wastes disk space but also decreases query performance because there will be more disk I/O as a result. SQL Server 2008 provides native data compression technologies that compress at the row and page levels, which helps to mitigate the performance and storage issues. Regardless of whether or not you decide to compress your data, it's a good idea to analyze your database to determine whether the data types are defined appropriately for the given data.

Unicode vs. ANSI

If you are new to the database world and haven't had a lot of experience programming, you may be curious about Unicode character strings versus ANSI character strings. To truly understand this, you must look to the origins of computers. The American National Standards Institute (ANSI) came out with a standard known as American Standard Code for Information Interchange (ASCII). This standard defines letters, numbers, and symbols that are referred to as a *character set*. The ASCII character set handles 256 different characters generally stored as 1 byte each within a computer. With only 26 letters in the English language, you may be wondering why anyone would need more than 256 characters. If the world spoke only English, no one would, but our friends in China struggled to figure out how to represent their thousands of characters within this 256-character limit. Unicode, however, allows the storage of 2 bytes per character. These 2 bytes allow for more than 65,000 different characters. All modern operating systems use Unicode, and SQL Server supports both the Unicode and ANSI character sets.

Living with NULL

NULL is not your annoying cousin; it identifies that a value does not exist in the database. Take the Pets table definition, for example:

```
CREATE TABLE [Pets]
(pet_id        INT                           PRIMARY KEY,
pet_name    VARCHAR(50)      NOT NULL,
pet_weight  INT                           NULL)
GO
```

In this scenario, it's OK that the pet weight is not entered. However, it is not acceptable for the pet to have no name. In the table definition, you see pet_name was defined with a NOT NULL keyword. This means that the absence of a value cannot be a valid value for the pet_name column. Conversely, pet_weight was defined as NULL, meaning that you could insert a value into the table and leave out the pet's weight. If you queried the newly entered data, you would see that pet_weight is NULL.

Data Manipulation Language

Most of what you'll do with T-SQL centers around the Data Manipulation Language (DML). DML consists of the four statements SELECT, INSERT, UPDATE, and DELETE. These are the four statements that you use to get data into a database, update and delete that data, and get it back out again.

SELECT

The SELECT DML statement allows users to retrieve data from the database. A simplified version of the syntax follows:

```
SELECT <select_list> FROM <table_source> [WHERE <search_condition>]
```

where the parameters are defined as follows:

- <select_list> specifies the columns that you want to return in the query.

- <table_source> is the table that you want to retrieve data from.

- <search_condition> is used to filter or scope the results that you are seeking.

The WHERE clause is optional. If you omit this clause, you will return all the rows from the given table. You can think of the WHERE clause like a Boolean expression. That is, the expression will be evaluated across every row in the table.

Basic SELECT Queries

Let's look at an example. If you wanted to return all the pets' names and weights, you would issue the following SELECT query:

```
SELECT pet_name, pet_weight FROM Pets
```

This statement would return the following result set:

pet_name	pet_weight
Zeus	185
Lady	155
Deno	50
Rex	44
Rover	15

If you wanted to narrow the result set, you could add a WHERE clause like the following:

```
SELECT pet_name, pet_weight FROM Pets WHERE pet_weight > 100
```

This WHERE expression would cause the result set to return only pets whose weight was greater than the value 100.

In the example, you explicitly asked SQL Server to return specific columns from the table. You could have used an asterisk (*) instead, and this would have returned all the columns in the table. To return all the columns in the Pets table, you would issue the following statement:

```
SELECT * FROM Pets
```

Sometimes tables have millions or billions of rows, and you don't really want to enumerate all of them at once. There are expressions like TOP that you can use to limit the result set. TOP specifies that only a specific number of results or percentage of results will be returned from the query. For example, SELECT TOP 3 * FROM Pets will return the first three pets stored within the table, as shown here:

Pet_id	pet_name	pet_weight	MicroChipID
1	Zeus	185	398BF49
2	Lady	155	191ABBC
3	Deno	50	790AG441

This limiting capability is also useful when used in conjunction with other clauses defined within the query. The ORDER BY clause is used to instruct SQL Server to order the result set in a particular way. You specify the columns to sort by and the direction of the sort as parameters of the ORDER BY clause. For example, if you wanted to know the top three lightest pets, you would issue the following query:

```
SELECT TOP 3 * FROM Pets ORDER BY pet_weight ASC
```

This would yield the following result:

Pet_id	pet_name	pet_weight	MicroChipID
5	Rover	15	A8719841
4	Rex	44	CDD81322
3	Deno	50	790AG441

The ASC parameter instructs SQL Server to order the results in *ascending* order, or lowest to highest. If you wanted to go the other way and order from highest to lowest, you could have specified DESC, which means *descending*.

A key value for relational databases is the fact that sometimes different tables hold data that is related to each other. This data can be combined and returned in a single result set. In this example, you have a Pets table and an Owners table. Pets have owners, so if you wanted to figure out which owners have pets with a weight greater than 100, you could accomplish this by joining the tables within the query. When you join together tables, you have the option of specifying what to do with the rows that are matched and those that are not matched. What happens depends on what kind of JOIN you include in your query. For example, if you wanted to know all the pets who have owners, you could execute this statement:

```
SELECT pet_name,owner_name FROM Pets
 INNER JOIN Owners
 ON Pets.pet_id=Owners.pet_id
```

This statement will yield the following results:

pet_name	owner_name
Lady	Bryan
Deno	Rob
Zeus	Rob

If you look at the data in both the Pets and Owners tables, you can see that two additional pets, Rex and Rover, were not displayed. This is because the Owners table does not have a matching pet_id for these two pets.

If you wanted to list all the pets regardless of whether they had an owner, you could issue a LEFT OUTER JOIN, which will always include the data from the table defined on the left side of the JOIN statement. The following is an example of listing all the pets and their owners, if they have any:

```
SELECT pet_name,owner_name FROM Pets
 LEFT OUTER JOIN Owners
 ON Pets.pet_id=Owners.pet_id
```

This statement will yield the following result:

pet_name	owner_name
Zeus	Rob
Lady	Bryan
Deno	Rob
Rex	NULL
Rover	NULL

Notice that NULL values result when owners do not exist. Rex has no owner name on record. The system doesn't make up a name where none exists. When no value exists, the system will return NULL.

■ **Note** INNER JOIN is the default join if you do not specify the join type.

There are other types of joins: RIGHT OUTER joins are similar to LEFT OUTER joins except they include the result set for the table to the right of the JOIN statement. A FULL OUTER join lists all results for both tables to the left and right of the JOIN statement. For more information on the different join types, see the SQL Server Books Online article "Using Joins" at http://msdn.microsoft.com/en-us/library/ms191472.aspx.

Paging Support

When you want to view a product catalog on a web page, you usually see the results returned from 1–25 for example. The actual query, though, might have returned hundreds or thousands of results. A lot of developers spent time writing complex code in the middle-tier web page layer or the database layer to parse the full query for the specified range. Starting in SQL Server 2012, native paging support is available that allows you to ask for specific ranges of rows to be returned. To illustrate, let's add a few more rows of data to our Pets table:

```
INSERT INTO Pets
VALUES(6,'Roscoe',55,'F5CAA29'),
(7,'Missy',67,'B7C2A59'),
(8,'George',12,'AA63BC5'),
(9,'Spot',34,'CC8A674')
GO
```

If you wanted to know the three heaviest pets, you could leverage the TOP T-SQL statement as follows:

```
SELECT TOP 3 pet_name,pet_weight FROM Pets ORDER BY pet_weight DESC
```

This would get the answer, but it would be difficult to find out the next three heaviest pets. This is where the OFFSET and FETCH statements work well. Consider the following statement, which uses OFFSET (0) to specify stating at the beginning and FETCH NEXT 3 ROWS to request only the three heaviest pets:

```
SELECT pet_name,pet_weight FROM Pets
    ORDER BY pet_weight DESC
        OFFSET (0) ROWS    FETCH NEXT 3 ROWS ONLY
```

Running this statement yields the same result as our TOP 3 statement:

pet_name	pet_weight
Zeus	185
Lady	155
Missy	67

If you wanted to know the next three, you would set the offset to start at the third result and fetch the next three. Notice the use of OFFSET (3) in the following example:

```
SELECT pet_name,pet_weight FROM Pets
    ORDER BY pet_weight DESC
        OFFSET (3) ROWS    FETCH NEXT 3 ROWS ONLY;
```

This would yield the following result:

pet_name	pet_weight
Roscoe	55
Deno	50
Rex	44

More information on OFFSET and FETCH is available in the ORDER BY documentation in SQL Server Books Online located at http://msdn.microsoft.com/en-us/library/ms188385%28v=SQL.110%29.aspx.

SELECT is arguably the most frequently used DML statement. Many different expressions and clauses are possible to use with SELECT. Mastering the use of this statement will be important in your daily use of SQL Server or any other database platform. SQL Server Books Online covers the syntax in the article "SELECT (Transact-SQL)" located at http://msdn.microsoft.com/en-us/library/ms189499.aspx.

INSERT

The INSERT DML statement allows users to write data into a database. A simplified example of the syntax follows:

```
INSERT <table_name> [(column list)]
VALUES( { DEFAULT | NULL | <expression> } [ ,...n] )
```

where the parameters are defined as follows:

- <table_name> is the table that you want to insert data into.

- <column list> is a list of specific columns you want to insert data into. This is optional.

- <expression> is the actual data that you want to insert. The type of data depends on the data type that is defined for the particular column.

Basic INSERT Queries

The following sample script will add more pets to the Pets table:

```
INSERT INTO Pets (pet_id, pet_name, pet_weight, MicroChipID)
 VALUES (10,'Roxy',7,'1A8AF59'),
(11,'Champ',95,'81CB910'),
(12,'Penny',80,'C710A6B')
```

Alternatively, you could have omitted the specific columns you wanted to insert. If you do this, SQL Server will assume that the first value will be for the first column definition, the second value entered will be for the second columns definition, and so on. For example, since you are inserting information into all the columns in the Owners table, you could issue this statement and omit owner_id, pet_id, and owner_name from the statement:

```
INSERT INTO Owners VALUES (4,5,'Frank')
```

Identity and Sequences

When the Pets table was defined, a primary key column for pet_id was created. Usually, a table has a primary key column that uniquely identifies the information for that specific row of data. Up until now, when an INSERT statement was given, we supplied this primary key. In a real-world application, the next available primary key might not be known, or it may require some T-SQL execution to obtain the next value. This is one of the scenarios where the IDENTITY property of the CREATE TABLE statement can help with automatically generating a value for the new row. Since we already have the Pets table, to use the INDENTITY property, we would have to drop the table and create it. To help illustrate the property create a new table called PetFood as follows:

```
CREATE TABLE PetFood
(pet_food_id int IDENTITY(1,1),
 food_name varchar (20));
```

Now, as data is inserted into the PetFood table, you do not need to specify the pet_food identity, as shown by the following T-SQL statement:

```
INSERT INTO PetFood VALUES('Lamb and Rice'),('Chicken'),('Corn')
```

To view the table issue a SELECT * FROM PetFood statement. This will yield the following result:

pet_food_id	food_name
1	Lamb and Rice
2	Chicken
3	Corn

Notice that you didn't have to figure out what the next available pet_food_id was when you inserted the data into the table. There is a good article on working with identity located at the following web site: www.simple-talk.com/sql/t-sql-programming/identity-columns.

IDENTITY is a powerful and useful property, but it is also limited in some areas. Perhaps the biggest issue with IDENTITY comes with its restriction to a single table. It is hard to share a common identity value across multiple tables in a single transaction. This is because the identity value is created after the insert. There are some ways to get around this, but a much better solution would be to use a SEQUENCE object. A SEQUENCE object can easily be used by more than one table because it's not bound to any particular table; rather, it's a separate independent object. To create a SEQUENCE object, use the CREATE SEQUENCE statement as follows:

```
CREATE SEQUENCE PetFoodIDSequence
    AS INT
    START WITH 1
    INCREMENT BY 1
```

Let's drop and re-create our PetFood table so we can use the new PetFoodIDSequence object:

```
DROP TABLE PetFood
GO
CREATE TABLE PetFood
(pet_food int DEFAULT (NEXT VALUE FOR PetFoodIDSequence),
 food_name VARCHAR (20));
GO
```

Now, we can insert our pet food as before using the INSERT statement:

```
INSERT INTO PetFood (food_name) VALUES('Lamb and Rice'),('Chicken'),('Corn')
```

Running a SELECT statement on the PetFood table will yield the same results as when we used the IDENTITY property.

▒ **Note** For more information on SEQUENCE read the following article: `http://www.databasejournal.com/features/mssql/sql-server-denali-sequence-object.html`.

UPDATE

The UPDATE DML statement allows the user to modify existing data within the database. A simplified definition follows:

```
UPDATE <object>
SET { column_name = { <expression> | DEFAULT | NULL }
[ WHERE <search_condition> ]
```

where the parameters are defined as follows:

- <object> is the table or view that is being updated.

- column_name is the name of the column of data that will be updated.

- <search_condition> is used to filter or scope the list of rows to update.

As an example, let's update the Owners table and change the ownership of dogs owned by Frank to Courtney. You can do this with the following UPDATE statement:

```
UPDATE Owners SET owner_name='Courtney' WHERE owner_name='Frank'
```

The WHERE clause is optional. However, if you do not specify a search condition, you will update every row. So, unless updating all rows is what you intend to do, you should always specify a WHERE clause.

DELETE

The DELETE DML statement allows users to remove data from the database. A simplified definition follows:

```
DELETE FROM <table_source> [ WHERE <search_condition> ]
```

where the parameters are defined as follows:

- <table_source> specifies the table that you want to remove items from.

- <search_condition> is used to scope the amount of rows that will be deleted.

The following example uses the DELETE statement to remove the pet named Penny:

```
DELETE FROM Pets WHERE pet_name = 'Penny'
```

The WHERE clause is optional. If you omit it, you will delete all rows in the specified table. Be very careful about omitting it. Omitting the WHERE clause and inadvertently deleting all data from a table is a common mistake. It's a mistake that you truly want to avoid making.

Transactions

Transactions enable users to create T-SQL batch statements that are either completely applied or do nothing to the existing data. When changes are applied, it is said that the transaction has *committed*. When the batch is stopped for any reason, such as by an error or being intentionally canceled, the transaction will be *rolled back*, and changes made within the transaction will not be made to the data.

Executing Transactions

The following example shows how to begin a transaction, execute some statements, and then commit the transaction. The example swaps the names of the two pets, Lady and Deno:

```
BEGIN TRANSACTION
UPDATE Pets SET pet_name='Lady' WHERE pet_id=3
UPDATE Pets SET pet_name='Deno' WHERE pet_id=2
COMMIT
```

Notice that the two UPDATE statements are bracketed by the statements BEGIN TRANSACTION and COMMIT. These two UPDATE statements form a transaction. Either they will both succeed or they will both fail. And if they succeed, they will both appear to other database users to have executed simultaneously. No other user but you will ever see both pets having the same name of Lady. You, as the person executing the transaction, are the only user with the ability to query the intermediate state between the two UPDATE statements. We'll talk more about this in the "Isolating Transactions" section.

If you are executing a transaction and change your mind or make a mistake, you can issue a ROLLBACK statement to undo the damage, for example:

```
BEGIN TRANSACTION
DELETE FROM Pets
ROLLBACK
```

This example deletes all data from the Pets table and then issues a ROLLBACK statement to undo that deletion. You can protect yourself by following this pattern. Wrap critical DELETE and UPDATE statements in a transaction. Then, you can roll back in the event you mistype, omit the WHERE clause, or otherwise make a mistake.

Isolating Transactions

When you issue a BEGIN TRANSACTION statement, you are telling SQL Server that from this point in the T-SQL batch, you intend to isolate the effect of the statements from the rest of the user connections. Each transaction lasts either until it completes without errors and a COMMIT TRANSACTION statement is issued or until errors are encountered and all modifications are erased with a ROLLBACK TRANSACTION statement.

To help illustrate the transactional isolation from the rest of user connections, consider the following case where there are two different connections to SQL Server. User1 is connected and issues the following statement:

```
BEGIN TRANSACTION
UPDATE Pets SET pet_name='Big Boy' WHERE pet_id=5
SELECT pet_name FROM Pets WHERE pet_id=5
```

At this point, the result set for the SELECT statement is as follows:

pet_name
Big Boy

User2 is connected to the same SQL Server and issues the following statement:

```
SELECT pet_name FROM Pets WHERE pet_id=5
```

The result set for User2's SELECT statement follows:

pet_name
Rover

User2 still sees the old value until User1 issues a COMMIT TRANSACTION statement.

This isolation is valuable and critical to maintain consistency of the database. As a user, you can change the behavior of the isolation. If User2 wanted to know the value even though User1 did not commit the transaction yet, User2 could manually set the transaction isolation level using the SET TRANSACTION ISOLATION statement.

To read the uncommitted data in the Pets table, User2 would issue the following code:

```
SET TRANSACTION ISOLATION LEVEL READ UNCOMMITTED
GO
SELECT pet_name FROM Pets WHERE pet_id=5
GO
```

This would return the uncommitted Big Boy value instead of the original Rover value. It is important to note that it is not a best practice to keep transactions open; they take up valuable server resources, and other users could be depending on the data being used within the transaction. In this example, User1 should commit or roll back the transaction as soon as possible.

There are many different isolation levels that can be set. SQL Server Books Online describes all of these in detail in the article "Set Transaction Isolation Level (Transact-SQL)" at http://msdn.microsoft.com/en-us/library/ms173763.aspx.

Deadlocks

Any time you have multiple users trying to access and update the same piece of data, you will run into problems. One user may have read a value and, based on that value, performed some work, when in reality the value was updated right after the original read and now causes problems for the user. SQL Server places locks at different database levels, such as at rows or the entire table itself. This makes the multiuser scenario possible.

A *lock* is a way to synchronize multiple user access to the same piece of data. Locks have different modes, such as shared or exclusive. Depending on the lock type and the actions each user is trying to perform, you may end up in a deadlock situation. *Deadlocks* occur when User1 holds a lock on a resource and is requesting access to another resource that User2 holds a lock on. User1 has to wait for User2 to release the lock. However, User2 is also requesting a lock on User1's resource. Thus, User1 and User2 are both waiting for each other to release the locks. In the end, SQL Server will choose one to be the victim and roll back that user's transaction. You can find an in-depth discussion on deadlocking in the SQL Server Books Online article called "Deadlocking" at http://msdn.microsoft.com/en-us/library/ms177433.aspx.

SQL Server does a good job of providing tools to debug deadlock situations. You can use SQL Server Profiler to capture a SQL trace. Figure 6-1 shows the output of SQL Server Profiler when a deadlock was encountered.

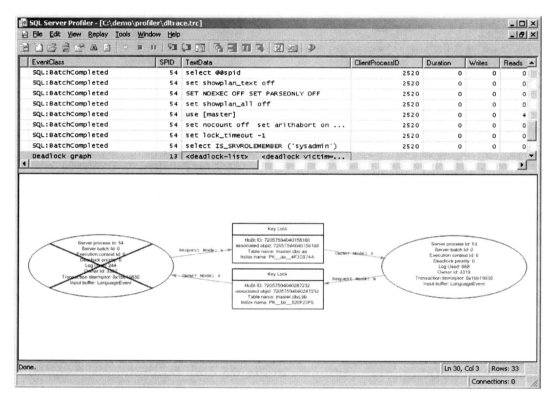

Figure 6-1. *SQL Server Profiler trace showing a deadlock event*

For a deadlock event, SQL Server Profiler displays the server process IDs that were involved with the deadlock, as well as the deadlock victim. Figure 6-2 shows a detailed view of the deadlock graph showing the actual T-SQL statement that was issued by the deadlock victim.

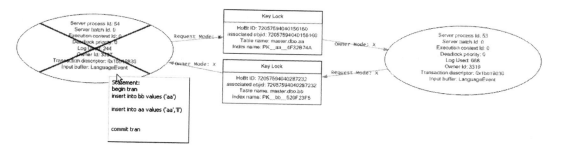

Figure 6-2. *Deadlock event showing T-SQL statement issued by the deadlock victim*

Alternatively, the Performance Data Collector feature in SQL Server 2008 captures locking as part of the Server Activity collection set. You'll learn more about SQL Server Profiler and the Performance Data Collector in Chapter 11.

Stored Procedures

A *stored procedure* is a block of T-SQL or .NET code that is stored within a database. This code is similar to other procedures in other languages because it accepts parameters as inputs and can provide output to the calling application or user. Stored procedures make building database applications easy.

Stored procedures contain a header and a body. In the header, you define the input and output parameters. In the body is the code. For example, the following CREATE PROCEDURE statement creates a procedure that will take a pet name and return the microchip ID for that pet:

```
CREATE PROCEDURE GetID
@name VARCHAR(50)

AS

BEGIN

SELECT MicroChipID FROM Pets WHERE pet_name=@name

END
```

Parameters are optional. In this example, you need to specify a name. To execute this procedure, you can issue the following statement:

```
EXEC GetID 'Roxy'
```

The return the value is 1A8AF59, which is the value of Roxy's microchip.

Creating Stored Procedures Using Templates

SSMS provides a template to use when creating a new stored procedure. To view this template, navigate to the Stored Procedures node within the Programmability node of the VetClinic database. Select New Stored Procedure from the context menu. This will open a Query Editor window with the following template:

```
-- =================================================
-- Template generated from Template Explorer using:
-- Create Procedure (New Menu).SQL
--
-- Use the Specify Values for Template Parameters
-- command (Ctrl-Shift-M) to fill in the parameter
-- values below.
--
-- This block of comments will not be included in
-- the definition of the procedure.
-- =================================================
SET ANSI_NULLS ON
GO
SET QUOTED_IDENTIFIER ON
GO
-- =============================================
-- Author:		<Author,,Name>
-- Create date: <Create Date,,>
-- Description: <Description,,>
-- =============================================
CREATE PROCEDURE <Procedure_Name, sysname, ProcedureName>
	-- Add the parameters for the stored procedure here
	<@Param1, sysname, @p1> <Datatype_For_Param1, , int> =
		<Default_Value_For_Param1, , 0>,
	<@Param2, sysname, @p2> <Datatype_For_Param2, , int> =
		<Default_Value_For_Param2, , 0>
AS
BEGIN
	-- SET NOCOUNT ON added to prevent extra result sets from
	-- interfering with SELECT statements.
	SET NOCOUNT ON;

	-- Insert statements for procedure here
	SELECT <@Param1, sysname, @p1>, <@Param2, sysname, @p2>
END
GO
```

Having the syntax already present is helpful, but SSMS makes working with templates easy by giving you a dialog box to use to fill in the values. To launch the Specify Values for Template Parameters dialog box, select this option from the Query menu in SSMS. Figure 6-3 shows this dialog box.

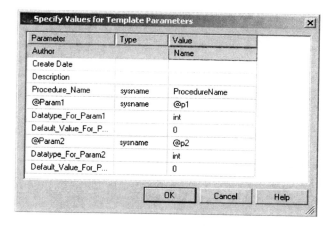

Figure 6-3. *Input dialog box for templates*

Once you fill the values in the dialog box and click OK, the template automatically updates the CREATE STORED PROCEDURE text in the Query Editor with the data you provided in the dialog box.

Templates make it very easy to create procedures. Many templates are available for SQL Server. To access the list of templates, select Template Explorer from the View menu in SSMS. This will launch a Template Browser window, shown in Figure 6-4.

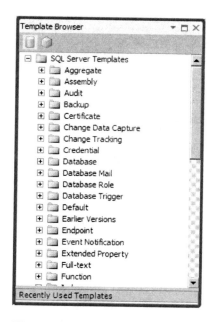

Figure 6-4. *Template Browser window in SSMS*

Note that there are two buttons on the top of this dialog box; the first one shows SQL Server templates, and the second shows Analysis Services templates. To use a template, simply double-click it, and the template will load in a new Query Editor window.

Modifying Stored Procedures

SSMS does a great job of enumerating all the stored procedures within the database. They are all listed under the Programmability node, which is under a specific database. To modify a stored procedure, you need to issue an ALTER STORED PROCEDURE statement. To modify the GetID procedure created earlier using SSMS, select Modify from the context menu of the GetID stored procedure. This will launch a Query Editor window with the ALTER STORED PROCEDURE text in it. The actual script generated by SSMS is as follows:

```
USE [VetClinic]
GO
/** Object:  StoredProcedure [dbo].[GetID]    Script Date: 04/29/2009 **/
SET ANSI_NULLS ON
GO
SET QUOTED_IDENTIFIER ON
GO
ALTER PROCEDURE [dbo].[GetID]
@name VARCHAR(50)
AS
BEGIN
SELECT MicroChipID FROM Pets WHERE pet_name=@name
END
```

SSMS saves you from a lot of typing when you are working with stored procedures.

System Stored Procedures

If you navigate around SSMS and the Programmability node as described earlier, you may notice a System Stored Procedures folder. There are quite a number of these, and each serves its own purpose within SQL Server. For example, the SQL Server Agent job scheduler does not have native DDL statements for creating jobs, so it uses system stored procedures to create and manage jobs. For a complete list, see the SQL Server Books Online article called "System Stored Procedures (Transact-SQL)" at http://msdn.microsoft.com/en-us/library/ms187961.aspx.

■ **Note** System stored procedures usually start with the characters sp_. Thus, it is a good idea to not start your stored procedures with the same three characters.

Functions

In many instances, you can accomplish a task using either a stored procedure or a function. Both functions and stored procedures can be custom defined and part of any application. They both can be written in T-SQL or .NET and contain a header and body. They can both accept parameters and provide output to the calling application or user.

Creating a Function

To illustrate, let's create a function that accepts a pet weight and returns a table that lists the pets who exceed that weight and their owners. The sample script is as follows:

```
CREATE FUNCTION GiantPets (@minWeight INTEGER)
RETURNS @retGiantPetsTable TABLE
(
pet_name      VARCHAR(50) NOT NULL,
pet_weight    INT                   NOT NULL,
owner_name VARCHAR(50) NOT NULL
)
AS
BEGIN
    INSERT @retGiantPetsTable
    SELECT p.pet_name, p.pet_weight,o.owner_name
    FROM Pets p, Owners o
    WHERE p.pet_id=o.pet_id AND p.pet_weight > @minWeight

    RETURN
END
```

Invoking a Function

Functions are designed with the idea that they will send their output to a query or T-SQL statement. With the exception of scalar functions, functions are called differently than stored procedures. Since the example function returns a table, you can call it as part of a SELECT statement by referencing it in the FROM clause, for example:

```
SELECT * FROM GiantPets(50)
```

This will return the following result set:

pet_name	pet_weight	owner_name
Lady	155	Bryan
Zeus	185	Rob

System-Defined Functions

The GiantPets function is a user-defined function. As with system stored procedures, SQL Server comes with many built-in functions. There are so many that they are grouped into different categories. *Scalar functions* use a single value or list of values, as opposed to data from multiple rows of a table. An example of a scalar function is GETDATE(), which returns the current date:

```
SELECT GETDATE()
```

Aggregate functions utilize multiple rows of data and return a value to the user. To find the average value for all the rows in a column, you use the AVG function as follows:

```
SELECT AVG(pet_weight) FROM Pets
```

There are also a lot of security-related functions. If you wanted to know whether the current user is a member of the sysadmin group, you would use the IS_SRVROLEMEMBER as follows:

```
SELECT IS_SRVROLEMEMBER('sysadmin')
```

This function will return 1 for true and 0 for false.

For a complete list of built-in functions, see the SQL Server Books Online article called "Functions (Transact-SQL)" at http://msdn.microsoft.com/en-us/library/ms174318.aspx.

Triggers

A *trigger* is a special kind of stored procedure that is executed when a special event happens within SQL Server. An event could include the execution of a given DDL or DML statement or a login to SQL Server. For example, if you wanted to make sure MicroChipID was valid before allowing a new pet to be added to the Pets table, you could create a trigger on INSERT. The script follows:

```
USE [VetClinic]
GO
CREATE TRIGGER ValidateMicroChip
ON Pets
FOR INSERT
AS

IF EXISTS(
SELECT MicroChipID FROM MicroChips
WHERE MicroChipID IN (
SELECT MicroChipID FROM inserted)
)

RAISERROR ('The chip was found!', 16, 1)
ELSE

BEGIN
    RAISERROR ('The chip was NOT found!', 16, 1)
    ROLLBACK
END

GO
```

Now, when you attempt to insert a new pet into the table using a microchip ID that is not in the MicroChips table, an error will be issued, and the pet information will not be added to the table, as shown in the following script:

```
INSERT INTO Pets VALUES (8,'Sushi',5,'0034DDA')
```

This will result in the following result:

```
Msg 50000, Level 16, State 1, Procedure ValidateMicroChip, Line 13

The chip was NOT found!

Msg 3609, Level 16, State 1, Line 1

The transaction ended in the trigger. The batch has been aborted.
```

Since the only valid microchip ID is 34BA123, if you used this value, the result would be as follows:

```
Msg 50000, Level 16, State 1, Procedure ValidateMicroChip, Line 10

The chip was found!



(1 row(s) affected)
```

Normally, you would not have to raise an error on a successful insert; this was done here only to help illustrate the code path that was executed in the trigger.

If you take a look at the trigger definition, you'll see that a table called inserted was referenced in the IF EXISTS clause. Within a DML trigger, SQL Server provides this table and a deleted table for DELETE triggers. Together, these tables allow your triggers to do something with the data and, depending on your business requirements, roll back any transactions. In this sample scenario, if the chip wasn't found, the trigger rolled back the transaction, causing the pet information not to be written to the table. For more information on the inserted and deleted tables, see the SQL Server Books Online article "Using the Inserted and Deleted Tables" at http://msdn.microsoft.com/en-us/library/ms191300.aspx.

Summary

In this chapter, you learned how to perform basic data retrieval and management using SELECT, INSERT, UPDATE, and DELETE DML statements. Remember that the definitions given in this chapter are simplified. The capabilities of these statements far exceed what was presented here, and you should study these in more detail when time permits.

SQL Server provides a robust dialect of the SQL language called Transact-SQL (T-SQL). With T-SQL, you can easily create reusable components such as stored procedures and functions. SQL Server provides many stored procedures and functions out of the box, making administering SQL Server very easy.

The concepts discussed in this chapter are all core to using the SQL Server relational database engine. Thus, a lot of the content is explained in much more detail within SQL Server Books Online. Table 6-2 provides links for all the articled cited in this chapter.

Table 6-2. *URLs for SQL Server Books Online Articles*

Article Title	URL
"Using Joins"	http://msdn.microsoft.com/en-us/library/ms191472.aspx
"Set Transaction Isolation Level"	http://msdn.microsoft.com/en-us/library/ms173763.aspx
"Deadlocking"	http://msdn.microsoft.com/en-us/library/ms177433.aspx
"System Stored Procedures (Transact-SQL)"	http://msdn.microsoft.com/en-us/library/ms187961.aspx
"Functions (Transact-SQL) "	http://msdn.microsoft.com/en-us/library/ms174318.aspx
"Using the Inserted and Deleted Tables"	http://msdn.microsoft.com/en-us/library/ms191300.aspx
"Identity Columns"	http://www.simple-talk.com/sql/t-sql-programming/identity-columns
"Understanding Sequence Object in SQL Server Denali"	http://www.databasejournal.com/features/mssql/sql-server-denali-sequence-object.html.
"ORDER BY Clause (Transact-SQL)"	http://msdn.microsoft.com/en-us/library/ms188385%28v=SQL.110%29.aspx

C H A P T E R 7

SQL Server Internals

SQL Server 2012 is a powerful and complex database platform. The relational engine itself is composed of many subsystems. One of these is the command parser, which takes the input from the connection, validates it, and parses it into an internal structure called a *query tree*. Another is the Query Optimizer, which takes the query tree and prepares the statement for execution. These preparation tasks include ensuring the user executing the query has enough access to the underlying database objects within the query and optimizing the query with respect to performance. Query optimization is cost based, and SQL Server chooses the execution plan that is best for the given statement.

As you can see, executing a query is complex, and many things are going on under the hood. As a database administrator, you can affect the performance of some of these functions based on what you find in a query's execution plan. You will learn more about execution plans in Chapter 13.

Even though you may optimize the execution of a query, the actual performance of the hardware that SQL Server uses is an important piece of the performance puzzle. In this chapter, you will learn the architecture of SQL Server databases, how SQL Server writes data to the physical disk, and important things about the services that are installed.

Databases

When you install SQL Server, five databases are automatically attached. Four of these are visible using SSMS, and the fifth one, the resource database, is invisible. The five databases and their definitions are as follows.

Master Database

The master database stores instancewide information, such as logins, endpoints, linked server information, and the server configuration. This database also contains the definition of all the databases that are attached to the instance of SQL Server. Needless to say, if the master database is corrupt or unavailable, SQL Server cannot be available for users.

Tempdb Database

SQL Server uses the tempdb database as a work area for grouping and sorting options, cursors, and other operational tasks. As you can imagine, these tasks consume a lot of disk I/O, so if your user data and tempdb are located on the same disk, there could be a lot of contention. For this reason, as a best practice, consider moving tempdb to its own set of physical disks.

Model Database

The model database is used as a template for new databases. Any objects created within this database, or database options that you set within it, will also exist on every new database that you later create.

The model database is required and cannot be deleted, because it is used by tempdb every time the SQL Server service starts. To see how the model database works, create a table in the model database using the following code:

```
USE [model]
GO

CREATE TABLE Sales
(i INT)
GO

USE [master]
GO

CREATE DATABASE SmartSalesDB
GO
```

Now, that you have created the new database, take a look at the tables within the SmartSalesDB database, as shown in the following code:

```
USE [SmartSalesDB]
GO

SELECT name,type_desc FROM sys.tables
GO
```

The results for this query are as follows:

name	type_desc
Sales	USER_TABLE

Here, the Sales table was created automatically, because it was defined in the model database.

MSDB Database

MSDB is used to store information for various components of SQL Server. Some uses include database backup and restore history, maintenance plans, and maintenance plan history as well as information about the SQL Server Agent job-scheduling service.

Depending on your implementation of SQL Server, MSDB might be your most heavily used system database outside of master. With any user-defined database, any time you make changes, you need to back up the database. MSDB is no exception, since actions such as changes to SQL Server Agent jobs, changes to policy management, or the creation of an Integration Services package will change MSDB.

Another important note is that there are special database roles defined in MSDB to support the various components. For example, `SQLAgentReaderRole` allows users in this role to view job execution information for all jobs but have full control only for the jobs the users own. Since so many components leverage this database, take caution about adding users to it.

Resource Database

You cannot, by default, see the resource database in SSMS. The resource database stores all system procedures, catalog views, functions, and other system-related objects in a read-only mode. Each instance of SQL Server has one `mssqlsystemresource.mdf` file and one `mssqlsystemresource.ldf` file located in the `Binn` folder of the SQL Server instance. You do not need to worry about backing up these files, because the only way they change is when a hotfix or service pack is installed.

Repairing Corrupt System Databases

When a user-defined database has an issue, the solution is straightforward: restore the database. When a system database has an issue, things can be more challenging. The SQL Server Books Online article called "Rebuild System Databases" does a good job of explaining the process of re-creating system; you can find it at `http://msdn.microsoft.com/en-us/library/dd207003(v=sql.110).aspx`. In summary, the `setup.exe` command-line executable has a switch that allows you to re-create the system databases. When you re-create the system databases, you will have to restore databases such as model and MSDB from backup to return to the last good state.

Writing Data to Disk

When SQL Server writes data to disk, it writes to one or more data files. There are two kinds of database files: data files and log files. As part of the commitment of a transaction, data is written to the transaction log file. This log file is a string of log records consisting of events such as modifying data, creating and dropping tables and indexes, and other transactional information. The log file is very useful in disaster recovery. If something bad happened when a user was in the middle of a transaction on server reboot, SQL Server would recover the database up until the last good transaction and roll back the last corrupt or incomplete transaction. Log files are traditionally given an `.ldf` extension. Database performance has a lot to do with the amount of data that SQL can write to the transaction log.

A data file with an `.mdf` file extension is the primary data file. If you have additional data files called *secondary data files*, these have `.ndf` file extensions. Data files contain data and metadata such as indexes and other database objects.

■ **Note** Nothing requires you to use the `.mdf`, `.ndf`, and `.ldf` file extensions. You can use whatever extensions you want. However, these are customary to SQL Server.

In a perfect world, you would load all your data into memory and forget the whole disk issue. Disks provide cheaper long-term storage and a much larger capacity than memory. Most of all, they store data in a persistent state. Generally, the more disks you have, the better performance you will get. However, this is true only to a certain point where the capacity of the hard disk controller or host bus adapter is reached. When objects are created in the database, they are written to a filegroup. A *filegroup* is an abstraction of underlying database files. For example, consider the following CREATE DATABASE statement:

```
CREATE DATABASE [Sales] ON  PRIMARY
( NAME = N'Sales', FILENAME = N'C:\DATA\Sales.mdf' ),
 FILEGROUP [OlderSales]
( NAME = N'Sales2', FILENAME = N'D:\DATA\Sales2.ndf'
 LOG ON
( NAME = N'Sales_log', FILENAME = N'M:\LOG\Sales_log.ldf' )
GO
```

In this statement, Sales is a database file that is located on the primary filegroup on the C drive. The Sales2 data file is located on the OlderSales filegroup. This filegroup is on the D drive. The log is called Sales_log and is located on the M drive.

Once these filegroups are configured, you can tell SQL Server where to create your database objects. To create a new table in the OlderSales filegroup, you can issue the following query:

```
CREATE TABLE Customers
(customer_id INT PRIMARY KEY)
ON [OlderSales]
```

You can also add more files within the same filegroup. If more files are added, SQL Server will stripe the writes across all files within the filegroup, creating an even write pattern. Depending on the kind of hard drives you have in your configuration, striping the writes could be a performance improvement. Another technique used to increase performance with respect to improving disk I/O is table partitioning. *Table partitioning* descibes the situation where portions of the table reside on physically different areas, but to the application or user, they appear as one single table. By moving parts of the table to different physical disks, SQL Server can parallelize the query and obtain the results more quickly.

▓ **Note** Filegroups have a default property that, when set to true, will act as a container for all the objects created that don't explicitly define a filegroup.

SQL Server Services

When you install SQL Server, you can have about ten services installed, depending on the options you selected. Some of these services are one per server, and some can be installed multiple times on the same server. By *server*, I mean an instance of the Windows Server operating system.

The following are the services that you might encounter:

SQL Full-Text Engine Filter Daemon Launcher. The SQL Full-Text Engine Filter Daemon Launcher service is installed once per instance of SQL Server. Within the SQL Server database engine is the powerful Full-Text Engine. This engine makes it easy for users and applications to search for keywords within the database. The Full-Text Engine has two roles: indexing support and querying support. This service spawns a process called `fdhost.exe`, which works with the word breaker functionality within Full-text Search. This service is necessary only when using the full-text features of SQL Server.

SQL Server. The SQL Server service can be installed one or more times within Windows Server. Each time a SQL Server service is installed, it's given another name called an *instance name*. To connect to a named instance of SQL Server, you would use the format `<servername>/<instance name>`. This service is for the relational database engine itself.

SQL Server Browser. The SQL Server Browser service is responsible for enumerating the available instances and port numbers back to the client that is requesting the information. There is one SQL Server Browser service per Windows Server. This service is beneficial when you have multiple named instances, because the alternative is to have clients manually input the port numbers on which the instances are listening.

Note If you try to connect to a named instance and the SQL Browser service is not running, you have to specify the port number within the connection string.

SQL Server Agent. SQL Server Agent is a job-scheduling service coupled with an instance of SQL Server. For every installation of the SQL Server service, there is one installation of the SQL Server Agent. You do not have to use this service; you can keep it disabled, but chances are unless your company has another job-scheduling tool that is the standard, you may end up using SQL Server Agent. SQL Server Agent is used to schedule maintenance jobs such as database backups and index maintenance. You will learn more about SQL Server Agent in Chapter 10.

SQL Server Integration Services 11.0. SQL Server Integration Services is an extract, transform, and load (ETL) platform for SQL Server. ETL tools are used heavily in data warehousing, because their task is to take data from all the disparate sources, transform the data into a common format, and load it into a database for further analysis. This service is installed one time per Windows Server instance, and it enables users to view current package execution status as well as view stored package information.

SQL Server Volume Shadow Copy Service (VSS) Writer: The Volume Shadow Copy Service (VSS) is a set of COM APIs that implement a framework to allow volume backups to be performed while applications such as SQL Server continue to write to the volumes. This service is what enables SQL to operate in the Volume Shadow Copy Service framework. There is one SQL Server VSS Writer service per Windows Server.

SQL Server Reporting Services: Reporting capabilities are heavily used in both business intelligence applications and the daily life of database administrators. SQL Server Reporting Services provides the core reporting services functionality, including hosting the Reporting Services service, report creation, and scheduling. You can install multiple instances of the report server on the same operating system.

SQL Server Analysis Services: When data is transformed and loaded into a database known as the *data warehouse*, it is primed and ready for analysis by a multidimensional engine such as SQL Server Analysis Services. This service is installed one time per Windows Server and is the workhorse for building multidimensional cubes. These cubes are used for purposes such as reporting and data mining by business analyst users.

SQL Server Distributed Replay Controller: The Distributed Replay Utility allows you to simulate a large-scale workload. In earlier versions of SQL Server, you could capture a SQL trace that contained statements from multiple clients against the database. This trace file could only replay events back to the server serially. To more accurately represent a replay workload, SQL Server 2012 introduced the Distributed Replay Utility feature. The SQL Server Distributed Replay Controller service is part of this feature and helps synchronize the clients in a distributed replay scenario.

SQL Server Distributed Replay Client: The SQL Server Distributed Replay Client service receives and instructions from the SQL Server Distributed Replay Controller service.

Single-User Mode

On a given production database system, the database accepts many requests from many different users. There comes a time when you, as a database administrator, may need to place the database in single-user mode. You may also need to start a database in that mode.

Single-user mode allows only one connection to the database. You would normally use this state when performing special maintenance functions such as issuing a `DBCC CHECKDB` command with the repair options enabled.

■ **Note** As soon as you place a database in single-user mode, any active connections within the database will terminate. Doing so is a really bad idea if users are not informed of this event.

Placing an Already-Started Database into Single-User Mode

To set a database that is already started to single-user mode, you can issue the following statement:

```
ALTER DATABASE [SmartSalesDB] SET  SINGLE_USER WITH ROLLBACK IMMEDIATE
GO
```

Three options are available when you change to single-user mode. The `ROLLBACK IMMEDIATE` option means connections will be closed immediately, and noncommitted transactions will be rolled back. If you want to give a delay before you do this, you can specify `ROLLBACK AFTER <X> SECONDS`, where `<X>` is an integer value. If you want to place the database only if there are no open transactions, use the `NO_WAIT` option.

If you want to have more than one connection to the database but need to limit the amount of users connected, you can put the database in a restricted state. This state is ideal for data imports and allows only members of the db_owner, dbcreator, and sysadmin roles to access the database. To set a database in restricted mode, you can issue the following query:

```
ALTER DATABASE [SmartSalesDB] SET  RESTRICTED_USER
GO
```

Remember to change the database setting back to `MULTI_USER` once you are ready. You can do this with the following script:

```
ALTER DATABASE [SmartSalesDB] SET  MULTI_USER
GO
```

Databases can be taken offline when you need to copy or move the database files. This is an extremely rare event, because there are other tools available, such as the Copy Database Wizard in SSMS, to move data and/or databases to new servers. To set a database offline, use the following script:

```
ALTER DATABASE [SmartSalesDB] SET OFFLINE
GO
```

Starting SQL Server in Single-User Mode

In some rare occasions, it may be necessary to start the SQL Server instance in single-user mode. If you are trying to recover a damaged master database or any other system database, you will need to put SQL Server in single-user mode. You can do this by starting the service with the -m command-line argument. To place the SQL Server instance in single-user mode, perform the following steps:

1. Stop all SQL Server services, and stop SQL Server Agent. You can stop these services through the Services applet in the Control Panel, through the command shell using the `NET STOP` command or through the SQL Server Computer Manager. For this example, you'll use the SQL Server Configuration Manager to stop these services. To launch the SQL Server Configuration Manager, select the application from the Programs ➤ Microsoft SQL Server 2012 ➤ Configuration Tools menu. Figure 7-1 shows the SQL Server Configuration Manager.

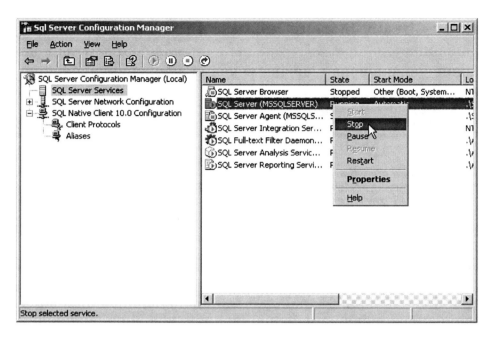

Figure 7-1. The Sql Server Configuration Manager

If you click the SQL Server Services node in the left tree, you will see a list of all the SQL Server–related services installed on your server. To stop the SQL Server service, simply right-click, and select Stop. It is a best practice to also stop the SQL Server Agent service when you want to put SQL Server in single-user mode. To do this, select Stop on the context menu for the SQL Server Agent service.

2. Modify the startup parameters. As with starting and stopping the service, there are a few ways to start the service with special parameters. You could navigate to the folder where the `sqlservr.exe` executable is located and start it by typing **sqlserve.exe -m**. Alternatively, you could add the `-m` parameter using the Startup Parameters tab in the Properties window of the SQL Server service. To modify the startup parameters of a service, click the Properties option in the context menu of the SQL Server service. Next, click the Startup Parameters tab. This will display the Startup Parameters tab, as shown in Figure 7-2.

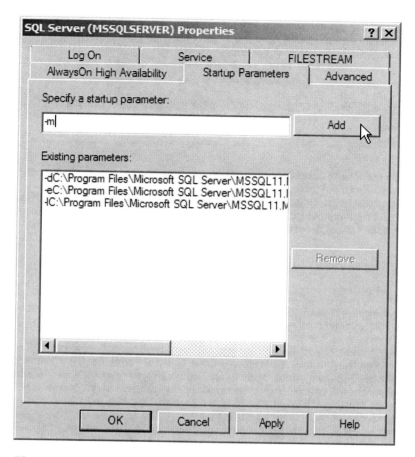

Figure 7-2. Properties dialog box in SQL Server Configuration Manager

The existing parameters define where the master database is located and where SQL Server should write error logs to. To add more parameters, simply add the parameter, in our case, **-m** to the "Specify a startup parameter" text box, and click Add. Next, click OK, and start the service by selecting Start from the SQL Server service context menu.

To test the new server state, launch SSMS and make a connection to your server. If SSMS has the Object Explorer tree open, try to click the New Query button. This will cause an error dialog box to pop up and show text similar to the following:

```
Login failed for user 'SERVERNAME\Administrator'. Reason: Server is in single user mode.
Only one administrator can connect at this time.
```

When you set SQL Server in single-user mode, it accepts only one connection, and since Object Explorer in SQL Server is one connection, by opening a New Query you are requesting another connection to SQL Server. Thus, you receive the failure message.

■ **Note**   To use SSMS with SQL Server in single-user mode, make sure only Object Explorer or a Query Editor window is open, but not both.

You can also use the command-line tool called SQLCMD to issue queries against this single-user server. You will learn more about SQLCMD in Chapter 10.

To remove the single-user restriction, go back to the Parameter Properties tab in the Properties dialog box of the SQL Server service in SQL Server Configuration Manager, and remove the -m parameter you added previously. Restart the SQL Server service, and it will allow multiple connections.

Summary

As a database administrator, you will become intimately familiar with all the system databases that are part of SQL Server. These system databases provide critical functionality to users and other components within SQL Server. Knowing special configurations, such as setting databases and the actual server instance to single-user mode, is important in certain rare situations.

When you install SQL Server, depending on the amount of components you select, you will see a bunch of new services within the Services applet in Windows Control Panel. Each of these services adds value to the user experience. Database administrators should be aware of how SQL Server sets up the accounts used for these services. A complete discussion of setting up these services is covered in the SQL Server Books Online article "Setting Up Windows Service Accounts" located at http://technet.microsoft.com/en-us/library/ms143504.aspx.

Table 7-1 lists some resources supporting the content discussed in this chapter.

Table 7-1. Resources

Title	URL
"Rebuild System Databases"	http://msdn.microsoft.com/en-us/library/dd207003(v=sql.110).aspx
"Setting Up Windows Service Accounts"	http://technet.microsoft.com/en-us/library/ms143504.aspx

CHAPTER 8

Database Backup Strategies

SQL Server 2012 and the Windows platforms it runs on are very stable and safe technologies that can offer you years of uptime and service. However, things do go wrong: Software can have errors. Hardware can break. Users can make mistakes. Any of these reasons and hundreds of others can lead to a loss of data that's important to you. To protect against the possibility of data loss, you're going to want some method of creating a copy of your database to store separately for use in the event of an emergency. This is called *backing up* the database. It's a fundamental task for people charged with administering databases and database servers to ensure that the databases in their charge get backed up appropriately.

There are a number of ways to back up your database, and each has its own strengths, weaknesses, and purpose. There are ways to back up only the parts of the database that have changed and ways to back up a record of the changes, called a *log backup*. SQL Server allows you to protect your backups with the same level of security that you protect your database, so you can encrypt backups. There are even ways in SQL Server 2012 to save space on backups by making the backup files smaller through compression. We'll cover the following in this chapter:

- Types of database backups
- Backing up the logs
- Automating the backup process
- Encrypting the backup files for security
- Compressing backups to save space
- Designing a backup plan

Defining the Types of Backups

You can back up a database in a number of ways. The different backup methods can be used together, separately, or as part of a complicated pattern designed to protect your data in the way that is best for your environment. To back up your database, you can use the following:

- Full backups
- Differential backups
- File and filegroup backups

Each of these backups protects data in slightly different ways by making a protected copy of that data. All of these types of backup operations write your data out to a file. That file can be on a different disk on your server, on another server, on portable media such as thumb drives, or it can be a specialized backup system, such as a tape backup system that writes out to specialized media resembling old-fashioned cassette tapes (although tape backup through SQL Server has been deprecated in SQL Server 2012 and soon won't be supported at all). Part of deciding on a backup strategy for your system is also picking the media, or what is called a *physical backup device*, on which to write your backup files.

When backups are run against the databases on your SQL Server 2012 instance, the users and applications connected to those databases are not interrupted. Most of the time, in fact, you will see minimum effects from running backups on reasonably active systems. If the system is under heavier loads, you might see significant performance degradation during some of the backup operations. Because backups don't take the systems down or offline, your backups may be run fairly frequently because you don't have to wait for all users to exit the system or kick the users off the system while you run backups. It's still a good idea to run the most intrusive backup operations, such as full backups, during off-peak hours when the user load is less.

More often than not, you won't be running backups manually. You will need to schedule the backup so that it occurs on an automated basis. The most common method of automation is using the scheduling process of SQL Server Agent. This is covered in detail in the "Automating the Backup Process" section.

To better understand which of the backup types might be applicable in your situation, we'll describe each of them in more detail.

Full Backups

A *full backup* creates a complete copy of all the data, structures, and code that are contained within the database when the backup operation is run. This copy of the database is done at the lowest possible level within the system, so it's not like running a query to retrieve data where some could be missed. All the data, all the code, and all the structure within the database will get backed up to the backup file. It is not possible for a successful backup to be taken of a database and miss data or change a stored procedure.

The full backup is the primary means of backing up a database. It's the foundation from which other backup types will operate. It's also the foundation from which a database restore (covered in Chapter 9) will be run. Because of this, no matter what other choices you make for backing up your data and logs, you must set up full backups to start.

A backup can be initiated through direct calls using the T-SQL scripting language or by having the graphical user interface (GUI) supplied with SQL Server 2012—SQL Server Management Studio (SSMS)—generate and run the T-SQL scripts for you.

Full Backup Using SQL Server Management Studio

To initiate a backup in SSMS, connect to your SQL Server instance, and expand the Databases folder. Select the database you want to back up, and right-click that database. This opens a context menu. Navigate through the menu to Tasks and then select Back Up. This launches the Back Up Database window shown in Figure 8-1.

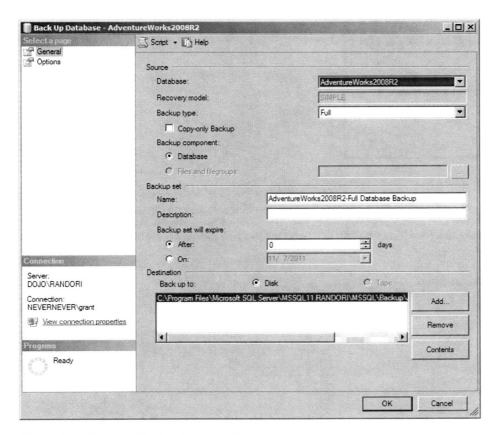

Figure 8-1. *The Back Up Database window*

There are two pages in the Back Up Database window that you can select on the left side of the screen. It opens on the default General page. The default values are the database you selected previously and a backup type of Full. The check box Copy Only Backup allows you to make a backup of the database that is separate from the normal chain of backups. We'll describe that in more detail in the section "Backing Up the Logs." You don't need to modify anything in the Source section of the window to create a full backup.

The next section of the window, "Backup set," is where you define the intended target of your backup. The options give you a full range of control over how you want to manage your backup. You can give it a name and a description to make it easier to understand the purpose and origin of the backup when you go to restore it (restoring is covered in detail in Chapter 9). You can also specify that a backup set expires after a certain number of days or on a specific date. For a simple backup operation, leave all these settings at the default values.

Finally, you need to specify a destination. You may have a default location already defined. If not, to add a location, click the Add button. This will open the Select Backup Destination dialog box, as shown in Figure 8-2.

Figure 8-2. Select Backup Destination dialog box

You can select either a specific file location or a backup device. A backup device is a predefined file or a tape backup system that is available to your server. In the window shown in Figure 8-2, a specific file has not been defined. Click the ellipsis button (…), which will open the Locate Database Files window, shown in Figure 8-3.

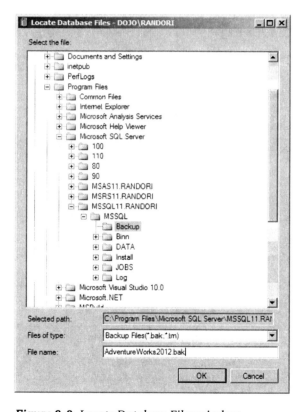

Figure 8-3. Locate Database Files window

Here, you can define the path and file name for the backup. Clicking the OK button for each of these windows will close them and take you back to the Back Up Database window shown in Figure 8-1. The Destination field will show the file you specified.

There is an additional function you can take advantage of that entails using multiple files for backups. This is referred to as *backup mirroring*. For very large databases, usually larger than 1TB in size, using multiple files to perform the full backup can speed up the process because multiple disks are being used. If you do want to mirror the backup files, you can add additional files using the same process used to add one. Just remember, you will need all the files to be available to perform a restore of the database.

From here, you can run a backup. Operations running against the database can continue uninterrupted, as described earlier. The backup operation itself will take longer to run as the size of your database increases. In addition, you can run one backup after another, all pointed to a single file. Since the default options are in operation, a new backup will be created within the file each time you run the backup operation. By default, SSMS will not overwrite the file with each new backup; it will instead append the backup to the file along with the other backups in your backup set. If you would prefer to change this behavior, when the Back Up Database window is open, click the Options page option on the left side of the screen to see all the options available, as shown in Figure 8-4.

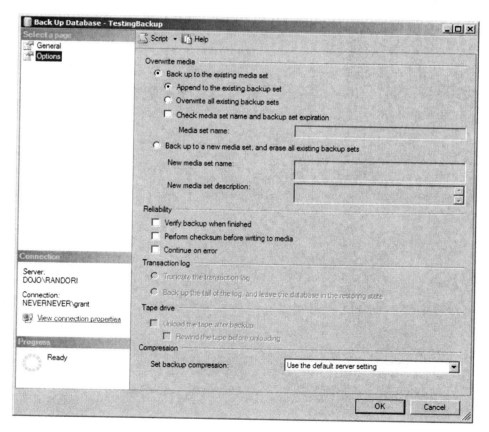

Figure 8-4. Back Up Database window's Options page

As you can see, the default option is to add, or *append*, the backup you're currently running to the existing file or device. The file or device in this context is referred to as a *backup set*. You can modify this so that instead it overwrites the file each time you run the backup. We prefer this methodology because it makes it easier to know exactly what is backed up where, visually. You don't need to open a file and peruse backups within it to see which backups are available, when they were created, and so on. We'll discuss looking through the backup sets in Chapter 9.

Other options that you should consider when running a backup include adding verification that the backup was done completely and correctly. You can do this by selecting the check box in the Reliability section of the Options page labeled "Verify backup when finished." This is a function of the `RESTORE` command and will be covered in more detail in Chapter 9. You can also validate that everything written to disk is written correctly by using the "Perform checksum before writing to media" option. This adds additional overhead to the backup process, so for very large systems, it might not be desirable. However, it also adds a layer of protection and safety to the backup process, helping to ensure that your backups are valid. At the very bottom of the screen, you can also see the settings for using compression with your backups. Increasingly often, managing disk space and trying to optimize the use of disk space has become more common tasks. SQL Server offers a method to help with this when using backups by adding the ability to compress the backups as you create them. Compression is only available in the Developer, Standard, and Enterprise versions of SQL Server. The other options available here are not generally used when performing a standard full backup.

Full Backup Using T-SQL

Although you can perform all your backup operations through Management Studio, most DBAs use T-SQL instead. Running your backup operations through T-SQL enables you to automate backups through scripting, which increases the flexibility of the backup process. Even the backup operations in Management Studio use T-SQL under the covers. You can always see the T-SQL being issued by the Management Studio GUI by clicking the Script button visible at the top of the Backup Up Database window (shown earlier in Figures 8-1 and 8-4).

To use T-SQL to back up the database, open Management Studio, and connect to the server as outlined earlier. Now, open a T-SQL editing window by clicking the New Query button visible by default on the toolbar. This will open a new window that looks like a blank white screen with a cursor blinking in it; this is the T-SQL editing window. Type the following to generate a full backup of the AdventureWorks2012 database:

```
BACKUP DATABASE AdventureWorks2012
TO DISK = 'c:\data\AdventureWorks2012.bak';
```

Clicking the Execute button will immediately back up the database to the disk location specified. You could also back up to a device. To do that, first you need to create a device. The following script creates a backup device that will allow you to back up to a file:

```
EXEC sp_addumpdevice
    @devtype = 'disk',
    @logicalname = 'MyBackupDevice',
    @physicalname = 'c:\data\AdventureWorks2008.bak';
```

And then you can use the device in a backup as follows:

```
BACKUP DATABASE AdventureWorks2012
TO MyBackupDevice;
```

Although this process seems simple, it can quickly become somewhat more complicated. Normally, we back up to a file that includes the date or date and time so that we can keep more than one backup file for a given database within a folder. A complete full backup script that includes the ability to overwrite a file looks like this (--basicbackup in the code download):

```
DECLARE @BackupLocation NVARCHAR(100) ;
SET @BackupLocation = 'c:\data\AdventureWorks2012_'
    + CONVERT(NVARCHAR(8), GETDATE(), 112) + '.bak' ;
BACKUP DATABASE AdventureWorks2012
TO DISK = @BackupLocation
WITH INIT ;
```

This command uses a variable, @BackupLocation, to define where we intend to store the backup file. We then get the current date and use the CONVERT function to turn into a format that looks like 'MMDDYYYY'. The output looks like this: c:\data\AdventureWorks2012_20111116.bak.

To add in the additional validation offered by getting a checksum as the backup runs, we'll need to modify the full backup script one more time (--fullbackup in the code download):

```
DECLARE @BackupLocation NVARCHAR(100) ;
SET @BackupLocation = 'c:\data\AdventureWorks2012_'
    + CONVERT(NVARCHAR(8), GETDATE(), 112) + '.bak' ;
BACKUP DATABASE AdventureWorks2012
TO DISK = @BackupLocation
WITH INIT, CHECKSUM ;
```

As we mentioned previously, compression for backups is becoming much more common. Adding compression through the command line is as easy as modifying the script to take it into account:

```
DECLARE @BackupLocation NVARCHAR(100) ;
SET @BackupLocation = 'c:\data\AdventureWorks2012_'
    + CONVERT(NVARCHAR(8), GETDATE(), 112) + '.bak' ;
BACKUP DATABASE AdventureWorks2012
TO DISK = @BackupLocation
WITH INIT,CHECKSUM, COMPRESSION, FORMAT ;
```

Two additional WITH words were added: COMPRESSION tells SQL Server that this backup is going to be compressed, and FORMAT makes SQL Server throw out the previously created file and reformat it completely, something necessary when switching from an uncompressed file to a compressed one or vice versa.

You are probably beginning to see the types of control you can exercise over your backup operations using T-SQL. For the rest of this chapter, with a few exceptions, we'll focus on using T-SQL to perform the backup operations.

Differential Backups

As databases get bigger, the amount of time it takes to perform a full backup increases, so you may find that your databases are too big for frequent full backups. You could also find that the backup runs for so long that it's running outside the off-hours you scheduled it for. Either or both of these combined could lead you to begin to use differential backups.

A *differential backup* is a process where only the changes since the last full backup are pulled from the database and backed up to the backup file or device. SQL Server places a marker in the database for the last time a full backup was run. This enables it to automatically track the changes that have been made since that backup. So, for example, if a full backup was run Sunday night and a differential backup was run on Monday night, only the data that had changed since the Sunday night backup would be included in Monday's file. A differential backup always take the last full backup as its starting point, so if you run another differential on Tuesday night, that new differential will have all the data that had changed on Monday and Tuesday, since the last full backup was Sunday night. This means that differential backups will get bigger as the date of the original full backup goes further into the past. Just remember that you need to have the full backup as a baseline, or you won't be able to restore the differential.

Creating a differential backup is not at all hard. The same basic syntax applies as for a full backup. Here is how a differential for the last full backup of AdventureWorks2008 could be created (`--differential` in the download):

```
DECLARE @BackupLocation NVARCHAR(100);
SET @BackupLocation = 'c:\data\AdventureWorks2012_' +
CONVERT(NVARCHAR(8),GETDATE(),112) + '_diff.bak';
BACKUP DATABASE AdventureWorks2012
TO DISK = @BackupLocation
WITH INIT, CHECKSUM, DIFFERENTIAL;
```

Looking at the script, you can see the two changes that were made in bold. We added `_diff` to the file name so that we mark the differential backup files appropriately and because we don't want to overwrite the full backup with a differential. If you accidentally did this and then tried to restore the database, your backup would be lost. The other change was in the `WITH` clause; the additional keyword `DIFFERENTIAL` changes the method of backup.

File and Filegroup Backups

For smaller databases, less than approximately 500GB in size, a full backup or a full backup with differentials should work just fine. As databases get bigger still, you might need to consider backing up only smaller parts of the database rather than backing up the entire database. You would still perform file or filegroup backups in conjunction with full backups. Backing up a file or a filegroup allows you to back up smaller pieces of the database, which means that the backup process runs faster. This approach does make the management of the backups more difficult. When you start backing up individual database files, you have to plan on restoring only individual files. This makes recovery operations much more difficult. However, the cost may be worth the benefit because it is possible to restore only the damaged file to a database, rather than restoring the entire database. Files can be stored in sets called *filegroups*. These can also be backed up individually from the database.

When a database is in simple recovery mode, the log data of completed transactions is not kept; you can perform a file backup only on those files that are marked read-only. You can only back up a file or filegroup of a database that has more than one filegroup in it.

To back up a file for a given database, you will need to know the logical file name, not the actual name, of the file you want to back up. When backing up a filegroup, you just need the name of the filegroup. You can get the logical file names for a database through the Database Properties window. Right-click the database in question, and select Properties from the pop-up menu. The Database Properties window will open. Click the Files tab to see the logical file names, as shown in Figure 8-5.

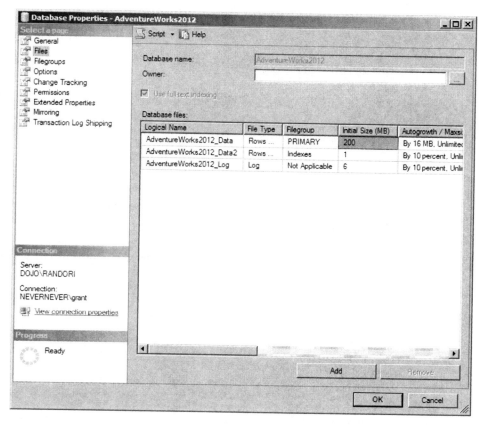

Figure 8-5. *Database Properties window displaying the logical file names*

Notice the Logical Name column in the "Database files" section of the window. Another way to get the information shown there is to go to the system management view **sys.database_files** and query it as follows:

```
SELECT   df.name
FROM     sys.database_files AS df;
```

Once you have the logical file name, you can use it in the backup script. Before a file backup of the AdventureWorks2012 database can be run, the database will need to be put into a recovery model other than simple. We'll use the full recovery mode since that is the most commonly used in production systems:

```
ALTER DATABASE AdventureWorks2012
SET RECOVERY FULL ;
```

Now, you can run the file backup like this (`filebackup.sql` in the download):

```
BACKUP DATABASE AdventureWorks2012
FILE = 'AdventureWorks2012_DATA'
TO DISK = 'c:\data\AdventureWorks2012_DATA.bak'
WITH INIT ;
```

This will back up just the file specified, `AdventureWorks2012_DATA`. If you want to back up multiple files in a file group, the syntax changes only slightly:

```
BACKUP DATABASE AdventureWorks2012
FILEGROUP = 'Primary'
TO DISK = 'c:\data\AdventureWorks2012_Primary.bak'
WITH INIT;
```

This will back up as many files as there are within the filegroup as a single backup file. It's important to remember that backing up files individually should be done only when necessary. A more standard approach is to use the more easily controlled mechanisms of the full backup.

A backup just marks a moment in time in the database. When you restore a backup, you restore to the point only when a backup was run. But your data is changing all day long. You can't run full backups all day, and the differential or file backups help only so much. To capture the changes in data over the day, you need to put log backups to work.

Backing Up the Logs

As data is manipulated within the database, a record of the edits that have successfully completed is kept in the database log. These edits are wrapped by what are called *transactions*. A transaction can contain a series of data changes or just one. These transactions are what are stored within the log. The log is maintained by the system to allow for the recovery of the database in the event of some type of shutdown of the system. Not all data will be automatically recorded to the disk; some may be in memory, waiting its turn to get to the disk, but the completed transactions will always be in the logs.

The data in a log can be kept until the next time everything gets written out to disk, an event referred to as a *checkpoint*. Keeping the log information only until a checkpoint is referred to as the *simple* recovery model. It's simple because to restore a database, you need only the backups, whether full, differential, or files. You can't use the log data in the recovery in any way, so you will not be able to restore transactional data. That data will be lost forever in the event of a catastrophe. Simple recovery is almost never used in production systems and certainly wouldn't be used in mission-critical systems.

The data in the log can be kept indefinitely, depending on disk space, until a special backup operation, called a *log backup*, is run. This approach of retaining the log is referred to as the *full recovery model*. There is also a recovery model called *bulk logged*; however, it behaves enough like full recovery for our purposes in this chapter that we'll ignore it. It's the full recovery model that allows for a more complete database recovery plan because the log allows for recovering to a point in time. Point-in-time recovery will be covered in detail in Chapter 9. Log backups are not cumulative. Each one captures the information in the log since the last log backup. As each backup is run, the entries backed up are removed. While the log is truncated internally, it doesn't change in size. You can store log backups in individual files or as a backup set.

Initiating Fully Recovery Mode

To get started with log backups, first you need to set your database to the full recovery model. In Management Studio, right-click the database to bring up the context menu, and then select Properties. This will open the Database Properties window for the database in question. Select the Options page, and you will see something similar to Figure 8-6.

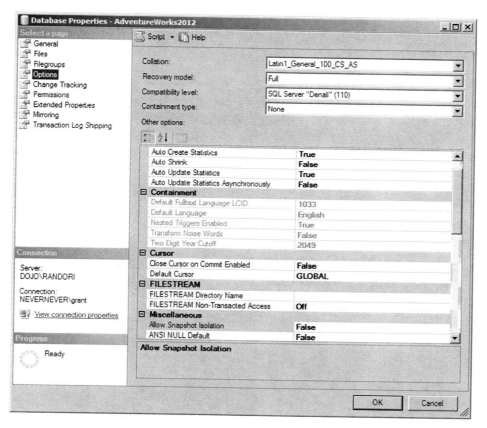

Figure 8-6. *Database Properties window showing the Options page*

Near the top of the page is a drop-down for the recovery model. Select Full from the list of three available models. Clicking the OK button will switch the database to the full recovery model. From this point forward, completed transactions will be kept in the log. Before you run out of disk space, it's time to learn how to back up the log.

Log Backup Using Management Studio

To back up the log for the database using Management Studio, perform the same actions as for backing up a database to open the Backup Database window. Right-click the database in question, and then select Tasks from the context menu. Next select Backup from the new menu choices. After the Backup Database window opens, select Transaction Log from the "Backup type" drop-down list. You will then have a window that looks something like Figure 8-7.

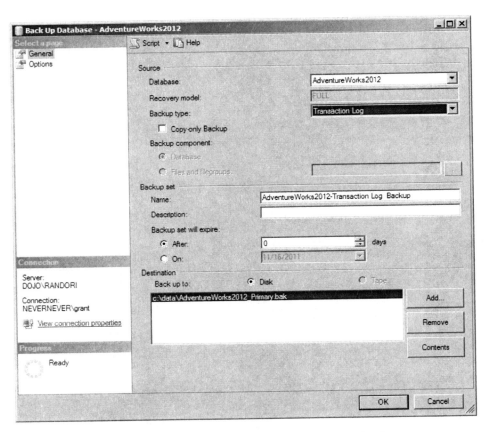

Figure 8-7. Back Up Database window ready for transaction log backup

To set the destination for the location you want to use, you may need to remove the most recently used location by clicking the Remove button. After that, you can click the Add button and select a disk or device to receive the backup file. The options are the same, and the Options page would look like it does in Figure 8-4. If you click OK, the log backup will run, and the log itself will be truncated, because all the entries that get backed up are removed.

Log Backup Using T-SQL

Just as the same mechanisms for backing up the log are used in Management Studio, the mechanisms in T-SQL look similar to those used for database backups. Open a query window in Management Studio, and type the following:

```
BACKUP LOG AdventureWorks2012
TO DISK = 'c:\data\AdventureWorks2012_log.bak' ;
```

When you execute this, it will append the log backup to the previously created log backup file. You can use the same options such as INIT, used previously to create a new file for each backup, and dynamically name the files to assist in managing your log backup files.

Backing Up a Copy of the Database

Once you begin using incremental backups and log backups, the changes recorded by each of those other backup types are based on the last full backup. This is important to know because sometimes, you're asked to make a backup of the database for testing, training, or some other purpose. You might want to back up a database prior to introducing new stored procedures or data structures or prior to an important data load. A full backup taken at this point in time would break the chain of backups; it would establish a new starting point for your log and incremental backup processes. To get around breaking the chain of backups, you can use the COPY_ONLY clause. A copy of the database or the log can be created, and neither method will affect the backup chain. To create a copy of the AdventureWorks2008 database, you would use the following syntax:

```
BACKUP DATABASE AdventureWorks2012
TO DISK = 'c:\data\AdventureWorks2012_Copy.bak'
WITH COPY_ONLY ;
```

This backup is just like any other backup, whether a full or log backup. It's just that the process of taking the copy-only backup doesn't affect the other backup types. Restoring a copy-only backup is the same as restoring any other backup (restores are covered in detail in Chapter 9).

Automating the Backup Process

Now that you have an understanding of the basics of database and log backups, you're going to want to automate the backup process. You'll have to decide the best schedule for your system to get maximum coverage through the various backup methods available to you. There are numerous for running processes automatically on Windows Server systems; some are built in, and some are available through third-party resources. SQL Server comes with its own scheduling software that we'll focus on using here, SQL Server Agent. Agent runs separately from the SQL Server software, yet it's an integral part of the SQL Server system.

To see SQL Server Agent, open SQL Server Management Studio, and connect to the server as previously explained. Once connected, you will see an icon at the bottom of the Object Explorer window, which is visible by default, labeled SQL Server Agent. If you have not configured the Agent to run automatically, you'll need to start it. Right-click the icon, and select Start from the context menu. Expanding this icon will show the information available as part of SQL Server Agent, as shown in Figure 8-8.

Figure 8-8. *SQL Server Agent viewed through Management Studio*

A number of options are available in SQL Server Agent, but we're concerned only with Jobs in this chapter. You can expand the Jobs folder and see any jobs that have already been created on your server. To create a new one to schedule backups, right-click the Jobs folder, and select New Job from the pop-up menu. This will open the New Job window, shown in Figure 8-9.

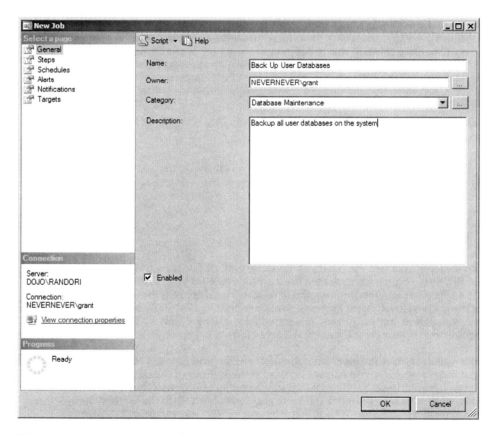

Figure 8-9. *New Job window showing the General page*

You can see a list of possible pages on the left and details regarding the page you have selected on the right. It opens by default on the General page. At the top of the window on every page is the opportunity to generate a script from the job by clicking the Script button; you can also open Books Online by clicking the Help button. In this window, you can also define a name for the job. The name should describe exactly what functions you expect the job to perform. In this case, type **Backup User Databases**. You also pick the owner of the job. The owner of the job defines the default user that the job will run as. You need to be careful that the user you pick has the appropriate privileges on the SQL Server system and on any of the drives, file shares, or backup devices you will be using in this automated job to back up your databases. We're setting the owner as **sa**, which means this job will run, by default, as the system administrator. You can also define a category, which will help you manage the various jobs that you create. We've selected Database Maintenance from the drop-down menu. You can also provide a more detailed description of the job that you are creating. Finally, you can set the entire job to be enabled or not through the Enabled check box. When you've completed defining the information on the General page, don't click the OK button because that will create the job, and this job doesn't do anything yet.

Click the Steps page on the left, which will change the New Job window to look like Figure 8-10.

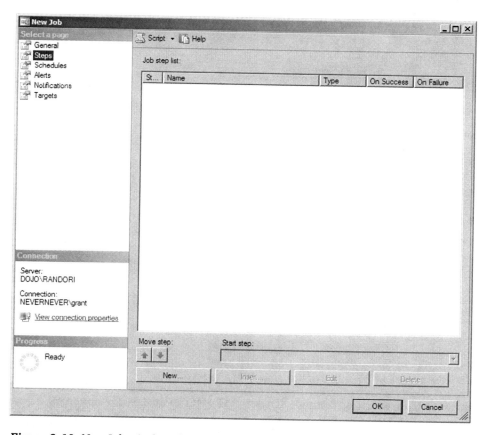

Figure 8-10. New Job window showing the Steps page

Since no steps have been created yet, nothing is displayed in this window. When steps have been created, this window will allow you to manipulate those steps by rearranging the order using the Move Step arrows and defining which step is the first step through the "Start step" drop-down box. You can add a step by clicking the New button or by clicking the Insert button when you have at least one step created. You can edit a script by clicking the Edit button or by double-clicking the step. Finally, you can delete a script through the Delete button.

Click the New button at this time to create a new step. This will open the New Job Step window visible in Figure 8-11.

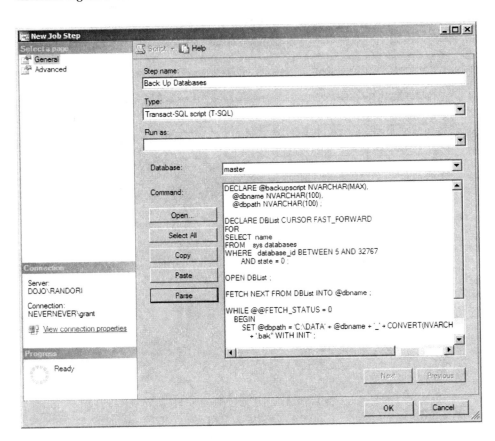

Figure 8-11. *New Job Step window*

In the New Job Step window, you will give each step a step name by typing it into the appropriate box. We chose Back Up Databases as the name of this step. You also have to define the type of command that the step represents. A large number of server-related subsystem types are available, but in this instance, you can use the default, which is "Transact-SQL script (T-SQL)". You have the option of changing the context under which this step is run; meaning which system user the step is executed as, by manipulating the "Run as" drop-down list. No changes were necessary for this step. You then pick the database where the script will run. Since we're running a query that will back up all the user databases in

172

the system, we need to run it from the master database where information that relates to the entire system is stored. Finally, you have to supply it with a command. You can type it in, open it from a file, or paste it in. You can parse the script to verify that it will run correctly. Here is the script used to back up all the user databases in the system (--backupalldatabases in the download):

```
--very simple query to back up user databases
DECLARE @backupscript NVARCHAR(MAX),
    @dbname NVARCHAR(100),
    @dbpath NVARCHAR(100) ;

DECLARE DBList CURSOR FAST_FORWARD
FOR
SELECT   name
FROM     sys.databases
WHERE    database_id BETWEEN 5 AND 32767
         AND state = 0 ;

OPEN DBList ;

FETCH NEXT FROM DBList INTO @dbname ;

WHILE @@FETCH_STATUS = 0
    BEGIN
        SET @dbpath = 'C:\DATA' + @dbname + '_' + CONVERT(NVARCHAR, GETDATE(), 112)
            + '.bak'' WITH INIT' ;
        BACKUP DATABASE @dbname TO DISK = @dbpath WITH INIT, CHECKSUM ;
        FETCH NEXT FROM DBList INTO @dbname ;
    END

CLOSE DBList ;
DEALLOCATE DBList ;
```

This script retrieves a list of databases from the system catalog view sys.databases. It eliminates the four basic system databases using their database IDs, and it makes sure that the databases it is backing up are online by checking that state = 0. It loads this list into a cursor and steps through the rows of the list, backing up the user databases one at a time.

Some other options are available in the New Job Step window. You can access them by clicking the Advanced page. The options this makes available are visible in Figure 8-12.

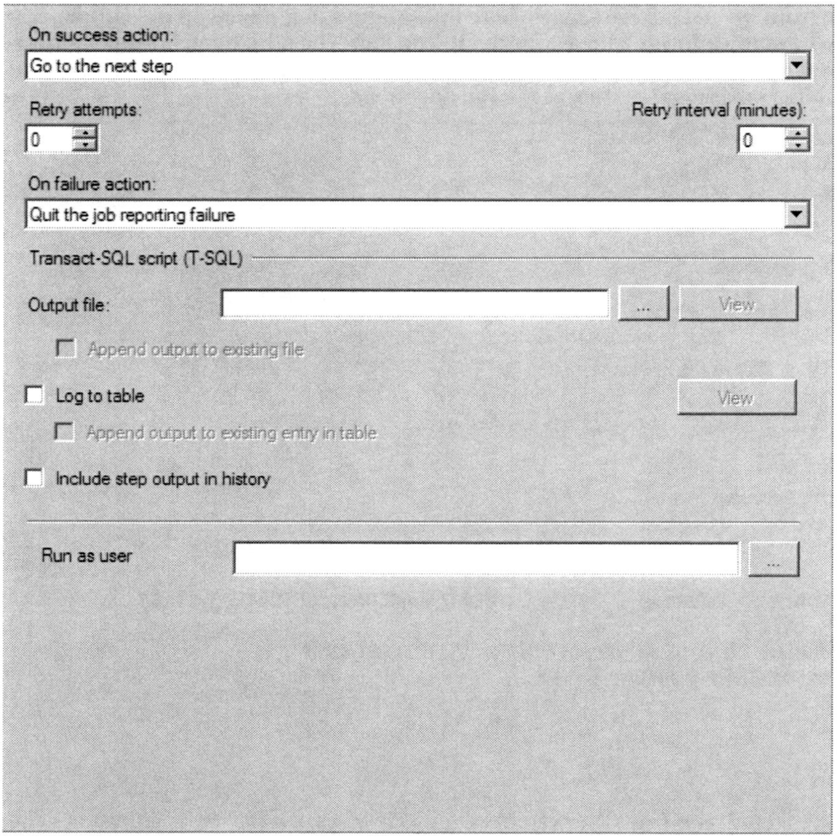

Figure 8-12. *New Job Step displaying the Advanced page*

The first thing visible at the top of the Advanced page is a flow control action. This allows you to control the behavior of jobs with multiple steps. By changing the "On success action" setting using the drop-down menu, you can control the next action. These are the values available and what they do:

- *Go to the next step:* This will cause the next step in order in a multistep job to be executed.

- *Quit the job reporting success:* This will prevent the following steps, if any, from being executed and will show the job as having been successfully completed.

- *Quit the job reporting failure:* This will prevent the following steps, if any, from being executed, but this will show the job as having failed to successfully complete.

For a single-step job like this, the default will work just fine. If the step were to fail to execute, you can have it automatically attempt to run again a defined set of times by changing the "Retry attempts" value to something greater than 0. You can have the retry wait a certain number of minutes by changing

"Retry interval (minutes)" to a value greater than 0. If the number of retries has been exhausted or the step is not set to retry and it does fail, the next flow control point is encountered, "On failure action." The drop-down has the same choices as the "On Success action" list, and they perform the same functions. They're just in a different order and respond to a failure of the step rather than a success. Since this is a T-SQL script, the section Transact-SQL script (T-SQL) is enabled. The first value is an output file, which will enable you to log the events that occurred during the execution of this step. In the case of the backup script, it will show all the databases backed up, or it will show any errors that occurred during the backup. You can create a new file every time it executes or have it add the data to an existing file, if any, by selecting the "Append output to existing file" check box. You can direct the output to a table in a database directly for later access. This will place additional load on your server to write and maintain the table. A job writes certain data, such as whether it succeeded, how long it took, and when it was run, to a log called the *history*. You can decide to have the output of the step included with the job history. This can make the history larger and hard to read, so we don't recommend it.

With the step finally defined, click the OK button. This will write it back to the job, and you will then see it in the New Job window, as shown in Figure 8-13.

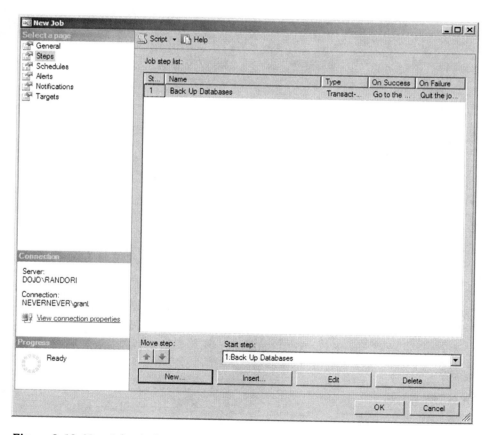

Figure 8-13. New Job window showing the Steps page with a step visible

The window has changed, and you can see that the step has a number and has been defined as the start step for the job. You can add other steps as needed to this job, but in this instance, this is the only step needed.

Click the Schedules page to determine when this automatic process will be run. The Schedules page will be empty, as the Steps page was before. You can create more than one schedule for a job so that it runs at varying times depending on the needs of your system. To create a new schedule, click the New button. You can also pick from a list of existing schedules. This allows you to create one schedule that, for example, executes once a week at 2 a.m. on a Sunday and apply that schedule to multiple jobs, all of which you want to start at 2 a.m. on a Sunday. However, it can be problematic to start lots of jobs at the same time. You can edit schedules on the list by clicking the Edit button. You can remove schedules from the list by clicking the Remove button. To practice defining a new schedule, click the New button. Figure 8-14 shows the New Job Schedule window that opens.

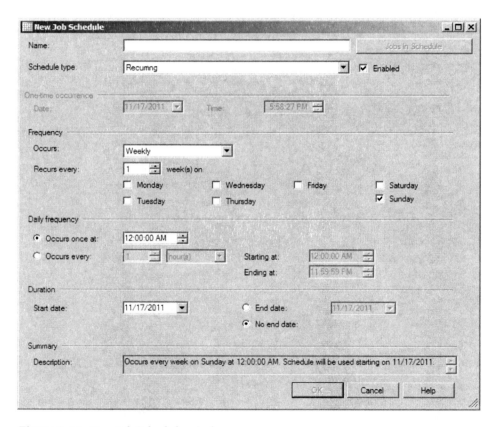

Figure 8-14. *New Job Schedule window*

To begin defining a new schedule, you have to give it a name, in this case **Weekly**. You then select from the "Schedule type" drop-down, which allows any of the following:

- *Recurring:* Runs on a schedule over and over as determined by the rest of the options defined in the Job Schedule window.

- *Start automatically when SQL Server Agent starts:* This will run any jobs associated when the SQL Server Agent service is started, usually just after SQL Server starts up.

- *Start whenever the CPUs become idle:* When all the CPUs on the system are no longer under load, this Agent job will be started.

- *One time:* Depending on the rest of the options defined, this will execute once and then never again.

If job is a one-time occurrence, that section would be enabled, and you could define a date and time for it to execute. This is a recurring job, so the Frequency section is enabled. The first option you have to choose is the frequency definition of the occurrence by selecting from the Occurs list:

- Daily

- Weekly

- Monthly

You can then pick the frequency of the occurrence. In this case, it's running every week on Sunday, but it could run on multiple days in the week with a varying number of weeks separating each execution. You then determine the daily frequency. In this case, it's executing once at 2 a.m., but you could have it run multiple times by choosing the "Occurs every" radio button. If this is selected, you need to determine the intervals between occurrences in hours, minutes, or seconds. And you can determine a start and stop time for multiple occurrences within the day or days that the schedule is firing. You can determine the day on which the process begins to run by selecting the Start date. You can also define a time for the job to stop running by defining an end date. In this case, you select the "No end date" radio button. This job will run once a week on Sunday at 2 a.m. and continue to do so until you do something about it. Click OK to close the New Job Schedule window.

You will now see that the Schedules page has the schedule that you just finished defining, as shown in Figure 8-15.

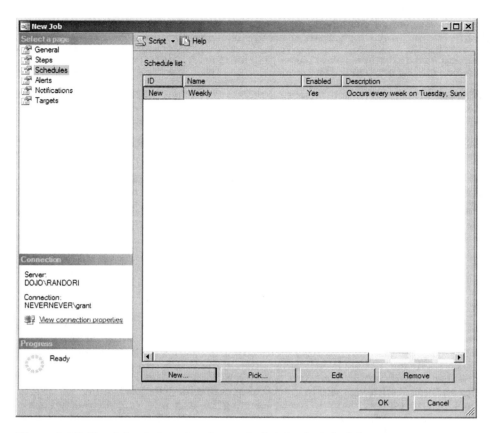

Figure 8-15. New Job window showing a schedule in the Schedules page

There are other pages available to the job—namely, Alerts, Notifications, and Targets—but they are outside the scope of this definition. With the completion of the schedule, you now have everything you need to back up your user databases once a week automatically. Click the OK button.

You can see the job you created by clicking the Jobs folder in the Object Explorer window just like the one shown in Figure 8-16.

Figure 8-16. List of jobs in the Object Explorer window

You can execute the job manually too by right-clicking the job and selecting the "Start Job at step" option. This will open a window with the steps on display. Just accept the default, the first step, and click OK. The job will start executing. Otherwise, it will execute based on the schedule defined.

Encrypting Backup Files for Security

SQL Server 2008 introduced the ability to encrypt your data using transparent data encryption (TDE). The idea behind this new tool is that you can encrypt the database without having to modify applications or change structures within your database. You would use this because it makes it impossible for someone to simply steal a copy of your disk and then have access to all your data. When a database has TDE enabled, the backups are also secured. With TDE, the encryption of the data as it's written to the database and the decryption of the data as it comes back out both happen in real time at a very low level (namely, at the page level) within the system. Pages are how data is stored on the disk, so as data is read or written on the disk, it goes through this decryption or encryption process prior to the information getting into memory or being sent to your application.

Once a database has been set to be encrypted, any backups of that database are also encrypted, automatically, through the use of certificates (a *certificate* is a security object that is generated, either by an external source or by SQL Server).

▪ **Note** You should test with a blank or dummy database until you understand thoroughly how encryption works. If you encrypt a production database and lose the key or password, you won't be able to retrieve them.

The syntax for backing up the database doesn't change. To see encrypted backups in action, use the following script to enable encryption on a test database. In the following example, we're using the AdventureWorksLT database (–**transparent data encryption** in the download):

```
USE master ;
GO
CREATE MASTER KEY ENCRYPTION BY PASSWORD = 'Chapter8Backup' ;
GO
CREATE CERTIFICATE Chapter8Certificate WITH SUBJECT = 'Chapter 8 Certificate' ;
GO
USE EncryptionTest ;
GO
CREATE DATABASE ENCRYPTION KEY WITH ALGORITHM = AES_128 ENCRYPTION BY SERVER
    CERTIFICATE Chapter8Certificate ;
GO
ALTER DATABASE EncryptionTest
SET ENCRYPTION ON ;
GO
```

Once this script is run, the database is encrypted. It's very important that you have a backup copy of the certificate and the private key that protects the certificate for use when restoring this database (covered in detail in Chapter 9). To back up the certificate and the private key, use the following script (**backupcertificate.sql** in the download):

```
USE [master] ;
GO
BACKUP CERTIFICATE Chapter8Certificate TO FILE =
'c:\data\Chapter8Certificate'
WITH PRIVATE KEY (FILE = 'c:\data\pkChapter8Certificate',
ENCRYPTION BY PASSWORD = 'Chapter8Backup') ;
```

You can run a normal backup to back up the database, because just as the encryption and decryption of the data are invisible to the users as they query the data, it's invisible to you as you manipulate backups. This will work just fine:

```
BACKUP DATABASE EncryptionTest
TO DISK = 'c:\data\EncryptionTest.bak' ;
```

The real work begins when you go to restore an encrypted backup. Read Chapter 9 for details.

Compressing Backups to Save Space

Backups can take up quite a bit of space. You may have more than one full backup of databases in your system stored on disk. Besides that, you could have multiple incremental backups for several of those databases. The log backups also take up quite a bit of room. Basically, it all adds up. Although disk drives are cheap and getting cheaper, you're unlikely to have an unlimited supply at hand. You also have to consider the time it takes to bring a new drive or mount point online, configure it, modify the backups to use it, and so on. Lots of time and money are being spent in maintaining these backup files. What if you could just make them smaller? SQL Server 2008 Enterprise introduced a mechanism for compressing backup files.

SQL Server 2012 Enterprise, Standard, and Developer editions support native backup compression. Compression can save you a lot of disk space. Because the backups are smaller and because writing the backup is the longest part of the backup process, the backup will be performed faster. Unfortunately, there is no free lunch here. You gain this at the sacrifice of processing power. Supporting the backup compression process places an added load on the CPUs of your system. There are a couple of other restrictions on the use of backup compression:

- A backup with compression cannot be in the same backup set as uncompressed backups.

- Older versions of SQL Server, prior to SQL Server 2008, cannot read compressed backups. All editions of SQL Server can restore a compressed backup file (restores are covered in detail in Chapter 9).

Backup compression is disabled by default, so it's necessary to turn it on before you use it. Making compression automatically available is very common on all enterprise systems, and we recommend it. You can enable backup compression on the server, which means that all database backups have compression enabled by default. To enable compression on the server, you need to change the server options. You can do this through a T-SQL command like this:

```
EXEC sp_configure
    'backup compression default',
    '1' ;
RECONFIGURE WITH OVERRIDE ;
```

The command `sp_configure` allows you to change server options. In this case, the query is changing the option `backup compression default`. It's setting the value to 1, which means true. If you wanted to turn backup compression off, you would set the value to 0.

You also have the ability to set the backup compression through SQL Server Management Studio. After connecting to the server, right-click the server in the Object Explorer window. This will open the Server Properties window. Select the Database Settings page, and you will see something similar to Figure 8-17.

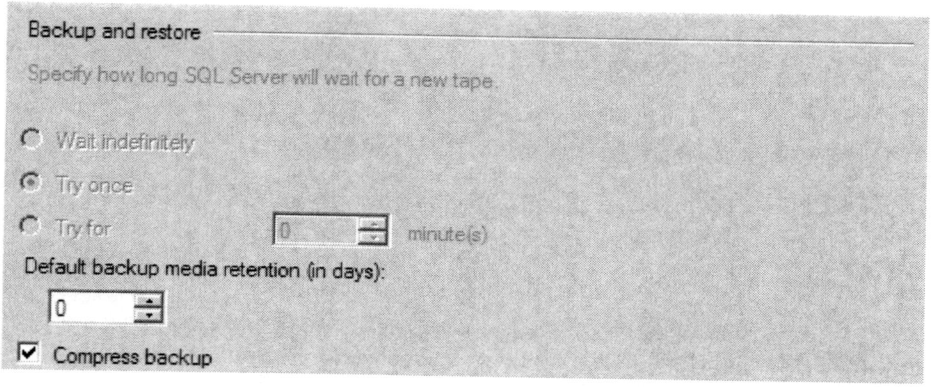

Figure 8-17. Server Properties window with Database Settings page displayed

You can enable or disable backup compression by selecting or deselecting the "Compress backup" option. Backup compression is enabled in Figure 8-17.

You can enable or disable compression directly during a single backup using T-SQL. You only need to introduce another `WITH` command to the T-SQL statement. Since the database is set to run compressed backups by default, you can use this command to back up the AdventureWorks2012 database without compression:

```
BACKUP DATABASE AdventureWorks2012
TO DISK = 'c:\data\AdventureWorks2012_uncompressed.bak'
WITH INIT, NO_COMPRESSION ;
```

If you have previously enabled default compression using one of the two mechanisms described earlier, use it again to make sure default compression is disabled. Now, you can run a backup with compression using this command:

```
BACKUP DATABASE AdventureWorks2012
TO DISK = 'c:\data\AdventureWorks2012_compressed.bak'
WITH INIT, COMPRESSION ;
```

For these two databases, the uncompressed file was 71767KB, and the compressed file was 14218KB for a compression ratio just slightly over 5:1. This is a real cost savings for data storage.

Backup compression should not be combined with other database compression schemes, such as row or page compression. Because the data is already compressed, you won't realize any space savings by compressing it again, but you will incur the overhead of processing the data in the attempt to compress it further. If you're encrypting your databases, you may see very little compression because the information stored inside an encrypted database doesn't have the kinds of simple patterns that compress well.

Designing a Backup Plan

With a more complete understanding of the options available to protect your databases through backups, you now need to design a backup plan. The driving factors behind a backup plan are very seldom technical. The business has to provide information defining the service-level agreement (SLA) for the implementation of a backup plan. The information you need to gather from the business includes the following:

- *Which databases or servers are vital to the business?* You should compile a list of servers and/or databases that your company determines to be vital to the continuity of the business itself. Those databases must then be as protected as possible. This is where you need to spend most of your time and effort.

- *What regulatory requirements might affect backups?* Some businesses operate under highly regulated rules that define the criteria for data, security, retention, and change management. The regulations defined will affect which processes you use with your backup plan.

- *How long you need to keep the data?* Simply having yesterday's backup is frequently not enough for most businesses. You may need to keep a week or two available for immediate access. You'll need to take this into account for your storage needs.

- *Do you need to encrypt the backups?* Just having the database protected isn't enough; you may need to protect the backup too.

- *Are there are industry or government regulations regarding backups?* You may have specific requirements outside your control that you must meet with your backup processes.

- *How much data can the company afford to lose?* Of course, the answer is zero, but there's usually a number of minutes that the company can live with. This will help you determine log backup schedules.

Once you've gathered all this information, and probably more, from the business, you'll need to examine your environment to ensure you can meet those requirements:

- *Disk storage*: Do you have the capacity to keep the backups you need without compression? How about with compression?

- *SQL Server edition*: Can you support the needs of the business on Standard edition, or do you need to get a copy of Enterprise?

- *Schedule*: Do you have lighter periods of time when you can run the backups to avoid any slowdowns for the users?

After you've determined that you have the technology in place to support the SLA for the business, you need to design a backup plan to support the SLA.

As an example, imagine a medium-sized database at about 200GB. The business has determined that the data in this database needs as much protection as you can provide through backup processes. The system is an online transaction processing (OLTP) system that modifies, deletes, or inserts 3GB to 5GB of data each day. You need to keep about a week's worth of data online. The business principals agree that they could deal with a five-minute data loss if they must.

To start with, 200GB will take a little while to back up on your system. Because of this, you decide to run one full backup a week, every Sunday. You can set up an Agent job to back up this database once a week. Because this satisfies the week of data online, you decide to overwrite the backup each week.

Since you need to be able to recover down to as close as possible to any kind of crash, but with no more than a five-minute data loss, you will need more backups. You couldn't run an entire week's worth of log backups. Instead, since you need to worry only about 3GB to 5GB of data changing each day, for a maximum of 35GB in a week, you decide to run an incremental backup every 12 hours during the week starting 12 hours after the full backup and ending 12 hours before. To track these backups over time, you create a new incremental backup with the date and time in the name to make recovering the as easy as possible. You can create a second Agent job to manage this operation.

Finally, to get as close to the five-minute limit as you can, you set the recovery model of the database to the full model. Since you need to keep only 12 hours of log available, you set the log backups to go to a single backup set with a 12-hour expiration so that it cleans itself out. Once the log is being kept, you need to set up a log backup routine to run every five minutes. All this data is a little more than you want to keep on your drives, so you enable compression. You'll need to create one other job that cleans out last week's incremental backups, because you chose to keep the files separate from a backup set. You now have a backup plan that looks something like the one in Table 8-1; it shows the type of backup being done followed by the frequency, and if there is an expiration for the backup, it outlines when that should occur.

Table 8-1. Backup Plan

Backup Type	Frequency	Expiration
Full	Once weekly	None; overwritten each week
Incremental	Every 12 hours	None; cleaned up each week
Log	Every 5 minutes	12 hours

There are other ways that this backup process could be laid out. It really depends on your system and the needs of your business. And that's just one database on one server. You may have multiple backup plans for different databases on a single server or a common plan for all databases. It's really up to the needs defined by your business.

Summary

Backups are a vital part of protecting the data that runs your business. Because of all the different types of backups, you have a lot of flexibility and power in establishing a backup plan that meets the needs of your business. You need a full backup as the foundation from which you can build more sophisticated backup routines. Remember that losing a backup of a database, even a well-secured database, could cause data loss unless the backup itself is encrypted. Data compression helps with speed and storage but comes at the cost of tying up the CPU.

As important as backups are, they're useless unless you know how to restore them. Chapter 9 shows how to get the data from your backups.

CHAPTER 9

Database Restore Strategies

Chapter 8 introduced the concept of backing up your database. Making a copy of the database and storing it separately from the original database is a wonderful safety mechanism. But it's an incomplete model. After you back up the database, you need to be able to bring it back and put all the structures and data from the backup onto your server for use again. This is known as a *restore*. Restoring a database is every bit as important as backing up the database. Without the backup, you have nothing to restore, but unless you can restore, you might as well have skipped the backup. There's an old saying, "your backups are only as good as your last restore."

Restores are much more complicated than backups. The simplest restore of an uncomplicated database requires more definition and code than the backup of that same database did. When you then bring incremental backups and log backups into the picture, restores get complicated fast. But without the restore process, you can't create a plan to recover your system in the event of something catastrophic occurring. This plan is called a *disaster recovery plan*.

Because this is a more complicated subject, a greater degree of detail will be required. The restore operation simply requires more from you than the backup did. We will cover the following in this chapter:

- Restoring a database with the Management Studio GUI
- Restoring a database with T-SQL
- Restoring differential backups
- Restoring log backups
- Restoring file backups
- Testing backups
- Developing a full disaster recovery plan

Restoring a Database from the Management Studio GUI

To the user, a database consists of tables with rows and columns of data. But to the Windows operating system on which the SQL Server instance runs, a database consists of some number of files. The number of files that represent a given database could be quite large as the structures and data maintained by that database grow. But the simplest default database consists of two files: a data file and a log file. These are defined on the model database, which is a database maintained by SQL Server explicitly for creating other databases.

To show the database restore in action, we'll create a basic database. You can follow along by opening Management Studio and connecting to a SQL Server instance that you can run tests against. Once you're connected, right-click the **Databases** folder in the Object Explorer window, and select New Database from the menu. The New Database window will open. Type a name for the database; we used RestoreTest. Make no other changes, and click the OK button. This will create a very simple database. Using one of the full backup methods outlined in Chapter 8, create a backup of the newly created database. Here's the script we used:

```
BACKUP DATABASE RestoreTest
TO DISK = 'c:\data\RestoreTest.bak' ;
```

To be sure that the restore operation works, modify the database by adding a simple table with this script:

```
USE RestoreTest ;
CREATE TABLE dbo.Table1 (Id INT, Val NVARCHAR(50)) ;
```

Once this script is run, you should be able to expand the **Databases** folder in the Object Explorer window, followed by the RestoreTest database and then the **Tables** folder. There you will see the table **dbo.Table1**. You cannot restore a database when other users are connected to it. You will need to log off the users and roll back or commit any outstanding transactions prior to performing the restore operation.

Just like backups, you can use the Management Studio user interface or T-SQL scripts to restore a database. For this simple restore, we'll use Management Studio. Right-click the RestoreTest database in the Object Explorer window. This will open the context menu. Open the Tasks menu folder and then the Restore menu folder. From the final list, select Database to open the Restore Database window, shown in Figure 9-1.

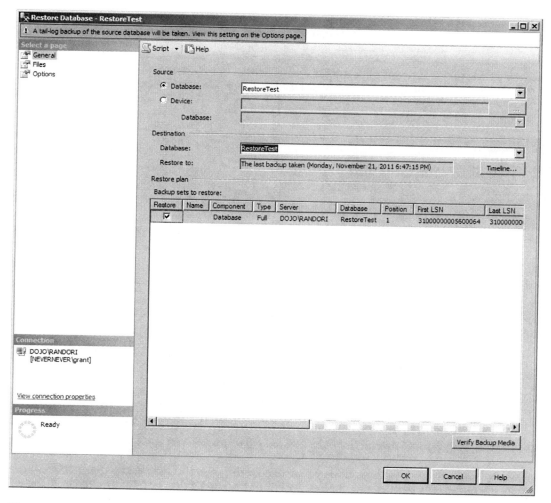

Figure 9-1. The Restore Database window opened for the RestoreTest database

As Figure 9-1 shows, the Restore Database window has three pages, General, Files and Options, which are listed on the left side of the window.

The General page opens by default. Because it was opened from a particular database, that database is already selected in the To Database drop-down list. If you wanted to restore to a different database, you can select other databases from there. The top section is basically for determining the source of the backup that you're going to use to restore the database in question. It's currently set to restore from a database, from known backups for that database. The second choice is "From device." You'll be using this mechanism frequently if you're restoring backups from other locations and other servers, a very common practice.

The next section is for defining the Destination. We have our database name, RestoreTest, but you'll note that you can type into that text box and change the name. We'll explain more about that later. You also have access to the Timeline from this section. That will be covered in detail in the section "Restore Log Backups."

Since the plan is to restore from a backup file created earlier, it's necessary to select the "From device" radio button at the top of the screen and then click the ellipsis button next to it. This opens the Specify Backup window visible in Figure 9-2.

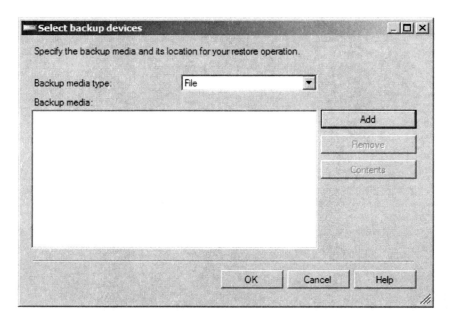

Figure 9-2. *The "Specify backup devices" window without a backup location defined*

The Backup Media drop-down box allows you to choose the source of the backup that will be used in the restore operation. The basic media choices are File or Backup Device. For this example, use the default, File. To add a file to the Backup location list, click the Add button. This will open the Locate Backup File window, shown in Figure 9-3.

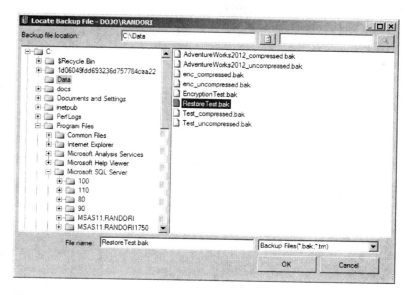

Figure 9-3. *Locate Backup File window with the file selected*

The Locate Backup File window is basically a file explorer window that lets you navigate through drives and shares to locate the file you want to access. In this case, you want to access the `RestoreTest.bak` file located in the path `C:\data`. Once the right file is selected, click the OK button to close the window and move the file into the Specify Backup window like it is in Figure 9-4.

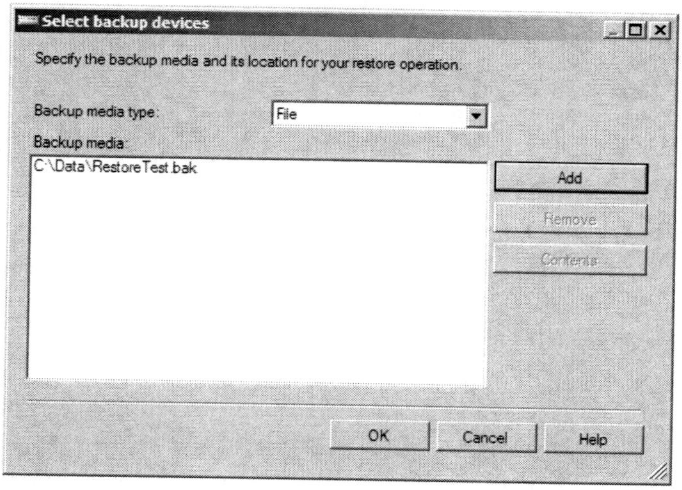

Figure 9-4. *The "Select backup devices" window with a backup location defined*

Since backups can be split across multiple files, you get the option of adding more files to the backup location list. You can also remove a file from that list by selecting the file and clicking the Remove button. You can put multiple backups into a single backup media set. If you do that, clicking the Contents button opens the Device Contents window, visible in Figure 9-5.

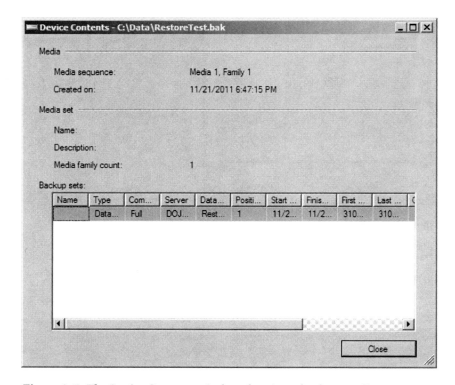

Figure 9-5. *The Device Contents window showing a backup media set*

The Device Contents window will show the information about a backup media set. This information isn't easily displayed in the window when the window is made narrow enough to fit onto the printed page. However, the information consists of the following:

- *Name*: The name, if any given to the backup

- *Type*: What was backed up—database or log

- *Component*: The kind of backup performed—full, incremental, and so on

- *Server*: The server from which the backup was taken

- *Database*: The database from which the backup was taken

- *Position*: The location of the file within the media set

- *Start Date*: The date on which the backup was started

- *Finish Date*: The date on which the backup was finished

- *First LSN*: The initial log sequence number (LSN)

- *Last LSN*: The final log sequence number included in the backup

- *Checkpoint LSN*: The LSN for the start of the Redo log

- *Size*: The size of the backup

- *User*: The user who performed the backup

- *Expiration*: The date on which the backup will expire, if one was specified

The data in the Device Contents window is purely informational. When you're finished reviewing the information, click the Close button. Back in the "Select backup devices" window, click the OK button to move the specified backup file to the Restore Database window, as shown in Figure 9-6.

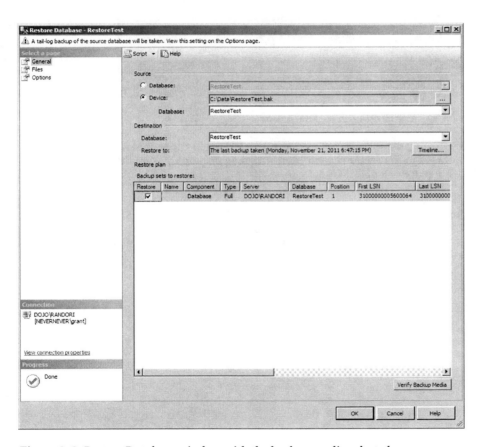

Figure 9-6. *Restore Database window with the backup media selected*

If the database is in simple recovery mode (explained in Chapter 8), you can simply click the OK button, and the database will restore. Once completed, a window stating that the restore completed successfully will appear. Once you click that new window, it will close, as will the Restore Database window. You will then have completed a successful restore of the database.

If, on the other hand, the recovery mode for the database is set to full or bulk logged, when you click the OK button, you'll get an error displayed at the top of the Restore Database window. If you click the error message, a complete description of the error will open in a new window. The window with the error message will have additional information explaining that the tail of the log for the database has not yet been backed up. The *tail* includes any transactions that completed since the last full, incremental, or log backup was done. Figure 9-7 shows an example of this error message.

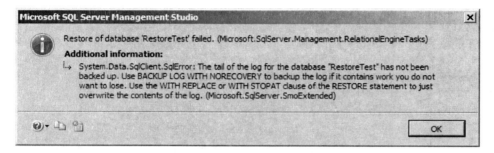

Figure 9-7. The restore failed error window and explanation

To complete the restore of a database in full recovery, you'll need to either deal with the log information (which is detailed in the section called "Restoring Log Backups") or, as the message suggests, use the RESTORE statement's WITH REPLACE clause.

Specifying Restore Options from the GUI

To get to the additional settings, options, and actions of the RESTORE statement in the Management Studio GUI, select the Options page on the left side of the Restore Database window. The new page will look like Figure 9-8.

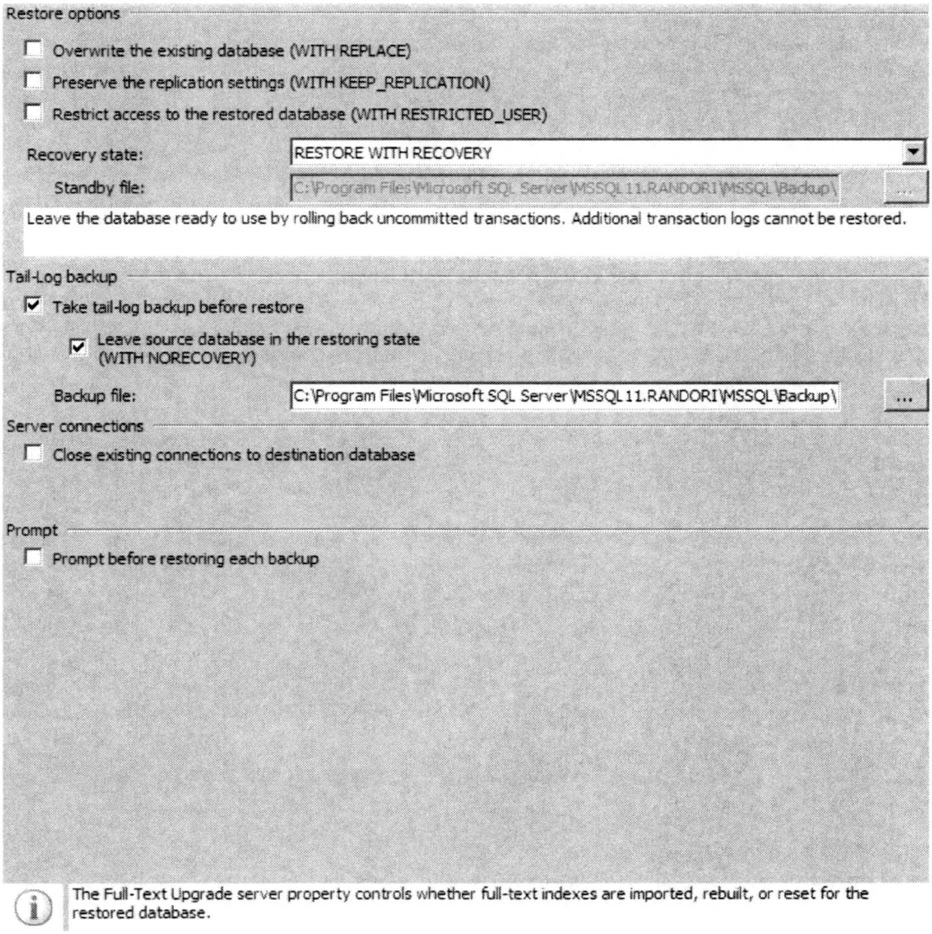

Restore options

☐ Overwrite the existing database (WITH REPLACE)

☐ Preserve the replication settings (WITH KEEP_REPLICATION)

☐ Restrict access to the restored database (WITH RESTRICTED_USER)

Recovery state: `RESTORE WITH RECOVERY` ▼

Standby file: `C:\Program Files\Microsoft SQL Server\MSSQL11.RANDORI\MSSQL\Backup\` ...

Leave the database ready to use by rolling back uncommitted transactions. Additional transaction logs cannot be restored.

Tail-Log backup

☑ Take tail-log backup before restore

☑ Leave source database in the restoring state (WITH NORECOVERY)

Backup file: `C:\Program Files\Microsoft SQL Server\MSSQL11.RANDORI\MSSQL\Backup\` ...

Server connections

☐ Close existing connections to destination database

Prompt

☐ Prompt before restoring each backup

ⓘ The Full-Text Upgrade server property controls whether full-text indexes are imported, rebuilt, or reset for the restored database.

Figure 9-8. *Restore Database window with the Options page displayed*

The Options page allows you to take very direct control over some aspects of the restore operation. The page is split into four sections: "Restore options," "Tail-Log backup," "Server connections," and Prompt. The "Restore options" section allows you to define behaviors of the restore. It also allows you to define the state in which the database is left when your restore is finished.

For now, don't worry about the recovery state. Leave the default option in place. We'll be covering the various recovery states in the "Restoring Differential Backups" and "Restoring Log Backups" Sections—same goes for the other options with the exception of Tail-Log backup. That option should be disabled before we continue.

The first restore option is the check box "Overwrite the existing database (WITH REPLACE)." The label both describes what the option does and tells which T-SQL command to use. You need to select this check box to restore a backup taken from a database in full recovery mode unless you perform a tail-log backup. This will replace the existing database with the database from the backup. The next option is "Preserve the replication settings (WITH KEEP_REPLICATION)." Until you're setting up replication on the server, you don't need to worry about this option for your databases; it is beyond the scope of this chapter. The next check box, "Restrict access to the restored database (WITH RESTRICTED_USER)," allows you to restore a database and bring it online but to bring it online so that only database owners—specifically, users belonging to the db_owner role—can access the database. This is a good way to restore a database but keep end users from it until you can verify that the restore worked properly.

A tail-log backup is a backup of the transaction log that captures any changes in the log since the last transaction log backup. If you have a database in Full Recovery mode, you should be using the tail log backup as part of your restore process to ensure you can recover to a point in time. But you don't have to run a tail log backup. You can do what we did, which is to disable this option and then use the WITH REPLACE command to simply put the new database on top of the other without regard to any other recovery.

The next option gives you the ability to kick any existing connections off the database prior to the restore. You can't run a restore while people are connected to the database. As attractive as this option is, I'd suggest you not use it if you don't have to. It can encourage mistakes in which you think you're restoring to one server but by accident restore to a different one. But if you do enable this, it will put all connections into rollbacks and then drop the connections completely.

The final check box on the window is "Prompt before restoring each backup." If you are performing multiple restores from multiple backups, this will pause between each file for you to verify that it should continue with the next step. This will slow down restores but give you more control over exactly what gets restored and when, because you can stop if there's a reason to not use the next file.

Once you select the "Overwrite the existing database" check box and deselect the Tail-Log check box, if it's checked, the restore is ready to run. Click the OK button, and the database should restore without error this time. Although you can do basic restores using the GUI, the full functionality of restores is exposed through the T-SQL statements.

If you now check the tables in the database, the table created just after the backup was done is no longer in the database. The restore was successful.

Restoring a Database Using T-SQL

Not all restore options are exposed through the GUI. You can't automate the GUI either. To get at the full set of options available to the restore operation and to begin to program and automate restore operations, you need to use Transact-SQL commands.

Executing a Simple Restore

In the previous section, you created a small blank database called RestoreTest and took a backup of that database. (When we say "take" a backup, that phrase is basically the same as saying "create a backup" of the database in question.) To perform the same restore that was defined with the GUI, including replacing the existing database, you simply need to run the following code (simplerestore.sql in the download):

```
RESTORE DATABASE RestoreTest
FROM DISK = 'c:\data\restoretest.bak'
WITH REPLACE ;
```

Just as in the earlier GUI procedure, this command will restore the database and overwrite the existing database.

Creating a Copy of a Database

You can do much more than simply restore your original database in its original location. What if you wanted to create a copy of the database? You could modify the procedure as follows and run it (--attemptrestore in the download):

```
RESTORE DATABASE WholeNewRestore
FROM DISK = 'c:\data\restoretest.bak' ;
```

All you did here was change the name. SQL Server will attempt to create a new database from the backup. Unfortunately, if you run this command, it will generate this error output:

```
Msg 1834, Level 16, State 1, Line 1

The file 'C:\Program Files\Microsoft SQL Server\MSSQL11.RANDORI\MSSQL\DATA\RestoreTest.mdf'
cannot be overwritten.  It is being used by database 'RestoreTest'.

Msg 3156, Level 16, State 4, Line 1

File 'RestoreTest' cannot be restored to 'C:\Program Files\Microsoft SQL
Server\MSSQL11.RANDORI\MSSQL\DATA\RestoreTest.mdf'. Use WITH MOVE to identify a valid
location for the file.

Msg 1834, Level 16, State 1, Line 1

The file 'C:\Program Files\Microsoft SQL
Server\MSSQL11.RANDORI\MSSQL\DATA\RestoreTest_log.ldf' cannot be overwritten.  It is being
used by database 'RestoreTest'.

Msg 3156, Level 16, State 4, Line 1

File 'RestoreTest_log' cannot be restored to 'C:\Program Files\Microsoft SQL
Server\MSSQL11.RANDORI\MSSQL\DATA\RestoreTest_log.ldf'. Use WITH MOVE to identify a valid
location for the file.

Msg 3119, Level 16, State 1, Line 1

Problems were identified while planning for the RESTORE statement. Previous messages provide
details.

Msg 3013, Level 16, State 1, Line 1

RESTORE DATABASE is terminating abnormally.
```

That's a lot of information to take in all at once. You can boil it down to the following rule: you can't create a database with the same file names and locations as an existing database. This is illustrated in the results with the statements that say a particular file and path "cannot be overwritten."

Fortunately, the error message provides the answer to the problem in the form of the suggestion "Use WITH MOVE to identify a valid location for the file." The MOVE keyword allows you to change the location or names of files when restoring a database. So, to create a new copy of the database, the following is the script that needs to be run (--newdbrestore in the download):

```
RESTORE DATABASE WholeNewRestore
FROM DISK = 'c:\data\restoretest.bak'
WITH MOVE 'RestoreTest' TO 'C:\Program Files\Microsoft SQL↵
 Server\MSSQL11.RANDORI\MSSQL\DATA\WholeNewRestore.mdf'
,MOVE 'RestoreTest_Log' TO 'C:\Program Files\Microsoft SQL↵
 Server\MSSQL11.RANDORI\MSSQL\DATA\WholeNewRestore_Log.ldf' ;
```

Notice that the MOVE operation doesn't move the file from one file location to a new file location. Instead, it uses the names RestoreTest and RestoreTest_Log. These are the logical file names used by SQL Server that match the logical file constructs with where the physical files are located. They're used in the restore operation to define a new location for the files. Running this script will create a new database with this output:

```
Processed 304 pages for database 'WholeNewRestore', file 'RestoreTest' on file 1.

Processed 2 pages for database 'WholeNewRestore', file 'RestoreTest_log' on file 1.

RESTORE DATABASE successfully processed 306 pages in 0.060 seconds (39.827 MB/sec).
```

The pages processed are the pages that data is stored on in the database. Each file is processed individually, and then the database is available for use.

Retrieving Logical and Physical File Names

You can get the logical names of the database files by looking at the Properties window through the Management Studio GUI. But you may not have an existing copy of the database available to gather this information from. Luckily, there's a method to retrieve the list of files that define the database from the backup file itself (filelistrestore.bak in the download):

```
RESTORE FILELISTONLY
FROM DISK = 'c:\data\restoretest.bak';
```

The output from this is a very extensive description of the files that define the database. Figure 9-9 shows some of the information available.

	LogicalName	PhysicalName	Type
1	RestoreTest	C:\Program Files\Microsoft SQL Server\MSSQL11.RAN...	D
2	RestoreTest_log	C:\Program Files\Microsoft SQL Server\MSSQL11.RAN...	L

Figure 9-9. *Partial output from the RESTORE FILELISTONLY command*

The information in Figure 9-9 is the most basic necessary for managing a database restore. The first column, LogicalName, is the logical file name that you would use if you needed to perform the MOVE operation. The next column, PhysicalName, is the actual file location of the database that was backed up. It's useful to verify whether the same drives and directories exist on the server where you're performing the restore or even whether there are already files in that location. The last column displayed here, Type, defines the file type, in this case one data file and one log file. Other types may be displayed, and since different types require different handling and definitions during the restore, it's good to know what kind you're dealing with. Table 9-1 explains the other information from the FILELISTONLY command.

Table 9-1. *The Remaining Output from FILELISTONLY*

Column Name	Description	Use
FileGroupName	The filegroup to which the file belongs	Largely informational for backup purposes
Size	Size of the file in bytes	Extremely useful information so you know if there's enough room on the drive
MaxSize	Max size of the file in bytes	Same as with the Size column
FileID	An identifier created by SQL Server unique within a database	Informational
CreateLSN	Log sequence number for the creation of the file	Used internally by the RESTORE operation
DropLSN	Log sequence number for a dropped file	Used internally by the RESTORE operation
UniqueId	A unique identifier assigned to the file	Informational
ReadOnlyLSN	Log sequence number that defines the read-only nature of the database	Used internally by the RESTORE operation
ReadWriteLSN	Log sequence number defining the read-write options of the database	Used internally by the RESTORE operation
BackupSizeInBytes	Size of the backup file	Another useful bit of information for copying files

Continued

Column Name	Description	Use
SourceBlockSize	Size of the blocks of the physical file	Used internally by the RESTORE operation
FileGroupID	Exactly what it says, the ID of the filegroup	Informational
LogGroupGUID	This value is not defined by Microsoft	Doesn't communicate anything useful
DifferentialBaseLSN	Defined in differential backups; marks the difference between the differential and log backups	Very useful for restores
DifferentialBaseGUID	Defined in differential backups; marks the difference between the differential and the full backup	Very useful for restores
IsReadOnly	Marks whether the file is read-only	Informational
IsPresent	Marks whether the file is actually in the backup	Useful if you're backing up different files and filegroups for the database
TDEThumbprint	Displays the encryptor thumbprint	Informational

Displaying General Information About a Backup

You can also display general information about the backup, in what's known as the *header*. The syntax is similar to that used in the other restore operations, as shown here (headerrestore.sql in the download):

```
RESTORE HEADERONLY
FROM DISK = 'c:\data\restoretest.bak';
```

Figure 9-10 shows part of the output from the header.

	BackupName	BackupDescription	Backup Type	Expiration Date	Compressed	Position	Device Type	UserName	ServerName
1	NULL	NULL	1	NULL	1	1	2	NEVERNEVER\grant	DOJO\RANDORI

***Figure 9-10.** Partial output from RESTORE HEADERONLY*

Like the FILEILISTONLY output, a lot more columns are available for the backup header. Most of them are more focused on describing the database or log being backed up and are not immediately applicable to the restore process, so we'll go over only the columns displayed here. Table 9-2 describes those columns.

Table 9-2. *Partial Output from RESTORE HEADERONLY*

Column Name	Description	Use
BackupName	The name given by the backup process, if any	Used to identify individual backups in addition to the backup file name
BackupDescription	If supplied by the backup process, a short description of the backup	Another opportunity to supply more information about the backup
BackupType	A numeric value that describes what kind of backup was done	Clearly useful for identifying the type of backup if the backup file name doesn't supply enough information
ExpirationDate	The date on which the backup will be expired	Needed to know if a backup will be expired or not
Compressed	A true/false field that determines whether a backup is compressed	Informational
Position	The number determining its location within the set, if the backup is part of a set	Necessary for restores from a backup set
DeviceType	A number that determines whether it's a virtual or physical device	Not used in restores
UserName	The user who performed the backup	Informational in restore operations
ServerName	The server from which the backup was taken	Informational in restore operations but might be useful to know if this will be a replace operation or not

Through the RESTORE FILELISTONLY and RESTORE HEADERONLY commands, it's possible to gather enough information to restore a full backup. You can overwrite an existing database, or you can create a new one by moving the files as you restore them.

Cleaning Up

Before continuing, if you've run the scripts to create these databases on the server, you should clean up by running the following script (`droprestore.sql` in the download):

```
USE MASTER;
DROP DATABASE WholeNewRestore;
DROP DATABASE RestoreTest;
```

Now, it's time to restore a differential backup.

Restoring Differential Backups

In Chapter 8, we introduced the concept of differential backups. These are backups that contain only the changes within the database since the last full backup. Restoring one of these backups is a two-step process. First, run the following script (`--setupdifferential` in the download):

```
USE DiffTest ;
CREATE TABLE dbo.DataChanges
    (DataChangesId INT IDENTITY(1, 1)
                        NOT NULL,
     DataValue NVARCHAR(50) NOT NULL,
     UpdateDate DATETIME NOT NULL,
     CONSTRAINT PK_DataChanges PRIMARY KEY CLUSTERED (DataChangesId)
    ) ;

INSERT  INTO dbo.DataChanges
        (DataValue, UpdateDate)
VALUES  (N'First Row', GETDATE()),
        (N'Second Row', GETDATE()),
        (N'Third Row', GETDATE()) ;

BACKUP DATABASE DiffTest TO DISK = 'c:\data\difftest.bak' ;

INSERT  INTO dbo.DataChanges
        (DataValue, UpdateDate)
VALUES  (N'Fourth Row', GETDATE()),
        (N'Fifth Row', GETDATE()) ;

BACKUP DATABASE DiffTest
TO DISK = 'c:\data\difftest_diff.bak'
WITH DIFFERENTIAL ;

DELETE  dbo.DataChanges
WHERE   DataChangesId = 3 ;
```

This script creates a database, DiffTest. It then creates and loads data into a new table, `DataChanges`. After this work, the script performs a full backup of the database to disk. Then more data is inserted, and a differential backup is taken. Finally, data is "accidentally" deleted, setting up the need to restore the database to the last good backup, the differential backup.

From here, it is possible to restore the database differential. The first step, because the differential is based on data changes since the last full backup, is to restore the previous backup. But, instead of simply restoring it, you need to leave it in a state that allows for the next backup to be applied. This means preventing the recovery of the database. *Recovery* is the process right at the end of restore in which uncommitted transactions, if any were captured by the backup, are rolled forward, and then the database is brought online for access by the users. To restore the database but prevent the recovery, you must run the restore from the full backup in this manner (`norecoverydiffrestore.sql` in the download):

```
RESTORE DATABASE DiffTest
FROM DISK = 'c:\data\difftest.bak'
WITH REPLACE, NORECOVERY ;
```

This will restore the full database, replacing the existing copy as you did in the original full backup restores; however, by using the `NORECOVERY` option, you prevent the database from recovering. This is even visible in the GUI. Once you run this script, click the Databases list in the Object Explorer window, and press the F5 key to refresh the list. You'll see something similar to Figure 9-11.

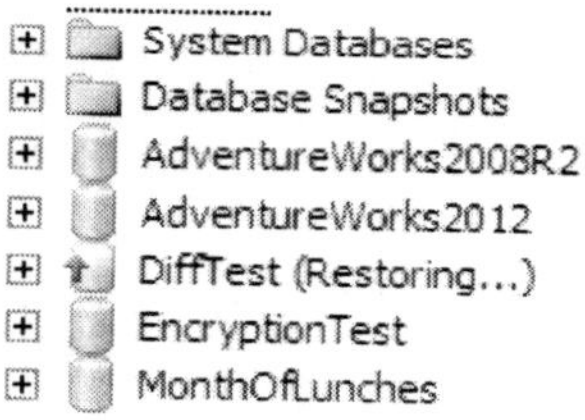

Figure 9-11. DiffTest database stopped at the point of recovery

The next step is to restore the differential backup. The syntax is identical to that of a full restore operation; only the source file is different (`diffrestore.sql` in the download):

```
RESTORE DATABASE DiffTest
FROM DISK = 'c:\data\difftest_diff.bak'
```

This command will restore the differential data and recover the database. If you refresh the database list again, you'll see that this database is online. If you select the data from the `DataChanges` table, you'll see that all the rows are back in place. To clean up before continuing, drop the DiffTest database (`cleanupdifftest.sql` in the download):

```
USE master ;
DROP DATABASE DiffTest ;
```

In the gaps between differential backups are the log backups. Restoring them is a similar process.

Restoring Log Backups

When a database is in full recovery mode, it's necessary to back up the logs independently from the database backups. When it's time to recover these logs, you can recover full log files, or you can actually recover to a specific point in time. For example, in the morning, say 3 a.m., you run your full backups. Following that, once every half hour, you back up the log. At 11:40 a.m., someone accidentally deletes important data. You act quickly and run a log backup. Now, you need to restore all the completed transactions up to 11:39. It's possible to do that with log backups.

Let's look at an example of restoring log backups. Begin by running the following script, which will set up the database and a set of backups. Be warned—the script will take more than two minutes to run (--setuplogs in the download):

```
CREATE DATABASE LogTest ;
GO
ALTER DATABASE LogTest SET RECOVERY FULL ;
GO

USE LogTest ;

CREATE TABLE BusinessData
    (BusinessDataId INT NOT NULL
                        IDENTITY(1, 1),
     BusinessValue NVARCHAR(50),
     UpdateDate DATETIME,
     CONSTRAINT pk_BusinessData PRIMARY KEY CLUSTERED (BusinessDataID)
    ) ;

INSERT  INTO BusinessData
        (BusinessValue, UpdateDate)
VALUES  ('Row 1', GETDATE()),
        ('Row 2', GETDATE()) ;

--Full backup
BACKUP DATABASE LogTest
TO DISK = 'c:\data\logtest.bak'

--create more business data
INSERT  INTO BusinessData
        (BusinessValue, UpdateDate)
VALUES  ('Row 3', GETDATE()),
        ('Row 4', GETDATE()) ;

--First Log Backup
BACKUP LOG LogTest
TO DISK = 'c:\data\logtest_log1.bak' ;

INSERT  INTO BusinessData
        (BusinessValue, UpdateDate)
VALUES  ('Row 5', GETDATE()),
        ('Row 6', GETDATE()) ;

--Second Log Backup
BACKUP LOG LogTest
TO DISK = 'c:\data\logtest_log2.bak' ;
```

```
INSERT   INTO BusinessData
         (BusinessValue, UpdateDate)
VALUES   ('Row 7', GETDATE()),
         ('Row 8', GETDATE()) ;
SELECT GETDATE();

--pause for two minutes
WAITFOR DELAY '00:02' ;

DELETE   BusinessData ;

--Final Log Backup, after the "accident"
BACKUP LOG LogTest
TO DISK = 'c:\data\logtest_log3.bak' ;
 GO
 USE master;
```

This script is very busy:

1. First, it creates a database and sets the recovery model to FULL.

2. It creates a table, BusinessData, and inserts some data.

3. The database is backed up using a full database backup, just like you would do in a production environment.

4. More data is inserted.

5. Then, a log backup is taken. This is modeling behavior that would occur during the normal production day.

6. More data is added.

7. Another log backup is taken.

8. A print statement shows the date and time (since there's no way to know when all this is taking place).

9. Then, more data is inserted

10. A delay of two minutes is added.

11. Finally, the "error" deletes all the data in the BusinessData table.

12. Then, an "emergency" log backup is taken. This final log backup will include the delete, but it will also include the last good data in the database.

If you are following along with the code, leave this Query Editor window open after running the query. You'll understand why a little bit later.

To begin restoring this database, first you'll need to restore the full backup. The restore operation will need to leave the database in an unrecovered state, just in the differential backup. The script would look like this (--norecoverylogrestore.sql in the download):

```
RESTORE DATABASE LogTest
FROM DISK = 'c:\data\logtest.bak'
WITH REPLACE, NORECOVERY ;
```

Just like in the differential backup, the database will be in a state labeled "Restoring . . . " in the GUI, as shown in Figure 9-12.

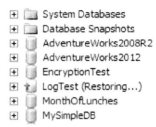

⊞ 🗀 System Databases
⊞ 🗀 Database Snapshots
⊞ 🗄 AdventureWorks2008R2
⊞ 🗄 AdventureWorks2012
⊞ 🗄 EncryptionTest
⊞ 🗄 LogTest (Restoring...)
⊞ 🗄 MonthOfLunches
⊞ 🗄 MySimpleDB

Figure 9-12. LogTest database in the "Restoring . . ." (or unrecovered) state

You now have the database back to its state as of the last full backup. But more data changes were made prior to the delete, so each of the log files will need to be recovered in the order in which they were taken. You also want to know the time when the final good query completed or when the problem query started. In the example case, the last good query, the INSERT statement, was finished just after November 25, 2011 at 5:34 p.m. You know this because you are able to get the date and time from the output of the PRINT statement. With this information, you can put together a set of restore operations that look something like the following (--pointintimelogrestore in the download):

```
RESTORE LOG LogTest
FROM DISK = 'c:\data\logtest_log1.bak'
WITH NORECOVERY;

RESTORE LOG LogTest
FROM DISK = 'c:\data\logtest_log2.bak'
WITH NORECOVERY;

RESTORE LOG LogTest
FROM DISK = 'c:\data\logtest_log3.bak'
WITH STOPAT = 'Nov  25 2011  17:49:30';
```

Each of the individual log restores, except the last one, completes its restore but does not allow the database to recover. The final log restore includes the information needed to stop before the time at which the delete occurred. Obviously, the more precisely you can determine the moment in time you want to restore to, the less data that will be lost. To verify that all the data was recovered, select BusinessTest from the table using a script similar to this one:

```
SELECT * FROM dbo.BusinessData AS bd;
```

You will see all eight rows of data returned, as shown in Figure 9-13.

	BusinessDataId	BusinessValue	UpdateDate
1	1	Row 1	2011-11-25 17:49:21.933
2	2	Row 2	2011-11-25 17:49:21.933
3	3	Row 3	2011-11-25 17:49:22.120
4	4	Row 4	2011-11-25 17:49:22.120
5	5	Row 5	2011-11-25 17:49:22.167
6	6	Row 6	2011-11-25 17:49:22.167
7	7	Row 7	2011-11-25 17:49:22.200
8	8	Row 8	2011-11-25 17:49:22.200

Figure 9-13. A complete data set after the log restore

You could have stopped the recovery at any point with one of the other log files, but none of these files covered the full time frame in which the error occurred. The full recovery that took place was because of the extra log backup taken after the error that caused the data loss. That tail backup provided the ability to recover to a point in time. Recovering individual file backups has slightly different requirements and implications than the previous restore types.

Before continuing, you may want to do some cleanup. Run the following script to remove the database used to test log recovery (`cleanuplogtest.sql` in the download):

```
USE MASTER;
DROP DATABASE LogTest;
```

Restoring File Backups

When you're dealing with very large databases or databases that have to be split across different disks for performance reasons, it can make more sense to back up individual files or filegroups rather than the entire database, as detailed in Chapter 8. It's then possible to restore the individual files or filegroups to the database. To see a filegroup restore in action, run the following script to prepare a database and backups (`--setupfile` in the download):

```
CREATE DATABASE FileTest ;

ALTER DATABASE FileTest
ADD FILEGROUP FILETESTFG ;

ALTER DATABASE FileTest
ADD FILE (
NAME = FileTest2,
FILENAME = 'c:\data\filetest2.ndf',
SIZE = 5MB,
MAXSIZE = 100MB,
FILEGROWTH = 5MB
) TO FILEGROUP FileTestFG ;
GO
```

```
USE FileTest ;

CREATE TABLE dbo.ft1
    (ID INT IDENTITY(1, 1)
            NOT NULL,
     Val NVARCHAR(50) NOT NULL
    )
ON  FileTestFG ;

INSERT  INTO dbo.ft1
        (Val)
VALUES  (N'Test') ;

BACKUP DATABASE FileTest
FILEGROUP = 'FileTestFG'
TO DISK = 'c:\data\FileTest_FileTestFG.bak'
WITH INIT ;

BACKUP LOG FileTest
TO DISK = 'c:\data\FileTest_Log.bak'
WITH INIT ;
```

This script creates a new database, FileTest. The script then adds a filegroup, FileTestFG, and adds a file to that group, FileTest2. From there, the script creates a table, ft1, and adds one row to the table. A backup of the filegroup is taken. Then, a backup of the end of the log (also known as the tail) is taken. When a file or group is not read-only, the tail of the log must be backed up if you will need to restore and recover the file or filegroup.

The restore operation itself is very simple. First, you restore the necessary filegroups or files. But the database should not be recovered because the log still needs to be restored. As shown earlier with log restores, until the final log is restored, the database should not be recovered. The final script should look as follows (filerestore.sql in the download):

```
RESTORE DATABASE FileTest
FILEGROUP = 'FileTestFG'
FROM DISK = 'c:\data\FileTest_FileTestFG.bak'
WITH NORECOVERY ;

RESTORE LOG FileTest
FROM DISK = 'c:\data\FileTest_Log.bak'
WITH RECOVERY ;
```

To verify that the file is back online, you can select a row from the table dbo.ft1. It seems easy, but the large databases that you'll be performing this type of operation on, if needed, will be much more complicated than this simple example. To remove the test database, run the following script (cleanupfiletest.sql in the download):

```
USE MASTER ;
DROP DATABASE FileTest ;
```

Testing Backups

In Chapter 8, we pointed out that in the Back Up Database window in SQL Server Management Studio there was an option called "Verify backup when finished" on the Options page. This option is visible about halfway down the page; it's shown in Figure 9-14.

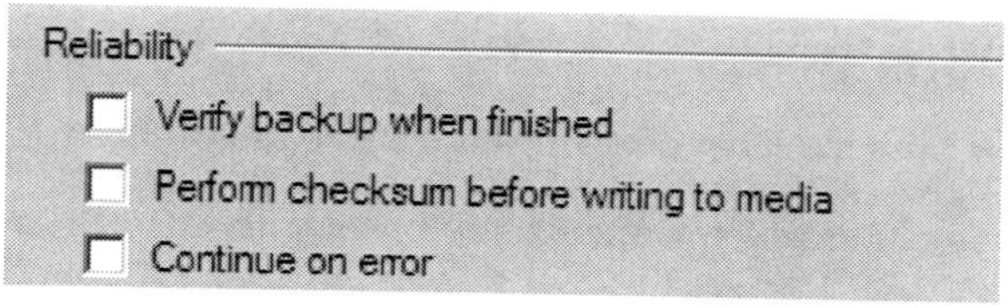

Figure 9-14. *Back Up Database window showing the Reliability options*

We didn't address this option in Chapter 8 because it's actually a function of the RESTORE command. The syntax looks like this:

```
RESTORE VERIFYONLY FROM DISK = 'somepath'
```

This command—and it's the same if you run it from the Back Up Database window in Management Studio—reads the backup file. It checks that the most of the file is readable and complete. It does not in any way actually restore the database. That makes VERIFYONLY a vital part of your backup and recovery strategy because it will help ensure that the backups you're creating are ready when you need them. To save time, you can also run RESTORE VERIFYONLY before attempting a backup. When VERIFYONLY finds no issues with the backup, it returns a success message. If there is a problem with the backup, an error is returned.

Just remember that parts of the file are not checked by the VERIFYONLY command, so using it does not provide as complete a verification that your backups are good and in place as actually running a restore. It's a good idea to restore your more mission critical databases to verify that your backups are working correctly.

Developing a Full Disaster Recovery Plan

Between Chapter 8 on backups and this chapter on restores, you have the basics to begin thinking about laying out a disaster recovery plan for your databases. A disaster recovery plan has to take many factors into account. Most of these are not technical issues. Rather, the factors that drive most of the decision making and planning around disaster recovery are related directly to the needs of the business. To arrive at a disaster recovery plan, you first need to ask a series of questions of both the business and information technology teams. We won't hit every possible question here, but we'll give you enough information so that you can plan for the worst kinds of disaster.

After you gather all the information about the technology and the business, you need to plan a backup and restore strategy that will answer all, or most, of the business needs that came up. You'll have to take into account the technology that you have available and its capabilities. You may need to purchase additional capacity in terms of tape backups or off-site storage. You also may have to make compromises because the technology can't do what you want or because you may not be able to afford it. All of this will help you define a plan for your disaster recovery.

Once you have the plan put together and implemented, you need to document it. You need to share that document with the business and with the various technology teams in your organization. Everyone should know what's expected of them, what they can expect of you, and what you can all expect in the event of an emergency. You then need to take that plan and practice it. Run through all the processes, both literally and as a desktop exercise. Make sure you've practiced performing the tasks necessary to support the plan.

Gathering Information About the Business

You may have a very thorough understanding of what your business does or what kind of information your business captures, stores, and presents in its databases. You may not. You need to develop a full understanding of which data is vital, which is important, and which is ancillary to the business. Here is a first set of questions to ask:

- What kind of data am I storing?

- How important to the business is this data?

- How much data is there? (In other words, how big are the databases?)

Once you ask these questions of the business, you'll understand whether you're storing transactional data from the sales force, test runs from the chemical plant, or demographic data from an outside source. You'll know whether the data stored is absolutely vital to the continuing operation of the company or whether it's easily replaceable by downloading the content from the vendor. You'll also know how much data you have to deal with.

With this information in hand, you need to ask more questions:

- How much information can be lost in a worst-case scenario?

- How much *downtime* (time without the database being online) can the business sustain?

- How many locations must we protect?

The initial answer to the first of these questions is almost always "none." But, if you push back, you'll find that the previous day can be lost, for example, or it may be only up to five minutes. Or you may, in fact, be working with a business that can lose no data.

The second question involves finding out just how long the servers and their data can be offline before it starts to hurt the business. And the third question is about how many different physical locations you have to cover in the event of a real emergency.

Then, you need to focus on the information services information. This where you ask questions such as the following:

- How much storage capacity is available?

- Is off-site storage of backups available?

- How fast is the network?

- How much budget do I have to work with?

These technical questions and the information provided go hand in hand with business information to help you make decisions about the disaster plan.

Establishing the Disaster Plan

Now that you know your basic requirements and capacities, you can start making plans. As a method for showing how a plan might work, we'll describe two scenarios for a business and technology and then suggest a possible disaster plan for each.

Scenario 1: Large Commercial Insurance Company

In scenario 1, you're supporting a large commercial insurance company. The type of information the company stores is quite diverse, but it primarily consists of information about the clients and the property that you insure. The amount of data is somewhat large, but it consists of multiple moderate-sized databases varying from 20GB to 300GB, for a total of about 1TB. The data itself is not terribly volatile, because the client base doesn't change very fast and because the number of transactions against the system (the amount of data being changed) is small on a daily basis.

The data is the company, though. Without full knowledge of what is insured, the company would be in serious trouble in the event of a claim. Further, the company has to meet certain regulatory requirements that detail certain types of data protection that you're required to provide. The company has a large storage area network from a major vendor, a fast network, quite a lot of spare capacity, and secondary backup systems (such as tape or mirroring) already installed. If the system lost no more than an hour of work in any given day, there would be minimal impact on the business. Since the business could be run entirely on paper if necessary, you can count on a day or two of recovery time if you really needed it.

With all this information, the backup plan might look something like this:

- Full database backups are taken once a week. One backup is kept on disk for recovery.

- Incremental backups are taken twice a day. Each one overwrites the previous.

- Log backups are taken once every half hour. These are accumulated between incremental backups but kept only for 24 hours.

- Copies are taken of the full backups each week and stored outside the company.

- Copies are taken of the incremental and log backups each day.

This backup plan will allow you to capture the data for the company described in the scenario and meet the basic business and regulatory requirements. The full and incremental backups provide basic recovery. The log backups taken once each half hour help ensure less than one hour of data would be lost in the event of a failure where the tail of the log could not be backed up. The off-site storage means that, in the event of a catastrophic disaster, no more than a week of data is lost to the company.

Scenario 2: Small Online Retail Business

In scenario 2, you're a DBA in a small to midsized online retail business. Everything the company does is dependent on sales, and all the sales come into the database by way of the Web. There are two different sets of data. First are the ongoing transactional data from the sales. There are a lot of transactions, and the data changes constantly during the day, but the database itself isn't that big—only 75GB. The second set of data contains the historical sales records, which are aggregated once a week into a large and growing data mart for reporting. The company leases storage and doesn't have much in the way of spare capacity. If the system goes down, so does the company. If data is lost in the transactional system, the company loses sales. If data is lost in the data mart, it hurts the company a bit, but it wouldn't be the end of everything. If the transactional database were to go down, you'd need to recover everything in as timely a fashion as humanly possible.

With this information, the backup plan might resemble this:

- Full database backups are taken once a week for the data mart, immediately following the aggregation load. No other backups are needed. One copy is kept online.

- For the transactional system, one full backup is taken each day, keeping only one online.

- During the day, an incremental backup is taken once every four hours, keeping only one online.

- Log backups are taken every five minutes but kept for only four hours.

This backup plan reflects the lack of space and the inability to store backups off-site. If the leased storage were to go offline, this business might have to close. A secondary backup system should be negotiated into the contract, or some other method of backup is necessary in the event of a catastrophic failure. The full backup taken daily and the incremental backups taken every four hours should help shorten the recovery time, because less changed data would have to be applied after the full backup was restored. The logs taken every five minutes help ensure a minimum of loss in the event of a complete failure of the database.

Testing the Disaster Plan

Having a disaster plan is not enough. The plan must be tested. First, you should be running backup verifications on the backups themselves. You need to know that your backups are structurally sound. This is especially important if your backups are getting shipped to off-site storage in the event of an emergency. You need some assurance that those backups are functional.

You need to practice restoring your databases. You should do this regularly. Restore the full backups on a regular basis to a test machine somewhere (not on your production system). When an emergency occurs, all the managers descend to your desk to see how things are going, and if that's the first time you've run a full restore, you might be in trouble. Performing restores regularly also tests the integrity of your backups. Run an incremental restore on a regular basis too. All the same rules apply. You'll want to use the logs to recover to a point in time even more often than using the incremental backups. This is the most common emergency process that you'll run into, and you need to prepare for it.

You should take one of the backups out of the off-site archive on a semiregular basis and see whether you can restore the database. This tests both the off-site storage mechanisms and the integrity of your backups. If possible, you should go to an off-site facility, either within your company or at one of the emergency backup companies, and see whether you can get a system installed, configured, and operational at the off-site facility. Be sure you can do the same for SQL Server and your backups.

All of this may sound a bit paranoid and over the top, but when the emergency occurs and you've already run the restore of the most vital systems three or four times that year, you'll be smooth and confident. You'll have the system, and the company, back online in a minimal amount of time. What's more, as the number and size of your databases grows, you'll need to completely evaluate any disaster recovery plans you've already created. These plans can, and should, change over time, so be prepared to go through the reevaluation exercise once a year at least.

Summary

Backups are one of the most important things you can do for your data, your server, and your company. But without the ability to restore the data, the backups are useless. Some of the more important points from this chapter bear repeating: Restoring a full database requires that you manage the files associated with that database, but you can get the information needed directly from the backup itself. Incremental and log restores require you to leave the database in a recovering state.

If you take nothing else away from this chapter, be sure that you're verifying your backups through the use of RESTORE VERIFYONLY and through occasional full restores. Taking a backup is simply not enough. You need to know that it will work. You must also restore your databases so that you know how to perform the operation and so you know that your backups are functional. With all this, you can protect the value that the data represents to your business.

CHAPTER 10

Common Database Maintenance Tasks

Database administrators perform a variety of tasks. Depending on how your organization is structured, your own roles and responsibilities will most likely differ when compared to DBAs at other companies. However, there are a few common database maintenance tasks that every DBA should be familiar with, regardless of your position. This chapter will introduce you to the core DBA maintenance tasks, such as moving databases and data, and other routine maintenance tasks, like index reorganization.

Backing Up and Restoring Databases

The abilities to back up and restore a database are fundamental skills all DBAs need to know. They're so important that a chapter in this book is devoted to each topic (Chapters 8 and 9). Keep in mind that a database backup is an online operation. This means that an end user can continue to make modifications to the database while the backup is being performed. Since a very large database backup will take time to complete, you may want to think about strategies for reducing the backup window. Backing up to disk is faster than backing up to tape. Features like backup compression also help reduce the amount of disk I/O that needs to be performed when creating or reading from the backup and thus will dramatically reduce the backup window.

Transaction logs contain all of the recent activity in the database and are used when restoring a database to a specific point in time. If you do not back up the transaction log, it will grow and eventually fill up your entire disk, causing you a lot of problems and potentially ending your job.

Note Managing your transaction logs is critical, and a good start is to make sure they are being backed up. A transaction log backup will truncate the log, freeing up space to be used by future transactions.

If you are responsible for the operating system, make sure this is backed up. Also, the system databases, such as master and msdb, need to be backed up, because they contain SQL Server instance related information.

Finally, practicing your disaster recovery plan is important. Set up a test environment to practice a failover scenario. Determine how long this recovery actually took and verify that it met your companies SLAs.

Moving Data

Whether you are supporting the developer who is writing an application or are moving data out to a disaster recovery site, there will be a time when you need to move data around. Moving data can be done in a variety of ways, but there are three common ways to move an entire database.

Moving a Database Using the "Detach and Attach" Method

First, you can detach a database from an instance of SQL Server and attach it to another instance. One use case for the "detach and attach" method is when you want to move a database but do not have enough free disk space to make a copy. A real-life example is a customer who had a 1.7-TB database to upgrade from SQL Server 2005 to SQL Server 2008. The customer did not own enough physical disk storage to make a copy of the new database, so the only option was to install SQL Server 2008 on new hardware, attach to the existing LUN where the database was stored, and attach the database.

■ **Note** When you attach a database to SQL Server, the database engine will update the database metadata to that of the version of the SQL Server This means that once you attach your database to a newer edition of SQL Server, you will not be able to attach it to any earlier version because the structure of the database will have changed.

You can detach a database via SSMS by right-clicking the database in Object Explorer and selecting Tasks and then Detach from the context menu. This will launch the Detach Database dialog shown in Figure 10-1.

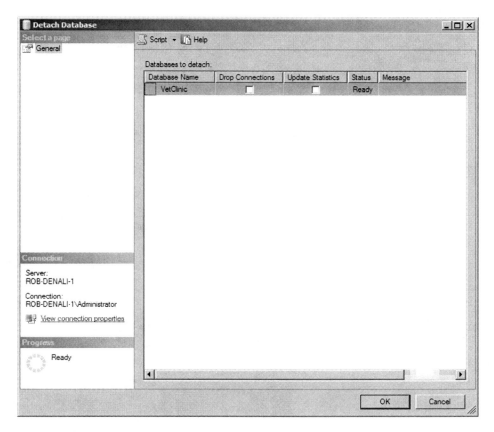

Figure 10-1. Detach Database dialog

If we simply click the OK button, the operation will fail if there are active user connections to this database. If we want to disconnect any users who are connected to the database, we can check the "Drop connections" check box. When this is checked, the dialog will first issue an `ALTER DATABASE [Database Name] SET SINGLE_USER WITH ROLLBACK IMMEDIATE` command to force the disconnect. If you are moving the database to a read-only location, you should check the update statistics check box so that information about the data and indexes is most current. This dialog uses the `sp_detach_db` stored procedure to perform the detach.

Now that the database is detached, it no longer shows up in Object Explorer. However, the database files still exist at the original location. In this scenario, we proceed by copying them to the server instance we wish to attach the database. Next, we connect to the destination server instance and launch the Attach Databases dialog by selecting Attach from the Databases node in Object Explorer. The Attach Databases dialog is shown in Figure 10-2.

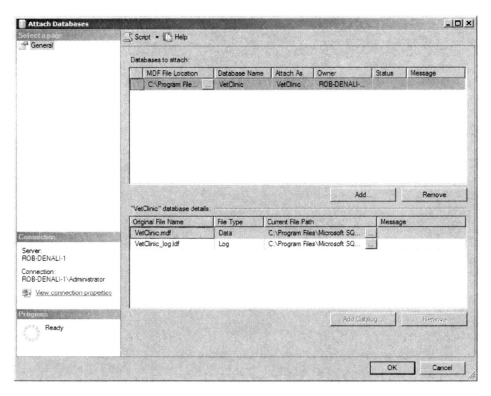

Figure 10-2. *Attach Databases dialog*

To attach a database navigate to the database files by clicking the Add button. When database files are selected, the dialog will populate the database details, as shown in the Figure 10-2. To attach the database, simply click OK, and the dialog will issue a `CREATE DATABASE . . . FOR ATTACH` statement that will perform the attachment.

Moving a Database Using the Copy Database Wizard

The Copy Database wizard allows you to copy databases and most of the objects that are outside of the database that the database may depend on. These objects are things like SQL Server login information and SQL Server Agent jobs. In this example, we are going to move the VetClinic database from the default instance to a named instance called DEV. To launch the Copy Database wizard select, Copy Database from the Tasks menu of the desired database. After the welcome screen page, the wizard will guide you through two additional pages where you enter the source and destination servers.

■ **Note**   Since the wizard creates a SQL Server Agent job to move the data, you will need SQL Server Agent running on the destination server. If you do not have SQL Server Agent running, you will receive an error message.

The next page, shown in Figure 10-3, asks you how to transfer the database.

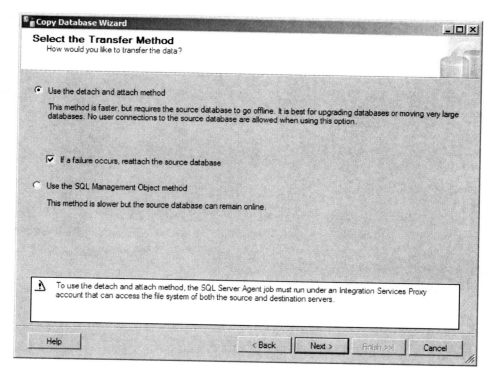

Figure 10-3. Select the Transfer Method page

There are two methods the wizard allows you use when moving databases. The first is the "detach and attach" method. This method uses the same idea that was described earlier in this chapter. The database is detached; a file copy occurs, and the database is attached to the new SQL Server instance. This option will disconnect any users that are connected to the database. If we cannot disconnect users, we have another option, and that is to use the SQL Management Object (SMO) method. Basically, you are using the SMO scriptor to script out the database and bulk copy the data from the source to the destination. SMO is a .NET API available for anyone to use to programmatically manage SQL Server. SSMS uses SMO extensively.

The next page in the wizard, shown in Figure 10-4, will allow us to select one or more databases to move or copy.

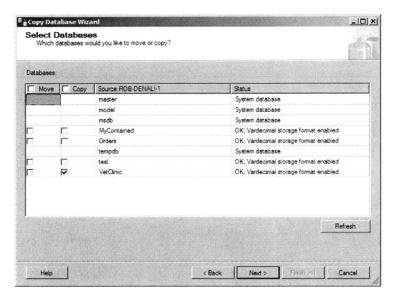

Figure 10-4. *Select Databases page*

The next page, shown in Figure 10-5, will allow you to specify the destination database configuration details.

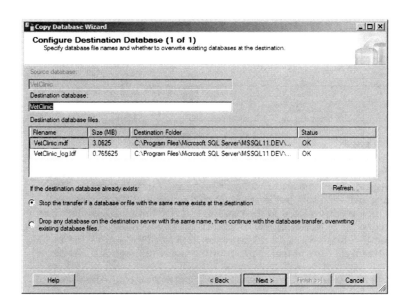

Figure 10-5. *Configure Destination Database page*

On this page, you can give the database a different name at the destination and optionally change the destination files and folders. In addition, you can specify what should happen if a database with the same name exists on the destination.

At this point, we have enough information about the database, but other objects not within the database that may need to be moved as well. The Select Server Objects page, shown in Figure 10-6, is the next page in the wizard, and it allows you to specify these objects. The most common objects to watch out for are SQL Logins. Database users of the copied database will be orphaned if you simply copy a database to a different server without moving any SQL Logins that are mapped to these database users.

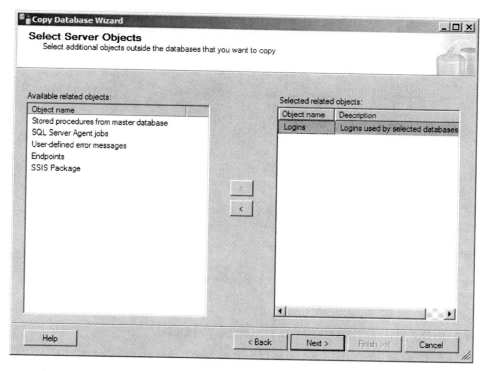

Figure 10-6. *Select Server Objects page*

This wizard creates a SQL Server Integration Services package that performs the actual work. The next page of the wizard, shown in Figure 10-7, shows the package configuration.

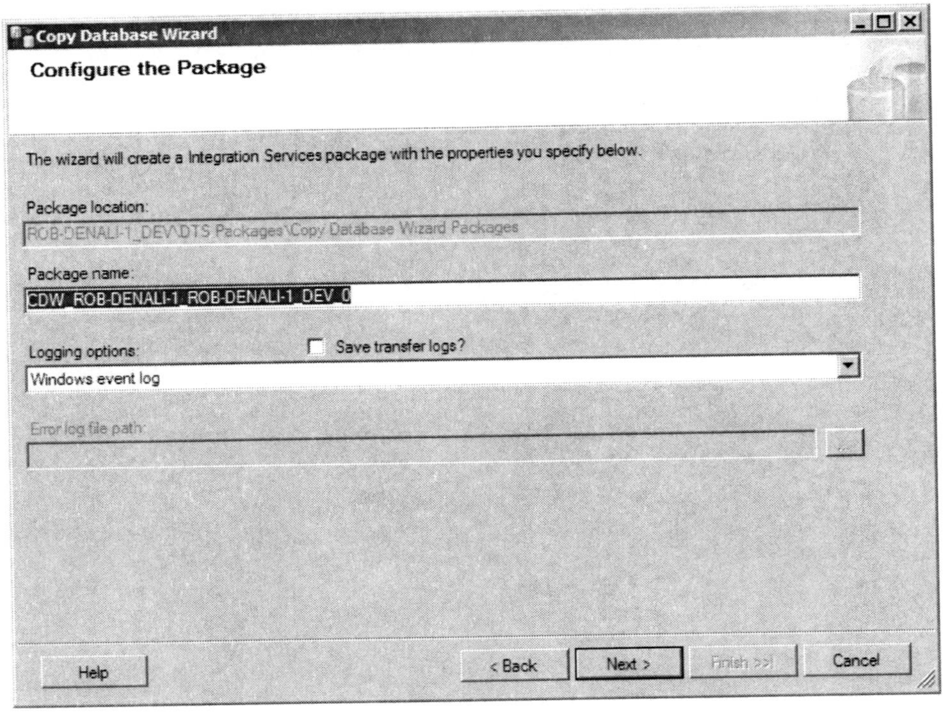

Figure 10-7. Package configuration

The next page in the wizard allows you to run the package now or schedule this copy for a specific time. After this page, the wizard provides you a summary.

Moving Data Using the Import and Export Wizard

The SQL Server Import and Export Wizard allows you to import or export data from SQL Server. The source or destination of these data include Microsoft Excel, Microsoft Access, Oracle, flat files, or any ODBC connection. In this example, we will load data from a text file into a table in our VetClinic database. The schema of the VetClinic includes a table called Pets that is defined with the following columns: pet_id, pet_name, pet_weight, and MicroChipID. We have a text file called dogs.txt that contains the following text:

```
pet_id,pet_name,pet_weight,MicroChipID
14,George,60,BN8XA
15,Betty,14,H73A1
```

To import data into the VetClinic database, select Import Data from the context menu of the VetClinic database in Object Explorer. This will launch the wizard, and the second page will ask for a data source. Selecting Flat File Source and entering the location of the dogs.txt file will populate the rest of the tabs within this page. The Choose a Data Source page is shown in Figure 10-8.

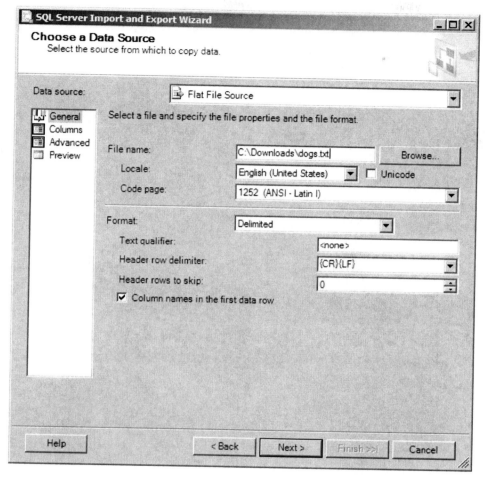

Figure 10-8. *Choose a Data Source page*

There are four tabs within this page: General, Columns, Advanced, and Preview. The General tab, which is shown in Figure 10-8, allows you to select the source file and any other information about the format of the text file such as if it had a header row or not. The Columns tab, shown in Figure 10-9, defines the rows and columns within the text file.

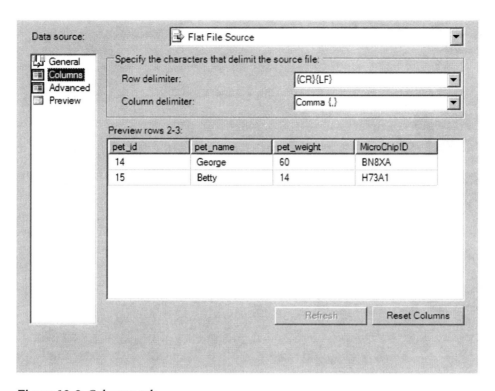

Figure 10-9. *Columns tab*

By default, the Columns tab selects a comma as the delimitor with a carriage return and line feed for the row delimiter. The Advanced tab, shown in Figure 10-10, is where you specify the data types that should be bound to the data you are importing.

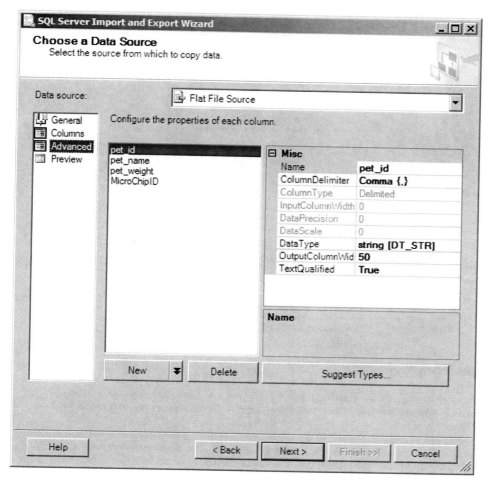

Figure 10-10. Advanced tab

Instead of going through each and every column and figuring out which data type it should be, you can have the wizard suggest data types by clicking the Suggest Types button. This will launch the dialog shown in Figure 10-11.

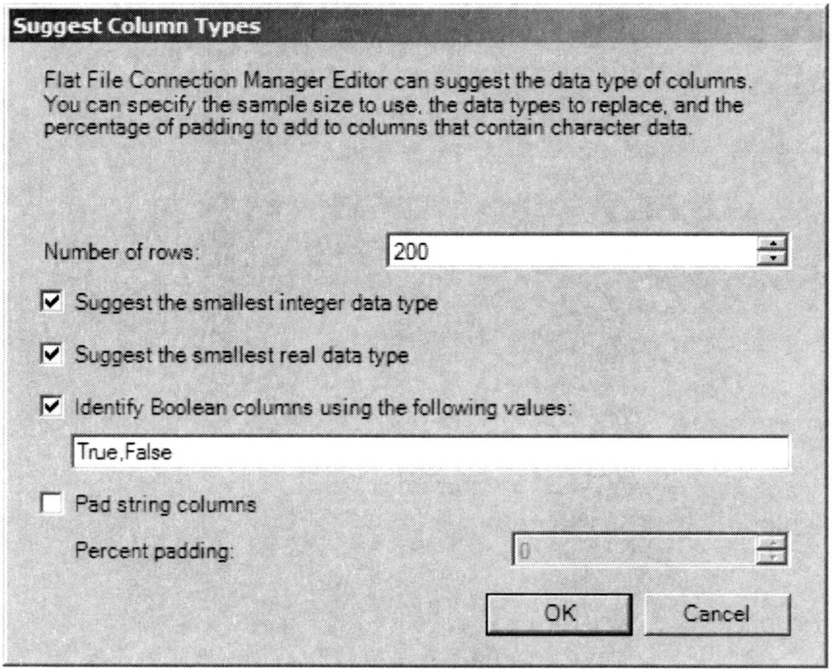

Figure 10-11. *Suggest Column Types dialog*

If you are inserting the data into an existing table, having the smallest data type isn't as important, since the table schema is already defined. However, the option is useful when you are creating a new table to receive the data.

The Choose a Destination page in Figure 10-12 allows you to select a destination to write the data. Note that the destination does not have to be a SQL Server instance. The destination can be a flat file, an Oracle database, or any of the other destination type available. Since we want to append this data to the existing VetClinic database, we select VetClinic from the Database down-down box.

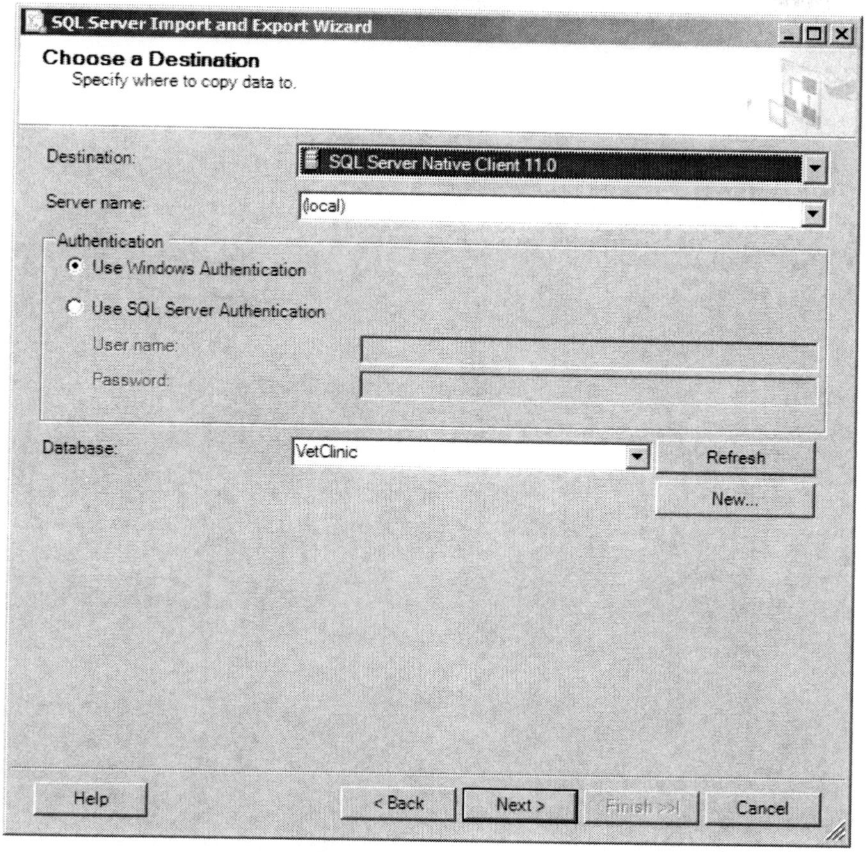

Figure 10-12. Choose a Destination page

Figure 10-13 shows the next page in the wizard, which prompts us to specify a destination table. We are prompted for a table, because we chose a database a destination. If we are appending data, we need to select the appropriate table; otherwise, our values will not map correctly. Once we do this, the bottom of the page will populate with a correct mapping, as shown in Figure 10-14.

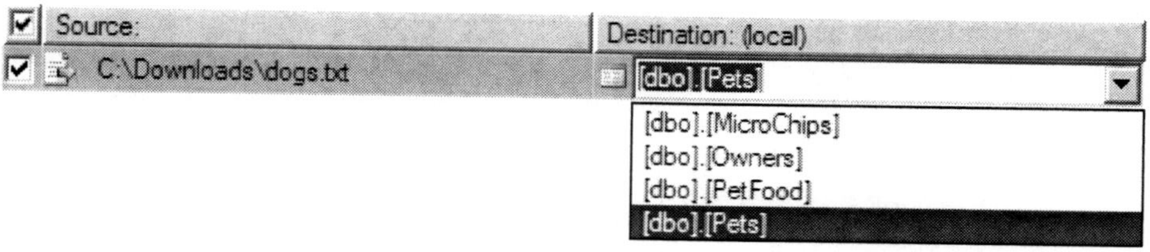

Figure 10-13. Destination table drop-down

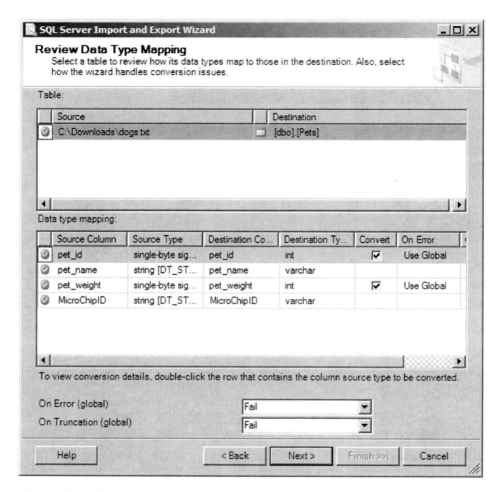

Figure 10-14. *Data Type mapping page*

The next pages in the wizard will allow you to import immediately or schedule the import to occur at a later time. If you run the import, you will see a status page that shows the results of the data movement. This status page is shown in Figure 10-15.

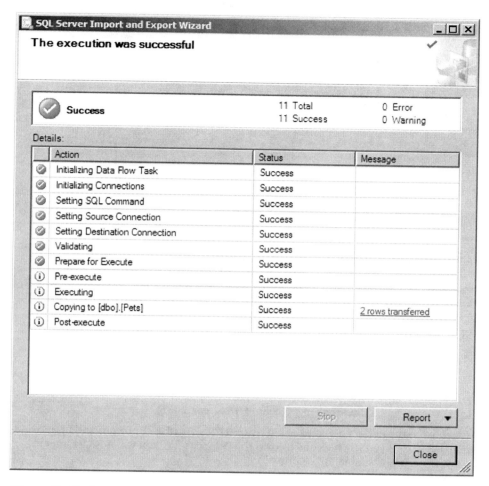

Figure 10-15. Execution status

Moving Data Using the Bulk Copy Program (BCP)

The Bulk Copy Program (BCP) is a command-line tool used to copy data between an instance of SQL Server and a data file. Where the Import and Export wizard can move data between multiple types of data sources, BCP only goes between SQL Server and a file. Issuing a BCP command without any parameters will give us a list of parameters. This list is shown in Figure 10-16.

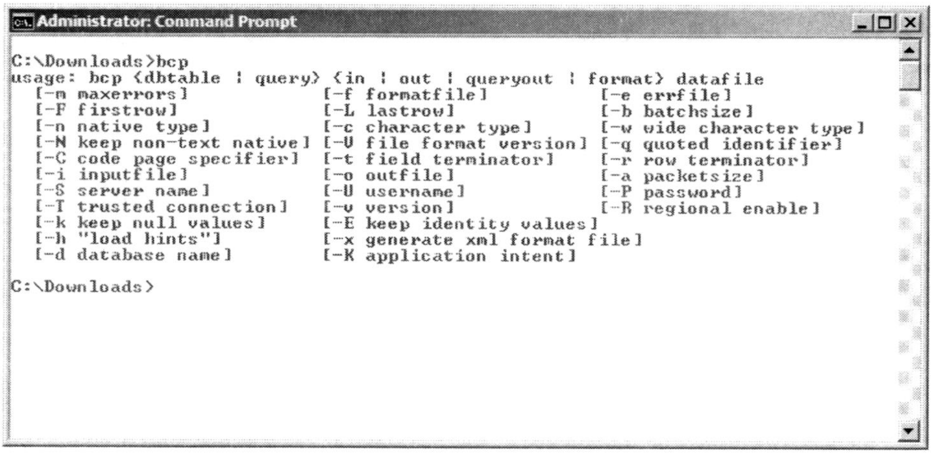

Figure 10-16. BCP.exe command line parameter list

Although its parameter list is relatively small, this little utility has been around for many iterations of SQL Server and is very powerful when used with the appropriate parameters. To move our data out of the database we can issue the following statement:

```
C:\Demo>bcp VetClinic.dbo.Pets out Pets.dat -T -c
```

```
Starting copy...
```

```
15 rows copied.
Network packet size (bytes): 4096
Clock Time (ms.) Total    : 1       Average : (15000.00 rows per sec.)
```

Here, we are connected to the default instance using trusted security (the -T option) and outputting the data to a file called Pets.dat. If you use notepad to view the Pets.dat file, you will notice that it's simply a plain text enumeration of the table, for example:

```
1     Zeus   185    398BF49
2     Lady   155    191ABBC
3     Deno   50     790AG441
4     Rex    44     CDD81322
5     Rover  15     A8719841
6     Roscoe 55     F5CAA29
7     Missy  67     B7C2A59
8     George 12     AA63BC5
9     Spot   34     CC8A674
10    Roxy   7      1A8AF59
11    Champ  95     81CB910
12    Penny  80     C710A6B
13    Fido   33     F82V
14    George 60     BN8XA
15    Betty  14     H73A1
```

To import data we can simply change IN to OUT and specify the destination server using the -S switch. For more information regarding BCP check out the SQL Server Books Online topic "bcp Utility" located at the following URL: http://msdn.microsoft.com/en-us/library/ms162802(v=SQL.110).aspx.

Checking Database Integrity

In SQL Server, a few key functions check the logical and physical integrity of the objects within the database. The most important function to be aware of is DBCC CHECKDB. "DBCC" is short for Database Console Command, and there are a number of DBCC commands that you will eventually use in your everyday DBA life. For a complete list see the article "DBCC (Transact-SQL)" located at the following URL: http://msdn.microsoft.com/en-us/library/ms188796.aspx.

DBCC CHECKDB checks the consistency of disk space allocation. When you issue a DBCC CHECKDB command, it actually executes three other DBCC commands: DBCC CHECKALLOC, DBCC CHECKTABLE, and DBCC CHECKCATALOG. Each of these can be executed individually as well, but if you issue DBCC CHECKDB, you are effectively already including them. Together, these commands check for issues like data purity where a value stored within the column falls outside the range of the data type defined for that column.

DBCC CHECKDB is a great tool to use as part of your maintenance routine for SQL Server databases. However, it is important to note the performance impacts that occur when you are running this command. DBCC CHECKDB may take a long time to run for very large databases and may use a lot of memory, CPU, and I/O bandwidth. DBCC CHECKDB makes heavy use of the tempdb database. All of these behaviors are expected because of the nature of what DBCC CHECKDB is doing to achieve its objective. Despite these issues with the command, there are some ways to mitigate. First, you could run this command with the parameter WITH PHYSICAL_ONLY. This only checks the physical structures of the database and does not check the internal logical structures. Alternatively, you could back up and restore the database on a separate system and then run the DBCC command. Although not a true representation of the production system, using a separate server is an option if your production system is maxed out already. Issuing a DBCC CEHCKDB (AdventureWorks2008R2) statement yields the following results, some of which are elided for brevity:

```
Service Broker Msg 9675, State 1: Message Types analyzed: 14.

Service Broker Msg 9676, State 1: Service Contracts analyzed: 6.

…

There are 1887 rows in 23 pages for object "sys.sysrscols".

DBCC results for 'sys.sysrowsets'.

There are 330 rows in 4 pages for object "sys.sysrowsets".

DBCC results for 'sys.sysclones'.

…
```

There are 181 rows in 2 pages for object "Person.vStateProvinceCountryRegion".

DBCC results for 'sys.xml_index_nodes_1765581328_256000'.

There are 195 rows in 3 pages for object "sys.xml_index_nodes_1765581328_256000".

DBCC results for 'Production.ScrapReason'.

There are 16 rows in 1 pages for object "Production.ScrapReason".

DBCC results for 'sys.xml_index_nodes_1765581328_256001'.

There are 301696 rows in 2151 pages for object "sys.xml_index_nodes_1765581328_256001".

DBCC results for 'sys.xml_index_nodes_526624919_256000'.

There are 9113 rows in 64 pages for object "sys.xml_index_nodes_526624919_256000".

DBCC results for 'HumanResources.Shift'.

...

There are 1764 rows in 70 pages for object "Production.vProductAndDescription".

DBCC results for 'sys.syscommittab'.

There are 0 rows in 0 pages for object "sys.syscommittab".

DBCC results for 'Sales.SalesTerritoryHistory'.

There are 17 rows in 1 pages for object "Sales.SalesTerritoryHistory".

CHECKDB found 0 allocation errors and 0 consistency errors in database 'AdventureWorks2008R2'.

DBCC execution completed. If DBCC printed error messages, contact your system administrator.

There are quite a few articles written on the subject of DBCC checks and very large databases. One such article is called "DBCC Checks and Terabyte-Scale Databases" located at the following URL: http://sqlcat.com/sqlcat/b/technicalnotes/archive/2009/08/13/dbcc-checks-and-terabyte-scale-databases.aspx.

Maintaining Indexes

If you have spent any time with relational databases, you have probably come in contact with indexes. Indexes are essential for driving peak query performance of SQL Server or any other relational database.

Indexes conceptually work like the index of a book. If you picked up a technical reference book looking for more information on the SELECT T-SQL command, you would go to the index and look up the page number where this function is referenced. Without an index, you would have to go to every single page in the book to see if it has this information. If the book is large, this could take a really long time. Indexes are discussed in more detail in Chapter 5.

SQL Server has a number of different types of indexes that can be used to optimize query performance. For a complete list of indexes, take a look at the article "Indexes" available at http://msdn.microsoft.com/en-us/library/ms175049(v=SQL.110).aspx. The most common types of indexes you will encounter as a DBA will be *clustered* and *nonclustered*. The key difference between these two is how SQL Server stores the data when you create an index of these types. A clustered index stores the data rows in order based on the clustered index key. The order is implemented as a B-tree index structure. For a clustered index, the data is stored on disk in this structure and thus only one clustered index can be defined on a table. If you want to create another index on the table, you can define a nonclustered index. A nonclustered index does not change the data as it is physically stored within the database. You can have many nonclustered indexes defined on a table.

Detecting Fragmentation

As data is added, modified, and removed from the table, indexes that are defined become fragmented. This fragmentation occurs as a result of the data not being in the place where the index thinks it should be.

When a fragmentation occurs, SQL Server takes longer to scan through the data to find the value. The degree of fragmentation can be found using the DBCC SHOWCONTIG command. To illustrate this function, let's create a test database, table, and sample data in the following script:

```
CREATE DATABASE Sales
GO
CREATE TABLE Customers (customer_id INT PRIMARY KEY,
customer_name CHAR(255) NOT NULL)
GO
INSERT INTO Customers VALUES(1,'user1')
GO
DECLARE @i INT
WHILE (@i<1000)
BEGIN
INSERT INTO Customers(customer_id,customer_name) VALUES(@i,'UserXXXX')

SET @i=@i+1
END
GO
```

We can issue the DBCC SHOWCONTIG command and pass the name of the table to look only at that table. If we omit the table name, the command will enumerate all indexes in the database. Here, we pass the name of the table that we've just created:

```
DBCC SHOWCONTIG('Customers')
```

This command yields the following results:

```
DBCC SHOWCONTIG scanning 'Customers' table...

Table: 'Customers' (2107154552); index ID: 1, database ID: 1

TABLE level scan performed.

- Pages Scanned................................: 36

- Extents Scanned.............................: 6

- Extent Switches.............................: 5

- Avg. Pages per Extent.......................: 6.0

- Scan Density [Best Count:Actual Count].......: 83.33% [5:6]

- Logical Scan Fragmentation ..................: 5.56%

- Extent Scan Fragmentation ...................: 66.67%

- Avg. Bytes Free per Page....................: 270.5

- Avg. Page Density (full)....................: 96.66%

DBCC execution completed. If DBCC printed error messages, contact your system administrator.
```

To interpret these results, you need to understand the concept of a database *page*. A page is the basic unit of I/O for the database. It consists of 8,096 bytes of information. SQL Server reserves 96 of those bytes for header information, which includes the page number, page type, the amount of free space on the page, and the allocation unit ID of the object that owns the page. An *extent* is a physically contiguous block of 8 pages. In our example, the data in the table is contained within 36 pages. Six extents were allocated to contain these 36 pages. In an ideal world, these six extents would all be right next to each other physically on disk such that when SQL Server was querying it could read all the pages sequentially.

The ideal sometimes happens, but over time, without any maintenance additional extents will be allocated to hold data, data will be removed from existing pages, and the number of switches required between the extents to access pages in the logical order of the index will increase. The Extent Switches property in the preceding output tells you this number and optimally should be equal to the number of extents minus 1. In our example, a value of 5 is optimal, because we have six extents.

Another important metric is Scan Density. Under ideal conditions, the best count is the same as the number of extent switches, assuming everything is linked contiguously on disk. Actual Count is the actual number of extent switches that were required for all the data given the current amount of fragmentation. Any best-over-actual ratio under 100 percent means some fragmentation exists. Typically, a value less than 40 percent indicates the need for defragmentation. The preceding output shows a ratio of 83.33 percent, so there is no compelling need to defragment.

`Logical Scan Fragmentation` is another item to look at. It shows the ratio of pages with a different physical order from the logical order. In this example, the `Logical Scan Fragmentation` is 5.56 percent. A percentage between 0 and 15 percent is acceptable. A database with a metric over 15 percent is a candidate for defragmentation. This counter gives an indication of a table's fragmentation level. If a table is fragmented, you will suffer unnecessary disk I/O, which will affect end user query performance.

Defragmenting Indexes

The main command used to remove fragmentation is `ALTER INDEX`. `ALTER INDEX WITH REBUILD` will drop and re-create all the clustered indexes. When the command is used with the keyword `ONLINE`, SQL Server will build a new index on the side, and when the new index is ready to be used, it swaps out the old index with the new one allowing users to continue to use an index on their queries. This is good to use when you do not want to lock users out of the underlying tables that are part of the index. However, there is a performance cost when rebuilding an index, so it should only be done when necessary.

In our example, we don't have a lot of data, so rebuilding of the index will be very fast, and we can issue the following statement:

```
ALTER INDEX PK__Customer__CD65CB85E1E35C48 ON Customers REBUILD
```

■ **Note** The name of the primary key will be different for you as SQL Server randomly generates the name because we didn't specify one. To list the indexes available on your table, execute `sp_helpindex 'Customers'`. This will show you the name of the primary key index on the `Customers` table.

After the `ALTER INDEX` statement is issued, if you run another `DBCC SHOWCONTIG` statement you will see significant differences, as shown here:

```
DBCC SHOWCONTIG scanning 'Customers' table...

Table: 'Customers' (277576027); index ID: 1, database ID: 9

TABLE level scan performed.

- Pages Scanned................................: 34

- Extents Scanned.............................: 5

- Extent Switches.............................: 4

- Avg. Pages per Extent.......................: 6.8
```

```
- Scan Density [Best Count:Actual Count].......: 100.00% [5:5]

- Logical Scan Fragmentation ..................: 0.00%

- Extent Scan Fragmentation ...................: 0.00%

- Avg. Bytes Free per Page....................: 229.4

- Avg. Page Density (full)....................: 97.17%

DBCC execution completed. If DBCC printed error messages, contact your system administrator.
```

At this point, we have no fragmentation in the primary key index.

Distribution Statistics

SQL Server stores information on the distribution of data in columns and indexes. This information includes things like the number of rows of data and a distribution of data within a particular column. This data is used by the query optimizer to select the most efficient query plan for retrieving the data. As a DBA, you need to understand how statistics are used and also how to update them manually when needed.

Understanding Distribution Statistics

Two catalog views provide additional information about statistics; they are sys.stats and sys.indexes. If we join these two tables, we can get a simple list of the statistics created on the tables.

To illustrate statistics, let's create a table that will include a lot of random numbers. The script to create this table is as follows:

```
CREATE TABLE LotsOfRandomNumbers
(number_generated INT,
seed INT,
random_number FLOAT)
```

Next, let's fill the table with 100,000 random values with the following script:

```
DECLARE @i INT
DECLARE @RNF FLOAT
DECLARE @RNI INT
SET @i=0

WHILE (@i <= 100000)
BEGIN
SET @RNF = RAND(@i)
INSERT INTO LotsOfRandomNumbers VALUES((CAST(0x7FFFFFFF AS int) * @RNF),@i,@RNF )
SET @i=@i+1
END
```

Since we want the range of values to include all possible integers, we use CAST(0x7FFFFFF). Next, let's create a nonclustered index on the number_generated column as follows:

```
CREATE NONCLUSTERED INDEX NC_number_generated ON dbo.LotsOfRandomNumbers(number_generated)
```

When we created the index, SQL Server created some statistics on the table that we could obtain by querying the sys.indexes and sys.stats tables. The following query joins these two catalog views into a simple result set that shows you a list of statistics created for the given table.

```
SELECT s.object_id,
   OBJECT_NAME(s.object_id) AS table_name,
   COL_NAME(s.object_id, sc.column_id) AS 'Column Name',
    s.Name AS 'Name of the statistics',
           s.auto_created as 'Is automatically created'
FROM sys.stats AS s
 INNER JOIN sys.stats_columns AS sc
 ON s.stats_id = sc.stats_id AND s.object_id = sc.object_id
WHERE s.object_id = OBJECT_ID( 'dbo.LotsOfRandomNumbers')
```

Issuing this query will result in the following:

object_id created	table_name	Column Name	Name of the statistics	Is automatically
341576255	LotsOfRandomNumbers	number_generated	NC_number_generated	0

We created the index, which created the statistics; however, if we issued a query against this data that didn't leverage the index, SQL Server would want to create some more statistics so that it could answer the query faster the next time. To demonstrate SQL Server creating statistics, issue the following query:

```
SELECT seed FROM LotsOfRandomNumbers WHERE random_number < .5
```

If you rerun the earlier query to report on statistics for the table, you will see the following result:

object_id automatically created	table_name	Column Name	Name of the statistics	Is
341576255	LotsOfRandomNumbers	number_generated	NC_number_generated	0
341576255	LotsOfRandomNumbers	random_number	_WA_Sys_00000003_145C0A3F	1

SQL Server has created a statistic, _WA_Sys_00000003_145C0A3F, with information on the random_number column. SQL Server Management Studio also enumerates statistics for given objects and provides a lot of the same information you can get via T-SQL statements. If we expand the Statistics node under the LotsOfRandomNumbers table, we can see our two statistics created, as shown in Figure 10-17.

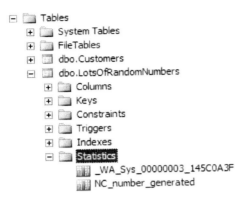

Figure 10-17. *Statistics node in SSMS*

You can view the properties of a statistic by selecting the statistic and choosing Properties from the context menu. This will launch the Statistics Properties dialog box shown in Figure 10-18.

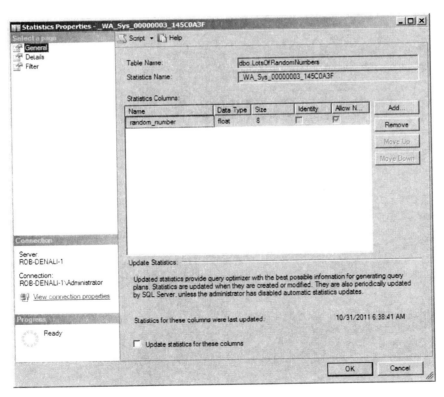

Figure 10-18. *General tab of the Statistics Properties dialog box*

From this panel, you can see the columns that are included, as well as an option to update the statistics. There are two database-level options related to statistics that are important: Auto Create Statistics and Auto Update Statistics. When we executed our previous script, SQL Server automatically created a new statistic for these data, because the Auto Create Statistics setting is true for the database.

Updating Statistics

When Auto Update Statistics is on, SQL Server will update statistics only when certain thresholds are met such as the number of rows in the table increase or decrease by 10 percent. Both of these database properties are enabled by default. Even though SQL Server will automatically update statistics, there may be cases when, according to SQL Server, the threshold hasn't been met, but the statistics are out of date and causing query performance problems. This can occur when the number of rows stays about he same, but there are many updates, deletes, and inserts to the table. Also, if you have a very large table, it may take a long time to achieve 10 percent, thus you may want to manually update statistics. You can do this via SSMS manually by checking the box. Alternatively, you could issue an UPDATE STATISTICS T-SQL statement as follows:

```
UPDATE STATISTICS dbo.LotsOfRandomNumbers
```

This statement allows you more granularity in how much of the data to sample in obtaining the statistics. If you have a very large table, updating statistics may take quite a while, and you may be better off updating just a sample of the data. For example, you could update the statistic and have SQL Server only sample 25 percent of the data by issuing the following:

```
UPDATE STATISTICS dbo.LotsOfRandomNumbers WITH SAMPLE 25 PERCENT, ALL
```

Executing this command takes noticeably less time than the previous UPDATE STATISTICS command. Keep in mind though that the statistics will be less effective given the smaller sample size.

Creating Maintenance Plans

A *maintenance plan* is a workflow of database-maintenance–related tasks that you define to run on demand or at a specific time via the SQL Server Agent job scheduling service. You can easily create a plan using the Maintenance Plan Wizard. This wizard is designed to give you a head start in building out your maintenance plan. When you are finished with the wizard, the end result is a maintenance plan that you can go back to and modify as you see fit. To illustrate, let's launch the Maintenance Plan Wizard from the Maintenance Plans container node under the Management node in Object Explorer. The first properties page will be Select Plan and is shown in Figure 10-19.

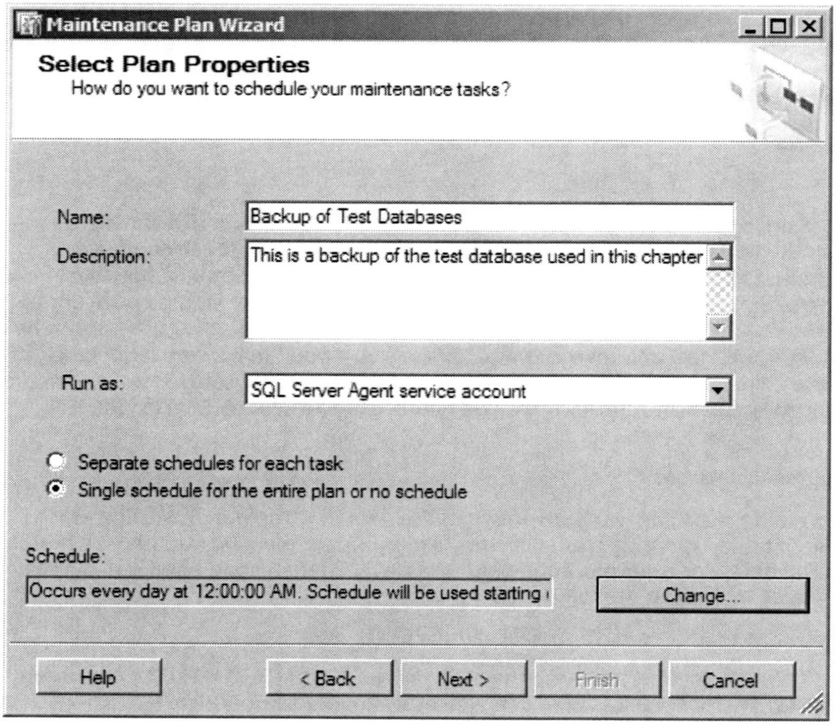

Figure 10-19. *Select Plan Properties dialog*

From this first page, we can specify if the tasks that we are defining should run on separate schedules or the same schedule. We can also specify which credentials should be used when the maintenance plan runs. The next page, shown in Figure 10-20, allows us to select which tasks should be included in this maintenance plan.

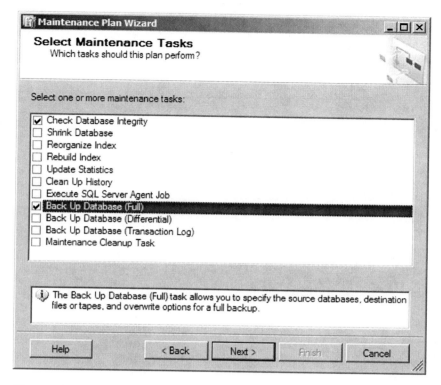

Figure 10-20. Select Maintenance Tasks page

Do not worry about adding the exact tasks you want the first time. When this wizard finishes, you can add, remove, and change tasks using the designer, which we will cover later in this section. For this demonstration, we will select the Check Database Integrity and Back Up Database (Full) tasks.

The next page in the wizard will allow you to change the order of execution of the tasks. By default, it checks the integrity first and then performs the database backup so there is no need to change the order for this particular example. The next two pages will ask us to provide details on the objects within the database that we wish to check the integrity of and back up. Figures 10-21 and 10-22 show the Check Database Integrity and Backup Database pages. Depending on which tasks you select, you will have a property page for each task selected.

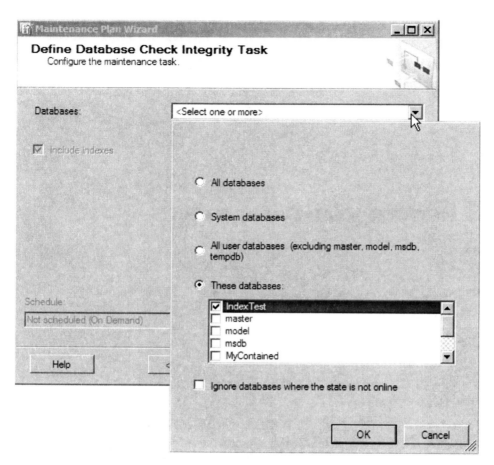

Figure 10-21. Check Database Integrity Task page

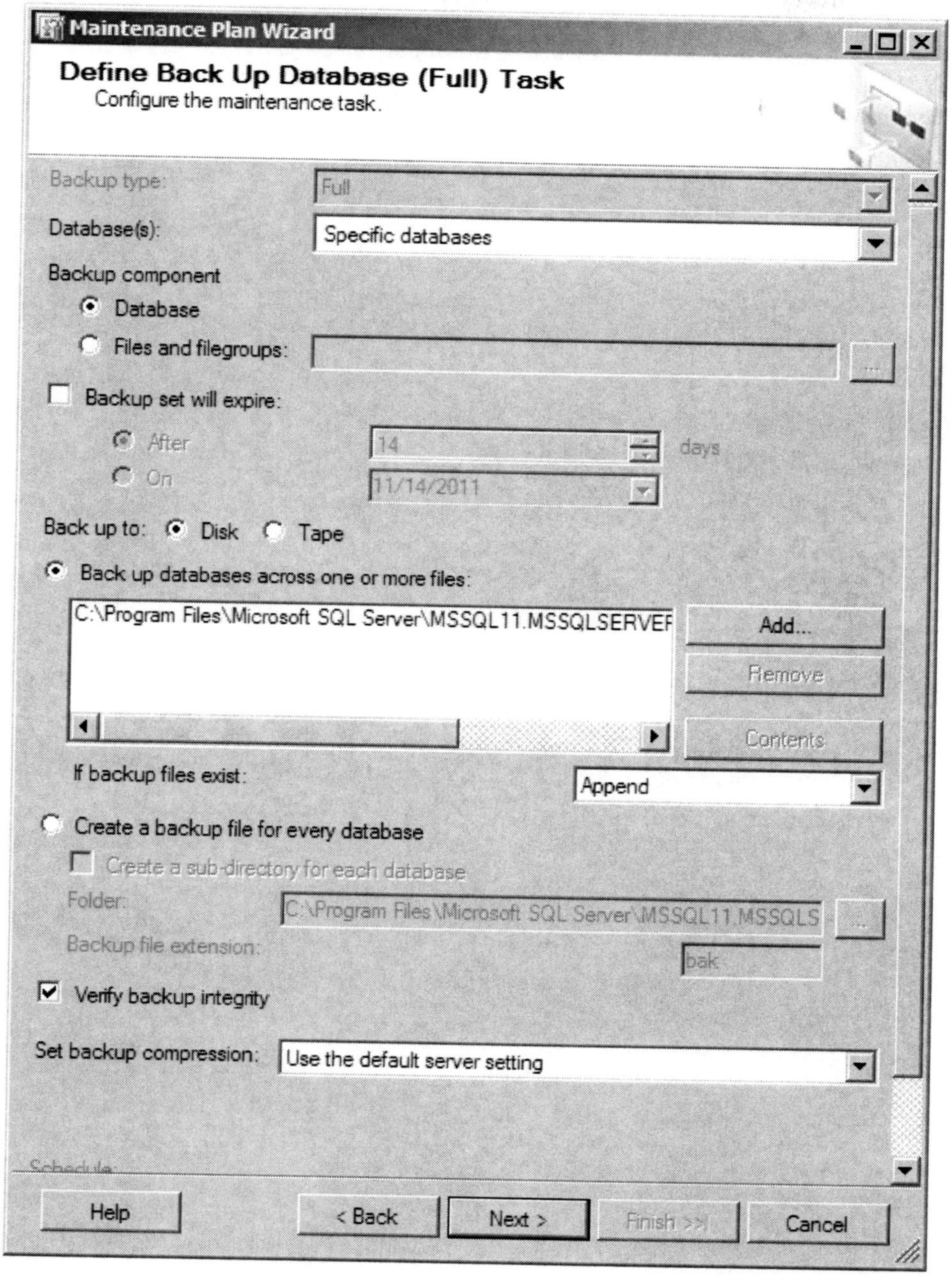

Figure 10-22. *Full Database Backup task page*

The next page in the wizard will ask you if you want to write a report of the maintenance plan execution. You also have the option of automatically sending this report via e-mail. Once we have completed the wizard, we can see our new maintenance plan by selecting Modify from the context menu of the maintenance plan we just created. This context menu is shown in Figure 10-23.

Figure 10-23. *Context menu of the Backup of Test Databases maintenance plan*

Modifying a maintenance plan will launch the maintenance plan designer in a document window within SQL Server management studio. From here, we can see a single subplan that was created by the wizard, as shown in Figure 10-24.

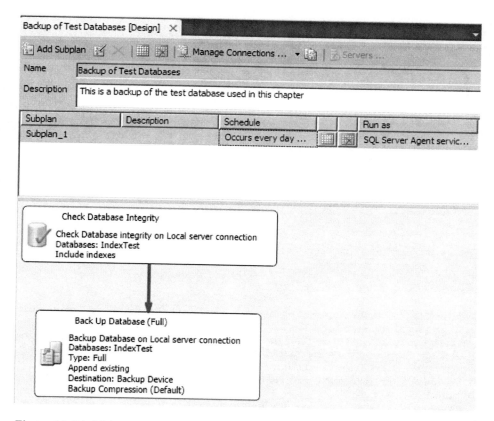

Figure 10-24. *Maintenance Plan created by the Maintenance Plan Wizard*

If we want to include additional tasks, we can simply drag and drop tasks onto the designer surface from the toolbox. If the toolbox is not shown in SSMS, you can select View Toolbox from the View menu. Here, you can see a bunch of maintenance tasks to include in the plan. By clicking and dragging, you can create a fairly complete maintenance plan, like the one shown in Figure 10-25.

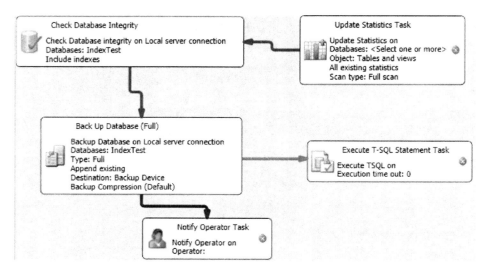

Figure 10-25. *Maintenance plan showing additional tasks*

The lines that join the tasks define the workflow for the plan, such as what path the task should take on failure or completion. Notice that Figure 10-25 has tasks with a red "X" icon. This tells you that more information is needed before the plan can successfully run. One of the pieces of information neeed is the server connection. By default, you are defining the maintenance plan to run against the current local server, but you can add remote servers to the list and have the maintenance plan perform the tasks against these servers. To add additional servers to run maintenance tasks against add them using the Manage Connections button.

Maintenance plans are an easy way to quickly define and implement your maintenance strategy. For more information read the article, "Maintenance Plans" located at `http://msdn.microsoft.com/en-us/library/ms187658(v=SQL.110).aspx`.

Scheduling Maintenance Tasks

SQL Server Agent is a Windows service that is installed when you install SQL Server itself. By default, it is not started, but if you want to leverage maintenance plans or features like Database Mail, you may need to start it. This can be done by connecting to the SQL Server instance, navigating to the SQL Server Agent node, and selecting Start from the context menu.

Previously, in Chapter 8, SQL Server Agent was discussed in depth as it relates to scheduling database backups. As a refresher, SQL Server Agent uses the concept of jobs and schedules. A job consists of one of more job steps. Each job step is a specific type. Types include T-SQL scripts, PowerShell scripts, and SQL Server Integration Services Package execution commands to name a few. You can define a job schedule and bind this schedule to run one or more jobs. DBAs use SQL Server Agent frequently to schedule routine maintenance of their SQL Server databases.

For more information on SQL Server Agent, check out the TechNet Webcast "SQL Agent in SQL Server 2005" located at `https://msevents.microsoft.com/CUI/EventDetail.aspx?culture=en-US&EventID=1032275577&CountryCode=US`. Although this webcast is based on SQL Server 2005, the core concepts are still the same with the latest version of SQL Server.

Creating Log Files

SQL Server creates a log file every time the server instance starts. It writes valuable information to this log file and is a great place to look at when you want to troubleshoot any issues with SQL Server. This information includes status from backup and restore operations, kernel messages, and server-level error messages. By default, the location of this error log is located in the following folder on the drive where your SQL Server instance is installed:

```
Program Files\Microsoft SQL Server\MSSSQL.n\MSSQL\LOG\ERRORLOG
```

Although you could use a text editor to view these error log files, there is a more useful Log File Viewer dialog within SQL Server Management Studio that is optimized for loading this potentially large amount of information. To view the error log using SSMS, enumerate the SQL Server Error Logs node under the Management node for the selected SQL Server instance. This node is shown in Figure 10-26.

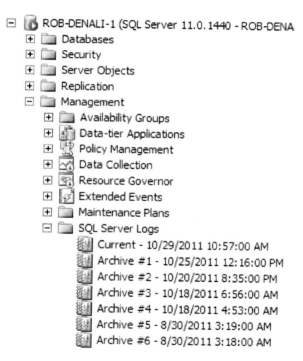

Figure 10-26. SQL Server Logs node in SSMS

To view the log, right-click the current log, and select View SQL Server Log. This will launch the Log File Viewer dialog shown in Figure 10-27.

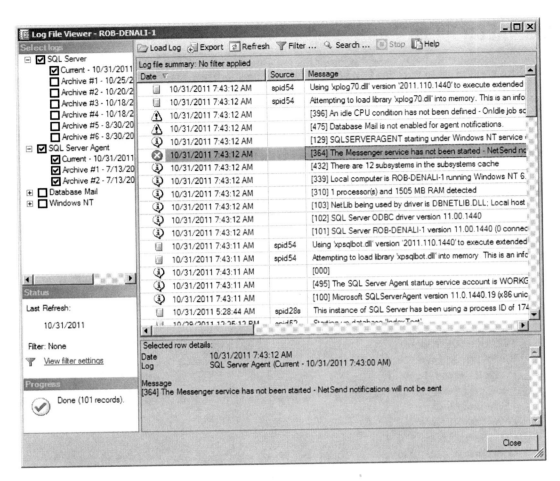

Figure 10-27. *Log File Viewer dialog*

This dialog will show you the current log file, because that is the node we launched it from in SSMS. The real power of this dialog is that we can add additional logs and look that the results in chronological time. For example, when we check the SQL Server Agent node, and all the SQL Server Agent logs are combined with the SQL Server engine logs. We can also add Windows NT logs by simply clicking the check box.

SQL Server keeps six log files with the file names ending in `.1`, `.2`, and so on. DBAs can force SQL Server to write to a new log file by issuing a `sp_cycle_error_log` command. However, under normal operating conditions, you usually do not need to do this unless you want to copy off the log to another location.

Summary

This chapter discussed some of the key maintenance tasks for DBAs. First, as a DBA, you sometimes move data. With SQL Server, there are a few ways to do this, each with its own pros and cons. Strategies that were discussed included moving data using the database "attach and detach" method, the Copy Database Wizard, and the Import and Export wizard. Next, this chapter covered the common maintenance tasks performed by database administrators. By far, the most common tasks for DBAs are backing up and restoring databases. These tasks are not covered in this chapter; rather, each has its own chapter in this book. Other common tasks that are the DBA's responsibility include checking database integrity, maintaining indexes, and creating maintenance plans.

Table 10-1 lists some resources supporting the content discussed in this chapter.

Table 10-1. Resources

Title	URL
"bcp Utility"	http://msdn.microsoft.com/en-us/library/ms162802(v=SQL.110).aspx
"DBCC (Transact-SQL)"	http://msdn.microsoft.com/en-us/library/ms188796(v=SQL.110).aspx
"DBCC Checks and Terabyte-Scale Databases"	http://sqlcat.com/sqlcat/b/technicalnotes/archive/2009/08/13/dbcc-checks-and-terabyte-scale-databases.aspx
"Indexes"	http://msdn.microsoft.com/en-us/library/ms175049(v=SQL.110).aspx
"Maintenance Plans"	http://msdn.microsoft.com/en-us/library/ms187658(v=SQL.110).aspx
"SQL Agent in SQL Server 2005"	https://msevents.microsoft.com/CUI/EventDetail.aspx?culture=en-US&EventID=1032275577&CountryCode=US

CHAPTER 11

SQL Server Security

Understanding the SQL Server security model and how to effectively implement and manage a secure SQL environment is important for a DBA. If your employer's data gets compromised, it's not just your job that is lost; it could also affect the lives of many people outside your company. You have probably heard stories of hackers obtaining the credit card information of thousands of helpless consumers. All these thefts could have been prevented had proper security measures been in place. SQL Server comes with a well-tested security model that enables DBAs to delegate access control from the server level down to the column level and, with the help of native encryption capabilities, to the individual column entries. In this chapter, you will learn how users are authenticated and authorized within SQL Server, and you'll learn some best practices to follow with respect to the security of your SQL Server instances.

Terminology

Before we dive deep into the security topic, it's important to first define some key concepts. To help in this discussion, imagine the scenario where you want to access your valuables that are in a safety deposit box. Safety deposit boxes, if you're not familiar, are metal boxes of different sizes that store valuables and are located in a vault at a bank. They usually require a key to open them. In addition, a bank will often ask for identification before allowing you to get your box.

Authentication

The bank needs to make sure you are who you claim you are. They do this by asking for identification, traditionally a driver's license. This action is called *authentication*. SQL Server makes sure you are who you claim you are by asking for credentials. You give SQL Server credentials in one of two ways. You can give SQL Server a username and password combination. SQL Server will take a hash of the password you supplied and compare it with a hash of the password that is stored in its internal tables. If the two hashes match for the given username, you are authenticated. This type of authentication is known as SQL Server authentication.

    The other way to authenticate to SQL Server is through Windows authentication. With this type, you do not need to type in a password; rather, since you are logged into Windows, SQL Server asks Windows to verify your identity via your Windows security token.

Authentication Mode

In an ideal world, you would use only Windows authentication. The main advantage with a pure Windows authentication environment is a streamlined administration experience—you don't have to manage yet another set of credentials. To tell SQL Server what authentication modes to support, there is a server property called Server Authentication. It has one of two possible settings: Windows Authentication and SQL Server and Windows Authentication mode (which is also referred to as Mixed Mode). When SQL Server is in Windows Authentication mode, users will not be able to log in using SQL Server authentication. If Mixed Mode is selected, SQL Server will accept both Windows-authenticated and SQL Server–authenticated logins. Since it is easier to show examples using SQL Server–authenticated accounts than to create a Windows user, this book's examples will use SQL Server in SQL Server and Windows Authentication mode. To see which authentication mode your server is using, launch the Server Properties dialog box in SSMS by selecting Properties from the context menu of a SQL Server instance. Click the Security page within the Server Properties dialog box to see the authentication mode setting, as shown in Figure 11-1.

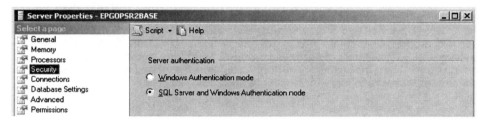

Figure 11-1. *Portion of the Server Properties dialog box showing the Security page*

Authorization

Getting back to the safety deposit box example, now that the bank has validated your identity using your driver's license, you are given the box. The box is locked with a key. Possessing this key authorizes you to open the box. In SQL Server, just because you have authenticated yourself and have a SQL Server login account, you do not necessarily have access to items contained within the server. The DBA has to explicitly authorize a user's access to objects within SQL Server. The DBA can grant access to one or more objects to a group of users or to a single user. You will learn more about granting permissions later in this chapter.

Server Instance vs. the Database

Databases within SQL Server are their own unique entities. SQL Server databases are designed to be easily detached from one server environment and reattached to another server without any extra work being done by a DBA. This concept is slightly different from what other database vendors implement, which is typically to marry the database and server instance more closely. With this independence come some additional security concepts to understand.

Databases have their own users called *database users* and their own roles called *database roles*. You will learn more about database roles later in this chapter. To authorize a SQL Server login access to a particular database, DBAs need to create a database user within the requested database, which maps to a SQL Server login. Database users are not shared among any databases on the server instance, but a single SQL Server login can map to one or more database users with each database user being in a different database.

■ **Note** In SQL Server 2012, database users can be directly provisioned within the database without an associated SQL Server login. You can read more about this concept in the "Contained Databases" section of this chapter.

In Figure 11-2, there is a single SQL Server login called Howard_Login. This login is mapped to two different database users. In the Sales database, Howard_Login is mapped to Howard_Sales_User. In the HR database, Howard_Login is mapped to Howard_HR_User.

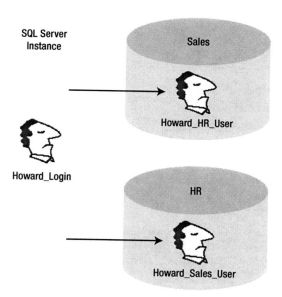

Figure 11-2. Representation of server login and database users

Since databases are their own unique entities, the permissions defined for Howard_Sales_User and Howard_HR_User can be different. In Figure 11-2's scenario, Howard logs in to SQL Server just once. He then has access to both the Sales and HR databases, with whatever permissions he has been given on each of those.

SQL Server Instance Security

Now that you have been introduced to the difference between a server instance and database with respect to a database user, it is time to dive into more detail around the security at the server instance level. A SQL Server login is also known as a *principal*, which is a generic term used to describe any entity that can request server resources. You may see the word *principal* being used throughout other publications including SQL Server Books Online. Some other principals within SQL Server include server roles, database users, database user roles, and application roles. In the Windows world, a principal can be a Windows domain group, a local group, a domain user, or a local user.

Creating a SQL Server Login

To create a new SQL Server login from SQL Server Management Studio (SSMS), navigate down the Object Explorer tree to the Logins node, which is a child of the Security node. Right-click, and select the New Login context menu item. This will launch the Login – New dialog box, shown in Figure 11-3.

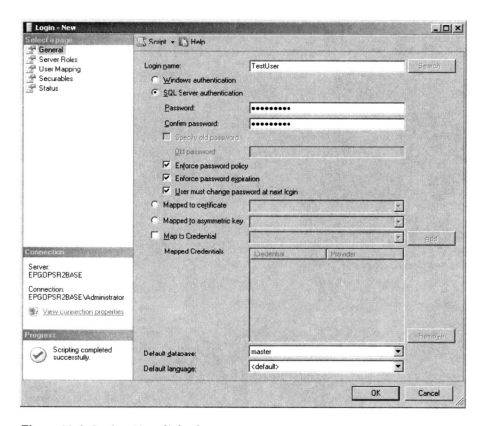

Figure 11-3. *Login – New dialog box*

The Login – New dialog box allows you to create four different types of logins. They are as follows: Windows authentication, SQL Server authentication, Mapped to certificate, and Mapped to asymmetric key. If you wanted to create a SQL Server login mapped to a Windows account, you select the "Windows authentication" radio button and type the Windows user account in the text box provided. This option does not require you to provide any password for the user. If you wanted to create a SQL Server–authenticated login, simply supply a login name and type a password. When you select the SQL Server Authentication radio button, you will notice three additional check boxes become available. "Enforce password policy" tells SQL Server to honor any Active Directory group policy configuration for passwords. "Enforce password expiration" tells SQL Server to remind users to change old passwords and to lock out expired logins. "Users must change password at next login" is self-explanatory. SSMS has a nice dialog box that pops up for the user if this option is selected and it's the first time the user has logged into SQL Server. The two other options, "Mapped to certificate" and "Mapped to asymmetric key", are used in advanced security scenarios like signing stored procedures.

SQL Server provides the ability to securely store credentials. These credentials are used for SQL Server Agent proxy accounts or for use with a cryptographic provider. The Map to Credential check box allows the DBA to add credentials that will be available to a given login for use with these specific features. If you are still wondering why you would ever want to store credentials to be used by a SQL Server login, consider this scenario. When you connect to SQL Server using SQL Server authentication, you have no identity to the Windows OS. If you want this SQL Server login to do something on the server that requires a Windows identity, using a credential solves the problem.

The dialog box in Figure 11-3 contains four other pages that have additional options. Using these other pages, you can add the login you are creating to server roles, map the login to database users, and configure other settings.

If you click OK on the General page, the login will be created. The T-SQL statement that creates a login is CREATE LOGIN. An example of creating the TestLo.gin login is as follows:

```
USE [master]
GO
CREATE LOGIN [TestLogin] WITH PASSWORD=N'PaSsWoRd!'
 MUST_CHANGE, DEFAULT_DATABASE=[master],
CHECK_EXPIRATION=ON, CHECK_POLICY=ON
GO
```

Server Roles

At the server instance level, there are nine fixed server roles that you can assign to a SQL Server login. *Fixed* means that you, as a DBA, cannot create your own server roles; rather, you have only the nine to choose from. In SQL Server 2012, database administrators can create their own server level roles. You will learn more about user-defined server roles later in this chapter. Assigning a principal to a server role allows that principal certain privileges within the SQL Server instance. Table 11-1 describes the nine fixed server roles.

Table 11-1. Fixed Server Roles

Server Role	Description
Public	This is the default server role for all logins. Any object that is granted public access will be available for all logins.
Sysadmin	Sysadmin has access to everything and can do any activity within SQL Server.
Serveradmin	This role can change server-wide settings and restart the SQL Server service.
Securityadmin	This role manages logins and their properties, including resetting passwords. Securityadmins can also manage database users.
Processadmin	This role can terminate processes that are running within SQL Server.
Setupadmin	This role can add or remove linked servers.
Bulkadmin	This role can issue a BULK INSERT statement.
Diskadmin	This role manages disk resources.
Dbcreator	This role can create, alter, drop, or restore any database.

Before you start assigning logins to various roles, it is important to know that, in reality, you probably will use very few of these roles. The most popular is the sysadmin role. The functionality of these roles has been superceded with the introduction of server permissions. Server roles are still relevant to learn and use, because in some cases, it is not possible to create a SQL Server login with enough server permissions to mimic a server role.

To add a SQL Server login to a server role, you can use the Server Roles tab in the Login – New dialog box (shown earlier in Figure 11-3). To add roles to a SQL Server login using T-SQL, you can use the sp_addsrvrolemember system stored procedure. For example, to give the dbcreator role to the Test,Login login, you can use the following script:

```
USE [master]
GO
EXEC sys.sp_addsrvrolemember @loginame = N'TestLogin', @rolename = N'sysadmin'
GO
```

■ **Note** It is not a best practice to arbitrarily give sysadmin access to SQL Server logins. Being a sysadmin is the highest elevated privilege within SQL Server, and its use should be highly discretionary.

Server Permissions

Before server permissions, if you wanted a login to be able to shut down the server, you needed to assign that login to the **serveradmin** role. Yet **serveradmin** imparts a number of other capabilities that you may not want to give that other user, such as the ability to change server-wide settings. With server permissions, you can now grant just the **SHUTDOWN** permission to a specific login, as shown in the following code:

```
USE master
GO
GRANT SHUTDOWN TO <login>
GO
```

where `<login>` is the name of the SQL Server login that you want to grant the **SHUTDOWN** permission to. There are 30 permissions that can be granted at the server instance scope. Table 11-2 shows a complete list of these permissions.

Table 11-2. *Server Permissions*

Permission	Applies to Securable
ADMINISTER BULK OPERATIONS	SERVER
ALTER	ENDPOINT, LOGIN
ALTER ANY CREDENTIAL	SERVER
ALTER ANY CONNECTION	SERVER
ALTER ANY DATABASE	SERVER
ALTER ANY EVENT NOTIFICATION	SERVER
ALTER ANY ENDPOINT	SERVER
ALTER ANY LOGIN	SERVER
ALTER ANY LINKED SERVER	SERVER
ALTER RESOURCES	SERVER
ALTER SERVER STATE	SERVER
ALTER SETTINGS	SERVER
ALTER TRACE	SERVER
AUTHENTICATE SERVER	SERVER

Continued

Permission	Applies to Securable
CONTROL	ENDPOINT, LOGIN
CONTROL SERVER	SERVER
CONNECT	ENDPOINT
CONNECT SQL	SERVER
CREATE ANY DATABASE	SERVER
CREATE DDL EVENT NOTIFICATION	SERVER
CREATE ENDPOINT	SERVER
CREATE TRACE EVENT NOTIFICATION	SERVER
IMPERSONATE	LOGIN
SHUTDOWN	SERVER
TAKE OWNERSHIP	ENDPOINT
VIEW DEFINITION	ENDPOINT, LOGIN
VIEW ANY DEFINITION	SERVER
VIEW ANY DATABASE	SERVER
VIEW SERVER STATE	SERVER
EXTERNAL ACCESS	SERVER

Each one of these permissions applies to one or more securables. A *securable* is a resource to which SQL Server regulates access. In Table 11-2, you can see that some securables are servers, some are logins, and some are endpoints. By using these permissions, you be very granular in what you allow other users to do.

Endpoints

An *endpoint* is a point of entry into SQL Server. Prior to SQL Server 2005, if you had a valid SQL Server login, you could connect via TCP/IP, shared memory, or any other protocol that was enabled on the server. With endpoints, you can now restrict what kinds of protocols a specific SQL Server login can connect by. Restricting available protocols reduces the area of attack for hackers. If you allow your sysadmin accounts to connect via shared memory only, you won't have to worry that someone remote will try to connect as sysadmin over a network connection. Shared memory clients can connect to only those server instances that are on the local server, so you have to be physically sitting at the machine or within a remote desktop session. As a best practice (and if possible to do within your organization), consider locking down access to sysadmin accounts.

In addition to the transport protocol, endpoints specify the payload. *Payloads* define the type of traffic that is allowed. For example, if you can create an HTTP endpoint that listens to SOAP traffic and assign the CONNECT permission to a specific SQL Server login, that SQL Server login can then submit SOAP queries via HTTP to SQL Server. Endpoints are highly leveraged by two key components within SQL Server: Service Broker and database mirroring. When you set up these features within SQL Server, you may notice additional endpoints created.

The sys.server_endpoints catalog view displays both system and user endpoints. Since there are no user-defined endpoints on the queried server, Table 11-3 simply shows the system endpoints that are available out of the box.

```
SELECT Name,Protocol_desc from sys.endpoints
```

The previous SELECT statement yields the information represented in Table 11-3.

Table 11-3. Endpoints

Name	Protocol_desc Value
Dedicated Admin Connection	TCP
TSQL Local Machine	SHARED_MEMORY
TSQL Named Pipes	NAMED_PIPES
TSQL Default TCP	TCP
TSQL Default VIA	VIA

By default, all SQL Server logins are granted CONNECT permissions to all the system endpoints listed in Table 11-3 with the exception of the dedicated administrator connection (DAC). The DAC is a special endpoint available only to members of the sysadmin role. It's a special single-user connection that is designed for an administrator to connect if he or she cannot connect via the normal connection method to SQL Server. The DAC is useful if a particular process ID within SQL Server is consuming too many resources, which, in turn, prevents additional user connections. With DAC, an administrator can always connect and troubleshoot any issues.

To help illustrate the power of endpoints, let's create a login, MyAppLogin, and allow it to connect only via shared memory. You do this by denying access to all the other protocols.

```
CREATE LOGIN MyAppLogin WITH PASSWORD='PaSsWoRd1'
GO
DENY CONNECT on ENDPOINT::[TSQL Default TCP] to MyAppLogin
GO
```

```
DENY CONNECT on ENDPOINT::[TSQL Default VIA] to MyAppLogin
GO
DENY CONNECT on ENDPOINT::[TSQL Named Pipes] to MyAppLogin
GO
```

You can test the ability to connect to SQL Server as MyAppLogin through SQL Server Management Studio. When you make a connection in SSMS, the connection dialog box has an Options button. Clicking that will allow you to select the Connection Properties tab. On this tab is a Network Protocol drop-down box. Here, you can force a certain protocol to be used when SSMS makes the connection to SQL. If you run the previous script and attempt to connect using TCP/IP with valid credentials, your connection request will fail. However, if you specify shared memory, the connection will succeed. This is illustrating the fact that you denied access to these endpoints for the MyAppLogin account.

Managing SQL Server logins and their memberships to each server role can be done using SQL Server Management Studio. There are also a number of system catalog views that help DBAs manage this information. For a complete list, read the "Security Catalog Views" article in SQL Server Books Online.

User-Defined Server Roles

SQL Server contains a plethora of permissions that a database administrator can assign to a particular login. In reality, once we have more than a few users managing permissions, this way becomes cumbersome. To address this, administrators can create a user-defined server role. These roles are defined at the SQL Server instance level, and specific server-level permissions can be assigned to a role. One scenario where user-defined server roles can be useful is when you have a requirement to give users elevated capability (such as the sysadmin role), but they only need a limited part of that role for thier jobs. With user-defined server roles, a system administrator can create a role that has specific elevated permissions like CONTROL SERVER. CONTROL SERVER is almost the same level as a sysadmin except that it obeys a DENY permission on an object. Given this, we can create user that has sysadmin-like access without being in the sysadmin role. If we wanted to prevent that user from modifying the server audits we can simply apply the DENY ALTER ANY SERVER AUDIT permission to the user-defined server role.

To illustrate user-defined server roles, let's consider the scenario where we want to create a new user-defined role that will contains logins who are database administrators. We want to make sure this group cannot change any audits that are defined but can perform all the other duties that a sysadmin can. First, we create the server role by issuing the CREATE SERVER ROLE statement as follows:

```
CREATE SERVER ROLE [DBA Role]
```

Next, we define the permissions assigned to this new role and add the necessary DENY permissions to restrict the user from changing audits or impersonating the auditor.

```
GRANT CONTROL SERVER TO [DBA Role]
GO
DENY ALTER ANY SERVER AUDIT TO [DBA Role]
GO
DENY ALTER ANY LOGIN TO [DBA Role]
GO
DENY IMPERSONATE ON LOGIN::CorporateAuditor TO [DBA Role]
GO
```

To add a login to a user-defined server role we issue the ALTER SERVER ROLE statement as follows:

```
ALTER SERVER ROLE [DBA Role] ADD MEMBER [Julie]
```

Given these statements, if we assigned our database administrator, Julie, to the DBA Role role, she could perform any administrative function except being able to change the audit. Since we denied this role the ability to change logins, she can't simply modify permissions on the group to give herself more privileges. Also, we denied the group the ability to change the server audits. This protects against a repudiation attack where the malicious user, or DBA Role member in this case, tried to cover up their tracks by tampering with the audit. Someone with CONTROL SERVER permission also has the ability to impersonate user accounts, thus, we want to ensure that this role doesn't have the ability to change the audit via the auditor's credentials, so we use DENY IMPERSONATE on the auditors login as well. The advantage with user-defined server roles is its flexibility when compared with the existing fixed server roles discussed earlier in this chapter. Now, organizations can create their own specific roles per their internal requirements.

Database Security

Database users are similar to SQL Server logins in that they are principals within the scope of a database. These users can be granted or denied specific permissions such as SELECT on a specific table. They can also be included in database roles. All database users are members of the public role. Thus, any permissions that are given to the public role will be in effect given to every database user.

Database Users

When you create a database, a few database users are created for you. One of them is dbo, which is the database owner; as the name implies, the role has permission to perform all activities within the database. Any member of the sysadmin fixed server role, who accesses a database is automatically mapped to the dbo user.

The guest database user is also always created. When SQL Server users log into a database where they do not have mappings, they are automatically mapped to the guest account. guest is created and is disabled by default. Thus, the default behavior for SQL Server logins that have no specific mapping is to not have any access at all to the database.

The sys and INFORMATION_SCHEMA views are created and used by SQL Server to provide you with views, dynamical management views, and catalog views of information about your database. An example of a catalog view is sys.database_princpals. This catalog view will show you information about database users and roles for the given database.

Schemas

When a database user is created, the user is assigned to a default schema. A *schema* is a logical collection of database objects. By grouping objects in a schema, a DBA can grant permissions to the schema that in turn would affect all the objects within the schema. If the user does not have a default schema, but the user is a member of a group that has a default schema, the default schema of the group will be used.

An Example of the "Wrong" Way

For example, assume you have two database users: DBAUser and DevUser. DBAUser is mapped to a SQL Server login who is a member of the sysadmin group. DevUser is a valid database user within the Accounting database. DevUser has no specific permissions granted, nor is it included in any database role other than `public`. The `DBAUser` user would like to give `DevUser` the ability to add tables to the `Accounting` database but is concerned about the security impact of this action.

The following script sets up the example I'm describing. It creates a database, a login, and a user named `DevUser`. Then the script grants the `CREATE TABLE` privilege to that user.

```
USE master
GO
CREATE DATABASE Accounting
GO
CREATE LOGIN DevLogin WITH PASSWORD='asdif983*#@YRfjndsgfD'
GO
USE Accounting
GO
CREATE USER DevUser FOR LOGIN DevLogin
GO
GRANT CREATE TABLE TO DevUser
GO
```

However, just having the `CREATE TABLE` privilege is not enough. If `DevUser` connected to SQL Server and tried to issue the following statement:

```
USE Accounting
GO
CREATE TABLE Customers
(id INT NOT NULL,
firstname VARCHAR(20) NOT NULL,
lastname VARCHAR(40) NOT NULL)
GO
```

then `DevUser` would receive the following error message:

```
Msg 2760, Level 16, State 1, Line 1

The specified schema name "dbo" either does not exist or you do not have permission to use it.
```

Just because `DevUser` has the permission to create a table within the `Accounting` database doesn't mean that user can start creating tables. The error message that comes back tells you that this user doesn't have access to a schema called `dbo`. By default, database users that are created without a default schema specified are assigned the `dbo` schema.

In this example, since the administrator never granted `DevUser` access to the `dbo` schema, `DevUser` cannot create objects within that schema. At this point, `DBAUser` could issue the following statement to grant `DevUser` the ability to add a table to the dbo schema:

```
GRANT ALTER ON SCHEMA::dbo TO DevUser
```

The "Right" Way

Granting the `ALTER` permission on the `dbo` schema to `DevUser` enables that user to create the table. However, by granting `ALTER` on this schema, `DevUser` can intentionally or unintentionally affect all the other objects within the dbo schema. For this reason, it is a best practice to create schemas that serve a specific purpose and grant permissions only to those users who need them. To correct this example, let's have the developer create their new Customers table in a schema called People. To start, the DBA will create the People schema and grant ALTER permissions to DevUser. The script is as follows:

```
CREATE SCHEMA People
GO
GRANT ALTER ON SCHEMA::People TO DevUser
GO
```

Now DevUser can issue the following statement to create the Customers table within the People schema:

```
USE Accounting
GO
CREATE TABLE [People.Customers]
(id INT NOT NULL,
firstname VARCHAR(20) NOT NULL,
lastname VARCHAR(40) NOT NULL)
GO
```

Four-Part Naming Convention

From the previous code sample, the table was created within the People schema. This can be seen by the two-part name People.Customers. You can create objects names using up to four parts. Formally the parts are as follows: Server.Database.Schema.Object.

■ **Note** There is another capability within SQL Server that allows you to link two SQL Servers together from a query perspective. When you reference another SQL Server instance within a query, you can create that SQL Server instance as a linked server to the current SQL Server instance that you are using.

For example, if you had created a linked server to the SQLPRODUCTION_2 server, you could issue a T-SQL statement that would create a table on the SQLPRODUCTION_2 server as follows:

```
CREATE TABLE [SQLPRODUCTION_2.Accounting.People.Customers]
```

More commonly, statements are executed within the current server context, so the first part is rarely used. The current database context is also usually defined earlier in the script (via a USE statement or via the default database in the connection string), so the second part is also not as common within scripts.

Default Schema

Previously, you learned that by default database users that are created without a default schema specified are assigned the dbo schema. The exception to this is if the user is mapped to a Windows group and that group has a default schema defined.

As a DBA, you can assign the default schema at user creation time. An example script is as follows:

```
CREATE USER DevUser FOR LOGIN DevLogin
WITH DEFAULT_SCHEMA = People
```

You might think of this statement as assigning the default schema.

Reassigning Schema Ownership

Prior to SQL Server 2005, there were essentially two schemas: dbo and another named after the user. Thus, if DevUser created the Customers table within his or her user schema, the two-part name for the Customers table would be DevUser.Customers. The problem with having application schemas based on usernames is that such a schema prevents you from ever deleting the underlying user. If DevUser leaves the company, you are stuck maintaining that user because of the objects within the user's schema. This behavior was a huge pain in the rear for many DBAs. And to circumvent the problem, the poor practice of creating all objects within the dbo schema came to be.

Since SQL Server 2005, you can now easily reassign the ownership of the schema, allowing you to drop the previous, underlying database user with ease. The following script will reassign the People schema to TestUser.

```
ALTER AUTHORIZATION ON SCHEMA::People TO TestUser
```

Having reassigned ownership of the People schema to TestUser, you may now drop DevUser.

Fixed Database Roles

There are two kinds of database roles: fixed and flexible. Fixed roles cannot be deleted and are provided within every database. Table 11-4 lists fixed database roles.

■ **Note** The msdb database contains additional fixed roles that are not found in any other database. These roles support the SQL Server Agent and SQL Server Integration Services features.

Table 11-4. Fixed Database Roles

Role Name	Description
db_owner	Other than sysadmin, no other role has a higher privilege within the database. Members of this role have full access to the database, including the ability to perform all configuration and maintenance activities on the database. They can even drop the database.
db_securityadmin	Members of this role can modify role membership and manage permissions.
db_accessadmin	Members of this role can add or remove database access to SQL Server logins.

Role Name	Description
db_backupoperator	Members of this role can back up the database.
db_ddladmin	Members of this role can run any Data Definition Language (DDL) command in a database.
db_datawriter	Members of this role can add, delete, or change data in all user tables.
db_datareader	Members of this role can read all data from all user tables.
db_denydatawriter	Members of this role cannot add, modify, or delete any data within the database.
db_denydatareader	Members of this role cannot read any data within a database.

In addition to using the UI in SSMS, numerous stored procedures and functions help DBAs work with database roles. The article "Database-Level Roles" in SQL Server Books Online does a good job at enumerating this list.

These fixed roles serve to define a general permission within the database. For example, the following script grants DevUser the db_datareader permission using the sp_addrolemember system stored procedure:

```
USE [Accounting]
GO
EXEC sp_addrolemember N'db_datareader', N'DevUser'
GO
```

In this example, DevUser would be able to read any table within the database regardless of whether they had SELECT permission defined.

■ **Note** There is an exception to this global grant behavior. If the DBA issued a DENY statement against DevUser on a specific object, that object would no longer be accessible by DevUser.

The global behavior of fixed database roles addresses some scenarios; however, to reduce the surface area for attack, it's better for you to grant specific permissions on objects to your users.

Database Permissions

If you are a database user in a database and are not a sysadmin or a member of the db_owner or db_datareader group, you will not be able to read any data within the database. To read data, an administrator needs to grant the user the SELECT permission. Similarly, if the user wants to add data to a table, they would need the INSERT permission. If the user wants to delete data, they would need the DELETE permission. There are many granular database permissions that you as an administrator can define for a given database user or role.

Also, there exists a permissions hierarchy within SQL Server. Some server-level permissions convey the rights of other permissions by implication. For example, if a database user is mapped to a login that was granted `ALTER ANY SERVER AUDIT` permission, this database user has the `ALTER ANY DATABASE AUDIT` permission even though that user might not have been explicitly given that permission. This implication also works within the scope of the database. For example, if a database user was granted `ALTER ANY ASSEMBLY`, the database user also has the `CREATE ASSEMBLY` permission, even without being explicitly given that permission. In both cases, `ALTER ANY SERVER AUDIT` and `ALTER ANY ASSEMBLY` are known as *covering permissions*.

SQL Server Books Online has an article called "GRANT Database Permission (Transact-SQL)." This article lists more than 60 possible database permissions and their covering database or server permissions. To help illustrate this concept, a sample of this list is shown in Table 11-5. Refer to the SQL Server Books Online article for the complete list.

Table 11-5. *Sample Database Permissions*

Database Permission	Implied by Database Permission	Implied by Server Permission
ALTER	CONTROL	ALTER ANY DATABASE
ALTER ANY ASSEMBLY	ALTER	CONTROL SERVER
ALTER ANY DATABASE AUDIT	ALTER	ALTER ANY SERVER AUDIT
ALTER ANY ROLE	ALTER	CONTROL SERVER
ALTER ANY SCHEMA	ALTER	CONTROL SERVER
ALTER ANY USER	ALTER	CONTROL SERVER
BACKUP DATABASE	CONTROL	CONTROL SERVER
CONTROL	CONTROL	CONTROL SERVER
CREATE ASSEMBLY	ALTER ANY ASSEMBLY	CONTROL SERVER
CREATE DATABASE	CONTROL	CREATE ANY DATABASE
CREATE PROCEDURE	ALTER	CONTROL SERVER
CREATE ROLE	ALTER ANY ROLE	CONTROL SERVER
CREATE SCHEMA	ALTER ANY SCHEMA	CONTROL SERVER
CREATE TABLE	ALTER	CONTROL SERVER
CREATE VIEW	ALTER	CONTROL SERVER

Database Permission	Implied by Database Permission	Implied by Server Permission
DELETE	CONTROL	CONTROL SERVER
EXECUTE	CONTROL	CONTROL SERVER
INSERT	CONTROL	CONTROL SERVER
REFERENCES	CONTROL	CONTROL SERVER
SELECT	CONTROL	CONTROL SERVER
SHOWPLAN	CONTROL	ALTER TRACE
TAKE OWNERSHIP	CONTROL	CONTROL SERVER
UPDATE	CONTROL	CONTROL SERVER

With SQL Server, you can grant permission to a user, revoke an existing permission from a user, or deny permission from a user. To grant permission, you use the GRANT statement. An example of granting SELECT on the Customers table is as follows:

```
GRANT SELECT ON Customers TO BusinessAnalysts
```

If you wanted to remove this permission, you would use the REVOKE statement as follows:

```
REVOKE SELECT ON Customers TO BusinessAnalysts
```

What if you had a user Bob who was part of the BusinessAnalysts group and you did not want him to have the SELECT permission? You could use the DENY statement as follows:

```
DENY SELECT ON Customers to Bob
```

Bob would still have all the permissions defined for business analysts, but he would be denied from reading data from the Customers table.

Flexible Database Roles

If your database consisted of just a couple of users, it would be very easy for you to manage permission for these users directly. However, in the real world, DBAs manage lots of users and, more commonly, many different types of users. A developer will have different requirements than a business analyst. If your organization has 35 developers and 70 business analysts, you have a lot of permissions to manage. To alleviate this burden, you can create a database role, add database users or other roles to this new role, and assign permissions to the role. Now, any time you have new developers, all you have to do is add their usernames to the role, and they have all the necessary permissions.

To create a database role, use the CREATE ROLE statement, as shown here:

```
USE AdventureWorks
GO
CREATE ROLE Developers AUTHORIZATION DevManager
```

```
GO
```

Here, you are creating a new role, **Developers**, and making the **DevManager** user the owner of this new role. As an owner, you can freely add and remove membership to the role.

To add users to the role, use the **sp_addrolemember** stored procedure as follows:

```
sp_addrolemember 'Developers', 'Bryan'
```

This assumes that there is a database user within the database named Bryan.

Once you defined a role, you can grant permission to the role using the **GRANT** statement as follows:

```
GRANT CREATE TABLE TO Developers
```

▓ **Note** Even though **DevManager** may be the owner of the **Developers** role, **DevManager** would still need the ability to grant the **CREATE TABLE** permission in order for the previous statement to work. To do this, the DBA would issue the **GRANT** statement with the **WITH GRANT OPTION** clause as follows:

```
GRANT CREATE TABLE TO DevManager WITH GRANT OPTION
```

Security Functions

Now that you know how to grant, revoke, and deny permissions, I'll introduce a series of functions that are designed to help you in managing security. Although most of this information is available in SQL Server Management Studio dialog boxes, the following functions and catalog views are useful if you prefer to issue Transact-SQL statements instead of using the UI.

fn_my_permissions() Function

In the "Flexible Database Roles" section of this chapter, you created a role called **Developers** that included a database user called **Bryan**. You also granted **CREATE TABLE** permission to this role. If Bryan wanted to know what permissions he had within this database, he could use SQL Server Management Studio or simply leverage the **fn_my_permissions** function as follows:

```
SELECT * FROM fn_my_permissions(NULL, 'DATABASE');
```

For Bryan, this query would return the information in Table 11-6.

Table 11-6. *Sample Results from fn_my_permissions() Function*

entity_name	subentity_name	permission_name
Database		CREATE TABLE
Database		CONNECT

This function also works at the server instance level. By replacing the **DATABASE** word with **SEVER**, the function will return the server-level permissions that are granted to the login.

HAS_PERMS_BY_NAME Function

Previously in this chapter, you learned how some permissions convey the rights of other permissions by implication. You also learned that users can be members of roles, and these roles can be members of other roles. In the end, if you wanted to really know what permissions a user had on an object, it would be difficult to trace through all these layers of indirection. The function tells you whether the current context has a specific permission. For example, if developer Bryan wanted to know whether he had SELCT permission on the Customers table, he could issue the following query:

```
SELECT HAS_PERMS_BY_NAME('Customers', 'OBJECT', 'SELECT')
```

This function will return a 1 or 0, indicating a true or false value, respectively.

If you wanted to know whether another user had a specific permission, you would have to be a sysadmin or have IMPERSONATE permission for the user in question. Provided one of those conditions are satisfied, you could find out whether Bryan has the SELECT permission by issuing the following:

```
EXECUTE AS USER='Bryan'
GO
SELECT HAS_PERMS_BY_NAME('Customers', 'OBJECT', 'SELECT')
GO
```

Contained Databases

Consider the case where you perform a database backup and restore it on a different server. Upon restoration, you may still need some additional objects in order for your application that is using the database to work properly. These objects may include SQL Server Agent jobs, SQL logins, linked server definitions, database mail configuration, replication setup, and a few others. Database administrators may have to create these objects before the database is useable. A contained database is a step toward alleviating this pain point. A *contained database* is the same as a traditional database with the exception that in addition to traditional database users you can create database users that are not mapped to any SQL login. This allows your database application to connect directly to the database without authenticating a login at the server level. Upon a failover, all you need is the database itself on the disaster recovery site, because the database contains the security information needed for the user. SQL Server 2012 introduces a partially contained database. A *partially contained database* is the same as a user-defined database except it also includes security information needed for authentication. In the scenario where you move a contained database, if your database leverages objects that exist outside the database such as agent jobs or linked servers, these objects would have to be created on the new server first before the database could be used on the new server.

Database movement is not the only use case for contained databases. Benefits for this feature revolve around separating the application development and management from the underlying database instance infrastructure needed to support it. A contained database makes administering applications easier, because there is no real dependency on the host instance.

To create a contained database you must first enable the "contained database authentication" system option as follows:

```
Sp_configure 'show advanced options', 1
RECONFIGURE
GO
Sp_configure 'contained database authentication', 1
RECONFIGURE WITH OVERRIDE
GO
```

Next, let's create a sample database and set the containment of this database to partial.

```
CREATE DATABASE Customers
GO
ALTER DATABASE Customers SET CONTAINMENT=PARTIAL;
```

Now that our database is partially contained, we can create database users without associated SQL logins. These users can be created with a password or they can be Windows principals. If you use Windows principal users, they do not need any existing access to SQL Server. For this example, assume we have created a local Windows user named, **"Bob"** on the server, **"ROB-DENALI-1"**. To create both a user with a password and a user from a Windows principal, we issue the following commands:

```
USE Customers
GO
CREATE USER [SalesRep1] WITH PASSWORD='pass@word1';
GO
CREATE USER [ROB-DENALI-1\Bob];
GO
```

To test our containment, assume we logged into a Windows client under Bob's credentials. Alternatively, you as a Windows administrator, can issue the **RUNAS** command and open a new command window under Bob's context. To do this, you can type the following in a command prompt:

```
C:\>RUNAS /USER:Bob "CMD.EXE"
```

Bob can now try to connect to SQL Server. Figure 11-4 shows a command shell window running under Bob's security context depicting Bob's attempt at connecting to SQL Server. Bob is using SQLCMD, which is the command line tool for connecting to SQL Server. In case you are not familiar with the command line switches, **-E** means connect via Windows Authentication, meaning connect as Bob in this case. **-S** **.** means the server name, and the period is an abbreviation for the local server. In the first attempt, notice that SQL Server failed to authenticate Bob.

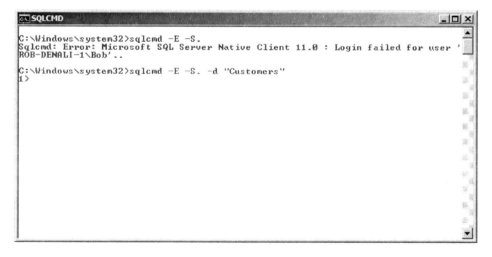

Figure 11-4. *Using SQLCMD to connect to a contained database*

This failure occurred, because we didn't specify an initial database to connect to, so it was implied that we were trying to connect to the master database. Since Bob doesn't exist as a SQL login in the master database, SQL Server rejected the connection request. In the second attempt at the sqlcmd command Bob explicitly states that he wishes to connect to the Customers database via the -d parameter in SQLCMD. Since Bob's account is provisioned in the database, the connection succeeds. You can see SQLCMD gives us 1>, which is the SQLCMD command prompt with a successful connection. This example used SQLCMD, but you can use whatever application or method you normally use to connect to SQL Server. There are no specific connection requirements or restrictions for accessing a contained database.

Summary

The security model for SQL Server is focused around the concepts of server instances and databases. Logins are defined at the server instance level and, by default, have no access to any particular database. If you want a login to access a database, you will have to create a database user that maps to that login. With contained databases, you no longer have to create a login for a user to have access to a database. This allows for easy database movement and application administration. Roles make security management much easier, since instead of defining permissions for everyone, you can simply assign permissions to the role.

The current security model of SQL Server has been around for many years, encompassing multiple versions. SQL Server is a well-tested and well-trusted database platform. As your experience with SQL Server increases, you will undoubtedly use the concepts and functions described in this chapter.

CHAPTER 12

Auditing, Encryption, and Compliance

According to the Privacy Rights Clearinghouse, more than 535 million records with sensitive information have been breached since January 2005. If you browse through the detailed report at www.privacyrights.org/ar/ChronDataBreaches.htm, you'll see that there are many kinds of breaches of stolen data. In some cases, there were stolen laptops; in others, it was in inside job by a disgruntled employee. This report yields an almost endless supply of breaches and stolen data.

As a customer of a business, you want to feel confident that a stolen laptop thousands of miles away will not have you repairing your credit report for years. Businesses need you, the customer, to have this faith.

The payment card industry is one such industry to come together and create a set of standards for its business practices. The Payment Card Industry Security Standards Council—an independent counsel originally formed by American Express, Discover Financial Services, JCB, MasterCard Worldwide, and Visa International in 2006—charters itself with the goal of managing the ongoing evolution of the Payment Card Industry Data Security Standard specification. This specification details technical and operational requirements that help companies prevent credit card fraud, hacking, and various other security vulnerabilities and threats.

PCI is just one type of regulatory compliance. There are many others spanning most major industries. For example, if your company is publicly traded, it will have to comply with the Sarbanes-Oxley (SOX) Act.

As a DBA, you may be asked to help in a compliance effort. Unfortunately, most of these regulatory compliances are vaguely written and are subject to interpretation. For this reason, many times companies will hire a third-party auditor to help them. Microsoft understands the importance of compliance and has some resources dedicated to the effort. Specifically, Microsoft has a senior program manager within the SQL Server group who is in charge of compliance strategy. When we began this book, the person in that position was J.C. Cannon. The following is an excerpt from an interview that we had with him:

> *Robert Walters: What is your role at Microsoft?*
>
> *J.C. Cannon:* I help customers understand how SQL Server can help them address their compliance needs and provide input to future releases of SQL Server that will improve its compliance capabilities.

Robert Walters: What is compliance?

J.C. Cannon: There is not a simple answer to this. I tell customers that, related to the database, it is the ability to manage data in a verifiable manner based on policy.

Robert Walters: My company is publicly traded, and management says we have to be SOX compliant. Can I select a box that makes SQL Server SOX compliant?

J.C. Cannon: Not at all. Becoming compliant with most regulations requires that a formal process be developed that includes a risk assessment, action plan, verification procedures, and remediation capabilities. No product can make an organization compliant by itself. Manual processes are also needed to perform the tasks that technology is unable to.

Robert Walters: How will SQL Server continue to address compliance in future releases?

J.C. Cannon: Microsoft has a strong commitment to compliance. SQL Server, along with other product groups, will continue to engage customers to determine the most important compliance features that are needed and add them to future releases.

Robert Walters: What advice do you have for folks new to the DBA profession as it relates to security and compliance?

J.C. Cannon: Start with reading the SQL Server 2008 Compliance Guide on our compliance portal at `www.microsoft.com/sqlserver/en/us/solutions-technologies/mission-critical-operations/security-and-compliance.aspx`. When developing a strategy for database compliance, you want to start by creating a set of actionable policies. Determine how you will implement those polices. Ensure you provide a means for validating that the policies are in compliance. The Policy-Based Management feature of SQL Server provides a strong mechanism for validating that database settings are set a certain way and remain that way. There is also a means for validating that those settings were in compliance over a period of time. SQL Server Audit provides a granular means for monitoring sensitive operations in a database. The logs generated by the auditing process can be sent to a central auditing server to make it easy to create consolidated reports. In general, SQL Server provides the best platform for building compliance solutions.

As you can begin to see from this interview excerpt, compliance is a hard problem. We can't solve it in this one chapter. But what we can do is make you familiar with the tools that are built into SQL Server to help you along the way.

Auditing in SQL Server

Auditing is the process by which you track events occurring within the database. These events could be almost anything, including the creation of new users, the insertion of data into a table, or the querying of data. The capability of auditing has been around in some form for a few versions of SQL Server, but its implementation was sketchy at best. Up until SQL Server 2008, there has never been any formal user interface for auditing.

In the past, SQL Server DBAs used Profiler, a performance tuning and optimization tool, to create and manage audits. Alternatively, they could roll their own auditing solutions using DDL triggers. Or they could forget the pain and drop some money on third-party auditing solutions.

With the worldwide effort around defining and enforcing compliance, SQL Server comes with native auditing support in all editions of the product. The majority of regulatory compliance agencies want some form of auditing, and chances are, if your company is going through the process of becoming compliant, either you will be involved with auditing via SQL Server or you'll be aware of it occurring using hardware-based auditing devices.

Auditing Objects

Auditing support in SQL Server consists of the following three objects:

- *Server audit*: Defines an abstract container, if you will, representing a specific audit that you want to perform. For example, you might want to create a *compliance audit* to ensure that you comply with a specific regulation.

- *Server audit specification*: Defines a specific, server-level item to watch and record as part of an audit. Perhaps you want to record failed logins as part of your compliance audit. You would create a server audit specification for that purpose.

- *Database audit specification*: Defines a specific, database-level item to watch and record as part of an audit. For example, you might want to log stored procedure executions as part of your compliance audit.

Figure 12-1 shows these three objects and the scope where these objects are defined.

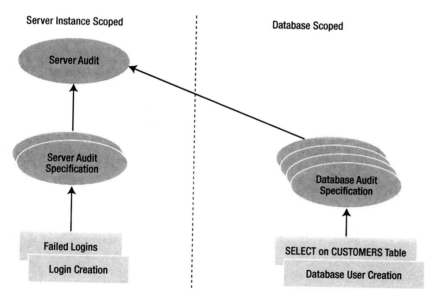

Figure 12-1. *The three auditing objects and their corresponding scopes*

The concept of *scope* is important to understand when you learn about auditing, because only through having a good understanding of instance scope versus database scope will you know which audit specification object to choose for a given purpose. If you are talking about something affecting a particular database, you are referring to a database-scoped object or action. If you are interested in auditing failed logins, you would create a server-instance–scoped audit specification, since logins affect all databases.

The idea of an *audit* as an abstract concept is also important to grasp. A server audit is an abstract object—a container, if you will—containing one or more audit specifications. When you enable or disable a specific audit, you are really enabling or disabling all of that audit's specifications. Likewise, when you specify a location at which to record audit data, that location applies to all specifications within an audit. This container concept will get clearer as you read through the following examples.

Server Audit Object

When you want to perform an audit, you have the option to write audit data to one of three places. First, you can write audit data to the Windows Application log. Next, you can write data to the Windows Security log. Finally, you can write audit data to the file system. Each one of these destinations has pros and cons, which will be explored later in this chapter.

To create an audit object, navigate down the Object Explorer tree to the Security node.

Select New Audit from the Audits node context menu. This will launch the Create Audit dialog box, shown in Figure 12-2.

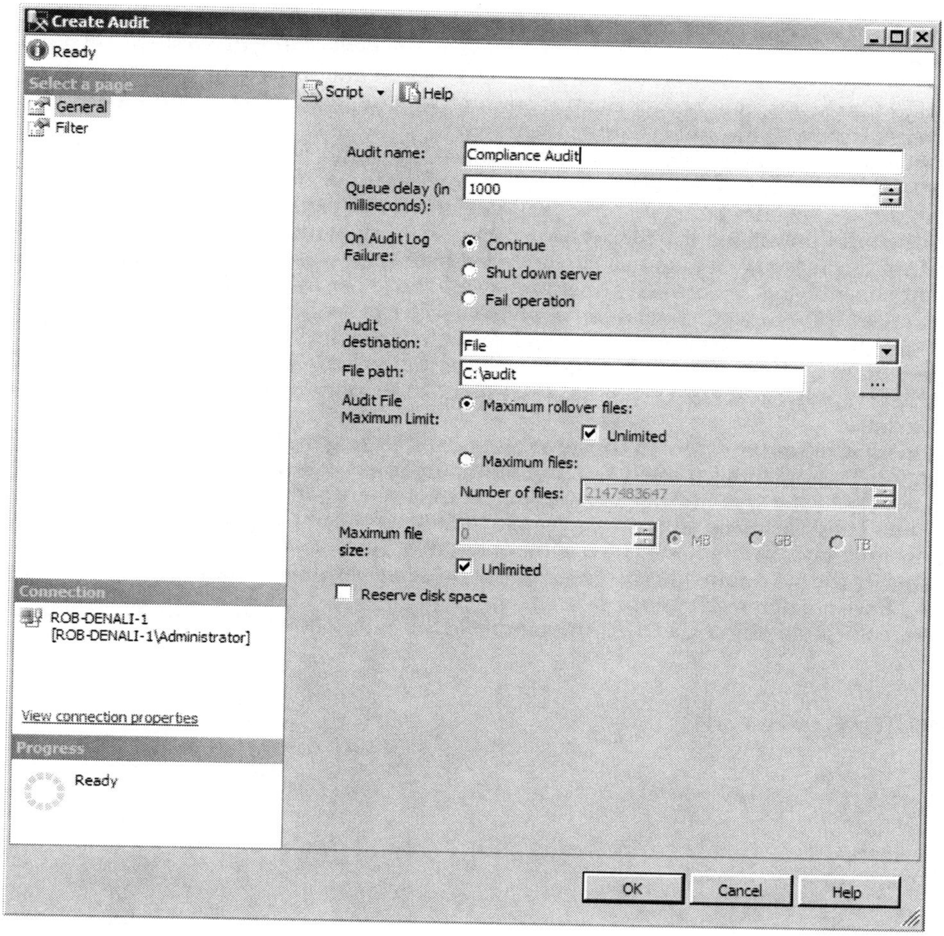

Figure 12-2. Create Audit dialog box

The audit name will be auto-generated for you, but you can easily change the generated name to something simple like Compliance Audit. A number of options are available when you create the audit object. The first is the queue delay. Since auditing is leveraging a service-broker–based eventing system called *extended events*, it is possible to configure the maximum amount of time you are willing to wait before auditing events are guaranteed to be written. Here's another way of thinking about the queue delay. If a meteor flew in from the sky and crashed through the roof into our data center right through our server and we had defined the queue delay to be 1,000, that meteor may cause us to lose one second's worth of auditing events, because the queue delay is in terms of thousandths of a second, or milliseconds. If the default queue delay of 1,000 milliseconds seems unacceptable, just consider the performance impact of making the queue delay smaller.

In some cases, auditing is so important that if SQL Server fails to write an audit event to the log, the SQL Server service will be stopped. This is what happens when you select the "Shut down server on audit log failure" option. Selecting, "Fail operation" will cause the transaction that caused the audit to be rolledback. The most unintrusive option is the default, Continue, which simply raises an error in the event log if SQL Server fails to write the audit event.

The "Audit destination" drop-down box allows you to choose File, Application Log, or Security Log. Where you write auditing information is extremely important. Auditing information can contain sensitive information such as Social Security numbers, salaries, and credit card numbers. Thus, you would not want to write this information in a place where other users might unintentionally have access to it. Writing to the Application log is easy, and you do not need to have an elevated privilege within Windows to see the Application log. A more secure solution would be to use the Windows Security log. Additional measures are in place to restrict the number of users who can see and erase the Security log. You can integrate your SQL Server auditing events with other auditing events from other servers by using tools such as Windows Audit Collection Services, which is part of the System Center Operations Manager (http://technet.microsoft.com/en-us/library/bb381373.aspx). These tools use the Windows Security log to obtain auditing data.

If you do not plan on using another tool to consume audit data, writing the audit data to the file system is the best option. For one thing, it's very fast, but more important, it is possible to protect against repudiation attacks by the sysadmin. A *repudiation attack* is where a malicious user does something they shouldn't and cleans up after themselves so their actions can't be tracked.

Selecting a file destination also enables a series of other options. Since it's the file system we are writing to, you can specify the maximum file size an audit can be as well as reserve the space up front so you are sure to always have enough room for the audit data.

You can also create the audit object via DDL. An example of this is as follows:

```
USE MASTER
GO
CREATE SERVER AUDIT [Compliance Audit]
TO FILE
(    FILEPATH = N'c:\audit'
)
WITH
(    QUEUE_DELAY = 1000,
     ON_FAILURE = CONTINUE
)
GO
```

Auditing can generate a massive number of events in a very short time. In most cases, we may not be interested in auditing everything but rather a subset of events based on a certain condition. Assume for a moment that we have an application that connects to SQL Server under a common SQL login, AppUser. Users who use this application do not directly connect to SQL Server but access the database via the AppUser account from the application itself. Our auditing requirements state that we are interested in auditing anyone that connects or tries to connect with an account other than AppUser. To do this, we simply add the search criteria or filter to the audit definition. In SSMS, the Create Audit and Audit Properties dialog has a Filter tab; alternatively, you can specify a filter for the above DDL as follows:

```
USE master
GO
ALTER SERVER AUDIT [Compliance Audit]
WHERE server_principal_id <> 268
GO
```

This filter will ignore any audits generated by the `server_principal_id` of 268. The number 268 is just an example. If you are filtering by the `server_principal_id`, the actual ID number of the principal you want to filter may be different. You can use the system view `sys.server_principals` to see a list of server principal IDs. A sample of using this view follows:

```
SELECT name,principal_id,type_desc FROM sys.server_principals
```

This view contains 13 columns including information on when the principal was created and modified last. For this discussion, the `name`, `principal`, and `type_desc` fields are most interesting. Following are some of the query results:

Name	principal_id	type_desc
Sa	1	SQL_LOGIN
Public	2	SERVER_ROLE
Sysadmin	3	SERVER_ROLE
...		
SQL2012-RC0\Administrator	259	WINDOWS_LOGIN
...		
Test	267	SQL_LOGIN

Here, you can see from the `type_desc` field what kind of principal each item is.

Server Audit Specification Object

Now that you have created a server audit object, you can start writing auditing events to it. In this example, let's audit all failed logins. Since logins affect more than one database, you need to create a server audit specification. To create a server audit specification, select New Server Audit Specification from the Server Audit Specifications context menu. This will launch the dialog box shown in Figure 12-3.

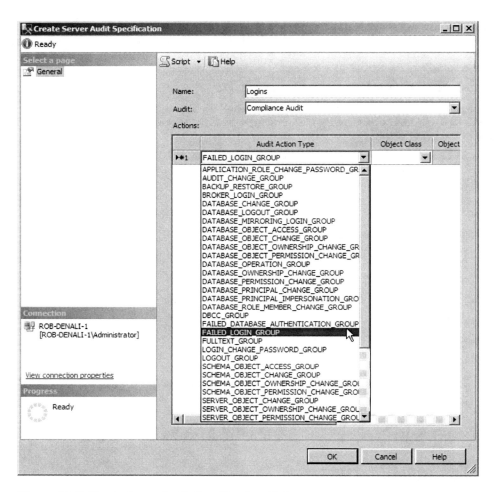

Figure 12-3. *Create Server Audit Specification dialog*

By default, a name is provided for you, but you can easily change this to something more meaningful. In our example, since we want to audit just failed logins, let's call it Logins. The Audit drop-down box contains all the server audit objects that are defined for the server. Notice that you can create as many server audit objects as you want. Since you created Compliance Audit, you can select this server audit.

The actions grid is where you specify what events or groups of events you want to record. To audit failed logins, select FAILED_LOGIN_GROUP.

If you click OK, the server audit specification will be created.

You can also create the server audit specification using DDL as follows:

```
USE MASTER
GO
CREATE SERVER AUDIT SPECIFICATION [Logins]
FOR SERVER AUDIT [Compliance Audit]
ADD (FAILED_LOGIN_GROUP)
GO
```

Now that you have both a server audit defined and a server audit specification, you can start an audit with these two objects. Note that auditing objects are not enabled by default since you may not be ready for the onslaught of auditing events after simply defining an audit. To enable the server audit specification, you can either select Enable Server Audit Specification from the context menu of the object or issue the following T-SQL statement:

```
ALTER SERVER AUDIT SPECIFICATION Logins WITH (STATE=ON)
GO
```

To enable the server audit, you can select Enable Audit from the context menu of the audit or issue the following T-SQL statement:

```
ALTER SERVER AUDIT [Compliance Audit] WITH (STATE=ON)
GO
```

Once you have enabled both the server audit and the server audit specification, you can test the audit by trying to make a connection to SQL Server using false credentials. Once you attempt to make this false connection, the audit event will be written to the audit log. You can view audit logs by selecting View Audit Logs from the context menu of your audit, Compliance Audit. Figure 12-4 shows the Log File Viewer dialog box with the failed login event.

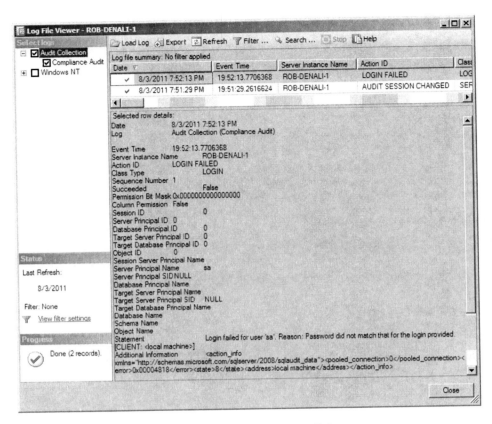

Figure 12-4. Log File Viewer dialog box showing an audit log

You cannot write auditing events directly to a table in SQL Server. If you really want to see them or push them into a table, you can use the fn_get_audit_file function. An example of using this function follows:

```
SELECT * FROM fn_get_audit_file ('c:\audit\*',null,null)
```

This yields a result set that includes a plethora of columns. Some of the more meaningful columns include the actual T-SQL statement that was executed and the calling context of the user.

Database Audit Specification Object

If you want to audit events that occur within a database, you will need to define a database audit specification. To create one, you can select New Database Audit Specification from the Database Audit Specification node of the Security node of a specific database in SSMS.

> **Note** Creating a database audit specification is only available on Enterprise edition and above.

Figure 12-5 shows the Create Database Audit Specification dialog box that opens.

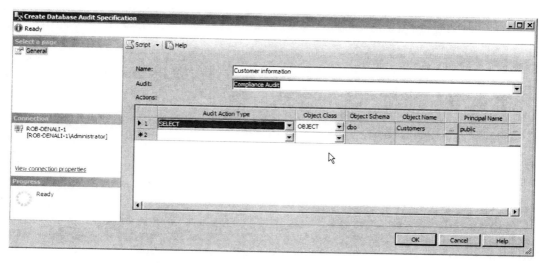

Figure 12-5. *Create Database Audit Specification dialog box*

Just like the server audit specification points to a server audit, so too can the database audit specification. In this example, select Compliance Audit to use the existing server audit that you created earlier.

The Actions grid is where you define which audit events or event groups you want to record. In addition to having groups of events, the database audit specifications have a handful of single events. Some of these are SELECT, INSERT, UPDATE, DELETE, and EXECUTE. If you want to audit anyone who issues a SELECT statement on the Customers table, select SELECT from the Audit Action Type list. Then, specify that the object class is an object. The object name is the object that is the target of the audit. In this case, you want the Customers table. If you want to audit all users, you can enter **public** for the principal name, or else you can specify a specific user or group to audit.

You can also create a database audit specification using the following T-SQL statement:

```
USE [Accounting]
GO
CREATE DATABASE AUDIT SPECIFICATION [Customer information]
    FOR SERVER AUDIT [Compliance Audit]
        ADD(SELECT ON Customers by public)
GO
```

In the previous chapter, you created the Accounting database. If you want to follow along and do not have this database created, execute the following script:

```
USE master
GO
CREATE DATABASE Accounting
GO
USE Accounting
GO
CREATE TABLE Customers
(id INT NOT NULL,
firstname VARCHAR(20) NOT NULL,
lastname VARCHAR(40) NOT NULL)
GO
```

Remember to enable the database audit specification once you are ready to start collecting events. You can do this by selecting Enable Database Audit Specification from the context menu of the specification or by issuing the following T-SQL statement:

```
ALTER DATABASE AUDIT SPECIFICATION [Customers Table]
    WITH (STATE=ON)
GO
```

■ **Note**   To turn off auditing but retain the audit definitions, simply use STATE=OFF in the preceding code.

Now, to test this audit event, try issuing a SELECT * FROM CUSTOMERS statement. If you view the Compliance Audit audit log, you will notice an additional entry for the SELECT statement. Notice that you can see both the calling context and the actual T-SQL statement that triggered the audit.

Previous editions of SQL Server did not display T-SQL stack information. For example, if you audited SELECT on a given table, an auditing event would be raised when you directly accessed the data via a SELECT statement and, as expected, via a stored procedure. With SQL Server 2012, T-SQL stack information is written to the additional information column of the audit log if applicable. You can test this by creating a stored procedure that runs a SELECT statement on the Customers table. Sample code is as follows:

```
CREATE PROCEDURE ViewCustomers
AS
BEGIN
SELECT * FROM Accounting.dbo.Customers
END
```

Now, if we execute the stored procedure and then looked at our auditing log, we see the following information in the additional information column for the SELECT audit event:

```
<tsql_stack><frame nest_level='1' database_name='Accounting' schema_name='dbo'
object_name='ViewCustomers'/></tsql_stack>
```

This additional information is helpful in determining the origin of the event that caused the audit to be raised.

COMPLIANCE AND THE PROBLEM WITH SYSADMIN

Although regulatory agencies' specifications for compliance don't specifically call out a SQL Server system administrator, they imply the need for protection against all users, and this includes system administrators. The problem with sysadmins is that they are, in some ways, running under the service account of SQL Server itself. You cannot protect data against the SQL Server service account, because SQL Server needs to have access to the protected data to serve to the users who have explicit access.

Although it is impossible to prevent a sysadmin from doing bad things to SQL Server or from reading data that they probably shouldn't, you can create an audit that will protect against sysadmin repudiation attacks. To set up this configuration, simply create a server audit that points to a folder on a file share where the SQL Server service account has Append Data permission only. Although the sysadmin could still stop the audit and do something inappropriate, the mere fact that the audit was stopped at all should be a red flag to an auditor. In most cases, this kind of configuration is acceptable to auditors.

User-Defined Audit Event

There are occasions when you want to write a custom event into the audit log. Consider the scenario where an application connects to SQL Server through a common single user account. The application may support multiple users but when these users access the data in SQL Server, the database server doesn't know the specific application user that is requesting data access to the database, because access is through a common user account. In this case, the application can write a user-defined audit event to ensure that, when auditors read the audit logs, they see the user who is connecting to the application who requested the data.

Writing a custom audit event is very straight forward. You can use the **sp_audit_write** stored procedure to write to an audit log. Before you can use this function, you need to create a server audit specification that contains the USER_DEFINED_AUDIT_GROUP. If you do not do this, the **sp_audit_write** stored procedure will not do anything but return success. To demonstrate this event, create a UserDefinedAudits server audit as follows:

```
CREATE SERVER AUDIT [UserDefinedAudits]
TO FILE
(       FILEPATH = N'C:\audit'
        ,MAXSIZE = 0 MB
        ,MAX_ROLLOVER_FILES = 2147483647
        ,RESERVE_DISK_SPACE = OFF
)
WITH
(       QUEUE_DELAY = 1000
        ,ON_FAILURE = CONTINUE
)
GO
ALTER SERVER AUDIT [UserDefinedAudits]
WITH (STATE=ON)
GO
```

Next, create the server audit specification `CustomAudits` and add the `USER_DEFINED_AUDIT_GROUP`.

```
USE [master]
GO
CREATE SERVER AUDIT SPECIFICATION [CustomAudits]
FOR SERVER AUDIT [UserDefinedAudits]
ADD (USER_DEFINED_AUDIT_GROUP)
WITH (STATE=ON)
GO
```

Now, with the audit defined, the server audit specification defined, and both enabled, we can utilize the `sp_audit_write` stored procedure as follows:

```
EXEC sp_audit_write @user_defined_event_id =  1000 ,
          @succeeded =  1
        , @user_defined_information = N'User Bob logged into application.' ;
```

The user defined event ID is any integer value you would like. It has no meaning other than what you make of it. The `@succeeded` bit can be used to determine if the event you are raising is a failure. The last parameter is a 4,000-character field where you can display any message you choose. After raising your event, you can view it by simply viewing the audit log in SSMS.

Encryption

Encryption is the process of obscuring information to make it unreadable to those who do not possess some special knowledge. The history of encryption dates far back to the days of Julius Caesar where he used a special algorithm called the *Caesar shift cipher* to protect military messages. The algorithm was quite simple. It was simply a shift of the alphabet three spaces to the left, as shown in Table 12-1.

Table 12-1. *Caesar Shift Cipher Alphabet*

Cipher	Alphabet
None	ABCDEFGHIJKLMNOPQRSTUVWXYZ
Shift cipher	DEFGHIJKLMNOPQRSTUVWXYZABC

To encrypt a message, you would just take each letter and match its cipher equivalent. For example, if you were to encrypt the word *bomb*, it would be *erpe*.

To decrypt a message, simply reverse the process, and look up the plain alphabet letter that aligns with the cipher letter. For example, the encrypted words *odcb grj* become *lazy dog*.

Encryption serves a critical role in some compliance requirements. Consider the case where a client computer sends a password over the network and the server authenticates the user based on this password. If attackers were to packet sniff the network, they would easily obtain the credentials the user used to log into the server. Alternatively, consider the case where one user sends an order over the network. The attacker intercepts the order and changes the shipping address to a house that is in foreclosure close to the attacker's location. There are countless scenarios where sending data and storing data in clear text is suboptimal. Encryption adds an extra layer of protection.

Before you dive into encryption in SQL Server, understanding a few concepts is important: plain text, algorithms, encryption keys, and ciphertext. In our order-changing scenario, the order itself is in plain text. It is, in fact, the sensitive data you are trying to protect. If you were to encrypt the order, you would need two things: an encryption algorithm and, depending on the algorithm, at least one encryption key. If you throw all three of these into a bowl, not only will you make a tasty soup but you'll have a stream of data called *ciphertext*. Ciphertext is the sensitive data once it's been encrypted. SQL Server leverages encryption functions that are part of the Cryptographic API. This API is part of the operating system and exposes a set of functions that allows you to encrypt and decrypt data.

Encryption Primer

To encrypt plain text, you need the plain text itself, an encryption algorithm, and an encryption key. Together, these will produce ciphertext (or in layman's terms, a bunch of binary data that doesn't look all that exciting). If you wanted to decrypt the ciphertext and determine the plain text, you could reverse this process and provide the ciphertext, encryption algorithm, and encryption key. Together, these would produce the plain text that you originally encrypted. If you use the same key for encrypting plain text as you do for decrypting the ciphertext, this key is referred to as a *symmetric key*.

Symmetric keys and their corresponding algorithms provide the best encryption and decryption performance, but there is an inherent problem with their use. If you use the same key to perform encryption as you do decryption, it is safe to say that the key material is sensitive information itself. You can't simply copy the symmetric key in the file system or database and call it secure. Anyone who can see the key can encrypt or decrypt the data. Symmetric keys are used extensively within SQL Server because of their performance benefit. However, there are ways of protecting symmetric keys, as you will learn later in this chapter.

An *asymmetric key* consists of two keys. One is called a *public key*, and the other is a *private key*. The idea is the encryption algorithms used with asymmetric keys take plain text and encrypt with the public key to yield the ciphertext. This ciphertext, or encrypted data, can be decrypted only by the private key. Conversely, you could encrypt plain text using a private key that will be decrypted only by an encryption algorithm plus the public key. With asymmetric keys, the private key is as sensitive as symmetric keys and should always be protected when stored. SQL Server also protects private keys.

A *certificate* is an asymmetric key with some extra metadata. This metadata defines attributes such as a certificate authority and an expiration date, to name a few. Certificates stored in SQL Server are not validated for expiration or against a certificate authority such as VeriSign for authenticity. Rather, certificates are used for a variety of reasons including protecting and managing encryption keys and signing modules in SQL Server.

Now that you are exposed to the basic definitions of these concepts, let's walk through an example of encrypting data.

Password-Based Encryption

In this example, say you work for a bank called ContosoBank that has a single table called Customers. The auditor requires you to encrypt the social_security_number column. There will be a single login called BankManagerLogin, which will be mapped to the BankManagerUser database user. Data stored in the Social Security number column will be encrypted such that only BankManagerUser will be able to decrypt the contents. The following is a script that will create the ContosoBank database as well as the Customers table and database user:

```
USE [master]
GO
CREATE LOGIN BankManagerLogin WITH PASSWORD='g4mqw9K@32!@'
GO
CREATE DATABASE ContosoBank
GO
USE [ContosoBank]
GO
CREATE USER BankManagerUser FOR LOGIN BankManagerLogin
GO
CREATE TABLE Customers
(customer_id INT PRIMARY KEY,
first_name varchar(50) NOT NULL,
last_name varchar(50) NOT NULL,
social_security_number varbinary(100) NOT NULL)
GO
GRANT SELECT, INSERT, UPDATE, DELETE ON Customers TO BankManagerUser
GO
```

If you read this script carefully, you may notice that the data type for the social_security_number column is a **varbinary**. Since ciphertext is binary, the only data type that will support storing encrypted data is **varbinary**.

Now, you need to create a symmetric key that will be used to encrypt the data. You can do this using the **CREATE SYMMETRIC KEY** statement as follows:

```
CREATE SYMMETRIC KEY BankManager_User_Key
AUTHORIZATION BankManagerUser
WITH ALGORITHM=TRIPLE_DES
ENCRYPTION BY PASSWORD='HighFeesRule!'
GO
```

The **AUTHORIZATION** parameter describes who the owner of the key is; in this case, it's the database user **BankManagerUser**.

You can use a number of different encryption algorithms. Some of the available options include DES, Triple DES, RC2, AES_128, and AES 256-bit. Each one of these algorithms has unique characteristics. Some are faster than others, and some are weaker encryption. DES, for example, can be broken in 22 hours. See http://en.wikipedia.org/wiki/Data_Encryption_Standard for more information. Every day, hackers and educators attempt to crack these encryption algorithms, so do some research before you place all your bets on using a specific algorithm.

When a symmetric key is created, it needs to be protected because simply leaving it in clear text within the database or file system defeats the purpose of encrypting your data. SQL Server will not allow you to create a symmetric key without first specifying how to protect it. In this example, you are encrypting it by a password. This also means that anytime you want to use this key, you will have to specify this password.

All encryption keys are visible in SSMS under the Security node of a specific database. There are also catalog views that return useful information. **Sys.symmetric_keys** returns a list of symmetric keys, the encryption algorithm defined for the key, and other useful information.

Now that you have created a symmetric key, you are ready to produce encrypted data. A number of functions within SQL Server allow you to encrypt and decrypt data. These functions simply pass parameters down to a call to Microsoft's Cryptographic API. The function used to encrypt plain text using a symmetric key is called **EncryptByKey**. To insert data into your table using this function, consider the following script:

```
EXECUTE AS USER='BankManagerUser'
GO
OPEN SYMMETRIC KEY [BankManager_User_Key] DECRYPTION BY PASSWORD='HighFeesRule!'
GO
INSERT INTO Customers VALUES (1,'Howard','Stern',
EncryptByKey(Key_GUID('BankManager_User_Key'),'042-32-1324'))
INSERT INTO Customers VALUES (2,'Donald','Trump',
EncryptByKey(Key_GUID('BankManager_User_Key'),'035-13-6564'))
INSERT INTO Customers VALUES (3,'Bill','Gates',
EncryptByKey(Key_GUID('BankManager_User_Key'),'533-13-5784'))
GO

CLOSE ALL SYMMETRIC KEYS
GO
```

The EXECUTE AS statement gives sysadmins or users with IMPERSONATE permissions the ability to change the execution context of the current connection. Since you want to simulate being the BankManagerUser, you issue the EXECUTE AS statement. In this example, we're using this statement to support the script. In the real world, the execution context would already be set by the user who is actually doing the encryption.

When you want to perform any encryption or decryption operation, SQL Server needs to have the key available in memory. The OPEN SYMMETRIC KEY statement will open the key and place it in memory. Notice, at the end of the script, the CLOSE SYMMETRIC KEY statement is given. This statement will release the memory used by the key.

Note The best practice when using encryption is to open all your keys first, perform your encryption or decryption work, and then issue the close statement. The reason for this is that opening the key requires permission checks and other operations that, if done at every encryption statement within your script, would hinder performance.

The EncryptByKey function takes the GUID of an open key and the plain text that you want to encrypt. Rather than typing the GUID of the key, you can use another function called KEY_GUID to obtain this for you. The EncryptByKey function will return the ciphertext or encrypted binary data.

At this point, if you issue a SELECT * FROM Customers statement, you would get the output shown in Table 12-2.

Table 12-2. *Sample Output from the Customers Table*

customer_id	first_name	last_name	social_security_number
1	Howard	Stern	0x006C4...BDD2C394E5
2	Donald	Trump	0x006C4...D98F3E2CBA
3	Bill	Gates	0x006C4...4A6EB6D8DE

To decrypt the data, you can issue the following statements:

```
OPEN SYMMETRIC KEY [BankManager_User_Key] DECRYPTION BY PASSWORD='HighFeesRule!'
GO

SELECT customer_id,first_name + ' ' + last_name AS 'Name',
CONVERT(VARCHAR,DecryptByKey(social_security_number)) as 'Social Security Number'
FROM Customers
GO

CLOSE ALL SYMMETRIC KEYS
GO
```

These statements will return your original table with the Social Security number decrypted, as shown here:

customer_id	Name	Social Security Number
1	Howard Stern	042-32-1324
2	Donald Trump	035-13-6564
3	Bill Gates	533-13-5784

Notice that, in the DecryptByKey function, you did not have to specify which key was used to encrypt the data. The reason for this is there is a thumbprint of the encryption key stored within the header of the encrypted data. Thus, to decrypt as long as you have the key opened in memory using the OPEN SYMMETRIC KEY statement, SQL Server will be able to figure out which key to use for you.

Certificate-Based Encryption

In the previous section, you encrypted data and protected the symmetric key by using a password. Although this is a perfectly acceptable way of protecting the key, the problem is that whenever you want to access the encrypted data, you will have to specify a password. If you are accessing the data from a script file or stored procedure, you will have to store the password in clear text in your script or stored procedure, which defeats the purpose of encryption. For this reason, a better approach would be to create a certificate and give the user, in our case BankManagerUser, access to the certificate. The certificate will then be used instead of a password to protect the symmetric key.

When you create a certificate, you need to protect that as well since certificates contain private keys. Certificates can be protected using a password or by using the database master key. There is only one database master key per user database. The purpose of this key is to protect keys like private keys where no explicit password is provided.

The following is how you create a master key. Before creating it, you should issue a REVERT statement to revert your current connection context to SYSADMIN if have been following along on your own SQL Server.

```
REVERT
GO
USE [ContosoBank]
GO
CREATE MASTER KEY
ENCRYPTION BY PASSWORD = 'Some!@Complex*@(39'
GO
```

Do not lose this password, because if you do, you won't be able to back up the key. Now that you have created the database master key within the ContosoBank database, you can create a certificate that will be used to protect the symmetric key.

```
CREATE CERTIFICATE BankManagersCert
AUTHORIZATION BankManagerUser
WITH SUBJECT='Bank manager''s certificate'
GO
```

There is no dialog box in SSMS that will allow you to create a certificate, so you will have to use the CREATE CERTIFICATE T-SQL statement. Now, you can create your symmetric key, protecting it with a certificate instead of a password. Since you are going to replace the protection, you need to open the key first, add the certificate protection and then remove the password protection. This will ensure that the symmetric key is never stored in cleartext for any duration of time. The following is an example:

```
OPEN SYMMETRIC KEY [BankManager_User_Key] DECRYPTION BY PASSWORD='HighFeesRule!'
GO
ALTER SYMMETRIC KEY BankManager_User_Key
ADD ENCRYPTION BY CERTIFICATE BankManagersCert
GO
ALTER SYMMETRIC KEY BankManager_User_Key
DROP ENCRYPTION BY PASSWORD='HighFeesRule!'
GO
CLOSE ALL SYMMETRIC KEYS
GO
```

Now that you have protected your key with a certificate, BankManagerUser does not need to specify a password to open the key. To confirm this, you can change your context to BankManagerUser by using the EXECUTE AS statement, for example:

```
EXECUTE AS USER='BankManagerUser'
GO
USE [ContosoBank]
GO
OPEN SYMMETRIC KEY [BankManager_User_Key] DECRYPTION BY CERTIFICATE BankManagersCert
GO
SELECT customer_id,first_name + ' ' + last_name,
CONVERT(VARCHAR,DecryptByKey(social_security_number)) as 'Social Security Number'
FROM Customers
GO
CLOSE ALL SYMMETRIC KEYS
GO
```

Encrypting data is a very important tool that can be used to add some protection above and beyond column-level permissions. SQL Server provides addition encryption capabilities such as the ability to encrypt the entire database. This is known as transparent data encryption (TDE).

Transparent Data Encryption

The encryption capabilities within SQL Server are powerful. However, they require application changes that may or may not be feasible in your environment. For this reason, SQL Server 2008 comes with an ability to encrypt the entire database. Technically, what happens when you enable encryption at the database level is that SQL Server encrypts data pages before it writes them to disk. Conversely, when data pages are read from the disk, they are decrypted and placed into memory. To the user, the experience with SQL Server is unchanged. They do not know the data is encrypted.

This type of encryption is termed *transparent data encryption* and protects against the attack in which someone copies the database files themselves and attempts to attach them to a SQL Server instance that they themselves control. As an added benefit, if you perform a BACKUP DATABASE operation on a database that has encryption enabled, the backup will be encrypted as well.

To enable encryption on a database, you need to create a database encryption key (DEK). A DEK is a symmetric key that the SQL Server service uses to encrypt and decrypt the database files. Since this is a symmetric key, it needs to be protected. You protect the DEK through a certificate that is created in the master database. This certificate contains a private key and needs to be protected as well. The certificate is protected by the database master key of the master database. This process is similar to encrypting specific data as described in the previous section of this chapter. To enable encryption on the ContosoBank database, use the following script:

```
USE master;
GO
--This database master key is created in master
-- and is used to protect the certificate
CREATE MASTER KEY ENCRYPTION BY PASSWORD = 'EOhnDGS6!7JKv';
GO
--This certificate is used to protect the database encryption key
CREATE CERTIFICATE MyServerCert WITH SUBJECT = 'My DEK Certificate';
GO
--You are now ready to create the Database Encryption Key
USE ContosoBank
GO
CREATE DATABASE ENCRYPTION KEY
WITH ALGORITHM = AES_128
ENCRYPTION BY SERVER CERTIFICATE MyServerCert
GO
ALTER DATABASE ContosoBank SET ENCRYPTION ON;
GO
```

There is a slight CPU performance hit when enabling TDE on databases. The actual amount depends on server hardware and many other factors. This should not prohibit you from enabling this useful feature. Perform testing and see for yourself that the benefits will most likely outweigh the performance hit.

Validating Server Configuration

Chances are if you work for a company that has gone through a compliance certification, you realize that it takes a lot of time and effort. Once you are considered compliant, staying in compliance is important. As a DBA, you may be asked to ensure server settings remain unchanged. Some of the properties that you need to ensure might be that databases must be encrypted or might be making sure a highly privileged function such as xp_cmdshell is disabled. SQL Server has a feature called policy-based management (PBM) that makes enforcing compliance easy. With PBM, you can create, deploy, and validate policies that enforce the configuration that you have defined.

The Need for a Policy

PBM models objects such as databases, tables, and logins within the SQL Server instance and provides a hierarchical structure of these managed targets. Each target has many characteristics. For example, the database target has properties such as autoclose, whether the database is encrypted, and so on. These targets have specific properties that are exposed through facets. When you create a policy, it is based on a facet. A *facet* describes some characteristics of a specific target that you can create a policy against.

To help illustrate these concepts, I'll show how to create a policy that will validate your security settings. The scenario for this example is as follows: Recently, a consultant was hired by your company to determine which kinds of things needed to be done to be PCI compliant. The consultant has tasked you with ensuring all servers in your organization match the given configuration:

- The common criteria mode should be enabled.

- SQL Server should be in Windows-integrated mode only.

- The xp_cmdshell extended stored procedure should be disabled.

- Cross-database ownership chaining should be disabled on every database.

- You manage 25 production SQL Server instances. Now, go and earn your paycheck!

Create Policy on a Local Server

First, let's create the policy on the local server to make sure it's what you want to deploy. To create a new policy, select New Policy from the context menu of the Policy node in the Management tree in Object Explorer. This will launch the Create New Policy dialog box, shown in Figure 12-6.

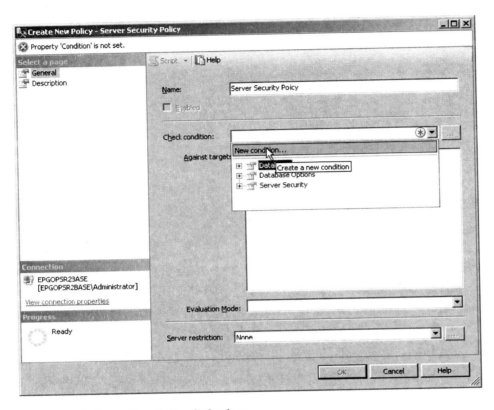

Figure 12-6. *Create New Policy dialog box*

After typing **Server Security Policy** in the Name text box, you need to select a check condition. A check condition is a lot like a `WHERE` clause in a T-SQL statement. It defines what, specifically, the policy is checking. Since you have not created a check condition for your server security settings, you need to select "New condition." This will launch the Create New Condition dialog box, shown in Figure 12-7.

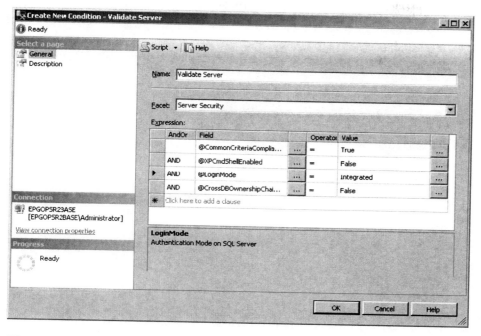

Figure 12-7. *Create New Condition dialog box*

Since you are interested in ensuring serverwide security settings are enforced, you need to select the Server Security facet. Notice that, when you open the Facet list, you are presented with a plethora of facets. Each one of these facets exposes a variety of parameters that you can use to create policies. Once you select Server Security, you will be able to build your logical expression.

The expression grid shown in Figure 12-7 builds the requirements. The common criteria switch should be enabled, XP command shell should be disabled, the login mode should be Windows integrated, and cross-database ownership chaining should be disabled. Once you click OK to create this new condition, control will return to the Create New Policy dialog box.

Had the Server Security facet applied to specific targets, such as tables or stored procedures, those options would be presented in the Against Targets list shown in Figure 12-6. Since the Server Security facet applies only to the SQL Server instance, there are no specific targets to apply this policy against. The next combo box is Evaluation Mode. The default is "On demand," which means that this policy will be created on the server, and nothing will be done with it unless you explicitly evaluate it. The next option is "On schedule," which schedules the evaluation of the policy using SQL Server Agent. If you had specified a policy that triggered on DDL events such as enforcing table names to be a certain format, you would see two additional execution modes: "On change: log only" and "On change: prevent." The log-only option allows a new table with the wrong name to be created; the prevent option rolls back the transaction, inhibiting the table from being created.

Click OK. You can see the new policy created in the Policies node in Object Explorer.

Evaluate the Policy

Having created a policy, you should evaluate it to see whether your server is in compliance. If you select Evaluate from the context menu of the Server Security Policy policy, you will launch the Evaluate Policies dialog box, shown in Figure 12-8.

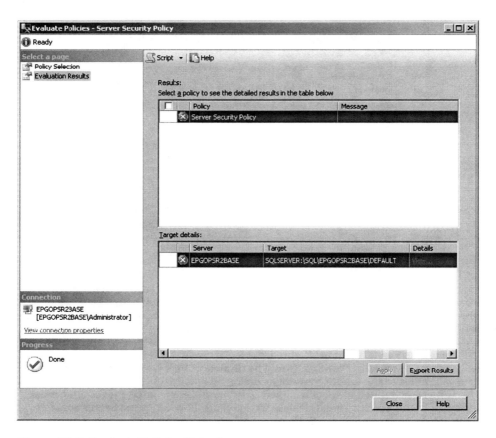

Figure 12-8. *Evaluate Policies dialog box*

In Figure 12-8, you can see that the policy that you created failed its evaluation. To view the details of the failure, click the View hyperlink in the Details column. Figure 12-9 shows an example of what you'll see. You'll get a list of the criteria, and that list will include a pass/fail result for each one.

▨ **Note** Some policy dialog boxes use a blue highlight against light blue hyperlink text. It is very hard to see on print and on the screen, but it's there; trust me.

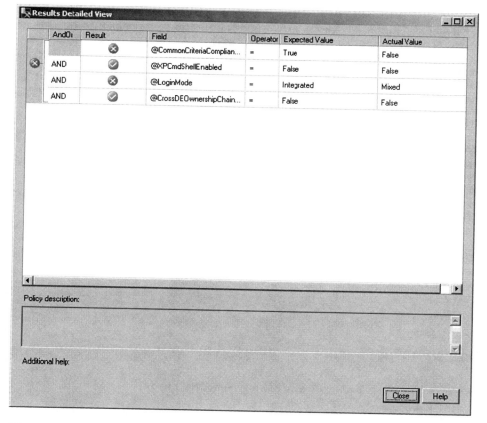

	AndOr	Result	Field	Operator	Expected Value	Actual Value
		⊗	@CommonCriteriaComplian...	=	True	False
⊗	AND	✓	@XPCmdShellEnabled	=	False	False
	AND	⊗	@LoginMode	=	Integrated	Mixed
	AND	✓	@CrossDBOwnershipChain...	=	False	False

Policy description:

Additional help:

| Close | Help |

Figure 12-9. *Details dialog box*

Figure 12-9 shows that the policy's evaluation failed because the common criteria switch was disabled and because the login mode was mixed and not set to integrated mode. You can see that having a policy is an easy and fast way to ensure your servers are in compliance.

In this example, you evaluated a single server. The real power of policy-based management comes with the easy ability to deploy and evaluate policies across multiple servers and multiple versions of SQL. You can create policies that check down level versions of SQL Server including SQL Server 2000, SQL Server 2005, and SQL Server 2008.

To evaluate multiple servers on demand, you can use the Registered Servers window in SSMS. This functionality has been expanded to include the concept of a central management server.

Using the Central Management Server

In the Registered Servers window of SSMS, there is a node called Central Management Server. A central management server (CMS) is not a special server or a new edition of SQL Server; rather, it's a SQL Server instance that you and your DBA team decide on to be the central management server.

Having a CMS server solves two problems. First, imagine the scenario where you are on a DBA team of five other people. Everyone is responsible for the 50 SQL Server instances your company owns. To make administration easier, you create a registered server list of all 50 SQL Server instances. You export this list and e-mail it to your DBA team. Your manager sees that you are proactive and really trying to save the company money by decreasing wasted time. Fast-forward a few days to when some new servers come online and some old ones are consolidated. Now, it's time to send out the registered servers list again, but this time, you forget because you are trying to troubleshoot a faulty backup on one of your servers. Your co-workers don't know the new server names and are stuck until they can get hold of you. Now, your manager doesn't think so highly, and in the words of Sir Topham Hat (from the children's series Thomas the Tank Engine), "You are causing confusion and delay!"

To solve this registered server fiasco, SQL Server has the capability to create a shared registered servers list, and that is the purpose of the central management server. Now, as you make changes to the registered servers list, everyone can see and leverage the same list.

The central management server allows you to group your servers. In Figure 12-10, SQL_DBA_1 is a SQL Server instance that is defined as a CMS. Within it is a folder called Production. Production contains two instances, SQLPROD_1 and SQLPROD_2.

Figure 12-10. Registered Servers view showing Central Management Server node

A few options are available in the context menu of the folders within the central management server. One of them, New Query, allows you to execute a query against all the instances within the Production folder. Another capability is the ability to execute policies. Imagine now how easy it is to determine whether all your servers are in compliance. It is almost just a right-click of a mouse button.

Summary

Compliance requirements come in many shapes and forms dependant completely on what kind of company you work for and who your company hired for an auditor. SQL Server exposes functionality that makes it easy for DBAs to become compliant and to maintain compliance. Table 12-3 lists some additional resources that you may want to peruse relative to what we've discussed in this chapter.

Table 12-3. *Further Resources on Auditing, Encryption, and Compliance*

Resource	Description
SQL Server Security web site	www.microsoft.com/sqlserver/en/us/solutions-technologies/mission-critical-operations/security-and-compliance.aspx
IT Compliance guide	http://technet.microsoft.com/en-us/regulatorycompliance/default.aspx

CHAPTER 13

Performance Tuning and Optimization

SQL Server 2012 and the Windows operating systems that it runs on perform very well storing, maintaining, and presenting data to your users. Many of the processes that make them run so well are built into SQL Server 2012 and the operating system. Sometimes, because of a variety of factors, such as data changes, new code, or poor design choices, performance can suffer. To understand how well, or poorly, your server is performing, you need to understand how to measure that performance.

A number of methods of collecting performance data are available, including the Performance Monitor utility in Windows and the dynamic management objects (DMOs) in SQL Server. All this server information can be automatically collected through the use of a utility built into SQL Server 2012, the data collector. But understanding how the server is performing is not enough. You also need to know how the queries running on the server are performing. You can gather this information using Extended Events sessions. Once you know which queries or processes are running slowly, you'll need to understand what's going wrong with them. Again, SQL Server provides a tool—*execution plans*, which allow you to look into the functions within a query. If you really need help with performance, another automated utility called the Database Tuning Advisor can help.

If this topic sounds large, it is. Entire books have been written about tuning the server and queries. This chapter will act as an introduction to the various mechanisms of performance monitoring and the processes available for tuning and optimizing performance. Some tools, such as the Resource Governor and data compression, can even help you automatically control performance on your server. The Resource Governor will help prevent any one process from consuming too many of the limited resources available on a server. Data compression will automatically make your data and indexes smaller, using fewer resources and, in some cases, speeding up the server.

Measuring SQL Server Performance

The metrics necessary to understand how your server is performing can be grouped into four basic areas: memory, central processing unit (CPU), disk input/output (I/O), and network. When your server is running slowly, one of these four elements needs tuning. To gather the information about these processes, and many more besides, the Windows operating system exposes what are called *performance counters* for your use. There are three ways to look at performance counters: using the Performance Monitor utility, using DMOs, and using the Data Collector.

Understanding Performance Counters

Before getting into the methods to look at performance counters, we'll discuss which performance counters are most useful to you. When you see the list of available performance counters, you're likely to be overwhelmed. Table 13-1 describes the most commonly used and useful performance counters, what they measure, and what represents potentially problematic measurement. Performance counters are grouped together by what are referred to as *objects*. Objects may have a particular application called an *instance*. Under this are the actual counters. To present the information, the Object(Instance):Counter format is usually used.

Table 13-1. System Performance Counters

Performance Counter	Measures	Problematic Values
Processor(_Total): % Processor Time	Percentage of time all the processors on the system were busy	Problematic if average value is greater than 75 percent
System: Processor Queue Length	Number of requests waiting on the processor	Problematic if average value is greater than two
Network Interface(Network card):Bytes Total/Sec	Rate at which bytes are transferred on the network interface card (NIC)	Problematic if average value is less than 50 percent of NIC capacity
PhysicalDisk(Per disk): Avg. Disk Queue Length	The number of requests waiting on the disk to finish	Problematic if greater than three times the number of spindles

These basic counters will show you the amount of time that the various system processes are spending working on your system. With the queue length of the processor and the disk, you can see whether some processes are waiting on others to complete. Knowing that a process is waiting for resources is one of the best indications you'll get that there is a performance problem. You can also look at the amount of information being sent over your network interface card (NIC) as a general measure of problems on your network. Just these few simple counters can show you how the server is performing.

To use these counters, you need a general idea of what constitutes a potential problem. For example, % Processor Time is problematic when a sustained load is 75 percent or greater. But you will see occasional spikes of 100 percent. Spikes of this nature are a problem only when you also begin to see the Processor Queue Length value grow. Understanding that the Average Disk Queue Length value is growing will alert you to potential problems with I/O, but it will also let you know that your system is beginning to scale and that you may need to consider more, or different, disks and disk configurations.

Several counters will show you the performance and behavior of SQL Server itself. These are available in the same places as the system counters, but as you'll see in Table 13-2, they are formatted slightly differently. You'll see these as SQL Server:Object(Instance):Counter.

Table 13-2. SQL Server Performance Counters

Performance Counter	Measures	Problematic Values
`SQLServer:Access Methods:` `Full Scans/sec`	Shows how often a full scan of a table, index, or temporary table is occurring on the server	Based on baseline measurement

`SQLServer:General`
`Statistics:`
`User Connections`
	Shows how many users are connected to the server	Excessive values beyond an established average

`SQLServer:Locks(_Total)`	Measure of total locks on the system	Values beyond a baseline should be cause for concern
`Lock Wait Time (ms)`	Shows how long the average lock is waiting on the server	This number should be as small as possible, but, again, compare it to a baseline
`Batch Requests/sec`	Shows how many requests (queries) are coming through the system per second	Only compare this to a baseline

The first counter listed in Table 13-2, `Full Scans/sec`, lets you know how many *full scans* (a complete read of an index or a table row by row) the system is experiencing. Large numbers here indicate poorly written queries or missing indexes. The second counter, User Connections, simply shows the number of user connections in the system. This is useful when combined with other measures to see how the server is behaving. Lock Wait Time is an indication that a lot of activity is occurring on the server and processes are holding locks that are necessary to manipulate data. This may suggest that transactions are running slowly. Finally, the counter `Batch Requests/sec` indicates just how much load the server is operating under by showing the number of requests in the system.

The counters displayed in Tables 13-1 and 13-2 are a very small subset of the total counters available, but these will give you a general indication of the health of your server. You would need to look at a number of other counters to get an accurate measure of a system's health. The counters mentioned here are the ones that are most likely indicative of a problem on the system. The idea here is that anything that is causing queuing, in other words, waits in the CPU or I/O, is a problem that needs to be identified and dealt with. Within SQL Server, growing numbers of scans or lock waits can also indicate deteriorating performance. So, although these counters won't provide an overall health for the system, they do act like a check on the pulse of the system, which is an early indicator of other problems. There are multiple ways to access these counters on your systems.

Performance Monitor

The Performance Monitor tool comes installed with all versions of the Windows operating system. This tool provides a graphical interface for accessing the performance counters introduced in the preceding section. The easiest way to access the Performance Monitor tool, often referred to as Perfmon because of the name of the executable file, is to click the Start menu on your server and click the Run icon. Type **perfmon**, and then click the OK button. This will open a window that looks like Figure 13-1.

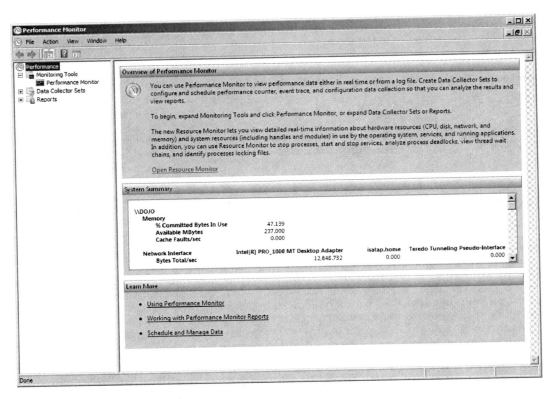

Figure 13-1. Performance Monitor suite

A number of tasks are possible with the Perfmon tool, including viewing performance monitor counters, creating logs of counters, and scheduling the capture of counters to files that can then be viewed through the Perfmon tool or imported into databases for more sophisticated data manipulation. I'll simply show how to view a few of the counters introduced in the previous section.

You first have to access the Performance Monitor tool. Click the icon on the left side of the screen labeled Performance Monitor. This will display a screen similar to Figure 13-2.

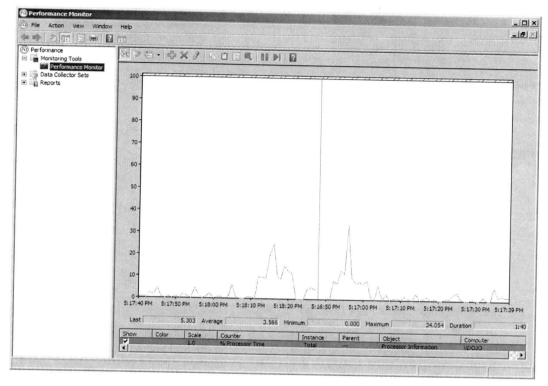

Figure 13-2. Initial Performance Monitor window

To add counters to the Performance Monitor window, click the plus icon near the center of the toolbar at the top of the window. This will open the Add Counters window, shown in Figure 13-3.

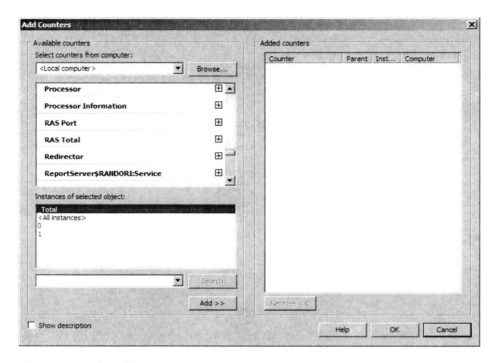

Figure 13-3. The Add Counters window in Perfmon

To select counters for a particular computer, you'll need to supply the name of the computer in the "Select counters from computer" combo box, or you can simply let the tool select from the local computer, as displayed in Figure 13-3. To supply the name, you can either type it or select from a list of computers on your network. Once that's done, you'll need to select one of the performance objects. As shown in Figure 13-2, the % Processor Time object has already been selected for you. To select additional counters, scroll within the "Available counters" window. For this example, select the object General Statistics, which will have your server's instance name in front of it so that it would read ServerInstance:General Statistics if you used the example name from Chapter 2. Scroll down until you find the User Connections counter, and then click it. Click the Add button to add this counter to the "Added counters" list on the right. When you're done adding counters, click the OK button.

Now the Perfmon window will show activity from the two counters selected. The window shows a set period of time, and you can see the variations in data across the period, as shown in Figure 13-4.

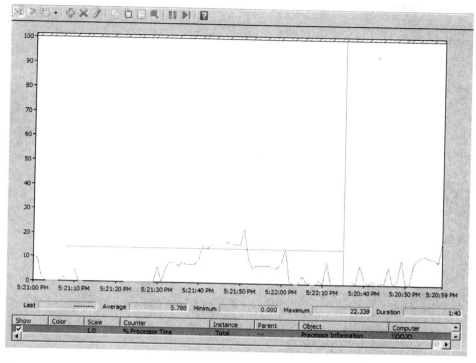

Figure 13-4. Perfmon displaying performance counters and activity

Looking at the screen displayed in Figure 13-4, you can see how the performance counters change over time. The data is collected and aggregated so that you can see important information such as the Last, Average, Maximum, and Minimum values. The duration, the amount of time on display, is also shown. You can see the list of counters that is currently on display. You can even highlight a counter by selecting it in the list and then clicking the lightbulb icon in the toolbar at the top of the screen.

With the Perfmon tool, you can further manipulate the display to show different types of graphs or raw data and change the properties of the counters displayed to adjust the color they're displayed in or the scale on which they display. You can also choose to have the Perfmon tool output to a log. There are other ways to get at performance counters, and one of them is within SQL Server using T-SQL.

Dynamic Management Objects

Introduced in SQL Server 2005, dynamic management objects (DMOs) are mechanisms for looking into the underlying structures and processes of the SQL Server 2012 system and, to a lesser degree, into the operating system. Of particular interest for looking at performance counters is the dynamic management view (DMV) `sys.dm_os_performance_counters`. This shows a list of SQL Server performance counters within the results of a query. It does not show the operating system performance counters. The performance counters for the operating system are not as easily queried as are those for SQL Server. Querying `sys.dm_os_performance_counters` is as simple as querying a table:

```
SELECT  *
FROM    sys.dm_os_performance_counters ;
```

This query will return all the performance counters at this instance in time. To see a specific counter or instance of a counter, you just need to add a WHERE clause to the query so that you return only the counter you're interested in, like this:

```
SELECT  *
FROM    sys.dm_os_performance_counters AS dopc
WHERE   dopc.counter_name = 'Batch Requests/sec' ;
```

This will return a data set similar to that shown in Figure 13-5.

	object_name	counter_name	instance_name	cntr_value	cntr_type
1	MSSQL$RANDORI:SQL Statistics	Batch Requests/sec		44973	272696576

Figure 13-5. *Results from query against sys.dm_os_performance_counters*

The column, cntr_value, shows the value for the counter being selected. If there were no other operations on the server and you were to run the query again, in this instance the counter would go up by 1 to become 44974 because even the query against the DMV counts as a batch request. Other values for other counters may go up or down or even remain the same, depending on what each of the counters and instances is recording. You can use this data in any way you like, just like a regular T-SQL query, including storing it into a table for later access. The main strength of the sys.dm_os_performance_counters DMV is that you can access the data in T-SQL and use the data it displays with the T-SQL tools that you're used to using.

Performance counters are not the only way to tell what is occurring within SQL Server. Another method of looking at performance data is the plethora of other DMOs. Detailing all the possible details for information that you could collect through queries against DMOs is beyond the scope of the book. The DMVs within SQL Server can be roughly grouped as either server DMOs or database DMOs. There are 17 different divisions of DMOs. We won't list them all, but we will list the groups directly used to access performance data about the system or the database:

- *Database*: These are primarily concerned with space and the size of the database, which is important information for understanding performance.

- *Execution*: The DMVs and dynamic management functions (DMFs) in this group are very much focused on the performance and behavior of the queries against the database. Some of these will be covered in the section "Tuning Queries."

- *Index*: Like the database-related DMOs, these are mostly about size and placement, which is useful information. You can also track which indexes are used and whether there are missing indexes.

- *I/O related*: These DMOs are mainly concerned with the performance of operations against disks and files.

- *Resource Governor:* These DMOs are not directly related to performance but are a means of addressing the settings, configuration, and behavior of the Resource Governor, which is directly related to performance. This is covered in detail in the section "Limiting Resource Use."

- *SQL Server operating system:* Information about the operating system, such as memory, CPU, and associated information around the management of resources is available to the DMVs and DMFs grouped here.

- *Transaction:* With the DMOs in this group, you can gather information about active transactions or completed transactions, which is very useful for understanding the performance of the system.

The ability to query all this information in real time or to run queries that gather the data into permanent tables for later analysis makes these DMVs a very important tool for monitoring the performance of the system. They're also useful for later tuning that performance because you can use them to measure changes in behavior. But real-time access to this data is not always a good idea, and it doesn't let you establish a baseline for performance. To do this, another way to collect performance data is needed. This is the Data Collector.

Data Collector

Introduced with SQL Server 2008, the data collector is a means of gathering performance metrics, including performance counters, from multiple SQL Server systems (2008 and above) and collecting all the data in one place, namely, the management data warehouse. The data collector will gather performance data, including performance counters, procedure execution time, and other information. Because it exposes a full application program interface (API), you can customize it to collect any other kind of information that you want. For our purposes, we'll focus on the three default collections: Disk Usage, Query Activity, and Server Activity.

The data collector is a great way to look at information over a long period of time so that you can provide information for tuning purposes. For example, you would want to start collecting data on a new application right away. This initial set of data is known as a *baseline*. It gives you something to compare when someone asks you whether the system is running slowly or whether the databases are growing quickly. You'll also have the ability to collect performance data before and after you make a change to the system. So if you need to know whether adding a new index, changing a query, or installing a hotfix changed the performance in the system, you'll have data collected that allows you to compare behavior before and after the change you introduced to the system. All of this makes the data collector a vital tool in your performance-monitoring and tuning efforts.

▪ **Caution** While experimenting with the data collector, use development, QA, or other test servers and instances. Don't take a chance on your production systems until you feel confident you know what you're doing. Although collecting performance data is important, collecting too much performance data can actually cause performance problems.

Setting Up the Data Collector

To begin using the data collector, you need to first establish security, a *login*, that will be used on all your servers for collecting data. You can approach this in two basic ways. First, you can have a single login across all your servers that have sysadmin privileges, which allows the login to do anything. Second, you can use the built-in data collector roles that are stored in the msdb system database. Detailing all the variations for setting up security for the data collector is beyond the scope of this book. For details, refer to "Data Collector Security" in Books Online.

Once the security is set, you'll need to establish a server as the host to the management data warehouse, where the performance data gathered through the data collector will be stored. When you have the server ready, open SQL Server Management Studio (SSMS), and connect to the server. Scroll down the folders available in the Object Explorer window to the **Management** folder. Expand this. It should look something like Figure 13-6, although if you haven't configured it, you may see a small red arrow like the one visible on the Resource Governor icon.

Figure 13-6. The Data Collector tool inside the Management folder

Once you have navigated to the Data Collector icon, as shown in Figure 13-6, you can begin to establish the management data warehouse. Right-click the Data Collector icon, and select Configure Management Data Warehouse from the context menu. This will open the welcome screen to the Configure Management Data Warehouse Wizard. Click the Next button to get past that screen, as shown in Figure 13-7.

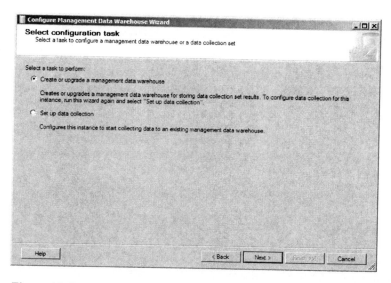

Figure 13-7. Management Data Warehouse Wizard's "Select configuration task" page

The default behavior is to create or upgrade a management data warehouse, which is exactly what needs to happen. The other option is to set up data collection on the server that you run this on. This is how you would set up the data collector, and there will be more on that later in this section. Click the Next button. This will open the next page of the wizard, shown in Figure 13-8.

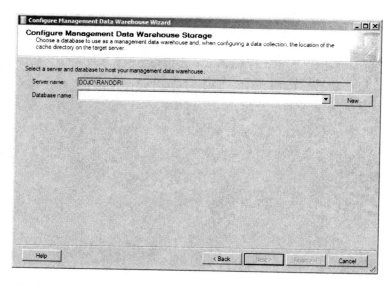

Figure 13-8. Management Data Warehouse Wizard's Configure Management Data Warehouse Storage page

This process is very simple. Either you select an existing database to act as the management data warehouse, or you click the New button to create one when the standard Create Database window opens. Which you do depends on your system. We strongly advise against placing the data collected for the management data warehouse into one of your online transactional systems. You could place it into an existing reporting or management system. If you choose to select a new database, another window, called Map Logins and Users, will open for setting up security. Adjust this as needed for the security within your system and finish the wizard. That's the entire process. Behind the scenes, more occurred than you can immediately see. Inside the database you selected or created, several tables were created that are used by the process to manage the collection and store the data. Stored procedures, views, user-defined functions, and other objects were also added to the database. All these objects are used to gather and present the data as it comes in from the various servers where you've enabled the data collector.

To configure the servers that will send their information to the management data warehouse, connect to those servers through SSMS. Navigate to the Management folder so that you can see the data collector, just like in Figure 13-6. Right-click and select Configure Management Data Warehouse from the context menu. This will again open the wizard's welcome screen. Click Next. This will open the Select Configuration Task page like in Figure 13-7. Click the radio button "Set up data collection," and click Next. This will open the Configure Management Data Warehouse Storage page, shown in Figure 13-9.

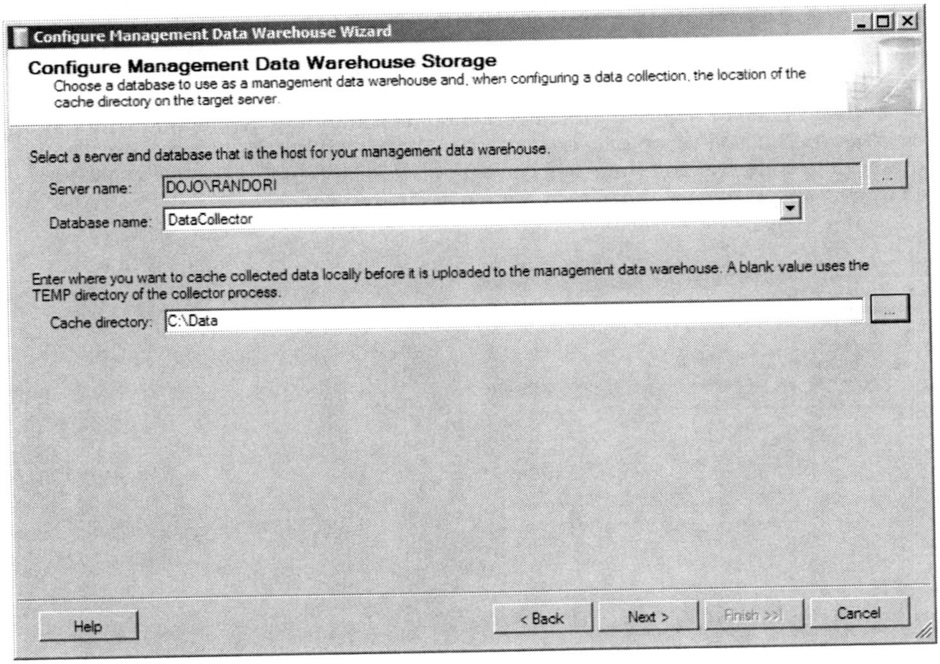

Figure 13-9. Configure Management Data Warehouse Storage page

From the server where you want to collect data, you must define the server where the management data warehouse is stored. Select the server by clicking the ellipsis button, which will enable the "Database name" drop-down. Make sure you select the database that you created previously. Finally, you need to define a directory for data to be cached while it waits for the process to pick it up for storage. Choose an appropriate location on your system. The default is to place it on the system drive (usually C:\). Depending on your environment, this is probably a poor choice. Instead, a storage collection that you can manage that won't affect other processes is a more appropriate location. The data collector is now configured and running.

Viewing the Data Collector Data

The data collector is now running on the server where you designated it. It's collecting the data and storing it in the cache directory you defined. To start to view this data, you need to first get it from the cache directory to the management data warehouse. All the collection jobs are set up and running, but they're not transmitting the data collected, and this transmission must be started. Initially, you can do this manually. Later, you may want to set up scheduled jobs through the SQL Agent to gather the data collector data. To get the data manually, right-click any of the defined data collection sets, and choose Collect and Upload Now from the context menu. This will take the data from the disk cache and load it into the management data warehouse. It's now ready for viewing. You should perform this step if you're following along to have data visible in the next steps.

The data is available in standard tables, so you could access it directly through SQL queries if you wanted. However, the data collector comes installed with a few standardized reports. If you right-click the data collector icon in the Object Explorer window, you can select Reports from the context menu and then select Management Data Warehouse from there. With the default install, three reports are available:

- Server Activity History
- Disk Usage Summary
- Query Statistics History

Server Activity History

If you select the first item in the list, Server Activity History, you'll see a window with a number of charts. All this information represents basic server-level data, showing information such as the amount of CPU or memory used, what processes are waiting when running inside SQL Server, and the aggregated number of activities over time. All of this information is very useful for performance monitoring and tuning. There are so many charts that we can't show them all in a single figure. The top half of the report will look like Figure 13-10.

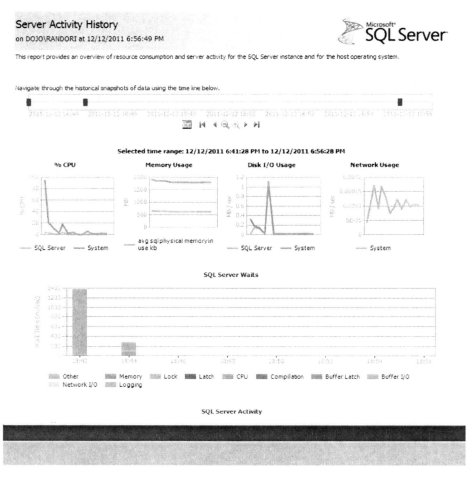

Figure 13-10. *Server Activity History report, top section*

At the top, you can see which server the data is being displayed for. Below that is the time period for which the data is being displayed, and you can modify or scroll through the various time periods using the controls provided. As you change the time period, the other graphs on the chart will change. Immediately below the controls, the time range currently selected is displayed. In the case of Figure 13-10, it's showing a time range between "4/24/2009 2:00AM" and "4/24/2009 6:00AM."

Next are a series of graphs showing different information about the system. Each graph, where appropriate, shows information about the operating system and SQL Server, color-coded as green and blue, respectively. These graphs are nice, but if you need detailed information, you need to click one of the lines. Figure 13-11 shows the detail screen for the % CPU for the system.

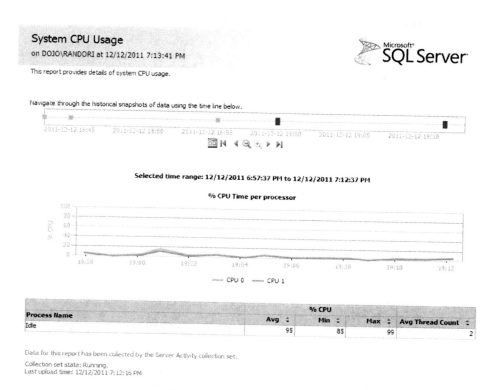

Figure 13-11. *% CPU Time per processor details report*

You can see that once more you have the ability to change the time frame for the report. It also displays a nice graph, even breaking down the behavior by CPU and, finally, showing aggregate numbers for % CPU over the time period. Each of the separate graphs in the main window will show different detail screens with more information specific to that performance metric. To navigate back to the main report, you click the Navigate Backward button located near the top of the window.

Back on the main window of the Server Activity History report, the bottom half of the report looks like Figure 13-12.

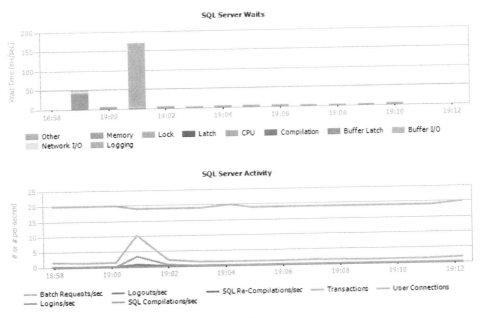

Figure 13-12. Server Activity History report, bottom section

Once again, these are incredibly useful reports all by themselves, showing the SQL Server waits broken down by wait type and showing SQL Server activity broken down by process type. With either of these reports, it is possible, as before, to select one of the lines or bars of data and get a drill-down menu showing more information.

■ **Note**   Initially, immediately after starting the data collector, your graphs might be quite empty. As more data accumulates, the graphs will fill in. You can also use the Timeline tool to zoom in on smaller time slices to get a more complete picture.

Disk Usage Summary

When you open the Disk Usage Summary report, you see a single graph. The report lists the databases over a period when the data collector was gathered. This allows you to see how the sizes of the databases are changing over time. Figure 13-13 shows the Disk Usage Summary report.

Disk Usage Collection Set

on DOJO\RANDORI at 12/12/2011 7:52:34 PM

This report provides an overview of the disk space used for all databases on the server and growth trends for the data file and the log file for each database for the last 4 collection points between 12/12/2011 6:41:58 PM and 12/12/2011 7:52:28 PM.

| Database Name ⬍ | Database | | | | Log | | |
	Start Size (MB) ⬍	Trend	Current Size (MB) ⬍	Average Growth (MB/Day)	Start Size (MB) ⬍	Trend	Current Size (MB) ⬍	Average Growth (MB/Day)
AdventureWorks2	4.06		4.06	0	1.00		1.00	0
AdventureWorks2008R2	199.75		199.75	0	42.25		42.25	0
AdventureWorks2012	4.00		4.00	0	1.00		1.00	0
DataCollector	100.00		100.00	0	10.00		10.00	0
EncryptionTest	4.00		4.00	0	1.00		1.00	0
LogTest	3.06		3.06	0	0.77		0.77	0
master	4.00		4.00	0	0.75		0.75	0
model	3.06		3.06	0	1.00		1.00	0
MonthOfLunches	8.00		8.00	0	12.06		12.06	0
MonthOfLunches2	4.00		4.00	0	1.00		1.00	0
msdb	24.44		24.44	0	19.63		19.63	0
MySimpleDB	3.00		3.00	0	1.00		1.00	0
ReportServer$RANDORI	5.06		5.06	0	6.88		6.88	0

Figure 13-13. Disk Usage Summary report

As you can see, the information is laid out between the data files, shown as the database sizes, and the transaction log, shown as the log sizes. Each one shows a starting size and the current size, which allows you to see a trend. Running this report once a week or once a month will quickly let you know which databases or logs you need to keep an eye on for explosive growth.

You can click the database name to open a new report, the Disk Usage for Database report, as shown in Figure 13-14.

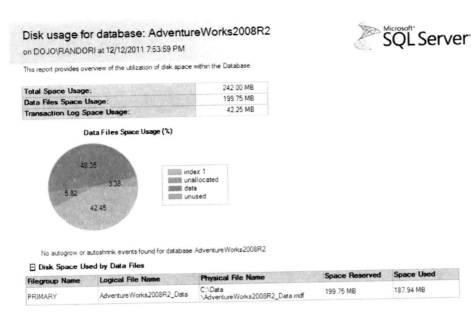

Figure 13-14. *Disk Usage for Database report*

The Disk Usage for Database report details how much of the space allocated to the database is being used and how much is free. It also shows whether the space used is taken up by indexes or data.

Query Statistics History

The most common source of performance problems in SQL Server is poorly written code. Gathering information on the performance metrics of queries is a vital part of performance monitoring and tuning. Opening the Query Statistics History report will display a window similar to Figure 13-15.

Selected time range: 12/13/2011 1:15:04 AM to 12/13/2011 5:15:04 AM

Top Queries by Total Duration

Rank Queries By:

| CPU | Duration | Total I/O | Physical Reads | Logical Writes |

Query #	Query	Executions / min	CPU ms / sec	Total Duration (sec)	Physical Reads / sec	Logical Writes / sec
1	SELECT CONVERT(int, ROW_NUMBER() OVER (ORDER ...	5	0	10	0	0
2	SELECT @operator=operator FROM core.snapshots...	301	0	5	0	0
3	SELECT packagedata FROM sysssispackages WHERE...	0	0	3	0	0
4	UPDATE [snapshots].[notable_query_plan] SET d...	3	0	2	0	0
5	SELECT @plan_handle AS plan_handle, @stateme...	3	0	2	0	0
6	SELECT [sql_handle], statement_start_offset, ...	0	0	1	0	0
7	insert #nt select distinct domain +N'\'+name, ...	0	0	0	0	0

Figure 13-15. *Query Statistics History report*

At the top of the report is the (by now familiar) time control so that you can determine the time period you're interested in viewing. The graph shows queries ordered by different criteria, such as CPU, Duration, Total I/O, Physical Reads, and Logical Writes. Clicking any one of these will change the display to show the top ten queries for that particular metric. In Figure 13-15, Duration has been selected, so the queries are ordered by the total duration of the query for the time period selected. This ability makes this tool incredibly useful because each of these metrics represents a possible bottleneck in your system. So, you may be seeing a number of waits on your system on the CPU in the Server Activity History report. If you then open the Query Statistics History report and sort by CPU, you can see the top ten worse offenders and begin to tune the queries (query tuning is covered in a later section called "Tuning Queries").

Clicking one of the queries will open the Query Details report, shown in Figure 13-16. At the top of the report is the text of the query. Depending on what was run inside the query, this can be quite long. Figure 13-16 shows only the bottom half of the report.

Query Execution Statistics

Average CPU (ms) per Execution:	7.2
Average Duration (ms) per Execution:	7.2
Average Physical Reads per Execution:	0
Average Logical Writes per Execution:	0

Average Executions per Min:	5
Average CPU (ms) per Sec:	0
Average Duration (ms) per Sec:	0
Average Physical Reads per Sec:	0
Average Logical Writes per Sec:	0

Total CPU (sec):	9.7
Total Duration (sec):	9.8
Total Physical Reads:	0
Total Logical Writes:	0
Total Executions:	1347

Query Plan Count:	1

View sampled waits for this query

Query Plans - Average Duration Per Execution

Plan 1

Rank Query Plans By Average Cost Per Execution:

CPU	Duration	Physical Reads	Logical Writes

Top Query Plans By Average Duration Per Execution

Plan #	Execution Count	Plan Creation Time	Average Cost Per Execution				Rate of Resource Use			
			CPU (ms)	Duration (ms)	Physical Reads	Logical Writes	Executions / min	CPU ms / sec	Physical Reads / sec	Logical Writes / sec
1	1347	12/12/2011 6:41:51 PM	7.2	7.2	0	0	5	0	0	0

Figure 13-16. Query Details report, bottom half

The Query Details report shows a lot of information about the query selected. Starting at the top of Figure 13-16, you can see the Query Execution Statistics area. This includes various information such as the average CPU per execution, the average executions per minute, or the total number of executions for the time period. All this information provides you with details to enable you to understand the load that this particular query places on the system. The graph in the middle of Figure 13-16 shows data about the different execution plans that have been created for this query. Selecting each of the different rankings will reorder the execution plans just as it did the queries in the Query Statistics History report. Execution plans are the way that SQL Server figures out how to perform the actions you've requested in the query. They're covered in more detail in the section "Understanding Execution Plans." Being able to look at the information in the Query Details report for a query and compare it to previous entries will be a powerful tool when you begin to tune queries.

Tuning Queries

Tuning SQL Server queries can be as much of an art as a science. However, you can use a number of tools and methods to make tuning your queries easier. The first thing to realize is that most of the time, when queries are running slowly, it's because the T-SQL code within them is incorrect or badly structured. Frequently, queries run slowly because a well-written query is not using an index correctly or an index is missing from the table. Sometimes, you even run into odd bits of behavior that just require extra work from you to speed up the query.

Regardless of the cause of the performance problem, you'll need a mechanism to identify what is occurring within the T-SQL query. SQL Server provides just such a mechanism in the form of execution plans. You'll also need some method of retrieving query performance data and other query information directly from SQL Server. You can capture query execution times using Extended Events. You may not have the time to learn all the latest methods and tricks for tuning your system, but you're going to want it tuned anyway. This is where the Database Tuning Advisor comes in. These three tools—execution plans, Extended Events, and Database Tuning Advisor—provide the means for you to identify queries for tuning, understand what's occurring within the query, and automatically provide some level of tuning to the query.

Understanding Execution Plans

There are two types of execution plans in SQL Server: estimated and actual. Queries that manipulate data, also known as Data Manipulation Language (DML) queries, are the only ones that generate execution plans. When a query is submitted to SQL Server, it goes through a process known as *query optimization*. The query optimization process uses the statistics about the data, the indexes inside the databases, and the constraints within and between the tables in SQL Server to figure out the best method for accessing the data that was defined by the query. It makes these estimates based on the estimated cost to the system in terms of the length of time that the query will run. The cost-based estimate that comes out of the optimization process is the estimated execution plan. The query and the estimated execution plan are passed to the data access engine within SQL Server. The data access engine will, most of the time, use the estimated execution plan to gather the data. Sometimes, it will find conditions that cause it to request a different plan from the optimizer. Either way, the plan that is used to access the data becomes the actual execution plan.

Each plan is useful in its own way. The best reason to use an estimated plan is because it doesn't actually execute the query involved. This means that if you have a very large query or a query that is running for very excessive amounts of time, rather than waiting for the query to complete its execution and an actual plan to be generated, you can immediately generate an estimated plan. The main reason to use actual plans is that they show some actual metrics from the query execution as well as all the information supplied with the estimated plan. When the data access engine gets a changed plan, you will see the changed execution plan, not the estimated plan, when you look at the actual execution plan.

There are a number of possible ways to generate both estimated and actual execution plans. There are also a number of different formats that the plans can be generated in. These include the following:

- *Graphical*: This is one of the most frequently used execution plans and one of the easiest to browse. Most of the time, you'll be reading this type of execution plan.

- *XML*: SQL Server stores and manipulates its plans as XML. It is possible for you to get to this raw data underneath the graphical plan when you need to do so. By itself, the XML format is extremely difficult to read. However, it can be converted into a graphical plan quite easily. This format for the execution plan is very handy for sending to coworkers, consultants, or Microsoft Support when someone is helping you troubleshoot bad performance.

- *Text*: The text execution plans are being phased out of SQL Server. They can be easy to read as long as the plan is not very big, and they are quite mobile for transmitting to others. However, since this format is on the deprecation list for SQL Server, no time will be spent on it here.

The easiest and most frequently used method for generating a graphical execution plan is through the query window in SQL Server Management Studio. Open Management Studio, connect to your server, and right-click a database. From the context menu, select New Query. A new query window will open. For this example, we're using Microsoft's test database, AdventureWorks2008R2. Type a query into the window that selects from a table or executes a stored procedure. Here's the query we're using (salesquery.sql in the download):

```
SELECT   p.[Name],
         soh.OrderDate,
         soh.AccountNumber,
         sod.OrderQty,
         sod.UnitPrice
FROM     Sales.SalesOrderHeader AS soh
JOIN     Sales.SalesOrderDetail AS sod
         ON soh.SalesOrderID = sod.SalesOrderID
JOIN     Production.Product AS p
         ON sod.ProductID = p.ProductID
WHERE    p.[Name] LIKE 'LL%'
         AND soh.OrderDate BETWEEN '1/1/2008' AND '1/6/2008' ;
```

You can run this query and get results. To see the estimated execution plan, click the appropriate icon on the SQL Editor toolbar. It's the circled icon on the toolbar in Figure 13-17.

Figure 13-17. *SQL Editor toolbar with the Display Estimated Execution Plan icon and tooltip*

This will immediately open a new tab in the results pane of the Query Editor window. On this tab will be displayed the estimated execution plan. Figure 13-18 shows the estimated execution plan.

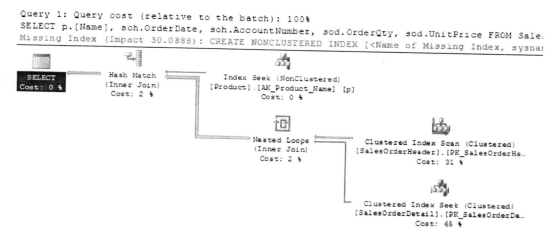

Figure 13-18. *Estimated execution plan*

The first thing to note is that the query was not executed. Instead, the query was passed to the optimizer inside SQL Server, and the output of the optimizer, this execution plan, was returned. There's a lot of information to understand on this execution plan. At the top of Figure 13-18, you see the text "Query 1: Query cost (relative to the batch): 100%." When there is more than one statement inside a query, meaning two SELECT statements, a SELECT statement and an INSERT statement, and so on, each of the individual statements within the query batch will show its estimated cost to the entire batch. In this case, there's only one query in the batch, so it takes 100 percent of the cost. Just below that, the text of the query is listed. Next, printed in green, is Missing Index information. This will only be visible if the optimizer has identified a potential missing index. In some instances, the optimizer can recognize that an index may improve performance. When it does, it will return that information with the execution plan. Immediately below this is the graphical execution plan. A graphical plan consists of icons representing operations, or operators, within the query and arrows connecting these operations. The arrows present the flow of data from one operator to the next.

There is a lot more to be seen within the execution plan, but instead of exploring the estimated plan in detail, we'll drill down on the actual execution plan. To enable the actual execution plan, refer to Figure 13-17. Use the icon second from the right of the figure to enable the display of actual execution plans. When you click it, nothing will happen, but it's a switch. It will stay selected. Now execute the query. When the query completes, the result set and/or the Messages tab will be displayed as it normally would. In addition, the Execution Plan tab is visible. Click that, and you will see something similar to Figure 13-19.

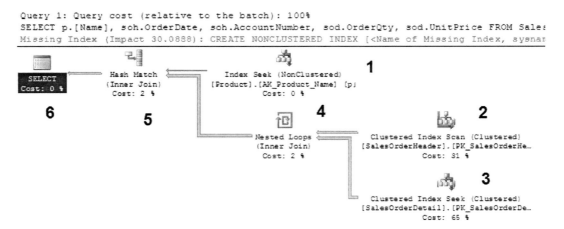

Figure 13-19. Actual execution plan, including operator order

The numbers displayed to the right of each of the operators were added and will be explained a little later. You'll see that this actual execution plan looks more or less identical to the estimated execution plan shown in Figure 13-18. In lots of instances, the statistics on the indexes and data within the database are good enough that the estimated plan will be the same as the actual execution plan. There are, however, large differences not immediately visible, but we'll get to those later.

Graphical execution plans show two different flows of information. They are displayed in a manner that defines the logical flow of data; there is a SELECT statement that has to pull information from a hash match operator, and so on. The physical flow of information is read from the top, right, and then down and to the left. But you have to take into account that some operations are being fed from other operators. We've shown the sequence that this particular execution plan is following through the numbers to the right of the operators. The first operator in sequence is the Clustered Index Scan operator at the top of the execution plan. This particular operator represents the reads necessary from the clustered index, detailed on the graphical plan, SalesOrderheader.PK_SaleOrderHeaderId. You can see a number below that: "Cost: 51%." That number represents the optimizer's estimates of how much this operator will cost, compared to all the other operations in the execution plan. But it's not an actual number; it represents the number of seconds that the optimizer estimates this operation will take. These estimates are based on the statistics that the optimizer deals with and the data returned by preceding operations. When this varies, and it does frequently, these estimated costs will be wrong. However, they don't change as the execution plan changes. The output from the Clustered Index Scan is represented by the thin little arrow pointing to operator 5. That arrow represents the rows of data coming out of the Clustered Index Scan operator. The size of the arrow is emblematic of the number of rows being moved. Because the next operation, Hash Match, relies on two feeds of data, you must resolve the feed before resolving the Hash Match operator. That's why you then move back over to the right to find operation 2, Index Seek. The output from 2, Index Seek, feeds into 4, the Nested Loop operator. Since the Nested Loop operator has two feeds, you again must find the source of the other feed, which is 3, the other Index Seek operator. Operations 2 and 3 combine in operation 4, and then output from operation 4 combines with that of operation 1 inside operation 5. The final output goes to operation 6, the SELECT statement.

It can sound daunting and possibly even confusing to explain how the data flows from one operator to the next, but the arrows representing the rows of data should help show the order. There are more than 100 different operations and operators, so we won't detail them here. In this instance, the operators that are taking multiple feeds represent the JOIN operations within the query that combines the data from multiple tables. A lot more information is available within the graphical execution plan. If you hover over an operator with the mouse pointer, you'll get a tooltip displaying details about the operator. Figure 13-20 shows the tooltip for Nested Loops (Inner Join).

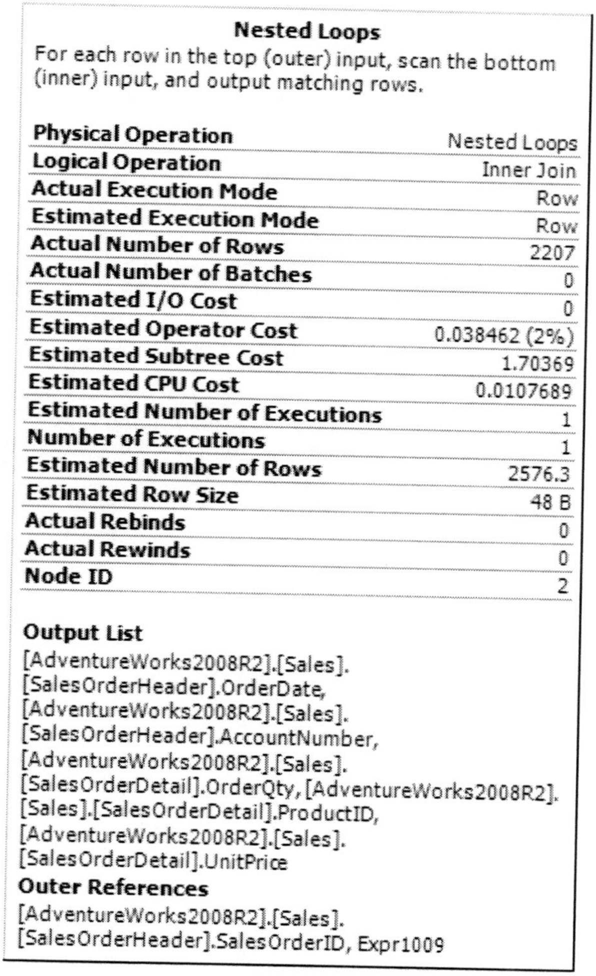

Nested Loops

For each row in the top (outer) input, scan the bottom (inner) input, and output matching rows.

Physical Operation	Nested Loops
Logical Operation	Inner Join
Actual Execution Mode	Row
Estimated Execution Mode	Row
Actual Number of Rows	2207
Actual Number of Batches	0
Estimated I/O Cost	0
Estimated Operator Cost	0.038462 (2%)
Estimated Subtree Cost	1.70369
Estimated CPU Cost	0.0107689
Estimated Number of Executions	1
Number of Executions	1
Estimated Number of Rows	2576.3
Estimated Row Size	48 B
Actual Rebinds	0
Actual Rewinds	0
Node ID	2

Output List
[AdventureWorks2008R2].[Sales].
[SalesOrderHeader].OrderDate,
[AdventureWorks2008R2].[Sales].
[SalesOrderHeader].AccountNumber,
[AdventureWorks2008R2].[Sales].
[SalesOrderDetail].OrderQty, [AdventureWorks2008R2].
[Sales].[SalesOrderDetail].ProductID,
[AdventureWorks2008R2].[Sales].
[SalesOrderDetail].UnitPrice

Outer References
[AdventureWorks2008R2].[Sales].
[SalesOrderHeader].SalesOrderID, Expr1009

Figure 13-20. Nested Loops tooltip

The tooltip gives you a lot more information about the operator. Each of the operator tooltips is laid out in roughly the same way, although the details will vary. You can see a description at the top window that names the operator and succinctly describes what it does and how it works. Next is a listing of measurements about the operation. In these measurements, you can begin drilling down on the operators to understand what each individual operator is doing and how well it's doing it. You can see some of the differences between the estimated and actual execution plans here. Near the top of Figure 13-20 is the measurement Actual Number of Rows and a value of 2207. Just below halfway down is the Estimated Number of Rows measurement and a value of 2576.3. This means that although there are an estimated 2576.3 rows being returned, the actual number of rows is a slightly less, at 2207. At the bottom of the tooltip are details about the operator: the output, the input, or the objects on which the operator is working. In this case, it was the output of the operator and the references used to do the loop join. When you move the mouse again, the tooltip closes.

You can also get a tooltip about the rows of information. Again, hover over the arrow instead of the operator. Figure 13-21 shows an example of the data flow tooltip.

Actual Number of Rows	2207
Estimated Number of Rows	2576.3
Estimated Row Size	48 B
Estimated Data Size	121 KB

Figure 13-21. Data flow tooltip

The data flow tooltip just shows the information you see. The actual plan shows the number of rows in addition to the estimated rows available in the estimated execution plan. It's useful to see how much data is being moved through the query.

Even more details about the operators are available. Right-click one of the operators, and select Properties from the context menu to open a properties view similar to the one shown in Figure 13-22.

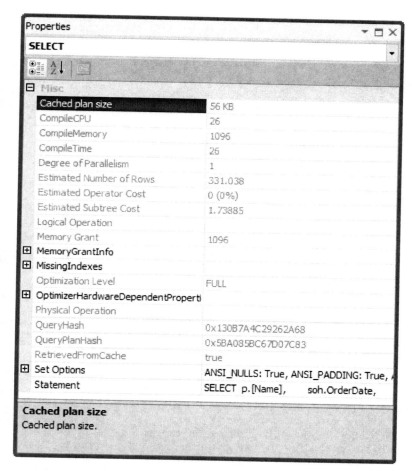

Figure 13-22. Execution plan operator properties

A lot of the information available on the tooltip is repeated here in the properties, and the Properties window has even more information available. You can open the pieces of data that have a plus sign next to them to get more information. All this is available to you so you can understand what's happening within a query. However, getting to the information from the graphical execution plan a little bit of work. If you want to deal with nothing but raw data, you need to look at the XML execution plan.

There are a few ways to generate an XML execution plan, but since even the graphical execution plans we've been working with have XML behind the scenes, it's possible to simply use a graphical plan to generate XML. Right-click inside the execution plan, and select Show Execution Plan XML. This will open a new window. Figure 13-23 shows a partial representation of an XML execution plan.

```
<?xml version="1.0" encoding="utf-16"?>
<ShowPlanXML xmlns:xsi="http://www.w3.org/2001/XMLSchema-instance" xmlns::
  <BatchSequence>
    <Batch>
      <Statements>
        <StmtSimple StatementCompId="1" StatementEstRows="331.038" Stateme
          <StatementSetOptions ANSI_NULLS="true" ANSI_PADDING="true" ANSI_
          <QueryPlan DegreeOfParallelism="1" MemoryGrant="1096" CachedPlar
            <MissingIndexes>
              <MissingIndexGroup Impact="30.0888">
                <MissingIndex Database="[AdventureWorks2008R2]" Schema="[!
                  <ColumnGroup Usage="INEQUALITY">
                    <Column Name="[OrderDate]" ColumnId="3" />
```

Figure 13-23. *The XML execution plan*

All the information available through the graphical part of the plan and from the properties of the plan is available within the XML. Unfortunately, XML is somewhat difficult to read. Primarily, you'll use the XML plans as a means to transmit the execution plan to coworkers or support personnel. But, you can write XQuery queries against the execution plans as a way to programmatically access the information available in the execution plans; that type of query is beyond the scope of this book.

Gathering Query Information with Extended Events

Extended Events are a mechanism for gathering and viewing detailed information about the queries being executed on your system, among other things. The events provide a means to gather this information in an automated fashion so that you can use them to identify long-running or frequently called procedures. You can also gather other types of real-time information such as users logging into or out of the system, error conditions such as a deadlocks, locking information, and transactions. But the primary use is in gathering information about stored procedures as they are executed and doing this over a period of time.

Extended Event sessions are created through T-SQL commands. You can learn the T-SQL necessary to set up the commands, but you can also take advantage of the graphical user interface that was introduced in SQL Server 2012. Extended Events offer a number of methods for output of the information gathered, and we'll focus in the two most common here. You can set up Extended Events to output to a live feed that you can watch through SSMS. You can also, in addition, set up the session to output to a file so that you can gather information over time and then report on it later at your leisure.

Extended Events operate, as we've already mentioned, within a construct called a session. A *session* is simply the definition of which events are being collected and what output you want for the events. Each event collects a default set of columns that represent information about itself. There are some columns that you can add in addition to the default columns as well as additional sets of data called *actions*. These can be expensive operations from a performance standpoint, and using them inappropriately can seriously impact your servers. Our suggestion is to stay away from actions until you're 100 percent sure you're collecting the right kind of information. The standard events and their columns will provide most of what you need anyway.

There are two graphical user interfaces that you can take advantage of for setting up Extended Event sessions. Both create the same sets of events and will start the same types of sessions. One is the standard interface used to create and edit sessions. The other is a wizard that walks you through the process of creating a session. We'll discuss both, but we'll spend most of our time working with the wizard. To get started with the wizard, navigate through the Object Explorer window in SSMS to the Management folder. Open that folder. Inside it is another folder called Extended Events. Expand this folder to see the folder inside labeled Sessions. Right-click the Sessions folder, and select New Session Wizard from the context menu to open the wizard shown in Figure 13-24.

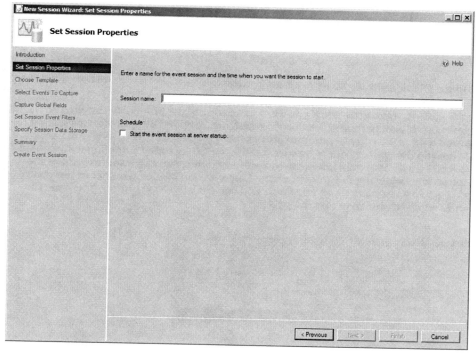

Figure 13-24. New Session Wizard for Extended Events

First, you supply a name for the session. This is a standard description and shouldn't require much thought. We're calling our session Gather Query Performance Metrics. You also have the option of starting a session when you start SQL Server. You can do this for gathering query metrics; just be prepared to deal with a lot of data. Once you've supplied a name, you can click the Next button to open the Choose Template page, shown in Figure 13-25.

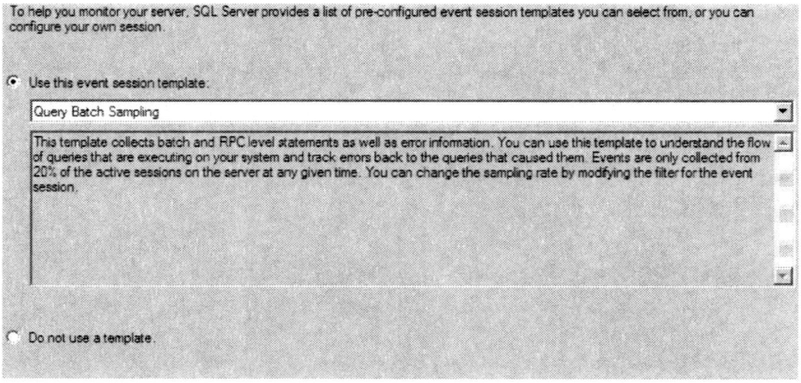

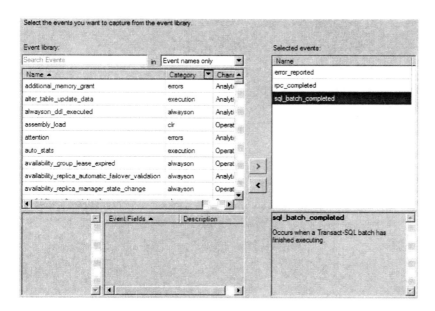

To help you monitor your server, SQL Server provides a list of pre-configured event session templates you can select from, or you can configure your own session.

⊙ Use this event session template:

Query Batch Sampling

This template collects batch and RPC level statements as well as error information. You can use this template to understand the flow of queries that are executing on your system and track errors back to the queries that caused them. Events are only collected from 20% of the active sessions on the server at any given time. You can change the sampling rate by modifying the filter for the event session.

○ Do not use a template.

Figure 13-25. *Choosing a template for the Extended Events session*

On this page of the wizard, you can decide if you want to use one of the Microsoft-supplied templates or put together your own particular session. The sessions supplied by Microsoft are a great foundation to get started with. Plus, you can edit the settings that they make for you, so you're not locked in. For a basic session that gathers query metrics, I think the Query Batch Sampling template that I have selected in Figure 13-25 is more than adequate as a starting point. You can even read about the session in the description just below the drop-down menu. Once you've decided whether or not you're using a template and selected a template if you need one, you can click the Next button. You'll see the Select Events to Capture window, shown in Figure 13-26.

Figure 13-26. *Selecting events for your Extended Events session*

Three events are already selected on the right side of the screen: `error_reported`, `rpc_completed`, and `sql_batch_completed`. Below each of the events is a description, so you don't have to try to decipher the names if they're not completely clear to you. On the left side of the screen is a list of all the possible events you could capture. You can use the Search Events text box to find events and filter the information in different ways by selecting from the drop-down box next to it. If you do select additional events, you can use the little arrow buttons in the middle of the screen to move events in and out of the Selected Evens list.

The next screen is Capture Global Fields, and it contains the actions we suggested earlier that you avoid. Click Next again to open the Set Session Event Filters window, shown in Figure 13-27.

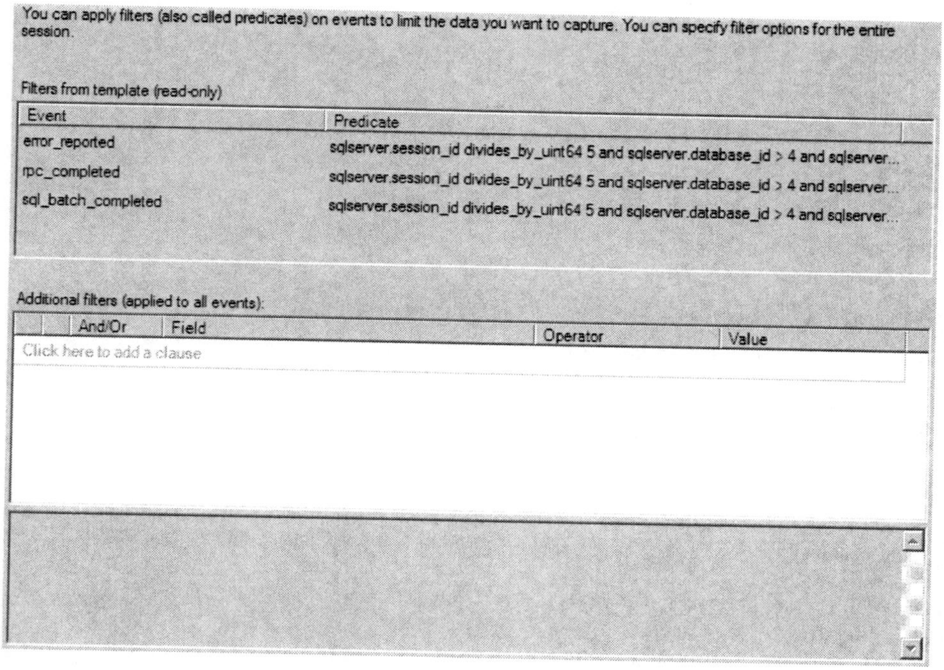

Figure 13-27. Set Session Event Filters in the Extended Events wizard

Three filters are already created for the three events in the template. You can add additional filters using the wizard page shown in Figure 13-27. You can't edit the filters for the template within the wizard, but you can edit them once the session is created using the standard session editor. If you hover your mouse over the Predicate column for the events, you can get a look at the filters already applied, as shown in Figure 13-28.

sqlserver.session_id divides_by_uint64 5 and sqlserver.database_id > 4 and sqlserver.is_system = false

Figure 13-28. Extended Event filter

The filter shown in Figure 13-28 tried to capture events only where the `session_id` is divisible by 5, therefore eliminating a substantial number of events but still capturing a representative sample. This is a valid method for gathering performance metrics on the system while keeping the overall amount of data collected low. If you're looking for more accurate information, you'd need to edit this filter after it is created. The rest of the filter is eliminating calls to the system databases.

Clicking the Next button will open the Specify Data Storage window, visible in Figure 13-29.

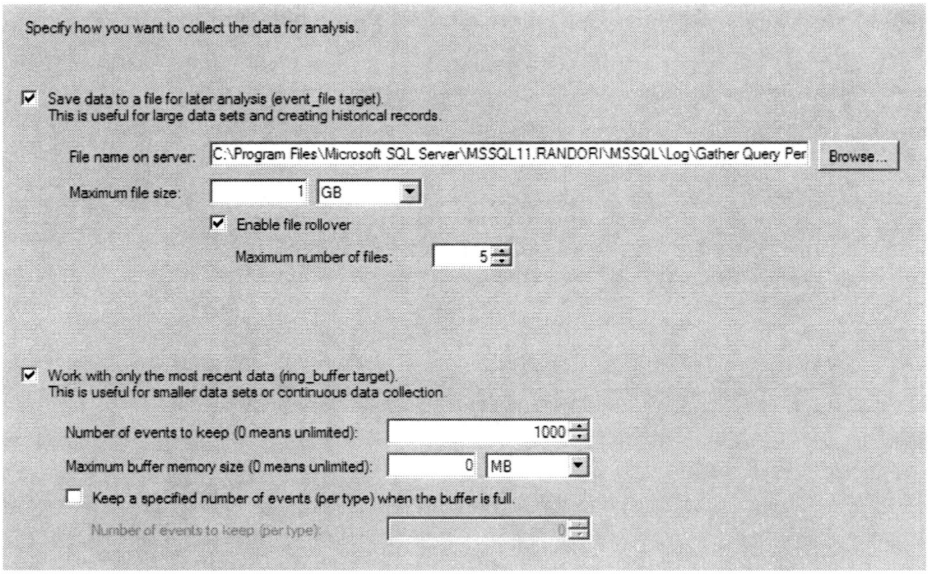

Figure 13-29. *Determining where the session will output through the Specify Data Storage window*

Finally, you need to determine where the information gathered during the Extended Events session will go. You can specify output to a file, to the window, or both at the same time. If you're trying to collect performance metrics about your system, you should plan on having this information go out to a file. You can then load that information into tables at a later date for querying and aggregating the information to identify the most frequently called or most resource-intensive query.

Clicking Next will bring up a summary window where you can see all the choices that have been made while setting up this session. The back button is always available, and you can use the window choices on the left side of the screen to go back to a previous step and edit it.

When you click the Finish button, the session is created, but it is not started. This means you can decide when you want to start the session. You do get the opportunity to start it from the wizard, but having the session created, but not started, is a great way to allow you to get into the session and make any adjustments you want without having to deal with data that doesn't meet your requirements. For the purposes of this example, we've started the session and launched the viewing window. The output is visible in Figure 13-30.

name	timestamp
error_reported	2011-12-15 19:37:06.7878998
sql_batch_completed	2011-12-15 19:37:06.7878998
error reported	2011-12-15 19:37:06.8699311

Event: sql_batch_completed (2011-12-15 19:37:06.7878998)

Details

Field	Value
attach_activity_id.g...	7FFFB470-0A04-4A29-B009-78DD891998E1
attach_activity_id.s...	4
batch_text	SELECT * FROM Person.Address AS a
client_app_name	Microsoft SQL Server Management Studio - Query
cpu_time	125000
database_id	9
duration	575195
logical_reads	342
physical_reads	0
query_hash	0
result	OK
row_count	19614
session_id	66
writes	0

Figure 13-30. Extended Events session output

The window is divided into two parts. At the top is a series of events as they occur. Selecting a particular event will open the details in the lower window. There, you can see all the metrics that make Extended Events so incredibly useful for performance tuning. You can see the query that was called in the batch_text column. And you can see the rows returned, the number writes and reads, and the duration of the query—all necessary pieces of information when determining if the query is running fast enough or not.

Using the Database Engine Tuning Advisor

Among the principal methods that SQL Server uses to maintain and control queries are indexes and the statistics on those indexes. Taking direct control over these indexes yourself can take a lot of time and effort and require education and discovery. Fortunately, SQL Server has a tool that will help you create indexes—the Database Engine Tuning Advisor (DTA). The DTA can be run a number of different ways to help you. You can capture a trace data set and send it to the DTA for analysis. You can pass a query from the Query Editor inside Management Studio straight into the DTA for analysis. Now, with SQL Server 2012, you can use the query plans that exist in the plan cache on a server as the base data for the DTA.

To see it in action, we'll run the DTA against the query used previously (`salesquery.sql` in the download):

```
SELECT  p.[Name],
        soh.OrderDate,
        soh.AccountNumber,
        sod.OrderQty,
        sod.UnitPrice
FROM    Sales.SalesOrderHeader AS soh
JOIN    Sales.SalesOrderDetail AS sod
        ON soh.SalesOrderID = sod.SalesOrderID
JOIN    Production.Product AS p
        ON sod.ProductID = p.ProductID
WHERE   p.[Name] LIKE 'LL%'
        AND soh.OrderDate BETWEEN '1/1/2008' AND '1/6/2008' ;
```

In the query window, right-click the query text, and select Analyze Query in Database Engine Tuning Advisor from the context menu. This will open the DTA in a window that looks like Figure 13-31.

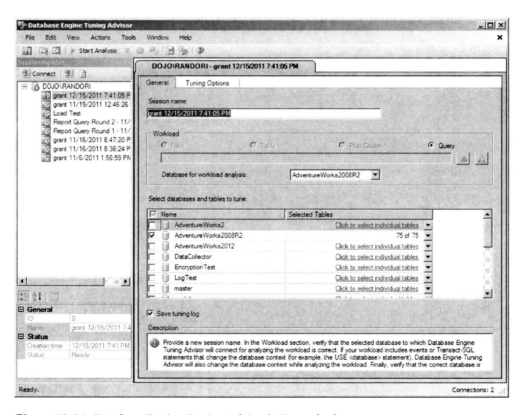

Figure 13-31. *Database Engine Tuning Advisor's General tab*

Figure 13-31 shows a simple example. With more complicated examples that include data from other databases that are being run based on the workload supplied by a trace, you would have more databases selected. In this case, it's a single query against a single database.

From here, you can move to the Tuning Options tab to adjust the possible changes being proposed by the DTA. For this example, we'll let the default values work. On the DTA toolbar, click the Start Analysis button, and a new tab showing the progress of the analysis will open. Once the analysis completes, another new tab showing recommendations from the DTA will open. Figure 13-32 shows the recommendations for the query.

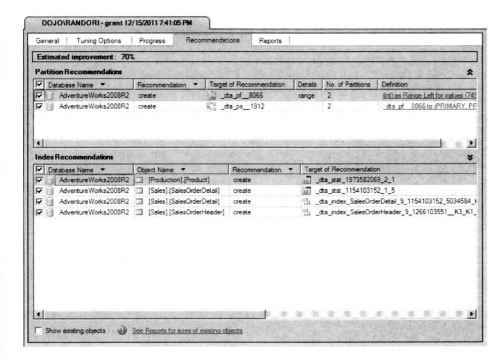

Figure 13-32. Database Engine Tuning Advisor Recommendations tab

For the query supplied, the DTA ran through the information in the query and the information in the tables, and it arrived at three indexes that it thinks will achieve a 70 percent increase in speed. You should take any and all recommendations from the DTA and test them prior to implementing them in production. It is not always right.

Managing Resources

Another way to control performance is to just prevent the processes from using as much of the CPU, memory, or disk space as possible. If any one process can't access very much memory, more memory is available to all the other resources. If you use less space on the disks, you will have more room for growth. SQL Server 2012 supplies tools that let you manage resources. The Resource Governor lets you put hard stops on the amount of memory or CPU that requests coming in to the server can consume. Table and index compression is now built into SQL Server.

Limiting Resource Use

The Resource Governor helps you solve common problems such as queries that just run and run, consuming as many resources as they can; uneven work loads where the server is sometimes completely overwhelmed and other times practically asleep; and the ability to say that one particular process has a higher, or lower, priority than other processes. The Resource Governor will identify that a process matches a particular pattern as it arrives at the server, and it will then enforce the rules you've defined as appropriate for that particular pattern. Prior to setting up the Resource Governor, you will need to have a good understanding of the behavior of your application using tools already outlined such as Performance Monitor, the Data Collector, and profile traces.

When you've gathered at least a few days' worth of performance data so that you know what limits you can safely impose on the system, you'll want to configure the Resource Governor. You can control the Resource Governor through SQL Server Management Studio or T-SQL statements. T-SQL statements are going to give you more granular control and the ability to program behaviors, and they are required for some functions, but using SSMS for most functions will be easier until you have a full understanding of the concepts.

The Resource Governor is not enabled by default. To enable it, navigate to the Management folder in the Object Explorer in SSMS. Right-click the Resource Governor icon, and select Enable from the context menu. The Resource Governor is now running.

The Resource Governor works by managing the resources available in *pools*. A resource pool describes how much memory and CPU will be available to processes that run within that pool. To create a new pool, you first have to enable the Resource Governor by right-clicking the icon and selecting Enable Resource Governor. Next, right-click the Resource Governor icon, and choose New Resource Pool from the context menu. A window similar to Figure 13-33 will open.

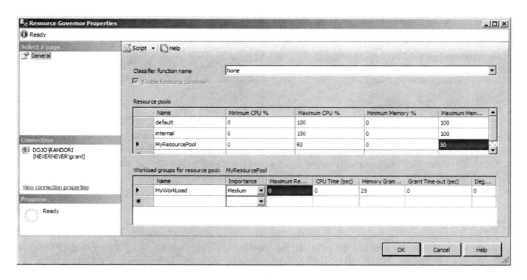

Figure 13-33. Resource Governor Properties window

We've created a new resource pool called MyResourcePool and placed limits on the Maximum CPU % of 60 percent and on the Maximum Memory % of 50 percent. This means that processes that run within the pool will be able to use only 60 percent of the processor power on the server and no more than 50 percent of the memory.

You define the processes that run within a pool by creating a *workload*. Figure 13-29 shows that we created a workload called MyWorkLoad. In the workload, you can further control the behavior of processes. These are the metrics you can control:

- *Importance*: This sets the priority of the particular workload within the resource pool. It doesn't affect behavior outside that pool. This is useful for specifying which workload gets more of the resources within the pool.

- *Maximum Requests*: This limits the number of simultaneous requests within the pool.

- *CPU Time (sec)*: Use this to put a limit on how long a process within the workload can wait for resources to be freed. Setting this limit gets processes out of the way if there's a lot of stress on the server.

- *Memory Grant %*: This one limits how much memory can be granted from the pool to any individual process within the workload.

- *Grant Time-out(sec)*: This is like the CPU time limit, but it limits how long the process can wait for memory.

- *Degree of Parallelism*: In systems with multiple processors, this limits how many processors can be used by processes within the workload.

Finally, to set up the Resource Governor to get it to recognize that processes belong to this pool and this workload, you need to define a function called a *classifier*. The classifier is a user-defined function that uses some sort of logic to decide whether the processes coming into the system need to be passed on to the Resource Governor. An example might be to limit the amount of resources available to queries run from Management Studio on your server. Inside the database you want to govern, you would create a function that looks something like this (governorclassifier.sql in the download):

```
CREATE FUNCTION GovernorClassifier ()
RETURNS SYSNAME
    WITH SCHEMABINDING
AS
BEGIN
    DECLARE @GroupName AS SYSNAME ;
    IF (APP_NAME() LIKE '%MANAGEMENT STUDIO%')
        SET @GroupName = 'MyWorkLoad' ;
    RETURN @GroupName ;
END
GO
```

You have to assign this to the workload only through the drop-down available in the Resource Governor Properties window, as shown in Figure 13-34. Now, when queries come in from SQL Server Management Studio, they will be limited, as defined by the workgroup and the pool, to the available resources. This will leave more resources for all other processes, thereby preventing their performance from degrading, which works out to be the same as improving it.

Leveraging Data Compression

Index and data compression are available only in the Enterprise and Developer editions of SQL Server. Data in SQL Server is stored on a construct referred to as a *page*. When you read data off the disk, you have to read a whole page. Frequently, especially when running queries that return large sets of data, you have to read a number of pages. Reading data from disk, as well as writing it there, are among the most expensive processes that SQL Server performs. Compression forces more data onto a page. This means that when the data is retrieved, fewer reads against the disk are necessary with more data returned. This can radically increase performance. Compression does not come without a cost, however. The process of compressing and uncompressing the data must be taken up the CPU. On systems that are already under significant stress in and around the CPU, introducing compression could be a disaster. The good news is that CPU speed keeps increasing, and it's one of the easiest ways to increase performance. No application or code changes are required to deal with compressed data or indexes.

You can compress a table or indexes for the table separately or together. It's worth noting that you can't count on the compression on a table or a clustered index to automatically get transmitted to the nonclustered indexes for that table. They must be created with compression enabled individually. Compression can be implemented at the row or page level. Page compression uses row compression, and it compresses the mechanisms that describe the storage of the page. Actually, implementing either of these types of compression is simply a matter of definition when you create the table. The following script (`createcompressedtable.sql` in the download) shows how it works:

```
CREATE TABLE dbo.MyTable
    (Col1 INT NOT NULL,
     Col2 NVARCHAR(50) NULL
    )
    WITH (
        DATA_COMPRESSION = PAGE) ;
```

This will create the table `dbo.MyTable` with page-level compression. To create the table with row-level compression instead, just substitute `ROW` for `PAGE` in the syntax. To create an index with compression, the following syntax will work (`createcompressedindex.sql` in the download):

```
CREATE NONCLUSTERED INDEX ix_MyTable1
ON dbo.MyTable (Col2)
WITH ( DATA_COMPRESSION = ROW ) ;
```

Using fewer resources for storage can and will result in performance improvements, but you will need to monitor the CPU on systems using compression.

Summary

To know how to tune your system, you first need to understand the baseline behavior that system. That's why you use tools such as Extended Events and the data collector on systems *before* you're having trouble with performance. Once you're experiencing performance issues, you use the data collected through these tools to understand where the slowdowns are occurring. To identify what is causing the slowdowns, you would use tools like Profiler to create a trace to capture the behavior of queries and procedures. You could also write queries against dynamic management views to see the performance information stored in the system.

Once you understand what's going wrong, you need to use execution plans to explore the behavior of the queries to find the processes that are running slowly and causing problems. With the Database Engine Tuning Advisor, you can fix some of the bad indexing on your system so that your queries will run faster. If you really need to, though, you can just limit the amount resources used by some processes through the Resource Governor. All this combines to enable you to tweak and tune the system to improve its performance and optimize its behavior.

This chapter only begins the process of explaining performance tuning. For more detail and a lot more information, check out Grant Fritchey's *SQL Server 2012 Query Performance Tuning* (Apress, 2012).

CHAPTER 14

Fault Tolerance

bWinInteractive Entertainment AG is a company that operates platforms for sports betting, casino games, and games of skill. The sports betting infrastructure supports about a million bets per day and hosts 100 Terabytes of information across 100 instances of SQL Server. During peak loads, SQL Server handles more than 30,000 database transactions per second. Imagine the amount of angry people there would be if the system went down after they placed bets. This would ruin the company's credibility in the industry. Designing fault tolerance in your environment is critical no matter what database platform you support or industry you are employed in. There is no doubt that bWin's solution involved highly available fault tolerant technologies. These technologies you will learn about in this chapter. If you are interested in reading more about the bWin case study, check out the following URL: www.microsoft.com/casestudies/Case_Study_Detail.aspx?CaseStudyID=4000001470.

Uptime is defined as the amount of time a computer system goes without crashing. For mission-critical database applications, keeping the systems running without failure is critical. As DBAs, we are always planning for disaster, because over time, everything fails. For example, hard disks have mechanical parts and will eventually fail. Not too long ago, hard disk manufactures proudly wrote the MTBF (mean time between failures) on their hard drives to distinguish the more expensive drives. To mitigate the hard drive failure problem, we could add more hard drives and employ RAID techniques like disk mirroring or disk striping. If a particular disk failed, it could be swapped out, and our data would still be available.

The mechanical spin of a disk is not the only thing to be concerned with in a datacenter. Over time, network cards, routers, switches, and anything electronic could fail for lots of reasons. For example, a poor solder joint on a board could loosen up because of the natural heating and cooling of the environment. Although most datacenters are climate controlled, one more risk still trumps our fine mitigation work: tornados, floods, earthquakes and other natural disasters occur and could instantly destroy a datacenter. For this reason, datacenters are usually replicated out to remote sites geographically far from the main datacenter. This geographical separation causes more challenges for DBAs and system administrators. Providing fault tolerance with remote datacenters is possible through SQL Server by leveraging Windows Server Failover Clusters. These kinds of remote datacenter clusters are called *geoclusters* or *stretch clusters* and will be discussed in more detail later in this chapter.

Defining a Service Level Agreement (SLA)

If you randomly ask DBAs at a few companies how they manage their databases, chances are you will get a variety of answers in return. Some have the DBAs solely focus on the actual database and its performance; they are hands off of the backend storage. Some DBAs are very much involved in the SAN architecture and understand its limitations. Despite these slight variations on the role of DBA, one concept is common among everyone in the IT world—uptime. The IT organization commits to the business a guarantee for the business applications (and databases) to be available, or up. This commitment is usually referred to as a service level agreement (SLA).

The "Nines"

When referring to the amount of uptime, or downtime, people refer to the nines. For example, if your customer would only allow about 8 hours of downtime a year, this would be considered three nines (99.9%). In other words, this application has to be up 99.9% of 365 days. Table 14-1 shows a list of common nines and their corresponding allowable downtimes per year.

Table 14-1. *Nines and Their Respective Downtimes per Year*

Availability %	Common Name	Downtime per Year
90%	One nine	36.5 days
99%	Two nines	3.65 days
99.9%	Three nines	8.76 hours
99.99%	Four nines	52.56 minutes
99.999%	Five nines	5.26 minutes
99.9999%	Six nines	31.5 seconds

In general, the more nines you are asked to provide, the more expensive the solution will be. Most groups in my travels are three nines, because the cost from this point upward is substantial.

Other Metrics

When thinking about SLAs, there are other discussions to have and decisions to make. First, you should think through the current size of your databases, their expected growth patterns, and the workloads for these databases. The workload analysis should include how much transaction log is created during peak times. The Performance Data Collector feature within SQL Server can help you capture historical server performance. You can read more about this feature in Chapter 13.

Within the topic of uptime, you may hear two additional metrics used to satisfy SLAs. The first, recovery point objective (RPO), is how much data can be lost. In the database world, think of a solution where your disaster recovery plan is to perform log shipping to a remote server. If you log ship every 5 minutes and your RPO is 5 minutes, your log shipping will not satisfy this requirement. Remember that for log shipping, you must also include the time it takes to file copy the log to the remote server. Thus our RPO would have to be more than 5 minutes to be satisfied.

The next metric is recovery time objective (RTO), and it defines how much time is allowed to pass in order for a restore of the database in case of a complete failure. "Complete failure," in this case, means recovering from a backup.

When databases go down, the outage can be planned or unplanned. Planned outages are usually known, and the end users expectations are set accordingly. These outages can occur because of deployment of operating system or database system patches, upgrades, or migrations. An unplanned downtime is a failure that occurs generally without warning. It can occur because of hardware or software failure or user error. Users can cause outages to database applications by accidently deleting data needed by the application to function properly. It is a best practice to grant users the fewest privileges possible. If a user needs to perform specific action that requires elevated privileges, consider writing the functionality within a stored procedure, executing the stored procedure as an administrator and just granting the user EXECUTE permission on that stored procedure.

Planning an effective recovery plan ahead of time eases the work necessary to recover from failure. SQL Server has a number of features that help you architect a highly available and fault-tolerant solution.

High Availability Features in SQL Server

Architecting a highly available SQL Server is not a simple click of a check box in SSMS. There are a number of different features and each one has its own pros and cons for a given situation. In the following sections, we will examine each of these major features.

Backup and Restore

Backup and Restore has been around since the first versions of SQL Server. As a DBA, being able to backup and restore your database is a key skill to master. From a high availability standpoint, database backups are usually the last line of defense against total data loss. It is critical that they are a part of your disaster recovery plan. This book devotes a chapter to each of these topics: Chapter 8 for backup and Chapter 9 for restore. Please refer to these chapters for an in-depth discussion of these topics.

Log Shipping

There are three types of database backups that you may incorporate into your disaster recovery plan: full, differential, and transaction logs. As you learned in Chapter 8, a full database backup is a point-in-time backup of all objects and data that reside in the database. A differential backup is a backup of the changes made to the database since the last differential or full database backup. In both of these backup types, it is important to note that, even though we are backing up the contents of the database within the data files, the information that is stored in the transaction log of the database is not backed up. There is a third backup type that is called transaction log backup. A transaction log backup does what its name implies; it backs up the transaction log of a particular database. Having a transaction log backup in addition to a full or differential allows us the most granular point-in-time restoration option available.

Log shipping is the automated process of continually backing up the transaction log from the primary server, copying the backup to a secondary or remote server, and restoring the database in either STANDBY or NORECOVERY mode. Using NORECOVERY puts the secondary servers in a state where no users can connect to that specific database. The STANDBY mode allows users connections, but these connections will be dropped when a new transaction log is applied to the database. You can configure this mode when you configure log shipping in SSMS.

Configuration

In this example we have two instances of SQL Server installed: ROB-DENALI-1 and ROB-DENALI-1\INST2. We have a database called UsedCars that we will create and use to configure log shipping. First, let's connect to the first instance and create our database.

To create the UsedCars database connect to the default instance via SSMS and open a new query editor window. Type the following code:

```
USE MASTER
GO
CREATE LOGIN BobLogin WITH PASSWORD='pass@word1'
GO
CREATE DATABASE UsedCars
GO
USE UsedCars
GO
CREATE USER Bob FOR LOGIN BobLogin
GO
CREATE SCHEMA Sales
AUTHORIZATION Bob
GO
CREATE SCHEMA Product
AUTHORIZATION Bob
GO
CREATE TABLE Product.Inventory
(car_id INT NOT NULL PRIMARY KEY,
car_make VARCHAR(50) NOT NULL,
car_model VARCHAR(50) NOT NULL,
car_year SMALLINT NOT NULL)
GO
CREATE TABLE Sales.Orders
(order_id INT NOT NULL PRIMARY KEY,
order_date DATETIME NOT NULL,
order_carsold INT REFERENCES Product.Inventory(car_id),
order_saleprice SMALLMONEY NOT NULL)
GO
INSERT INTO Product.Inventory VALUES (1,'Saab','9-3',1999),
(2,'Ford','Mustang',2003),(3,'Nissan','Pathfinder',2005)
GO
```

■ **Note** This is the same code used to create the UsedCars database in Chapter 4, so if you went through the example in that chapter, you may already have this database created.

To configure log shipping in SSMS, right-click the UsedCars database, and select Ship Transaction Logs from the Tasks context menu. This will launch the UsedCars Database Properties dialog with the Transaction Log Shipping panel open. This context menu is just a shortcut to the panel in the Database Properties dialog, shown in Figure 14-1.

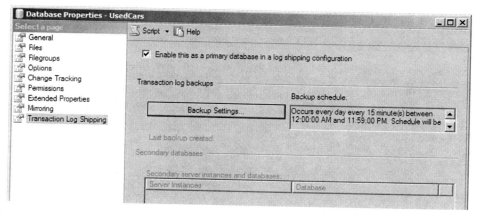

Figure 14-1. Transaction Log Shipping panel in Database Properties dialog

When the "Enable this as a primary database in a log shipping configuration" check box is checked, the Backup Settings button will be enabled. There are not a lot of default settings, so to enable transaction log shipping, you will have to supply a lot of answers to the dialog. The Backup Settings dialog is shown in Figure 14-2.

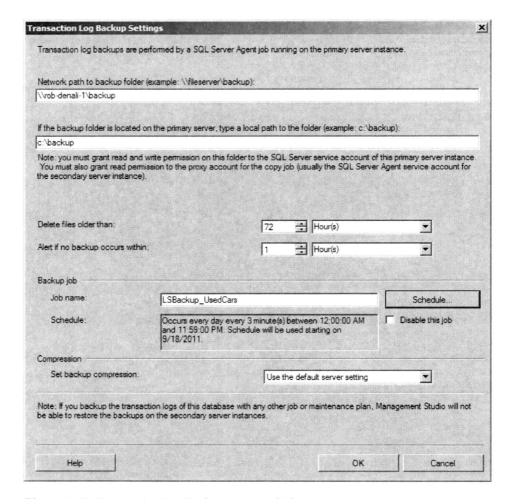

Figure 14-2. Transaction Log Backup Settings dialog

This dialog requires the following information:

- *"Network path to backup folder"*: This location needs to be a network share so that the secondary servers can connect and copy the transaction log backup. You need to make sure there are read permissions on this share for the SQL Server Agent account on the secondary machine. Alternatively, you can define a proxy account on the secondary server so that you do not have to use the SQL Server Agent account. For this particular configuration we are log shipping between two instances on the same machine and our SQL Server Agent account is running as the Network Service account. We do not have to worry about any additional permissions for this configuration. To create a share, you can use Windows Explorer or open a Command Shell and type **NET SHARE Backup=C:\backup**.

- *Local path to the backup folder.* If the backup folder is on the same server as the primary server, type in the path. In our case, it's C:\Backup.

As soon as those two pieces of information are entered, the OK button is enabled. There are default settings for the other information in this dialog that are important to note. Backing up the transaction log, in most cases, doesn't take much disk space. However, over time, a bunch of transaction log backups can take a lot of space. By default, a SQL Server Agent job will delete transaction log backup files older than 72 hours. Also, you will be alerted by default if, for any reason, a transaction log backup fails to happen within an hour.

The Schedule button will launch the schedule dialog of the SQL Server Agent. By default, the job will execute every 15 minutes.

Starting in SQL Server 2008, database backups can be compressed. The Transaction Log shipping feature leverages the same BACKUP DATABASE statement and can thus compress the transaction logs before they are written to the file share. The "Set backup compression" drop-down will allow you to either force compression or just do whatever is already defined at the server instance.

Clicking OK on this dialog will enable us to add secondary servers. We can add a secondary server by clicking the Add button under the "Secondary server and instances" grid control. Adding a secondary server launches the dialog shown in Figure 14-3.

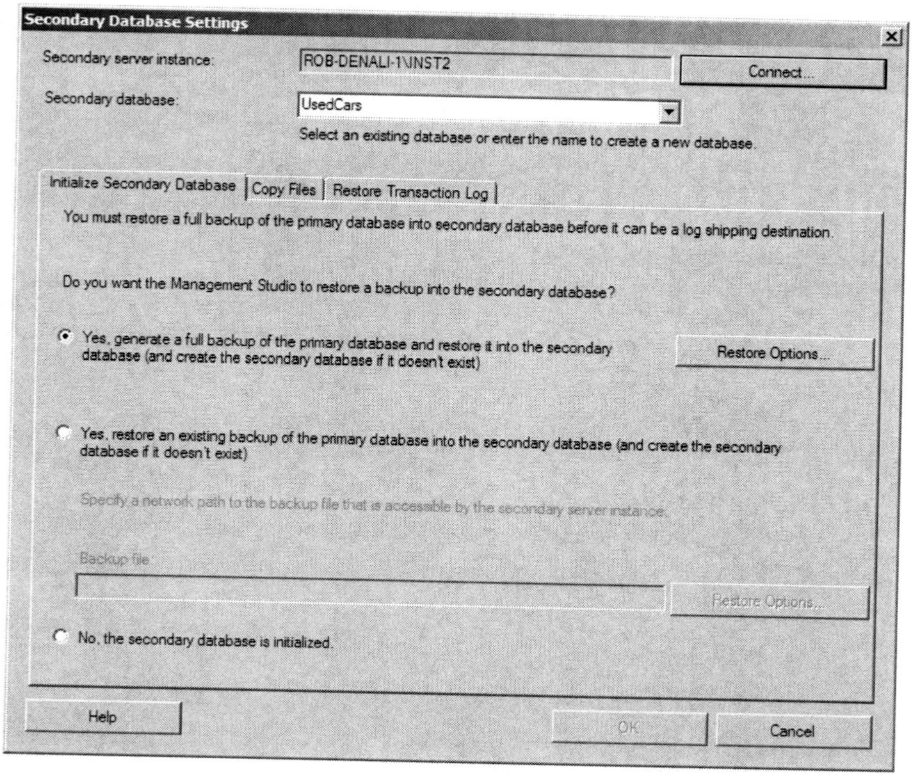

Figure 14-3. The Secondary Database Settings dialog's initialize panel

To add a secondary database, connect to the SQL Server instance by clicking the Connect button. This will launch a connection dialog. Once connected to the secondary server, we can enter a name for the database in the Secondary Server combo box.

The Secondary Database Settings dialog has three panels: Initialize Secondary Database, Copy Files, and Restore Transaction Log. In the Initialize Secondary Database panel, shown in Figure 14-3, you can tell SSMS to take a full backup now or use an existing backup. In order for Transaction Log Shipping to start, a backup of the database needs to exist on the secondary.

Transaction Log Shipping is a three-step process: backup, file copy, and restore. Details about the File Copy process are defined in the Copy Files panel shown in Figure 14-4.

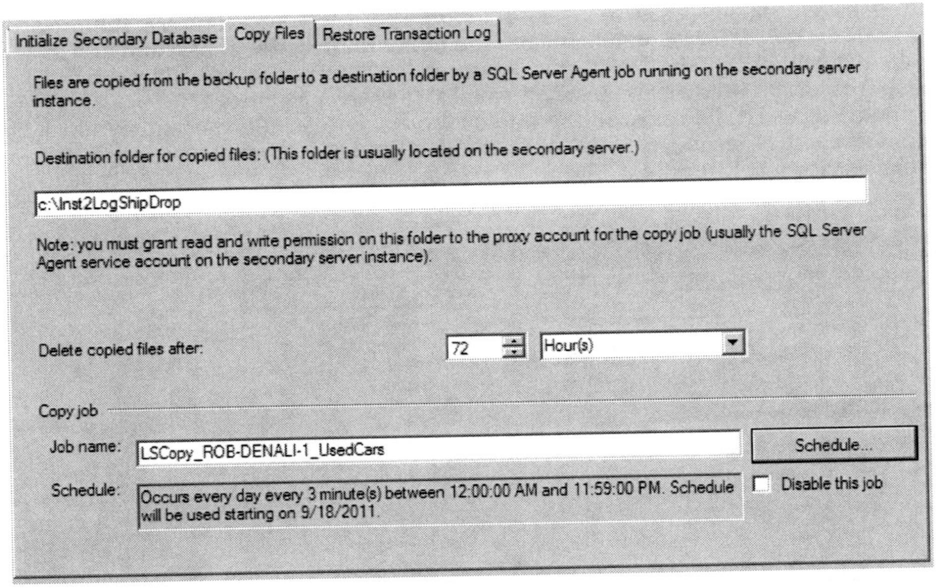

Figure 14-4. Secondary Database Settings dialog's Copy Files panel

In this panel, we define the destination folder where the secondary server will restore the transaction logs. We can also specify the time to automatically delete files and schedule the job that performs the file copy itself.

In the Restore Transaction Log panel, shown in Figure 14-5, we can specify how we want the secondary database to act with regard to clients.

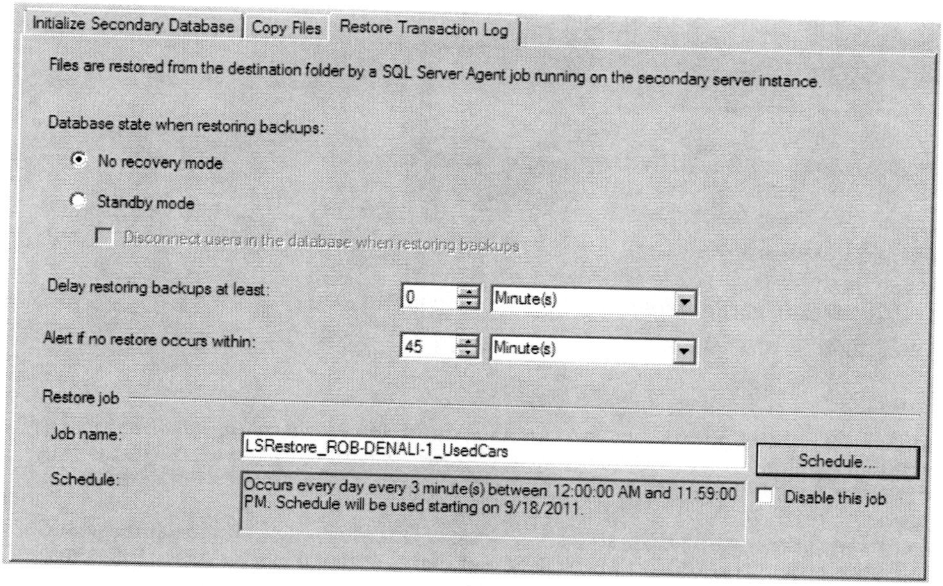

Figure 14-5. *Secondary Database Settings dialog's Restore Transaction Log panel*

If we specify "No recovery mode", the database will not be available to clients on the secondary servers. If we select "Standby mode", users can make active connections to the database on the secondary server.

We can make one more configuration decision regarding Transaction Log Shipping and that is if we want to have a monitor server. By default, SQL Server Agent job information is stored on the primary and secondary servers. A monitor server stores the same information in a central place for easy reporting. In the scenario where we have one secondary, it's not that useful. However, if we have multiple secondaries and multiple transaction log shipping sessions, a monitor server is useful. To configure a monitor server, check the "Use a monitor server instance" check box, and click the Connect button to configure the monitor server. The monitor server can be any SQL Server server; it does not have to be a separate installation of SQL Server.

Now that we have answered all the questions, we can go ahead and start transaction log shipping by clicking the OK button.

A few tables and stored procedures provide status and configuration information on your log shipping configuration. More information can be found in the article, "Monitoring Log Shipping" in SQL Server Books Online located at `http://msdn.microsoft.com/en-us/library/ms190224.aspx`.

SQL Server also has an out-of-the-box report available to view the status of your transaction log shipping jobs. To access this report, select the Transaction Log Shipping Status report from the Standard Reports menu of the Reports menu of the SQL Server instance context menu. A sample report is shown in Figure 14-6.

Figure 14-6. *Sample Transaction Log Shipping Status report showing an alert*

Pros and Cons

One of the key advantages of log shipping is that you can have multiple secondary servers. Before SQL Server 2012 and AlwaysOn Availability Groups, there wasn't an easy way to replicate across more than one secondary. The performance impact is relatively minor, because it's only that of a database backup on the production server.

There are a few cons with transactional log shipping. Since we are shipping a single database, it does not include automatically all the server objects like SQL Server logins and SQL Server Agent jobs that may be related to the database being shipped. For applications that leverage multiple databases, this solution may not be the best in a failover situation. Also, there is no concept of automatic failover, since all we are really doing is creating some SQL Server Agent jobs to do a database backup, file copy, and database restore.

Replication

When the scope of the data that we want to replicate is almost the size of the database, we use features like log shipping or database mirroring to ensure we have two or more copies of the data. If what you are looking for is a subset of the data to be replicated, you could use one of the three types of replication: snapshot, merge, and transactional. In a high availability scenario, we could replicate only those tables and objects that are absolutely necessary for our applications to work. Replication usually isn't the main solution for high availability, but it is important to have a basic understanding of this technology as it is widely used for other scenarios. For an in-depth review of replication, check out the Books Online article, "SQL Server Replication" located at `http://msdn.microsoft.com/en-us/library/ms151198(v=SQL.110).aspx`.

In a replication solution, there are three common components: a publisher, a distributor, and a subscriber. A *publisher* is the source of the replicated data, and it defines one or more publications. Each publication contains one or more articles. These articles define which particular data and objects such as stored procedures, views, and user-defined functions should be replicated. A *subscriber* uses a subscription that either pushes or pulls the source data. The *distributor* is a database instances that keeps track of the subscriptions for various publishers. In some cases, the subscriber gets its data directly from the publisher, and in other configurations, it gets its data from the distributor. In the case of a local distributor, a single distributor can act as both the publisher and the distributor. This is a common configuration. If the distributor is on a separate database server instances, it is known as a *remote distributor*.

Snapshot Replication

Snapshot replication is used when refreshing the entire dataset is easier than replicating portions of it. Consider the scenario where we have an online product catalog. The database that the web page uses to get the information might be getting this data from other database instance in the manufacturing group. Since the web pages will never update the product catalog, they can receive a fresh copy of the catalog when needed.

Snapshot replication is also used as an initial step in other forms of replication. Just as a full database backup is restored on the secondary before log shipping can begin, snapshot replication can be used as the initial dataset for transactional replication.

Merge Replication

Merge replication will send only the changes made to the data at scheduled intervals. Consider the scenario where we have sales people connecting to our corporate network periodically to update the Sales database. The orders that the sales people enter are unique, so updating these within the same database doesn't lead to many conflicts. The new updates and inserts done by the sales people are merged in with the data created by the other sales people. If a conflict does occur, there are ways to detect and resolve conflicts automatically.

Transactional Replication

Out of the three core replication topologies, transactional replication is the most popular one to implement from a high-availability standpoint. Transactional replication replicates data from the publisher to the subscriber each time a transaction completes at the publisher.

■ **Note** If you consider transactional replication as part of your high availability story, it is important to note that there is no automatic failover of clients using any replication topology. Setup and troubleshooting of replication is more difficult than other technologies like database mirroring.

Database Mirroring

Database mirroring takes the concept of log shipping and builds it inside the SQL Server engine. Instead of periodically packaging up the transaction log and sending it to a secondary server, database mirroring opens a connection to the remote server and sends the transactions themselves. Since it's built within the SQL Server engine, database mirroring can perform synchronous two-phase commits with a secondary server. Database mirroring also supports automatic failover via passing a failover partner parameter in the connection string.

Motivation and Benefits

Database mirroring resolves some of the downfalls of log shipping. The idea behind log shipping is to periodically send the transaction log out to secondary servers, so those servers have an exact copy of the primary database. Given the transaction log backup time—the time it takes to copy the log file to the secondary server and restore the backup on the secondary server—you can imagine that there is no way for us to have an exact replica on the secondary. This is one of the downfalls of log shipping; it is not possible to guarantee a transactionally consistent secondary server. In addition, it is not possible to perform an automatic failover. Upon a failure of the primary, someone would have to tell the secondary that it's now the primary. In addition, applications that connect to a primary server will have to know where the secondary server is and reconnect the application to that secondary. It is out of these deficiencies with log shipping that database mirroring was born.

▪ **Note** Database mirroring, similar to log shipping, provides protection at the database-level instance. The database that is the source of the mirror is the called the *principal*. The destination of the mirror is called the *mirror*. Together, this setup is called the *database mirroring session*. With database mirroring, you can only have one mirror in the database mirroring session. This is one of the more significant limitations of database mirroring. Some DBAs use log shipping when they want more than one remote copy of the.

Modes of Operation

Database mirroring has two modes of operation: high safety and high performance. You can think of high-safety mode as a synchronous mode and high-safety mode as asynchronous. In high-safety mode, transactions are committed on both the principal and mirrored servers, which decreases the overall performance but ensures that you will always have two copies of the same data. In high-performance mode, the mirror database makes the best effort to keep up with the transactions sent from the primary. There can be a lag in this configuration. However, the performance improvements with asynchronous communication will most likely outweigh the risk of the small data loss in the event of a total failure.

There is another mode of operation that is a variation of high-safety called high safety with automatic failover. This configuration is the same as high safety, except that there is another separate SQL Server instance called the *witness server*. The witness server's job is to know if the principal database is offline. It will issue an automatic failover if it can not connect to the primary and it has a connection to the mirrored database. The SQL Server instance that is the witness server does not have to be dedicated. You can easily leverage an existing SQL Server instance for this role.

Configuring Database Mirroring

Similar to when you use log shipping, you must perform a full database backup on the primary, copy the backup to the mirrored server instance, and restore the database using the `WITH NO RECOVERY` option within the `BACKUP DATABASE` statement. Once the database is restored to the mirrored server, you can configure mirroring for the database by selecting Mirror from the Tasks menu or the specific database node in Object Explorer. For this example, we will mirror the UsedCars database from the default instance on `ROB-DENALI-1` to the named instance, `ROB-DENALI-1\INST2`. On our test machine, we created a folder C:\backup\dm to hold the database backup. Next, we connected to the default instance, ROB-DENALI-1, and issued the following statement using the Query Editor in SSMS:

```
BACKUP DATABASE UsedCars FROM DISK='c:\backup\dm\UsedCars.bak'
```

If, at this point, the SQL Server instance we are mirroring to was on a remote server, we would copy the backup file to that server. In this example, the SQL Server named instance resides on the same physical machine, so we do not need to copy the backup file.

Connect to the INST2 named instance, ROB-DENALI-1\INST2, using SSMS and restore the UsedCars database with the following statement. Before you execute the statement, make sure that the directory C:\data exists. Create that directory if necessary.

```
RESTORE DATABASE UsedCars FROM DISK='c:\backup\dm\UsedCars.bak'
WITH MOVE 'UsedCars' TO 'C:\data\UsedCarsInst2.mdf',
MOVE 'UsedCars_log' TO 'C:\data\UsedCarsInst2.ldf',
NORECOVERY;
```

If you refresh Object Explorer, you can see that the UsedCars database node is shown as "UsedCars (Restoring . . .)". At this point, we can connect back to the default instance and select Mirror. This will launch the database properties dialog with the mirroring label preselected. This dialog is shown in Figure 14-7.

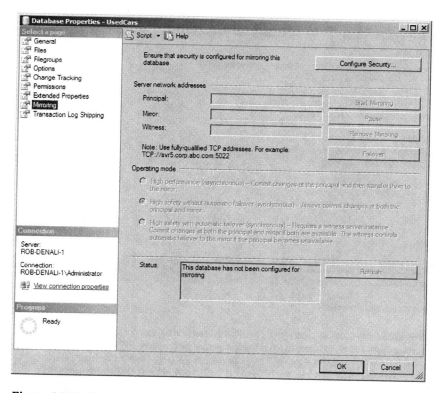

Figure 14-7. Mirroring panel of the Database Properties dialog

The first thing that needs to be done is to configure security. Once you've done that, the other sections including the server network address and operating mode will be enabled and available for editing.

Clicking the Configure Security button will launch the Configure Database Mirroring Security Wizard. The first page will ask you if you wish to include a witness server to enable the synchronous mode with automatic failover. In this example, we will configure asynchronous mirroring, so a witness is not needed and we will select No.

The next page in the wizard, shown in Figure 14-8, will define information about our primary instance such as the TCP/IP listener port that will be used.

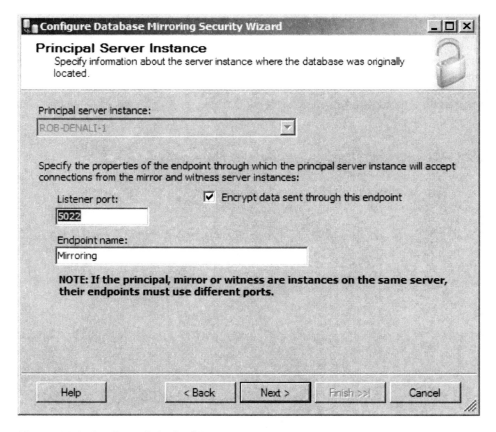

Figure 14-8. *Configure Principal Server Instance*

The default listener port is 5022 and can be changed. Database mirroring uses a feature called endpoints within SQL Server. At a high level, endpoints define an entry point into SQL Server. An endpoint defines a protocol, such as shared memory, TCP/IP, or named pipes, and a payload, such a TDS. Once an endpoint is defined, you can lock down who specifically can access that endpoint. In database mirroring, an endpoint is created and only the SQL Server instances involved with the database mirroring session can connect to it. The endpoint name in the case of this example mirroring configuration is given a generic name of Mirroring. This can be changed to something more descriptive.

The next page in the wizard will configure the mirror server instance. Similar to the way you defined the Principal Server instance in Figure 14-8, you will define a listener port on that server instance and provide an endpoint name.

Since database mirroring will define endpoints on both the principal server and mirror server instance, the wizard will next ask you for the service accounts for these instances. This wizard page is shown in Figure 14-9.

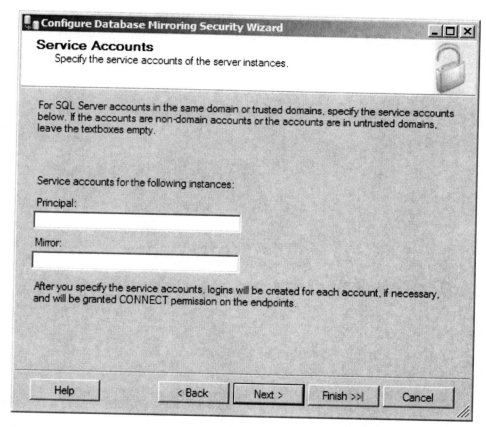

Figure 14-9. Specifying service accounts wizard page

After setting the accounts, the wizard has enough information to create the mirror. After completing the wizard, you will be prompted with a dialog box asking if you wish to start the mirroring session. If you elect to do so, you will see the dialog indicated that the mirrors are being synchronized.

Alternatively, you could script this whole process. A good article on scripting a database mirroring creation is located at www.sqlservercentral.com/articles/Database+Mirroring/72009/.

At this point, the database mirroring session should be enabled and running. There is a database mirroring monitor that is available to see the health of your mirror. It can be accessed via the Launch Database Mirroring Monitor context menu command under the Tasks menu of the database container node in object explorer.

■ **Note** There are a few moving parts to setting up database mirroring. If you have been following along and run into problems, they are most likely caused by security settings. You should use a domain account for the principal and mirror service accounts. Also, if you are having connectivity issues, check out the SQL Server Books Online topic "Use Certificates for a Database Mirroring Endpoint" located at the following URL: `http://msdn.microsoft.com/en-us/library/ms191477(v=SQL.110).aspx`. And for more information on Database Mirroring in general, check out the Books Online section on database mirroring at the following URL: `http://msdn.microsoft.com/en-us/library/ms365599.aspx`.

AlwaysOn Failover Clustering

SQL Server 2012 introduces a new technology called AlwaysOn Failover Clustering. Log shipping and database mirroring work at the database instance level. With those technologies, you can fail over a specific database and have the other databases still online in the primary server. One of the biggest differences in those two technologies versus failover clustering is that failover clustering is a protection of the SQL Server instance itself. If a failure occurs in a SQL Server and its clustered, the whole instance will be failed over. SQL Server leverages Windows Server Failover Clustering to enable this capability, and the resulting new feature set is termed AlwaysOn Failover Clustering.

In the clustering world there are active and passive nodes. Active nodes are servers that have active connections and are doing work. Passive nodes are not handling any active user workload. On an active node, the SQL Server service is started, and there are active user connections. On a passive node, the SQL Server service is stopped, and the server is waiting for a failover. In a configuration where there are two servers with one being active and the other being passive, this is said to be an active/passive configuration. Upon a failure of the active node, the passive node will start the SQL Server instance and allow users to make connections. This is possible since both servers share a common disk. A common disk also means a single point of failure, so in most clustering designs, the disk architecture has redundancy and fault tolerance. This shared storage must be in the form of a storage area network (SAN), iSCSI targets or both.

The example where we have one active and one passive is known as a two-node cluster. SQL Server supports as many cluster nodes as Windows Server supports. In Windows Server 2008, SQL Server supports up to 16 nodes. Typically, most enterprises have between two and four nodes in a cluster. When a cluster has more than two nodes, the remaining nodes are always passive and failed over when the other passive nodes are not available.

You may be thinking that it would be a waste of electricity to keep multiple passive nodes running and essentially not doing any work. This is the case, and some IT departments end up creating active/active clusters. In this configuration, you may have server A with databases 1, 2, and 3 fail over to server B and server B databases 4, 5, and 6 failover to server A. The important thing to note is that in the event of a failure, servers A and B need to assume the workload of all the databases, so we need to make sure that the hardware can support this load.

Typically, in our scenario, servers A and B are located within the same datacenter. In geoclustering (sometimes called stretch clustering), your cluster server nodes can be spread across different subnets. This means that you could failover to another geographical place in the world. SQL Server 2012 supports geoclusters via Windows Server 2008 R2.

From a performance perspective, enabling clustering doesn't impact SQL Server performance as much as it did in earlier versions. Prior to SQL Server 2012, `tempdb` had to be placed on the shared drive as well, which caused performance issues if your applications heavily used `tempdb`. Now, this is no longer the case, and even in a failover cluster configuration, `tempdb` can be located on a local drive to the node.

Failover clustering is one of the most popular high-availability features used within IT departments today. Proper setup clustering depends on a variety of factors including the shared disk infrastructure, networking configuration, and Windows Server versions. Diving in and walking through a failover clustering setup is beyond the scope of this book. However, if you are interested in learning more check out the SQL Server Books Online topic "Create a New SQL Server Failover Cluster" at the following URL: `http://msdn.microsoft.com/en-us/library/ms179530(v=SQL.110).aspx`.

AlwaysOn Availability Groups

The AlwaysOn Availability Group feature has evolved from database mirroring. While the plumbing is much different with Availability Groups, the idea is similar to database mirroring. With AlwaysOn Availability Groups, we can specify one or more databases to fail over as a group. Now, when a failover occurs or we manually issue a failover, all the databases defined within the Availability Group will be failed over together. This failover can occur to a failover partner known as an availability replica server, just like in database mirroring; however, unlike database mirroring, AlwaysOn Availability Groups allow you to have multiple availability replicas, up to four.

Availability replicas can be written to asynchronously or synchronously. The primary role availability replica is the host of the database and supports read and write queries. The secondary role availability replica supports active user connects and read-only queries. One of these availability replicas can be defined as the failover partner. A great user scenario for connecting to a secondary role availability replicas would be for reporting and database backups. Since these connections need to be read-only, if a user submits a write query, the query will simply fail.

Configuring an AlwaysOn Availability Group

Before you can configure an AlwaysOn Availability Group, there are a few prerequisites. First, the servers that host the SQL Server instance must be clustered together. Instead of using a witness server as with the database mirroring feature, AlwaysOn Availability Groups leverage the internode health and failure detection capabilities native within Windows Server failover cluster feature. One significant difference between setting up failover clustering for AlwaysOn Availability Groups and for a failover cluster is that AlwaysOn Availability Groups have no requirement of a shared disk. Thus, the setup involved with creating a cluster of Windows Servers is simple.

In the example to follow, we have four servers. The first is called DENALI-DC and it's a domain controller of the consoto.lab domain. The second, third, and fourth are SQL-EAST, SQL-WEST, and SQL-SOUTH respectively. Our objective is to create an Availability Group of three databases, DatabaseA, DatabaseB, and DatabaseC with SQL-WEST as the primary role availability replica and SQL-EAST and SQL-SOUTH as a secondary role availability replicas.

There is a domain user called CONTOSO\SQLService. The SQL Server instances for all three SQL Server servers are using this domain account for their SQL Server service account.

Creating a Windows Server Failover Cluster

The first step is creating a Windows Server failover cluster group with SQL-EAST, SQL-SOUTH, and SQL-WEST. This step doesn't have anything to do with the SQL Server instance; rather we are creating the Windows Server failover group containing these three Windows servers.

To create a Windows server failover cluster, each Windows server needs to have the Failover Cluster role installed. You can install this via the Server Manager. Once this is role is installed, you can create a cluster by using the Create a Cluster wizard. This wizard can be launched in Server Manager by selecting Failover Cluster Manager under the Server Manager node and then clicking Create a Cluster hyperlink in the Actions pane.

The second page in the wizard is the Select Servers page. On this page, we add all the servers that are to be a part of this cluster—in our example, SQL-EAST, SQL-SOUTH, and SQL-WEST. This page is shown in Figure 14-10.

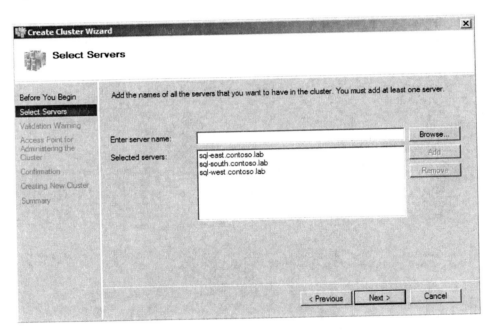

Figure 14-10. Select Server page in the Create Cluster Wizard

The next page in the wizard asks you about validating the cluster. Prior to Windows Server 2008, if you wanted to set up a failover cluster, you had to run it on specific hardware. All that changed, and you can set up a cluster on almost any hardware. You can skip this validation test and choose No.

A virtual IP is created for administering the cluster. This next page asks you for this virtual name and is shown in the Figure 14-11.

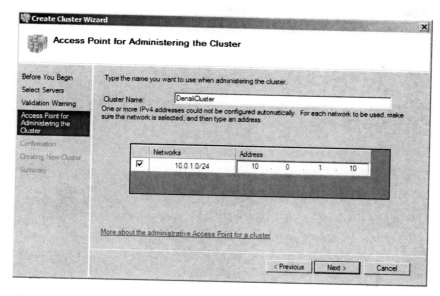

Figure 14-11. Access point for cluster administration

After the confirmation page, the wizard forms the cluster. Upon successful completion, the Summary shown in Figure 14-12 is displayed.

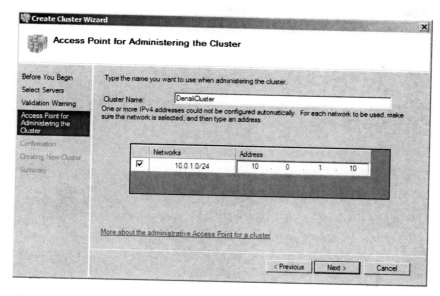

Figure 14-12. Successful cluster failover page

Configuring the SQL Server Instance

Now that we have all three Windows servers in a failover cluster, we need to enable the AlwaysOn Availability Groups feature within each SQL Server instance. To do this, we connect to each server: SQL-EAST, SQL-WEST, and SQL-SOUTH and launch the SQL Server Configuration Manager found under the Configuration Tools folder within Microsoft SQL Server 2012. When the SQL Server Configuration Manager launches, click the SQL Server Services node, then select the Properties context menu of the SQL Server service account. Click the AlwaysOn High Availability tab, and check the Enable AlwaysOn Availability Groups check box, as shown in Figure 14-13.

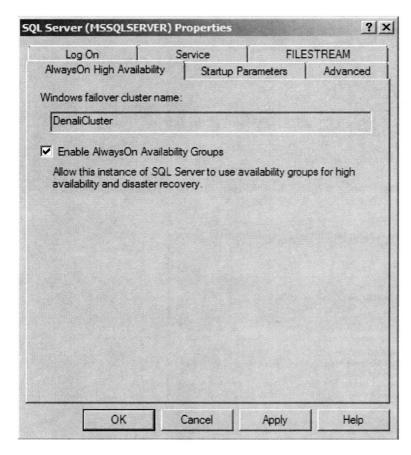

Figure 14-13. Enabled AlwaysOn Availability Groups check box

Restart the SQL Server service, and now, your SQL Server instance is ready for AlwaysOn Availability Groups.

Creating an Availability Group

Connect to the SQL-WEST instance using SSMS and create the sample databases as follows:

```
USE MASTER
GO
CREATE DATBASE [DatabaseA]
GO
CREATE DATBASE [DatabaseB]
GO
CREATE DATABASE [DatabaseC]
GO
```

Next, we need to take a full database backup of these databases. If we do not do this first, the Availability Group Wizard will not allow us to create the availability group with these databases. On the SQL-WEST server backup all three databases. For simplicity, we can create a folder, C:\Backup, and issue the following statements within SSMS:

```
USE MASTER
GO
BACKUP DATABASE DatabaseA TO DISK='C:\backup\DatabaseA.bak'
GO
BACKUP DATABASE DatabaseB TO DISK='C:\backup\DatabaseB.bak'
GO
BACKUP DATABASE DatabaseC TO DISK='C:\backup\DatabaseC.bak'
GO
```

Next, launch the New Availability Group wizard by selecting it from the context menu of the Availability Groups node within the Management node in Object Explorer. The first question the wizard will ask is for an Availability Group name. Type **TestAG**, and click Next.

The Select Databases page shown in Figure 14-14 is where we can select one or more databases to be part of the Availability Group. Select DatabaseA, DatabaseB, and DatabaseC, and click Next.

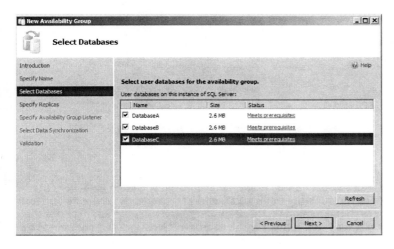

Figure 14-14. *Select Databases page*

The next page is where we define the replicas. This page is shown in Figure 14-15, and here, we can specify each secondary availability replica and whether or not the data will flow asynchronously (i.e., high safety) or synchronously (i.e., high performance). Click the Add Replica button, and add SQL-EAST and SQL-SOUTH. Next, change the Replica mode for SQL-SOUTH to "High performance" by clicking the Replica Mode drop-down for SQL-SOUTH. Notice that there are three options for Replica Mode: Automatic Failover, High performance, and High safety. You can only have two server instances involved with automatic failover in this example that would be SQL-WEST, the primary, and SQL-EAST, the secondary automatic failover partner.

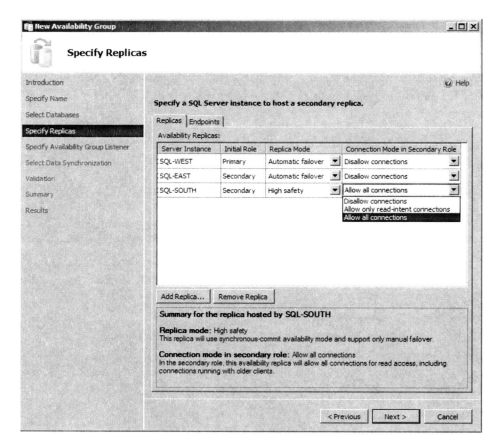

Figure 14-15. Specify Replicas page

The fourth column, "Connection Mode in Secondary Role," determines if you want give users the ability to connect directly to the secondary availability replica. "Disallow connections" is the default and does not allow any active connections to that database on the secondary server. Note that this is for the database itself, not for the SQL Server instance that is hosting the database. Users can still connect to the SQL Server instance; they just can't use the database that is part of this availability group. The next option is "Allow all connections," which, as the name implies, will allow users to connect to and use the database. However, if the user issues a write query, the query will fail. To mitigate the end users' frustration with their application periodically erroring out, there is another option called, "Allow only read-intent connections." When this option is selected, an extra parameter is required on the connection string to signal to the user who connects that he or she will be issuing read-only queries. This is mainly to force the users to know the expected behavior.

For this example, we will select "Allow all connections" for the SQL-SOUTH server instance, and click Next.

From a client perspective, it's easy to enable automatic failover. While using database mirroring, we had to specify the failover partner in the connection string. In this case, you can define an availability group listener, which is essentially a virtual IP that users connect to. In the event of a failure, the users still connect to this virtual IP, but now, they are being served by the secondary instance. The clients do not have to change or add anything to the connection string to achieve this behavior. The next page in the wizard, Figure 14-16 allows you to specify this availability group listener.

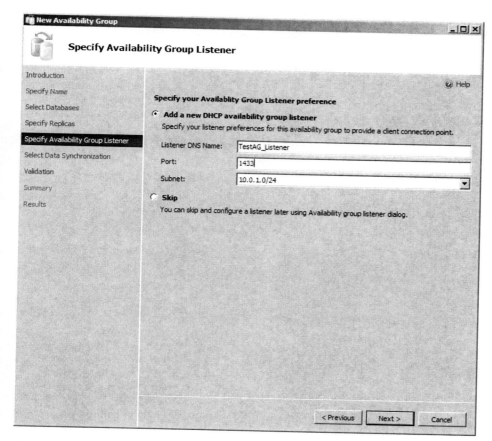

Figure 14-16. Specify the Availabilty Group Listener dialog

The wizard can also handle the initial data synchronization for you. The next page in the wizard, shown in Figure 14-17, allows you to specify a network share on SQL-WEST to obtain the backup from or to skip the initial data synchronization altogether.

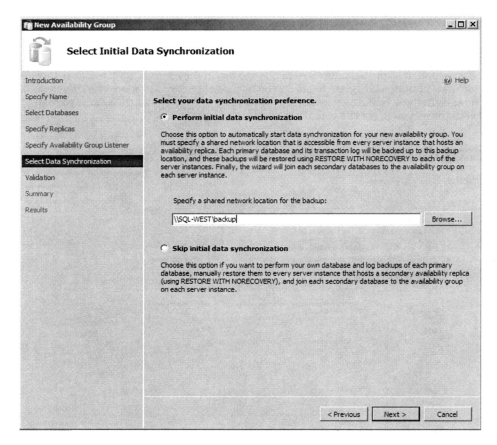

Figure 14-17. *Data Synchronization page*

The wizard will then perform a validation check to see if it can access the network share, if there is enough free disk space, and so on. Once this validation checks out, the wizard will provide you a summary of your selections. When you click Finish, the wizard will create your availability group.

If you go back to Object Explorer, you will see a new node under the Availability Groups node within the Management node of Object Explorer. By right-clicking and selecting Show Dashboard, you can see the overall health of the group including synchronization status and any issues that need to be addressed.

Summary

This chapter introduced the concept of SLA and the importance of fault tolerance within your environment. There are many different solutions to help with fault tolerance: some are hardware based, and some software. It would take many books to cover all the possibilities, and there are books on the market that deep dive into the topic of high availability. To read more about this topic, check out Allan Hirt's books *Pro SQL Server 2005 High Availability* and *Pro SQL Server 2008 Failover Clustering*, available from Apress. Allan may be updating the high availability book for SQL Server 2012, but if this doesn't happen, the SQL Server 2005 book is a great primer on the topic. In SQL Server 2012, there are key advancements to high availability including AlwaysOn Availability Groups and AlwaysOn Failover Clustering. Look for IT departments to heavily leverage these features for their SQL Server high availability solution.

CHAPTER 15

Cloud Computing for the DBA

Imagine for a moment that there was no electric company. The utility wires carrying electrical current from the street to your business would be nonexistent. Since we need electricity to power our critical devices and appliances, like computers and coffee makers, we would need to build a power source. To do this, first we need to decide on renewable sources like solar and wind power or nonrenewable sources like coal or gas. After obtaining all the necessary building permits and capital, we are ready to start construction of the power generator.

Let's assume that we have created enough power capacity to handle our load. Life is grand, and our online widget sales business is taking off. To handle this success, we acquire more servers, which in turn, require more power from our power generators. Now, we must build out additional power sources to accommodate this new demand. As you can see, power supply and consumption are huge burdens for our business. Thankfully, in reality, we have electric companies that simply provide us more power when we need it. On the flip side, if we do not need to power those new servers anymore, the power company does not give us that electricity. In the end, the power company simply bills us for the power consumption we actually use.

This is the main idea behind cloud computing, where the cloud vendor is providing us with computing and storage power in the form of servers running in their datacenters. If we need more computing power, we can easily ask for it, and likewise, if we no longer need the computing power, we can decommission it on the fly. This service-based approach allows us to focus more on our business problems than on the technical issues that result from our application of technology to solve those problems.

There is much talk today about the true definition of "cloud computing." As with any new technological concept, a myriad of definitions are available for you to read. Different people may have different opinions on what cloud computing is. For this book, we will define cloud computing as it's defined by the National Institute on Standards and Technology (NIST). The NIST defines cloud computing as ". . . a model for enabling ubiquitous, convenient, on-demand network access to a shared pool of configurable computing resources (e.g., networks, server, storage, applications, and services) that can be rapidly provisioned and released with minimal management effort or service provider interaction . . . ." The complete definition can be found at the following web address: http://csrc.nist.gov/publications/nistpubs/800-145/SP800-145.pdf. According to this document, some essential characteristics, like on-demand, self-service, and rapid elasticity, are needed to support the cloud model. The definition also defines three service models for cloud delivery. These three service models form the basis of what you, as the cloud computing consumer, can purchase in today's marketplace.

Cloud Service Models

BuyCarsFromMePlease is a new fictitious startup company that sells used cars on the Internet. You have been hired by the founders to manage all things technical. The first tasks are to ensure that you have a web site up and host a simple catalog of used cars from the neighborhood dealers and private owners. As a technological guru, you hired the phone company to provide you the Internet access and purchased and provisioned the web servers, database servers, and network. You also configured security and published the online catalog web application to the web servers. In a nutshell, you have implemented a complete on-premise solution.

Within a short period of time, the management team has hired a few contractors to come in and make modifications to the web application. Since there is no more money to purchase hardware, you look for alternative ways to provide these contractors with development and test environments.

Infrastructure as a Service

Some cloud vendors like Amazon.com and RackSpace offer the ability to host a variety of operating systems for you to use in their datacenters. The vendor provides you remote access to these images and then it's up to you to patch the operating system and install and maintain your application. In this case, the vendor is providing the network, physical server, and storage for you, and you worry about the rest. Under the covers, your operating system is hosted in a virtual machine environment, which allows easy provisioning and decommissioning of operating system images. You pay for only what you use.

Infrastructure as a service (IaaS) is one solution that would provide the contractors with a cheap sandbox to play in.

Software as a Service

The management team at BuyCarsFromMePlease has now asked you to provide e-mail, calendaring, and messaging for all the employees of the company. Before you go out and purchase an additional server to host Microsoft Exchange, consider what options are available in the cloud. With software as a service (SaaS) cloud service model, the provider not only takes care of the infrastructure, but also manages the servers, databases, security, and the actual application. You (as the consumer) use the application. Hotmail and Gmail are good real-world examples of SaaS implementations today. Microsoft has all of its office applications bundled up into an offering called Office 365 (http://office365.microsoft.com). Office 365 is a subscription-based service that combines Microsoft Office web applications (i.e., Excel, PowerPoint, Word, and OneNote) with online tools like SharePoint, Exchange, and Lync to provide you with a great experience in collaboration and productivity. Office 365 is a pure SaaS offering. Other than Internet connectivity, there is no additional infrastructure for you to worry about supporting.

Platform as a Service

Somewhere in the middle of IaaS and SaaS lies a cloud service offering known as platform as a service (PaaS). To understand PaaS is to comprehend the core user scenarios PaaS provides a solution for. Consider the scenario where the management team of BuyCarsFromMePlease has decided to run a television advertisement during the Super Bowl. The Super Bowl event in the United States is watched by tens of millions people worldwide. The management team is expected at least 1% (about 1 million) of the expected 100 million viewers to visit the company's website during the Super Bowl. To handle this workload on the premises, we would have to purchase additional hardware, rack the units, ensure adequate power and cooling, set up networks, manage security, and install operating systems, software patches, and applications. After the Super Bowl ended and the demand subsided, we would still have all this excess capacity in our datacenters.

A better solution would be to take our application, web page files, databases, and support DLLs and publish them to a server in the cloud. When the application is published, we would simply tell the host to spin up 200 more instances of the web host to accommodate the new demand from the Super Bowl ad. When the Super Bowl ends and the demand returns to normal, you can change the instances down to just a few. This is elastic computing, and this is the value of PaaS.

With PaaS, the cloud service vendor manages the network, storage, and virtualization as with IaaS, but it also manages the operating systems, patching, database servers, and security. As consumers of PaaS ,we focus on solving our own business problems. In the case of BuyCarsFromMePlease, we build the web page and deploy it to the cloud. Microsoft's PaaS offering is known as Windows Azure.

Figure 15-1 shows an overview of the three cloud servicing models discussed in this chapter. Notice how the vendor manages more or less as you move throughout the service models.

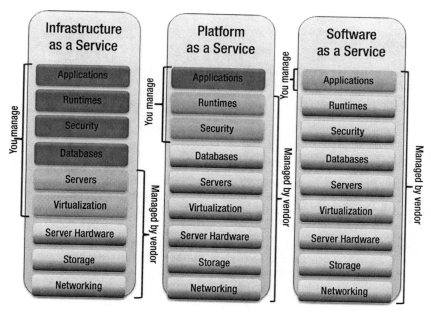

Figure 15-1. Cloud service models

Windows Azure

Windows Azure is Microsoft's platform for running applications in the cloud. The Windows Azure platform, shown in Figure 15-2, consists of five main components: Compute, Storage, Networking, Identity, and Marketplace.

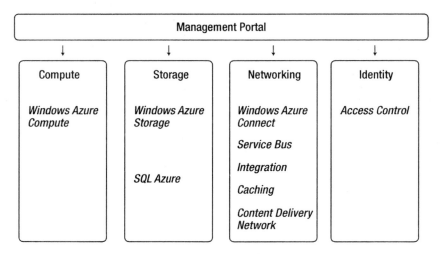

Figure 15-2. Windows Azure platform

It is important to note that any of the services in Figure 15-2 can be leveraged independently. For example, if your application just needs to store a large amount of information, you can just use the blob store within Windows Azure Storage service.

Roles

The Windows Azure Compute service contains three types of roles:

- A Web role can be thought of as an instance of Windows Server running Internet Information Server. A deployed web application to this role can immediately take advantage of the load balancing and scalability that is inherent in the Windows Azure architecture.

- A Worker role is similar to an instance of Windows Server without Internet Information Server configured. Leverage this role where you want to run code just like the code used within a Windows Service.

- The Virtual Machine (VM) role is a recent addition to the Windows Azure platform. This role allows you to upload your own Windows Server 2008 R2 Standard or Enterprise edition image and have it run inside the Windows Azure platform.

The VM role sounds a lot like IaaS. However, it's not a full IaaS solution. Even though you have full control over the operating system and can make a remote desktop connection to the hyper-v image, certain restrictions, such as lack of persisted state, may make your implementations different than those servers running on premises.

An overview of the Windows Azure VM role can be found at the following web site: http://msdn.microsoft.com/en-us/library/gg433107.aspx. The VM role is not the end answer for a true IaaS offering. Features within this space are constantly being added, and by the time you read this, Microsoft may have additional IaaS options for running your virtual machine in its datacenter.

Storage

Windows Azure Storage provides a storage options including a message queue, blob storage, and table storage. An in-depth discussion on data storage options can be found with the TechNet Wiki article, "Data Storage Offerings on the Windows Azure Platform" located at the following web site: `http://social.technet.microsoft.com/wiki/contents/articles/data-storage-offerings-on-the-windows-azure-platform.aspx`. As a DBA, you may hear about table storage in Azure.

■ **Note**   Table storage within Windows Azure is not the same as the functionality provided with SQL Azure.

Table storage in Windows Azure is simply a collection of row-like entities, which can each contain up to 255 properties. With table storage, there is no schema, no way to represent relationships, no way to perform join operations, no stored procedures, no triggers, nor any relational database management–type functions.

What Azure Table storage can do is scale, and it does this extremely well. Unlike SQL Azure, a Windows Azure Table can be up to 100TB in size. These tables can be propagated via Windows Azure content delivery network (CDN) halfway around the world, such that your Asian customers see the same query performance as your European customers. The CDN also enables developers to deliver high-bandwidth content including a smooth streaming of media. More information on the CDN can be found at the following web site: `www.microsoft.com/windowsazure/cdn`.

AppFabric

One of the differentiators of Windows Azure as compared with other PaaS providers is Windows Azure AppFabric (AppFabric). The AppFabric contains functionality related to networking and identity management. One component of the AppFabric is the service bus. This feature enables Azure applications to interact with applications both on and off premises. It does this without complex firewall configurations. The service bus can also be used to facilitate communication between two separate private networks.

The AppFabric Access Control feature provides identity management and access control to web applications and services. It integrates with enterprise directories, such as Active Directory, and web identities, like Windows Live ID, Google, Yahoo!, and Facebook. Using Access Control the integration is seamless and enables your applications to exercise complete control over the level of access that each user or group has defined.

Case Study: OCCMundial.com

Headquartered in Mexico City, OCCMundial.com connects jobs seekers with job opportunities and eases the hiring process for businesses. One of the competitive advantages of OCCMundial is a recommendation system called OCCMatch. This system matches job openings to candidate resumes. Before adopting the Windows Azure platform, the existing ASP.NET application was hosted on a few dozen Windows Server 2008 machines with a SQL Server 2005 database server. The existing on-premise solution could scale to compute 25,000 resumes against 20,000 job offers. While this was good for the inception of the technology, OCCMundial wanted to scale the application to connect 1.5 million resumes with 80,000 job listings. To do this, given the current configuration, they would have to spend almost half a million dollars on hardware upgrades alone. Leveraging Windows Azure, OCCMundial.com spins up to 200 compute nodes, allowing it to execute millions of OCCMatch operations in parallel. Its new Windows Azure design allows the company to process 1.5 million resumes two to three times per week.

In this example, OCCMundial had an existing .NET web application leveraging SQL Server. Porting this to Windows Azure was straightforward, because Visual Studio supports both on-premise and cloud based applications.

Case Study: 3M

3M is a science-based company and has developed thousands of innovative products including Post-It Notes and Thinsulate insulation. One area of science that 3M works in is visual attention models. Consider the case where you are designing a new company logo, or web site, or hotel lobby. The question may be asked of how people would respond to these designs. To what areas of the new logo are people first drawn, and which areas are not noticed? These questions are really important to designers. 3M has developed a web-based application called the 3M Visual Attention Service (VAS). The VAS is a service where designers can upload a picture or graphical design and get, in return, a heat map of which areas of the image were most likely to attract a viewer's attention. A sample of the result is shown in Figure 15-3.

Figure 15-3. Visual hot spots using 3M's Visual Attention Service

For designers to reliably leverage this application, 3M needed to build out a scalable infrastructure. Additional computing resources would also be needed at peak times before the holiday season. Rather than build out the datacenter to meet these requirements, 3M leveraged Windows Azure and SQL Azure for the solution.

The VAS application was written with a Silverlight browser plug-in which allows the end-user to edit and modify the images they submit to the VAS engine. The VAS application relies on the Access Control Service of Windows Azure to handle authentication to the system. Images that are uploaded are managed in a SQL Azure database and in Windows Azure blog storage. A big benefit to 3M is that the concern over daily database management is nonexistent, because SQL Azure has built-in data protection, self-healing, and disaster recovery. A detailed architectural view of the solution is shown in Figure 15-4.

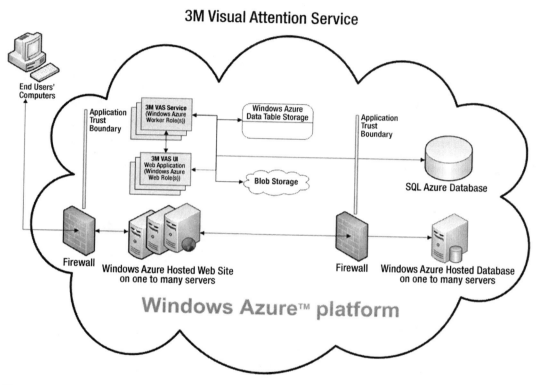

Figure 15-4. *3M VAS solution architecture*

The architecture allows for easy dynamic scaling with Windows Azure compute resources. At times of high volume, administrators can simply change the number of Web and Worker roles needed to fulfill the demand. In the end, 3M pays just for what compute resources it needs.

Since the inception of Windows Azure in 2009, Microsoft continues to invest in the platform. While Windows Azure and developing applications for the cloud are topics outside of the scope of this book, many books and articles have been written on the subject. For a quick overview of the features within Windows Azure, check out the following web site: www.microsoft.com/windowsazure/features. Microsoft has a plethora of free webcasts, videos, virtual labs, and podcasts available on topics around Azure including security, the AppFabric, SQL Azure, and many others. Check out this information at www.microsoft.com/events/series/azure.aspx.

SQL Azure

Up until now, we have been talking mostly about the Windows Azure platform in general. One important piece of Windows Azure is SQL Azure. SQL Azure is *not* a default install of SQL Server running inside a virtual machine on the public Internet. While it may be tempting to think of it this way, it's not correct. SQL Azure is a flavor of the traditional Microsoft SQL Server integrated within the Windows Azure platform. The end result is a cloud-based relational database service that offers enterprise-class availability, scalability, and security and is self-healing.

Understanding SQL Azure

With SQL Azure, you can, with a click of a button, provision and deploy relational databases solutions. These solutions come with manageability, high availability, scalability, and a familiar development model out of the box. SQL Azure database abstracts the logical administration from the physical administration. With respect to database administration, you continue to administer databases, logins, users, and roles, but Microsoft administers the physical hardware, such as hard drives, servers, and storage. For example, you will not find any command or statements that involve the disk in SQL Azure. Commands like `xp_fixeddrives` do not exist in the SQL Azure world, since Microsoft takes care of everything to do with disk provisioning and usage. This can also been seen within the CREATE DATABASE statement. It has been simplified to the following syntax convention:

```
CREATE DATABASE database_name
{
    (<edition_options> [, ...n])
}

<edition_options> ::=
{
    (MAXSIZE = {1 | 5 | 10 | 20 | 30 | 40 | 50} GB)
    |(EDITION = {'web' | 'business'})
}
```

A DBA should not worry so much about job security, because there is still plenty to manage. Even though we no longer are concerned with the physical environment, we will still be managing your applications with respect to security, query tuning, index management, and everything that's logical. Using SQL Azure, we won't be concerned with high availability or disaster recovery, because a SQL Azure database is automatically replicated to three different areas within the Microsoft datacenters.

The SQL Azure platform also manages load balancing, and in case of a server failure, it fails over transparently. Patching and upgrading of the server are all done automatically and transparent for us. This may sound like the holy grail of database servers. In some scenarios, it is, and in others, not so much. SQL Azure has a sweet spot, and it revolves around these core scenarios:

> *Web applications:* The cloud and Windows Azure specifically is a prime scenario for web application hosting. With SQL Azure as a relational database store, application developers can store transactions, content, and streaming media—all in a highly available and fault-tolerant environment.

Departmental applications: SQL Azure is a great target for Tier 2, Tier 3, and Microsoft Access applications and for those applications that use SQL Server Express edition. SQL Azure provides an excellent opportunity to organize these various smaller applications into one place. This also makes it easier to audit and control access to the content.

Data hubs: Consider the scenario where you have remote sales force staff members querying catalogs and creating orders on their phones or laptops. These data need to be uploaded to a corporate server, and fresh product data needs to be sent from corporate to our remote employees. With SQL Azure and the Sync Framework, you can create sync between the remote employee's phone or laptop, a SQL Azure database and the on-premise database. You can read more about the SQL Azure Data Sync from the following web site: `http://social.technet.microsoft.com/wiki/contents/articles/sql-azure-data-sync-overview.aspx`. There are links off of this page to webcasts and articles that go in depth on the subject.

Independent software vendor software plus services: Software vendors can write hosted software solutions without the concern of building out infrastructure to support it. Microsoft's Azure platform is not only about you writing your own applications for your own business needs. There is an online marketplace established where you can write applications and sell them or subscribe to real-time information feeds from commercial data providers and leverage this information in your own application. For more information on the Windows Azure Marketplace, check out `www.microsoft.com/windowsazure/marketplace`.

Getting Started

To sign up for Azure or to leverage the free trial offer check out the following website: `www.microsoft.com/windowsazure`.

The free trial requires the use of a credit card in case you go over your allocated time or disk space allowance.

■ **Tip**   Other offers not requiring a credit card pop up occasionally. The best thing to capture these would be to do a web search for something like "Windows Azure Free No Credit Card". Be careful that the web site you find is from Microsoft.com.

If you click the Buy button on the Windows Azure web page, you will be presented with three offers:

- *Pay as you go*: Pay as you go is self-explanatory; you only pay while you are using computing power or disk space.

- *Subscription*: If you want to save more money and make a six-month commitment to the platform, you can check out the reduced cost by looking at the subscriptions.

- *Member offers*: Special deals for people who are MSDN subscribers. In some cases, if you have MSDN already, you may have free access to Azure for a given duration. Check the MSDN web site for the latest offerings, because things like this change much fast than text within this book!

■ **Note** When you sign up for Azure, you will need a Windows Live ID. Live ID is a single sign-on service developed by Microsoft. It was formally known as Microsoft Wallet and Microsoft Passport. Existing Hotmail and MSN users automatically have Windows IDs associated with their accounts. If you do not use Hotmail or MSN, you will have to create a Windows Live ID at www.live.com.

As you make your way through the registration pages, you will be asked for a subscription type. In Azure, subscriptions are the billing boundary. Within a subscription, there is an account owner and a service administrator. These can be assigned to different Windows Live IDs, or to the same one. In general, the account owner will be responsible for the billing, whereas the service administrator is responsible for provisioning and managing the technical piece of Azure (i.e., deploying applications, creating SQL Azure databases, etc.). If you are just kicking the tires of Azure, you will probably use the same Live ID account for all of these accounts.

Assuming you have subscribed to Azure, there are two main web portals to note. Account owners will be interested in the Microsoft Online Services Customer Portal (MOSCP); see http://mocp.microsoftonline.com. This web site will show you the subscriptions you are currently using and an option to purchase more services and subscriptions. The MOSCP is shown in Figure 15-5.

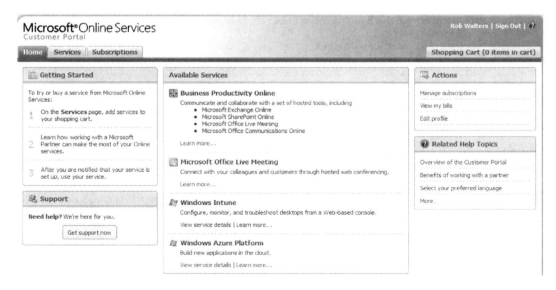

Figure 15-5. Microsoft Online Services Customer Portal

Service administrators and those wishing to do something technical with Azure will leverage the Management Portal (`https://windows.azure.com`). This web site is the primary portal for creating and managing anything Azure related: SQL Azure databases, Windows Azure Compute and Storage, deploying applications, and so on. This portal is shown in Figure 15-6.

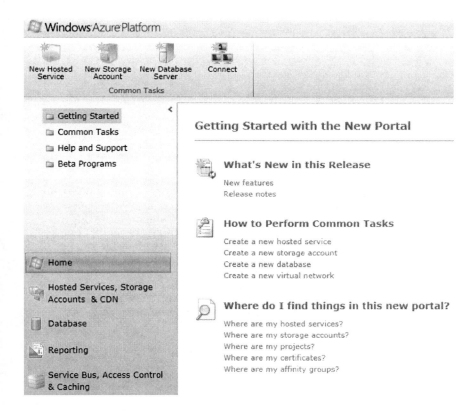

Figure 15-6. *Windows Azure Management Portal*

To get started with SQL Azure, we create a SQL Azure Server. A SQL Azure Server is a logical grouping of databases and acts as the central administrative point. Each SQL Azure Server has a fully qualified domain name, which gets created when you create a new server. This name is in the form `servername.database.windows.net`. The server name is automatically generated for you, and you will not be able to change this name.

Let's go ahead and create a new SQL Azure Server. If we click the New Database Server button on the Management Portal, the Database node will be displayed. From this node, we can either create a new SQL Azure Server or create a new SQL Azure Database. On the left-hand side of the portal, you will see a list of the subscriptions the currently logged in Windows ID has assigned to it. If you are using the free trial, you may only see one subscription. To create a database, we need to first create the SQL Azure Server. If you click the Create a new SQL Azure Server button, you will be presented with the dialog shown in Figure 15-7.

Figure 15-7. SQL Azure Create Server dialog

When we create a new SQL Azure Server, it's bound to a subscription. The subscription drives the price and all that monetary good stuff. Once we select a subscription, we are asked in what region we want the server to be placed. This depends on where the majority of the users who are accessing this instance of SQL Azure will be. Our options for this location include, North Central US, South Central US, North Europe, West Europe, East Asia, and Southeast Asia. The next page will ask for us for an administrator login and password. This is similar to the **sa** user found in on-premise SQL Server.

SQL Azure was developed with security in mind. By default, there is no external access to any of the databases that you create. The next page will ask you to define firewall rules to enable access to your SQL Azure server. By default, there are no rules. Figure 15-8 has been populated with a few sample rules to depict how you may want to enable certain scenarios like access from your home network.

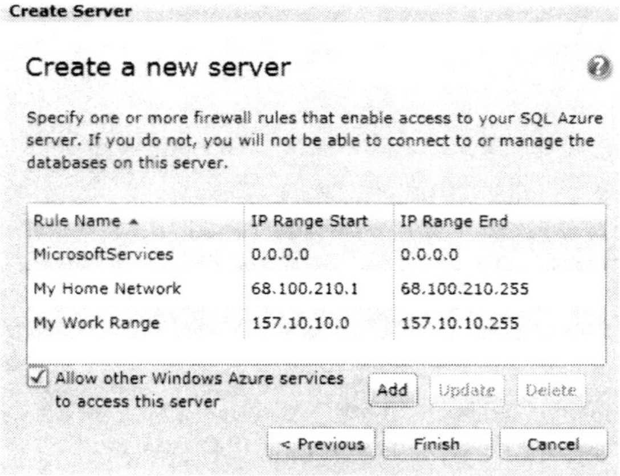

Figure 15-8. Firewall rules page of the SQL Azure Create Server dialog

When you click the Finish button, your SQL Azure Server will be created. Information about the server can be displayed by clicking the server name under the Subscriptions tab in the Management Portal. You will notice that there is already a `master` database created for us. The Properties tab on the right side of the screen shows important information about your new SQL Azure Server. An example of this information is shown in Figure 15-9.

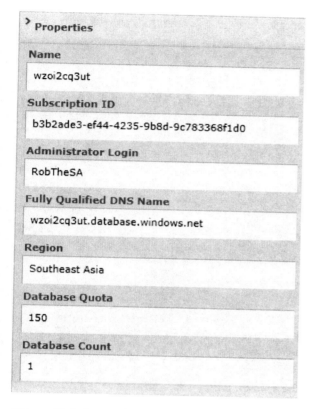

> Properties

Name

wzoi2cq3ut

Subscription ID

b3b2ade3-ef44-4235-9b8d-9c783368f1d0

Administrator Login

RobTheSA

Fully Qualified DNS Name

wzoi2cq3ut.database.windows.net

Region

Southeast Asia

Database Quota

150

Database Count

1

Figure 15-9. *Properties panel of a SQL Azure Server within the Management Portal*

From the example, the SQL Azure Server is called `wzoi2cq3ut`. One of the big advantages with SQL Azure is that it uses Tabular Data Stream (TDS) over the TCP/IP protocol. This is the same TDS protocol that is used by on-premise SQL Server. Thus, if we have an existing application that wants to leverage SQL Azure, all that is needed is to change the server name in the connection string from the on-premise name to the fully qualified DNS name of the SQL Azure Server.

■ **Note**   Before you connect to the SQL Azure Server from your location, be sure to click the Test Connectivity button in the Management Portal. If your IP isn't defined within the firewall IP range, it will fail to connect.

Leveraging TDS over TCP/IP also means that we can connect and manage SQL Azure databases using familiar tools, including SQLCMD and SQL Server Management Studio 2008 R2 and above.

Managing a SQL Azure Database

At this point, we could continue using the Management Portal to create our database, but we can also use SQL Server Management Studio. To connect to our SQL Azure Server, we simply put the fully qualified DNS name in the connection string, as shown in Figure 15-10.

Figure 15-10. Connection dialog of SQL Server Management Studio

Provided your local IP is within the firewall and you supplied the right login and password, you should see the familiar Object Explorer enumerated with various database-level objects. Note that SQL Azure only supports SQL Authentication at this time. One of the things you will notice after a successful connection is the Object Explorer tree does not contain a lot of the nodes it contains when connected to on-premise SQL Server. This is because a SQL Azure database is not the same as an on-premise SQL Server. When you connect to a specific SQL Azure Server, you will see all your databases within that server. From a physical perspective, this is a façade, because in reality, these databases are physically spread across the environment to various nodes. Each node services many databases, so it is unlikely that any of your databases are on the same physical server. This architecture allows for SQL Azure to load balance and automatically move databases within the cluster and to take advantage of the available capacity and to maintain the published service level agreement (SLA).

■ **Note** Currently Microsoft provides a 99.9% SLA per month for the SQL Azure platform. More information about SLA can be viewed in the following web site: www.microsoft.com/windowsazure/sla.

With Microsoft taking care of the physical placement of the database, you won't find any stored procedures that deal with the file system. Some other objects you may notice missing are SQL Server Agent. There is no job scheduling service available in SQL Azure at the time of this writing. A workaround would be to leverage a Windows Azure Compute node or an on-premise SQL Server Agent that would make a call to the SQL Azure database. Connecting to a SQL Azure database via SQL Server Management Studio yields the Object Explorer tree shown in Figure 15-11.

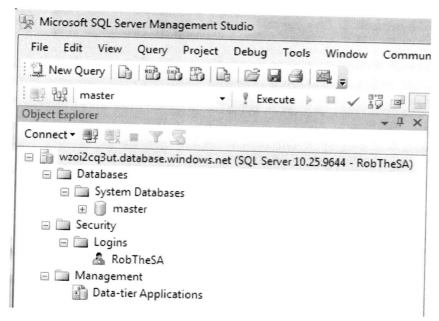

Figure 15-11. *Object Explorer connected to a SQL Azure database*

You'll notice in Figure 15-11 that the build number for SQL Azure is different from that of the current SQL Server releases. SQL Server 2008 starts with 10.00 and SQL Server 2008 R2 starts with 10.5. Currently in SQL Azure, the build is 10.25. SQL Azure updates on its own schedule about every 3–6 months, so the version numbers will always be different than what you will find on an on-premise SQL Server installation

From SSMS, we can create a new database by selecting Create Database from the context menu of the Databases node or by using the `CREATE DATABASE` command within a New Query window. While the amount and quality of dialogs may be increased in later versions of SQL Server, the Create Database context menu item simply puts a template script in the Query Editor window. To create a database, let's issue the following command in the query editor window:

`CREATE DATABASE MyTestDB`

Upon a refresh of the Object Explorer, we can see the newly created database.

Migrating Data into SQL Azure

There are many ways to get data into a SQL Azure database. You could run a script that contains a bunch of `INSERT` statements or explore some other ways, including these:

- *The bulk copy utility* (`BCP.exe`): BCP is a command-line tool that has been around for a long time. Out of the box, it can upload data to a SQL Azure database. More information on the BCP tool can be found here: `http://blogs.msdn.com/b/sqlazure/archive/2010/05/21/10014019.aspx`.

- *SQL Server Integration Services (SSIS)*: SSSIS is a powerful tool for creating simple and complex dataflows. To SSIS SQL Azure is just another datasource. Keep in mind that, since OLE DB is not supported with SQL Azure, to use SSIS, you will have to use the ADO.NET library.

- *SQL Azure Migration wizard*: CodePlex is an open source community that provides free tools to the public based on the Microsoft platform. One of the projects on CodePlex is the SQL Azure Migration Wizard. This wizard will help you migrate SQL Server 2005/2008 databases to SQL Azure. Not only will the wizard move the database, it has the ability to analyze trace files against Azure. This is very important for application compatibility testing.

To get some real data in SQL Azure, let's use the free SQL Azure Migration wizard available for download at the following web site: `http://sqlazuremw.codeplex.com`. The zip file will expose the `SQLAzireMW.exe` application. Launching this will run the wizard.

One of my favorite databases is `pubs`. It's still available bundled with Northwind and available as a free download at `http://archive.msdn.microsoft.com/northwind`. After downloading this zip file, simply connect to a local SQL Server instance and run the `INSTPUBS.SQL` script against your server, and you will have `pubs` and party like its 1999 all over again.

To get `pubs` in SQL Azure, we could have executed the script directly against our SQL Azure database, but we would need to make a slight modification to the script to remove the `USE` statements. Changing database contexts via an existing connection to SQL Azure is not something you can do. You would need to break the connection and reconnect to the other database to perform this action in SQL Azure. For purposes of demonstration, let's assume the `pubs` database is installed in an on-premise SQL Server. When we launch `SQLAzureMW.exe`, we are presented with the wizard screen shown in Figure 15-12.

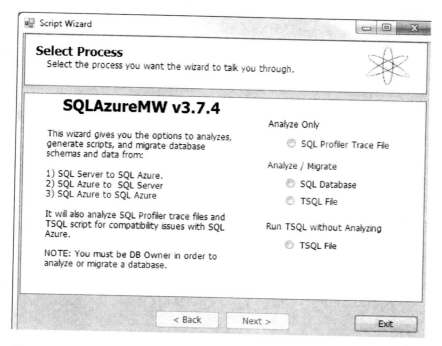

Figure 15-12. SQLAzureMW Select Process page

To migrate our PUBS database, click the SQL Database button, and click Next. At this point, we will be asked to connect to the source SQL Server that has the database we want to migrate. Provide the necessary connection information, and select "pubs" from the "Select source" page in the wizard. The next page will allow us to select which objects we want to migrate over. By default, this wizard will migrate all database objects including stored procedures, tables, user defined data types, and views. After this page, the wizard will confirm that you are ready to start generating the SQL Script. While the wizard is generating the script, you will see the status of the migration. This is the first step in the migration, and the wizard is essentially scripting the objects and using BCP.exe to push out the data into a file on the local directory. The Results Summary page is displayed in Figure 15-13.

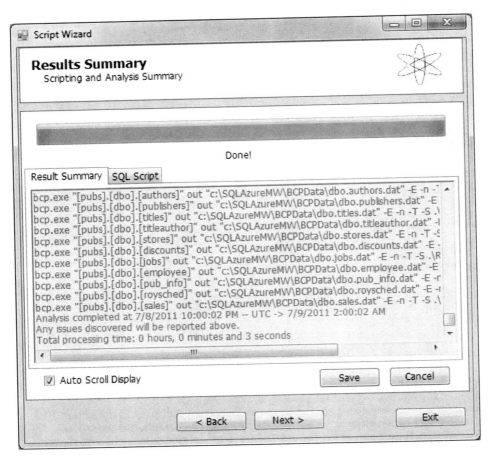

Figure 15-13. Results Summary page for the first step in migration

Next, the wizard will ask you for the location of the SQL Azure database. Remember that "User name" in this case is not just the administrative user name we defined but includes "@servername" at the end of the username, as shown in Figure 15-14.

Figure 15-14. *Connection dialog*

After connecting to the SQL Azure server, you will be asked to which database to add pubs. Since we do not have pubs, we can click the Create Database button on the Setup Target Server Connection panel and create a new database called pubs. The next page will execute the script and BCP of the original data against the new SQL Azure database. Results of this are shown in Figure 15-15.

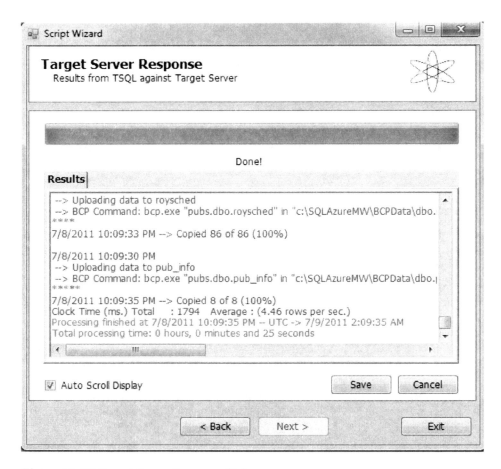

Figure 15-15. Target Server Response dialog

Now, we have a copy of pubs living in our SQL Azure database!

Understanding SQL Azure specific views

A few system views are only available on a SQL Azure database. If you connect to your SQL Azure Server and enumerate the system views within the master database, you will see these. You can notice these special SQL Azure–only ones by a small lock on the bottom right side of the view icon.

To return information about the bandwidth used by each database, we can use the sys.bandwidth_usage view. When we copy the pubs database to SQL Azure, we see exactly how much bandwidth was consumed since that operation. This view returns two rows for every database with one row showing data ingress and the other showing data egress. The results for a SELECT * FROM sys.bandwidth_usage is shown in Table 15-1.

Table 15-1. Sys.bandwidth_usage Results

time	database_name	direction	class	time_period	quantity
2011-07-08 19:00	pubs	Egress	External	OffPeak	76
2011-07-08 19:00	pubs	Ingress	External	OffPeak	169

The quantity field is in kilobytes (KB).

The sys.database_usage returns one row for each day of your subscription. The view returns the type of database (i.e., business or web) and the maximum number of databases of that SKU type that existed for that day. This view is useful to give you a guesstimate of the cost per day of the SQL Azure database.

The sys.firewall_rules view returns the list of firewall rules associated with the SQL Azure database. Running a query of this view would show us the firewall rules we defined in Figure 15-8.

The sys.dm_db_objects_impacted_on_version_change view is a database-scoped view that provides early warning for objects that will be impacted by version upgrades. Version upgrades happen, and with SQL Azure, you need to stay current. Even though Microsoft does everything possible to remain backward compatible, there is some chance that things may break if not tested.

Backing Up and Restoring Data with SQL Azure

At the time of this writing there is no way to easily backup and restore your database within SQL Azure. You may be curious as to why such a fundamental maintenance task is missing from the standard capabilities of SQL Azure and the answer lies in the fact that a SQL Azure database inherently is highly available. Multiple copies of your database are created automatically as soon as you create the database. These multiple copies protect you from loss of the entire database. Server failures and failover happen automatically for SQL Azure databases and require no interaction or configuration on your part.

However, the story is still incomplete. What if someone calls you and says, "I accidently dropped a table can you restore a backup"? This is where there is no good answer as of yet. Your database as a whole is protected, but there is no good way to restore a single object such as an inadvertently dropped table.

Right now, you can use SSIS or an SQLCMD script to automate the data creation or regeneration. You may also look into creating a database copy. Of course, you would need to make a copy before this disaster happens. To create a database copy, simple execute the following command: CREATE DATABASE Pub2 AS COPY OF Pubs. Note that this will create a separate database of the same size as your original database. If you are counting your pennies, maintaining a separate database may add up in cost and will certainly add up in storage space if your databases are large.

There is system view called sys.dm_database_copies. This view will show information on the status of the copy operation. For relatively small databases, there won't be a lot of useful information here, because the copy would happen so quickly the percentage_complete data would be meaningless. If the database failed to copy, the error_state column would reflect this.

Storing More Than Relational Data

The first effort with SQL Azure is to develop a highly scalable and robust relational database engine that can work with your Windows Azure applications and with on-premise data. Microsoft is not stopping at relational data. At the time of this writing, the SQL Azure Reporting feature is in Community Technology

Preview (otherwise known as beta release). The first iteration of SQL Azure Reporting Services will include the ability to create and execute reports based off of data stored in Windows Azure or a SQL Azure database. Although the first version won't be at feature parity with the on-premise SQL Server Reporting Services, it's a step in the business intelligence direction. Although there is no official word on details regarding Microsoft's story for SQL Server Analysis Services in the cloud, you can bet there is something in the works.

Summary

Cloud computing is a technology that's been around for some time. Rapid advancements in technology reduce the costs of building powerful datacenters, enabling companies like Amazon, Microsoft, and Google to intentionally design datacenters to rent out excess capacity. These offerings are more mature now and moving beyond the Infrastructure and Software as a Service spaces into Platform as a Service. This is where Microsoft has placed its bets with Windows Azure.

SQL Azure, which is a component of the Windows Azure platform, is a cloud-based highly scalable relational database based on SQL Server. In this chapter, we explored how to get started with SQL Azure and some of the issues and benefits of this platform. Keep in mind that this technology is evolving at a rapid pace, and limitations discussed in this chapter may no longer be limitations shortly after this book is published. For the latest information, always check the web sites.

SQL Server Private Cloud

Today, customers are heavily embracing virtualization technology. In the previous chapter, we discussed the various cloud deployments including Infrastructure as a Service (IaaS). IaaS gives IT the ability to quickly spin up an operating system environment in a fraction of the time it would normally take to procure new hardware and install an operating system and applications. Private cloud computing holds similar characteristics to public cloud computing. For one thing, both are elastic. By "elastic," we are referring to the capability to quickly and easily spin up and down new operating system environments. The big difference between public and private clouds is that private clouds occur within a corporate firewall and sometimes leverage existing hardware. Private clouds are shielded from the theoretical insecurities of the Internet. For this reason, many companies are quicker to adopt a private cloud infrastructure. In fact, according to the online article "Sizing of the Datacenter" located at www.ctoedge.com/content/sizing-state-data-center?slide=13, the Association of Data Management Professionals (www.afcom.com) estimates that 70% of customers are planning on or are currently implementing a private cloud-based solution.

When creating a SQL Server Private Cloud there are four pillars that make up the benefits of this architecture. These pillars are as follows:

- Resource pooling

- Elasticity

- Self-service

- Control and customization

Building out a private cloud infrastructure is complex and beyond the scope of this book. In this chapter, we are going to explore conceptually what makes up a SQL Server private cloud and how you can prepare for building one.

THE FIVE STAGES OF CLOUD COMPUTING

Gartner published an article called, "Roadmap from Virtualization to Cloud Computing" in March of 2011. This article defines five stages of cloud computing, each driven by different requirements, generating different benefits, and requiring different efforts.

In stage 1, server virtualization, companies simple look to consolidate their servers. In the database world, consider taking multiple physical servers hosting SQL Server and virtualizing them into a few virtualization hosts. Hypervisors like Microsoft Hyper-V support these physical to virtual migrations easily. For more information on converting physical machines to virtual ones, read the "P2V: Converting Physical Computers to Virtual Machines in VMM," located at http://technet.microsoft.com/en-us/library/cc764232.aspx. By reducing the amount of hardware you are using you immediately see the benefits of reduced energy consumption and physical space reduction. Given these benefits, simply virtualizing physical servers doesn't provide any relief from an IT management standpoint.

In stage 2, distributed virtualization, companies are leveraging more of the flexibility and speed inherent within the hypervisor itself. For example, Microsoft Hyper-V contains a feature called Live Migration. This allows an operating system environment running within a Hyper-V host to be moved to another Hyper-V host with no downtime, no dropped connections, and no disruptions. Live Migration allows you to easily make hardware updates and repairs and keep your SLAs intact.

Stage 3, private cloud, is the focus of this chapter and suggests a transformation of how IT within an organization is perceived and run. Traditionally, when an internal customer requests IT resources, IT has to go out and procure new hardware and install and patch the operating systems, among many other tasks. Ideally, the internal customer could request these resources, and they would be automatically provisioned based on preexisting IT configurations. This concept of self-service IT is one of the biggest benefits of a private cloud. Although you do not need to enable a self-service model in your own private cloud, having one helps out with standardization of virtual machine configurations. Some additional benefits of the private cloud are usage and metering. To ensure your end users are utilizing your infrastructure effectively, you can charge for its use. Usually, within companies, those charges are funny money, and no real dollars exchange hands, but billing for services keeps the IT requests for resources relevant.

Stage 4, hybrid cloud, is the concept of leveraging the public cloud when you need additional resources during peak times while still leveraging your on-premise private cloud solution. Some analysts predict that hybrid cloud computing will be a big trend within the next ten years as companies get comfortable with implementing private cloud solutions. To aid in the movement between private and public cloud computing, Microsoft has a product call Microsoft App Controller. App Controller's purpose is to allow customers to oversee both on-premise and cloud-based services. It will allow a business team to build its own system on a private cloud, scale it out to Azure if it needs more resources, and take it back in house seamlessly. It does this with IT managing the processes along the way.

Stage 5, public cloud, offers an almost limitless resource for us to use. In Chapter 15, we covered Windows Azure and SQL Azure, Microsoft's public cloud-based Platform as a Service offerings. In addition to private companies, governments are also heavily involved in leveraging the power of cloud computing. In the United States, President Obama has initiated the Cloud First strategy for government IT. The basic concept of Cloud First is to encourage cloud computing for IT projects within the government. The complete Federal Cloud Computing Strategy document is located at www.cio.gov/documents/Federal-Cloud-Computing-Strategy.pdf. Many people within the government have bought into the benefits. Richard Spires, chief information officer at the U.S. Department of Homeland Security, said the agency could save eight to ten percent of IT costs by moving to cloud infrastructure services. New network and storage services can be added in one week, as compared to up to 18 months if done in house.

Virtualization

Virtualization of the operating system plays a key part in architecting a private cloud solution. SQL Server is one particular workload that has unique characteristics, which need to be taken into account when virtualizing SQL Server. For one thing, the biggest contention within a database is disk I/O. When we virtualize a database, we need to make sure the I/O we obtain from within the operating system environment is pretty much what we had on a physical server. There are tools you can use to obtain I/O metrics based on a typical SQL Server workload. SQLIO is one such tool, and more information can be found at the following URL: http://technet.microsoft.com/en-us/library/cc966412.aspx. One of the limitations of running inside a virtual machine host is that your virtual machines are limited in using multiple host bus adapters. This could also cause your disk I/O to suffer. Provided your SAN engineers have convinced you that all will be well in the virtual world, there is one other thing to note when virtualizing a database. If your existing SQL Server implementation currently leverages more CPUs than your hypervisor can give per virtual machine, it is probably not a good idea to virtualize this workload.

Resource Pooling

In a SQL Server private cloud environment, consolidating databases is the prime objective and a benefit of resource pooling. This pillar maps to Gartner's Stage 1, server virtualization. By simply virtualizing your SQL Server instances, you achieve a reduction in operational expenses, reduction in energy costs, and a reduction in physical space required for hardware. When it comes to databases, we don't really want to perform a physical to virtual machine action on them without proper planning.

For one thing, before we set out on an effort to consolidate databases, we need to know which databases we want to consolidate. Even though we may have a master list, there could be other SQL Servers in our environment that popped up without our knowing. This concept, known as "SQL Server sprawl" comes from a variety of factors such as users getting frustrated at the time it takes to acquire new databases to power users ignoring corporate policies and installing software on their own. Whichever the case, it is important to know of all of our SQL Server installations. Microsoft has a free tool called the Microsoft Assessment and Planning (MAP) toolkit to make this inventory task really easy.

Discovering SQL Server Sprawl

The MAP tool is not meant to be an auditing tool. It doesn't secretly send information back to Microsoft, so you don't need to worry about Steve Ballmer knocking on your door after you use it demanding more money. The tool's original design was to scan your network and tell you which PCs were upgradable to the latest versions of Office and Windows. From a business standpoint, it would make sense that Microsoft would invest in this free software for you to see which PCs are able to be upgrade.

The plumbing of the tool though was seen as a great value to other products like SQL Server. In fact, in the latest version of MAP, the tool can inventory Windows and Linux environments as well as Oracle, MySQL, and Sybase. The MAP tool can be downloaded from the following URL: www.microsoft.com/map.

When you launch the MAP tool, its default tab is "Discovery and Readiness," and this tab is shown in Figure 16-1.

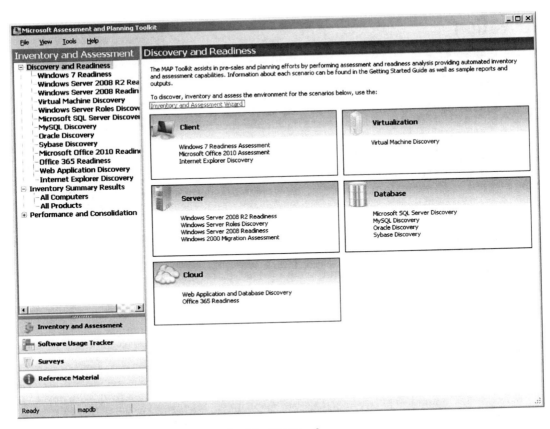

Figure 16-1. Discover and Readiness tab of the MAP tool

From this tab, you can click Inventory and Assessment Wizard to launch a wizard that will guide you through the process of scanning your environment. The wizard will first ask you which scenario you are targeting. This is shown in Figure 16-2.

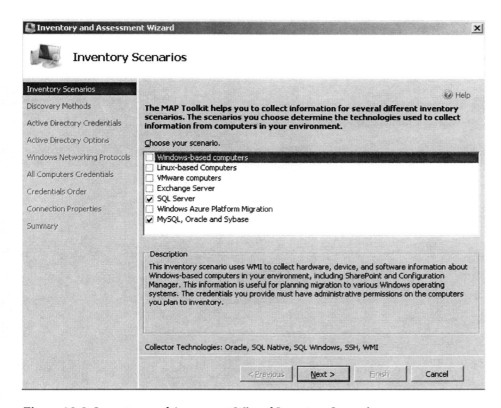

Figure 16-2. Inventory and Assessment Wizard Inventory Scenarios page

Depending on the scenario you select, the wizard will leverage many different technologies to use to obtain information. The most common is the Windows Management Instrumentation (WMI). Once we select the scenario, the next page asks you which methods to use in discovering your environment. This is shown in Figure 16-3.

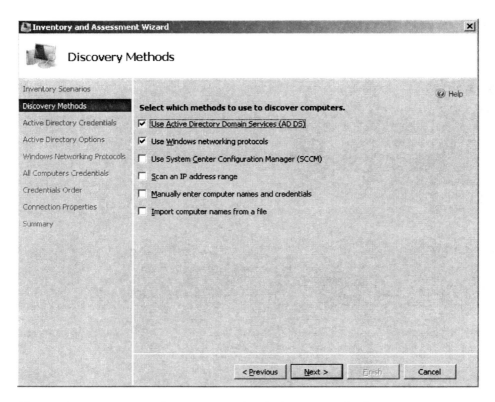

Figure 16-3. *Inventory and Assessment Wizard Discovery Methods page*

From this page, you can see that Active Directory is an option. This would be the best option if you have Active Directory deployed in your organization. Alternatively, you can specify an IP range, specify names from a text file and a few other options. Depending on which methods we chose, the wizard will either ask us for Active Directory credentials or standard username and passwords for those computers we selected to query. These credentials are not stored anywhere other than memory for the duration of the scan. After completing this information, the wizard will start scanning. Depending on which options you selected, this could take hours or days. The result though is worth the effort. For SQL Server scenarios, there are three reports that are generated. The first two are Excel files, and the third is a summary document written in Word that basically summarizes at a high level the information from the first two Excel files. Excel file number one is called SQL Server Assessment, and it contains three tabs: Summary, DatabaseInstance, and Component. The Summary tab displays a summary of the count of instances and components found in the scan. Information from the Summary tab is shown in Figure 16-4.

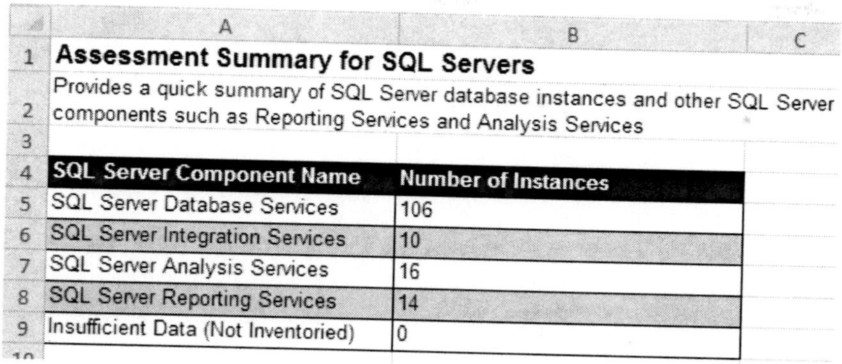

A	B	C
Assessment Summary for SQL Servers		
Provides a quick summary of SQL Server database instances and other SQL Server components such as Reporting Services and Analysis Services		
SQL Server Component Name	**Number of Instances**	
SQL Server Database Services	106	
SQL Server Integration Services	10	
SQL Server Analysis Services	16	
SQL Server Reporting Services	14	
Insufficient Data (Not Inventoried)	0	

Figure 16-4. Summary tab in SQL Server Assessment report

Table 16-1 shows the information presented in the DatabaseInstance tab. Begin with the spreadsheet shown in Figure 16-4. Look at the bottom of the window. You should see a tab named DatabaseInstance.

Table 16-1. Sample Content of DatabaseInstances Tab

Column Name	Sample Value
Computer name	SQLPROD-1.contoso.lab
SQL Server instance name	MSSQL$MAPS
SQL Server product name	Microsoft SQL Server 2008
SQL Server version	10.1.2531.0
SQL Server service pack	SP1
SQL Server edition	Enterprise Edition
Clustered?	No
SQL Server cluster network name	<blank>
SQL Service state	Running
SQL Service start mode	Auto
Language	English (1033)
SQL Server subdirectory	MSSQL 10.MAPS

Continued

Column Name	Sample Value
Current operating system	Microsoft Windows Server 2008 Enterprise
Operating system service pack level	Service Pack 2
Operating system architecture type	32-bit
Number of processors	2
Number of cores	0
Number of logical processors	4
CPU	Intel(R) Xeon(TM) CPU 3.20GHz, 32 bit
System memory (MB)	3583
Logical disk drive name	`C:`
Logical disk size (GB)	330
Logical disk free space (GB)	230
Recommendations	Consider upgrading to Microsoft SQL Server 2008 R2
Machine type	Physical
Number of host processors	Not applicable
WMI status	Success

The Component tab lists similar information to Database Instances, except it lists the components (e.g., Reporting Services, Analysis Services) that are installed for each server as well as the server specifications, like the number of processors and RAM.

The second Excel file, SQL Server Database Details, goes into depth on the databases within each instance. It contains six tabs: Overview, SQLServerSummary, DatabaseSummary, DBInstanceSummary, DBInstanceProperties, and DBUserDetails. This spreadsheet contains a plethora of information and a summary of each tab is in Table 16-2.

Table 16-2. SQL Server Database Detail Excel File Tab Summary

Tab	Description
Overview	For each SQL Server version, this lists the number of instances found and total databases within each instance.
SQLServerSummary	For each server inventoried, it lists all SQL Server instances and user databases within each instance.
DatabaseSummary	Lists detailed information (data file size, log file size, number of tables, number of views, number of functions, etc.) for each database within each instance.
DBInstanceSummary	Lists information like SQL Server service pack information, CLR version, and default collation.
DBInstanceProperties	Lists the SQL Server server configuration properties (affinity mask, AWE enabled, filestream access level, etc.) for each SQL Server instance inventoried.
DBUserDetails	Lists user names, roles, and logins for all databases that were inventoried.

Before any consolidation work is performed, we need to know the exact environment we are dealing with. The MAP tool is a fantastic and free way to get a grip on what SQL Server instances are running in your environment.

Upgrading SQL Server

One of the best practices when building out a consolidated SQL Server environment is to upgrade your database servers to the latest release. This will buy you a longer support cycle for the product. Versions like SQL Server 2000 are completely out of support, and dragging them into a new consolidated environment is not the best choice. However, there are circumstances that will prohibit you from upgrading. These include the vendor support for the applications that are the front end for databases not supporting a release more current than, say, SQL Server 2000. Also, internal business decisions to sunset the application could mean your choice is simply to migrate the physical SQL Server 2000 server to a virtual one and call it good enough.

Whenever you decide to upgrade the database servers, there are two important tools to be aware of in the upgrade process. These tools are the Microsoft SQL Server Upgrade Advisor (Advisor) and SQL Server Upgrade Assistant (Assistant).

The Advisor tool can be run from a desktop and points to the server instance you wish to upgrade. The tool goes through a check of potential issues you may encounter given the server you wish to upgrade. Examples of some of the potential issues include the use of deprecated statements like the *= and =* join syntax or extended stored procedures that were pulled from the product.

After the tool evaluates the server, it provides useful reports like the one shown in Figure 16-5.

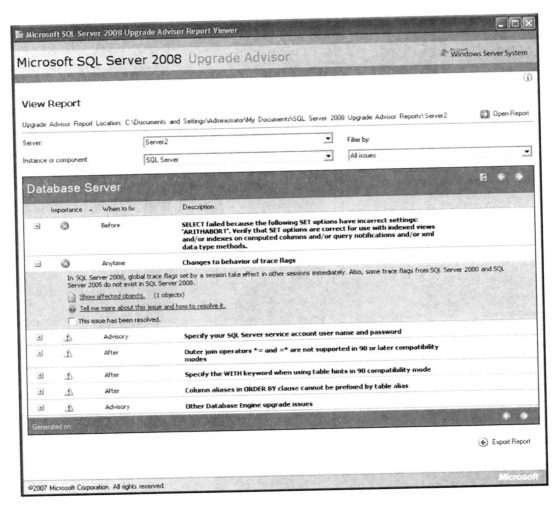

Figure 16-5. SQL Server Upgrade Advisor's instance report

If you sat for a moment and thought about situations where this tool may fail you could probably find quite a few. For example, if we were using encrypted stored procedures the tool could not obtain the text to parse to evaluate and so on. This tool is not meant to be the final check in whether or not you can upgrade; rather, it's meant to give you a rough idea of the work involved in upgrading to the latest version. A more thorough tool used in application compatibility testing is the Assistant tool.

The SQL Server Upgrade Assistant is a joint development effort by Scalability Experts and Microsoft. The Assistant tool can be downloaded for free at www.scalabilityexperts.com/tools/downloads.html.

The Assistant tool more thoroughly tests for compatibility than the Advisor. This tool requires more resources, primarily time, to effectively use. The idea behind the tool is to capture a SQL trace of a live production workload (or a complete set of functional tests within a test environment) and replay this trace against a separate upgraded instance of SQL Server. Since the tool is capturing a SQL trace, it will capture every statement that goes against the source database. This allows the tool to trap errors, like using undocumented DBCC commands, which the Advisor tool will not capture. When the SQL trace is replayed against the new environment, a detailed line-by-line comparison will be presented, as shown in Figure 16-6.

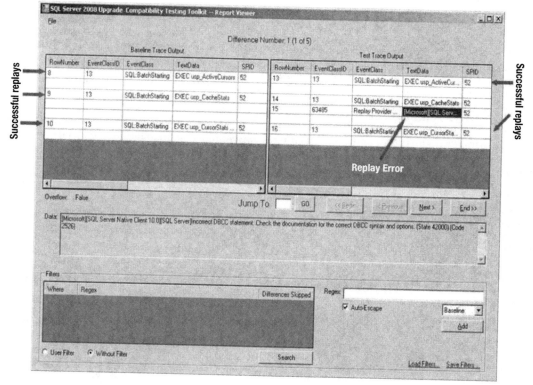

Figure 16-6. SQL Server Upgrade Assistant's Report Viewer

When developing a private cloud environment for SQL Server, as someone in the DBA role, your tasks will heavily center on the database inventory and consolidation piece. The magic of a private cloud has almost everything to do with the infrastructure—the flexibility of the operating system, the hypervisor, and disk subsystems. One of the other major pieces of resource pooling is taking the physical servers and virtualizing them. Products like Microsoft System Center Virtual Machine Manager (SCVMM) have this capability. SCVMM adds a ton more value and features on top of the Hyper-V platform and is a major component in architecting a private cloud infrastructure.

Elasticity

Elasticity is, perhaps, the most important component of a private cloud. Imagine if someone in your organization comes to you and asks for a new database server to be provisioned. If you don't have the server room, you would have to buy new hardware, install the operating system, install SQL Server, and patch and maintain this new server. When the users are finished with the database, you would repurpose the server. In a private cloud environment, we would simply spin up a new virtual machine with SQL Server running. When the customer was finished with the database, we could easily delete the virtual machine image. In this section, we will look into specific features that will support an elastic environment of SQL Server database servers.

Making creating new virtual machines easy may lead to virtual machine sprawl. Even worse, each one of these virtual machines could be configured differently, causing a management nightmare. One way to mitigate this nightmare is to use virtual machine templates. A virtual machine created from a template could contain all the applications and settings needed for a specific function. For a database, we could have a template that installs SQL Server in a certain directory with certain defaults that are common in our organization. SQL Server supports virtualization templates by allowing a SQL Server installation to be Sysprepped. "Sysprep" is short for "System Preparation Utility." Essentially, when you Sysprep a SQL Server instance, you install all the bits on the operating system but don't complete the install. By having a Sysprep image of an operating system with a Sysprep install of SQL Server, we can deploy this same image many times, and from this image, we can make an installation legitimate by completing the install. By using Sysprep, we avoid having to install the SQL Server bits after every new operating system created. There are some restrictions in using Sysprep with SQL Server. For more information read the article, "Considerations for Installing SQL Server Using Sysprep" at the following URL: http://msdn.microsoft.com/en-us/library/ee210754(v=SQL.110).aspx.

Even without a Sysprep image of SQL Server, you could tell the virtual machine host to run an unattended install of SQL Server after a new virtual machine is created. The end experience is the same, but with Sysprep except your new virtual machine of SQL Server will take a bit longer to get ready, because SQL Server has to install the bits on the operating system.

As mentioned in the previous section, Microsoft System Center Virtual Machine Manager (SCVMM) is the primary tool used within Windows Server to create a private cloud environment. SCVMM allows you to create virtual machine templates. Assume now that you have set up SCVMM and have deployed a few Hyper-V host machines.

In a traditional SQL Server deployment, we often see failover clustering used as a high-availability solution. These requirements don't change when a database lives within a virtual machine. Fortunately, you can define guest failover clusters for the virtual machines as well as cluster the virtualization hosts. If you are interested in setting up a shared disk resource within a Hyper-V virtual machine, read the following blog post: http://blogs.technet.com/b/mghazai/archive/2009/12/12/hyper-v-guest-clustering-step-by-step-guide.aspx. The article "Hyper-V: Using Hyper-V and Failover Cluster" located at http://technet.microsoft.com/en-us/library/cc732181(WS.10).aspx describes the requirements for using Hyper-V and failover clustering.

In a virtualized environment, you are sharing the same physical server (virtualization host) for multiple operating systems and database instances. If something bad happens on the virtualization host or if you need to upgrade a piece of hardware, taking the host offline could affect a lot of users and applications. For the unexpected downtime of a virtualization host, you can cluster the virtualization host as mentioned earlier in this section. For planned downtime, you can leverage a feature within Hyper-V called Live Migration. Live Migration moves a running virtual machine to another virtualization host with no downtime. This means your database users will be unaffected by this operation.

One of the biggest limitations with virtualization is memory use. If each virtual machine takes 4 GB and you only have 32 GB on the virtualization host, you can only run six to seven virtual machines. We know that SQL Server loves to use memory and that it will free memory that is not used over time. Earlier

versions of SQL Server introduced the ability to add hot memory and CPUs. These features, combined with Hyper-V Dynamic Memory found in Windows Server 2008 R2 SP1, allow you to specify a default minimum and maximum RAM size for a virtual machine. When you launch a virtual machine, the minimum RAM will be reserved, and as the activities within that virtual machine require more memory, more will be allocated up to the maximum value. As the virtual machine releases the memory, the memory will be freed to the virtualization host. Dynamic Memory allows you to stuff in more virtual machines per virtualization host—about 40% more virtual machines per virtualization host. For more information on Hyper-V Dynamic Memory, check out the following URL:
http://technet.microsoft.com/en-us/library/ff817651(WS.10).aspx.

Self-Service

If you consolidate your databases and virtualize them, you are moving one step in the cloud direction. By leveraging virtual machine templates, we make management a lot easier. At this point, if you configured your environment with SCVMM and a few Hyper-V hosts, you could call it a private cloud. However, we can optimize that cloud a bit more. As of now, if a user asks us for a virtual machine of SQL Server, we would do the heavy lifting of finding out specifically the size they are looking for, finding the VM host with enough space, and creating the virtual machine. However, SCVMM 2007 introduced a self-service portal (www.microsoft.com/en-us/server-cloud/system-center/virtual-machine-manager-self-service-portal.aspx). This portal contains a web page that allows the end user to request IT resources such as a database server with 2GB RAM and 500GB storage. The portal runs this request by the IT administrator to confirm it. Upon confirmation, a new virtual machine with the requested configuration is automatically provisioned on a host that has enough space for the requested virtual machine.

Control and Customization

If popping up another virtual machine is easy and doesn't require buying new hardware, internal customers may kept requesting resources. Perhaps their requests are without merit. To keep the virtual machine farms from getting out of control, you can assign costs per virtual machine template. Usage and charge reporting are available out of the box with SCVMM. As a DBA, you may be on the receiving end of this charge-back model by requesting the resources from IT.

Implementation Options

So far in this chapter, we've explored the key concepts and features within SQL Server, Microsoft's Hyper-V, and Microsoft System Center Virtual Machine Manager that enable you to build a SQL Server private cloud environment. If you went ahead and installed and configured these products on your own, you would be self-building the solution. To build out your own private cloud, start with reading the Hyper-V deployment guides located at www.microsoft.com/en-us/server-cloud/private-cloud/hyperv-cloud-deployment.aspx. Note that, to get to the guides, click the Build Your Own menu on the left-hand side of the page, and click the Step 2 tab. If you do not want to do this on your own, you can hire a Microsoft partner as well; credible partners are listed on the web site.

There are two additional ways to get a private cloud up and running. Certain hardware manufactures provide fast track architectures that modify the guidance suggested by the Hyper-V cloud deployment based on their hardware architectures For example, if you have an HP shop, check out HP's "Cloud Foundation for Hyper-V" at the following URL:

http://h71028.www7.hp.com/enterprise/us/en/partners/microsoft-cloud-foundation.html?jumpid=ex_r2858_us/en/large/tsg/microsoft_cloud. Dell's Hyper-V Cloud fast track is located at http://content.dell.com/us/en/enterprise/d/cloud-computing/microsoft-hyper-v-cloud-fast-track.aspx.

If you want the "Easy Button" approach to SQL Server in a private cloud, you can take a look at an appliance. A few hardware vendors like HP are coming out with database consolidation appliances that are essentially all the components we have discussed in this chapter preconfigured in a box. The HP Database Consolidation Appliance is available in half- or full-rack configurations. The idea is if you need more space, you can add more racks. For more information on the HP Enterprise Database Consolidation Appliance, check out the following URL: www.microsoft.com/sqlserver/en/us/solutions-technologies/Appliances/HP-dca.aspx.

Summary

This chapter presented a conceptual view of the applications, components, and capabilities of a SQL Server private cloud environment. Unless your organization is extremely small, chances are you will probably have another IT person helping you with or primarily responsible for a SQL Server private cloud architecture. The content in this chapter will help you work alongside that person or team, enabling you to play a part in bringing the benefits of cloud computing into your own environment and under your control.

Where to Go Next?

The great part about SQL Server and other Microsoft products is the amount of love that is given to the development and user communities. Many different resources are available for you to learn more about SQL Server. Some of these resources are in the form of online webcasts, some are white papers, and some are users groups. Perhaps the most important resource that you should get familiar with immediately is SQL Server Books Online.

Visit SQL Server Books Online

SQL Server Books Online is the one-stop shop for all documentation on SQL Server from Microsoft. If you chose not to install it from the SQL Server media, you can browse SQL Server Books Online at `http://msdn.microsoft.com/en-us/library/ms130214(v=SQL.110).aspx`. SQL Server Books Online not only covers the relational database engine but also covers all the components within the server, including Reporting Services, Analysis Services, and Integration Services. This documentation also provides detailed information on all the documented statements, including DML, DDL, and DCL statements. In addition, this detailed information gives examples of how to use the particular features.

SQL Server Books Online contains tutorials to make it easier to learn SQL Server. You can find these tutorials at `http://msdn.microsoft.com/en-us/library/ms167593.aspx`.

Keep Up with Public SQL Server Websites

Many websites host information regarding SQL Server. Most of these carry great information and will benefit you on your journey to become the best DBA on the planet. The following are the websites that we tend to frequent:

> *SQL Server Central*: SQL Server Central provides a lot of great articles and sample scripts. This website requires you to register before you can completely view the contents. The hassle of registration is well worth the prize. You can find this website at `http://www.sqlservercentral.com`.

> SQL Server World Wide Users Group: Similar to SQL Server Central, this website provides great articles and sample scripts. This website also requires registration. You can find this website at `http://www.sswug.org`.

SQL Skills: Paul Randal and his wife, Kimberly Tripp, are amazing presenters and educators and have a lot of valuable content on their website. If you have an opportunity to see them at a conference, you should take the time. Their presentations are well worthwhile. You can find this website at
`http://www.sqlskills.com`.

SQL Server Customer Advisory Team: This website provides blogs and other documents such as best practices on various topics within SQL Server. The website content is updated by members of the SQL Server Customer Advisory Team. This team is a special group of elite individuals inside the SQL Server product team who travel around the globe and handle issues from the largest of SQL Server implementations. You can find this website at `http://SQLCat.com`.

Microsoft TechNet: TechNet is a fantastic resource for both live and recorded webcasts on all Microsoft technologies including SQL Server. This website also contains troubleshooting information and various how-to videos. You can find this website at `http://technet.microsoft.com/en-us/sqlserver/default.aspx`.

Attend a Conference

A few conferences take place on a yearly basis. Microsoft TechEd is a conference that showcases the latest Microsoft technologies including SQL Server. You can obtain information about TechEd and view videos at `http://www.microsoft.com/events/TechEd`.

The Professional Association for SQL Server (PASS) is an independent, not-for-profit association dedicated to supporting, educating, and promoting the Microsoft SQL Server community. This organization holds public conferences every year, and it is said to be the largest gathering of SQL Server professionals in the world. If you attend the annual conference, you will have the opportunity to attend many presentations on a variety of SQL Server–related topics. There are usually many companies demonstrating their products in the exhibit hall. If you have the budget to attend only one conference a year, this is the one to attend. You can find more information at `http://www.sqlpass.org`.

Find a Local Users Group

If you live near a city, chances are you may be close to a local SQL Server users group. Although there is no officially published list from Microsoft, you can find one by checking out the Professional Association of SQL Server (PASS) website. It offers a list of PASS chapters located at
`http://www.sqlpass.org/PASSChapters.aspx`.

Attending users groups is a great way to learn more about SQL Server. In addition to the knowledge gained from the presentation, you will meet other DBA geeks just like yourself. Sometimes headhunters are there looking for DBA skills just like the ones you have! If you really want to push yourself and learn topics, you can also volunteer to present on a topic. This will force you into submersing yourself into the material for a week and delivering it to the group. User groups usually meeting once a month for most of the year.

SQL Saturday is another way to meet SQL Server users and learn more about the product. For a listing of SQL Saturday events check out the following URL: `http://www.sqlsaturday.com`.

Create a Lab System and Practice

Being a DBA is a lot like learning math for the first time. You can't just read a book and expect to be an expert. For that reason, you should always have an instance of SQL Server around to kick the tires and experiment with features on. If you want a more formal walk-through, a few hands-on labs are available free of charge from Microsoft. These hands-on labs actually put you into one of Microsoft's virtual machines already preloaded with SQL Server and all the other tools that you will need for the lab. You can find the SQL Server hands-on labs at http://technet.microsoft.com/en-us/virtuallabs/cc164207.aspx. Some of the labs available at the time of this writing include the following: Transparent Data Encryption, Authoring Reports Using SQL Server Reporting Services, and Using SQL Server Resource Governor for Predictable Performance. Microsoft is constantly adding labs. Check back often for more labs to be offered including some targeting the SQL Server 2012 release.

Create a virtual machine using Virtual PC 2007

If you do not want to install SQL Server on your personal machine consider creating a virtual machine (VM) and installing SQL Server on the VM. Microsoft Windows Server 2008 comes with VM technology called Hyper-V that allows you to create virtual machines. Windows Server with Hyper-V requires a 64-bit platform to run on. If you are still using 32-bit you can experiment with SQL Server in a VM by using Microsoft Virtual PC 2007, which is a free download at http://www.microsoft.com/downloads/details.aspx?displaylang=en&FamilyID=04d26402-3199-48a3-afa2-2dc0b40a73b6.

■ **Note**   At the time of this writing, the final Operating System and platform support for SQL Server 2012 has not been finalized so there is a possibility that you will not be able to run SQL Server 2012 on a 32-bit platform. If this is the case Virtual PC will not work for you and you will have to either install SQL Server 2012 directly on your desktop, server or on a 64-bit hypervisor like Hyper-V. There is still a lot of 32-bit hardware out in the wild so if I were in Las Vegas I would put my money on 32-bit support.

With Virtual PC, you create a virtual drive that in reality is just a file that lives on your local file system. From this virtual drive, you run another operating system or install a new operating system via an ISO image. Microsoft has also released free evaluation versions of Windows Server 2008 in ISO format, so you could easily create a Virtual PC machine running Windows Server 2008 Standard edition with the Evaluation edition of SQL Server 2012 installed. All of this is free for a limited duration. You can download the Windows Server 2008 evaluations from http://www.microsoft.com/windowsserver2008/en/us/trial-software.aspx.

To get a time-bombed SQL Server environment set up through Microsoft Virtual PC 2007, perform the following tasks:

1. Install Microsoft Virtual PC 2007 from the link mentioned earlier.

2. Download the ISO version of Windows Server 2008 using the link mentioned earlier.

3. Launch Microsoft Virtual PC 2007, and select File ➤ New Virtual Machine Wizard.

4. This will launch the New Virtual Machine Wizard.

5. On the Options page, select the "Create a virtual machine" radio button.

6. On the Virtual Machine Name and Location page, give a proper name for your Windows and SQL installation.

7. On the Operating System page, select Windows Server 2008. If this option is not available, select Other.

8. On the Memory page, adjust the memory to at least one or more gigabytes. If you try to give the Virtual PC less than a gigabyte of memory, your operating system performance may be hindered.

9. On the Virtual Hard Disk Options page, select "A new virtual hard disk."

10. On the Virtual Disk Location page, choose a location that is different from the hard drive where your local operating system is installed. This could be an external USB drive but not a USB memory stick. Figure 17-1 shows this page populated with a location on an external USB drive.

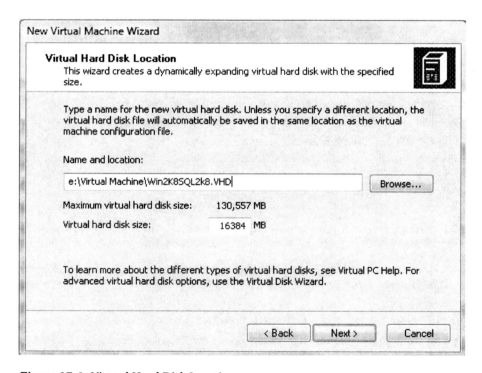

Figure 17-1. Virtual Hard Disk Location page

11. Clicking Next will bring you to the end of the wizard. When you click Finish, a new virtual machine will be created for you that has no operating system installed.

To tell the Virtual PC to use the ISO image you downloaded, perform the following tasks:

1. On the Virtual PC Console, click the virtual machine that you created, and click the Start button. This will launch a separate window that runs the new operating system. On the screen you will notice the power-on self-test that the virtual BIOS does, and after that, the OS will try to perform a network boot via the PXE technology.

2. At this point, you can bind the new ISO image to the virtual machine. You do this by selecting "Capture ISO image" from the CD menu on the Virtual PC console.

3. Navigate to the ISO image, and click the Open button.

4. To stop the PXE boot, hit Ctrl+C.

At this point, Virtual PC will start installing the Windows operating system from the ISO file you specified. From here you can finish installing Windows Server 2008, and when you're done, you can install SQL Server 2012 just as if you were on your load machine. Note that Virtual PC 2007 has an option on the CD menu to use the physical drive. This allows Virtual PC to use the CD-ROM drive on your client machine.

Get Certified!

Certification is that piece of paper that sets you apart from the other job applicants who have the same amount of experience as you. Sometimes employers such as consulting firms require you to obtain one, but more than likely, you will want to get one to prove to your employer that you know your stuff. Microsoft, like other software and hardware vendors, has certifications for most of its products. You can find more information about SQL Server certifications at http://www.microsoft.com/learning/en/us/certification/cert-sql-server.aspx.

Summary

Over the years, Microsoft has evolved the SQL Server product from a relational database engine to a complete data management platform. Today, SQL Server customers are managing petabytes of data and witnessing 100,000+ transactions per second throughput all at an affordable total cost of ownership. SQL Server 2012 is the latest and most significant release of Microsoft's database platform. In this book, we've scratched the surface and explored keys to database administration. Being a great DBA comes with a lot of practice and continual education. It is imperative that you take the time to perfect your skills by learning which style works best for you. Previously in this chapter, you'll find links to SQL Server user groups and online hands on labs. Take advantage of these great, free resources. Have fun and good luck in your rewarding career as a SQL Server database administrator!

Index

CPSIA information can be obtained at www.ICGtesting.com
Printed in the USA
LVOW121218090612

285379LV00004BB/1/P